uf

flying visits
SWITZERLAND

CADOGANguides

Contents

08

Reference

About the author

Norman Renouf was born and educated in London, England, and has travelled extensively since the age of 16. Having first worked in financial institutions, in both the UK and USA, he decided to become a freelance travel writer and photographer in 1990. Since then, he has written numerous travel guides for major publishers as well as articles for magazines and newspapers, covering destinations from the Arctic Circle to Gibraltar and as far east as Moscow and Tallinn, Estonia, and the mid-Atlantic region of the USA, where he now lives.

Cadogan Guides
165 The Broadway,
Wimbledon, London
SW19 1NE, UK
info@cadoganguides.co.uk
www.cadoganguides.com

The Globe Pequot Press
246 Goose Lane, PO Box 480, Guilford,
Connecticut 06437–0480, USA

Copyright © Norman Renouf 2004

Cover design by Sarah Gardner
Book design by Andrew Barker
Cover photographs: (front) © John Miller, © Jon Arnold images, © Royalty-Free/CORBIS and © Tim Thompson/CORBIS (train); (back) © John Miller and © Royalty-Free/CORBIS.
Maps © Cadogan Guides, drawn by Map Creation Ltd
Managing Editor: Natalie Pomier
Series Editor: Linda McQueen
Editor: Dominique Shead
Design: Sarah Gardner
Proofreading: Catherine Bradley
Indexing: Isobel McLean
Production: Navigator Guides

Printed in Italy by Legoprint
A catalogue record for this book is available from the British Library
ISBN 1-86011-134-3

The author and publishers have made every effort to ensure the accuracy of the information in this book at the time of going to press. However, they cannot accept any responsibility for any loss, injury or inconvenience resulting from the use of information contained in this guide.

Please help us to keep this guide up to date. We have done our best to ensure that the information in this guide is correct at the time of going to press. But places and facilities are constantly changing, and standards and prices in hotels and restaurants fluctuate. We would be delighted to receive any comments concerning existing entries or omissions. Authors of the best letters will receive a copy of the Cadogan Guide of their choice.

Introduction

Switzerland, with more than 70 per cent of its land covered by the Alps, attracts visitors from around the world to its famed alpine scenery and winter sports opportunities. However, this small, landlocked country, just 15,941 square miles (41,288 sq km) and with around 7.5 million inhabitants, has far more to offer visitors than just mountains and snow.

Its cultural diversity, shown in language, architecture and cuisine, is also a major attraction. The large swath of central, north and eastern Switzerland, with Zürich both the largest city and the country's financial centre, is dominated by the German influence. Contrastingly, the French style of life is predominant in the western and southwestern region, with Geneva and Lausanne being the main cities. Interestingly, the Valais area divides its loyalties, while places like Biel/Bienne – to the northwest – split their character. Altogether different, though, is the only region in Switzerland below the Alps: Ticino, sunnier and more luxuriant in its flora, is Italian in character and has a strong Mediterranean feel.

As might be expected, such diversity demands a flexible political system. Bern, on the central plains, is the capital of the Swiss Confederation and the seat of the Federal government that governs under a constitution accepted on 29 May 1874. The country is divided into 26 cantons, three of which are divided in turn into half-cantons, which each have their own constitutions and elected regional assemblies. Unlike in many countries referenda are an established method of government here, with constitutional amendments and Federal legislation subject to them.

How to Use This Guide

Being so small (it is easily possible to go north to south in 3–4 hours, and west to east in about 8 hours by train), having few international airports and with many places so close to each other, Switzerland is one of the easiest countries in Europe to travel in. It has a fully integrated public transport system that is clean, efficient and runs on time regardless of sometimes extreme weather conditions.

Main and Secondary Destinations

In fact, there are only three regular **direct flight destinations** from the UK – Basel, Geneva and Zürich – with only the latter two being directly accessible from North America. Surprisingly, none of these is the capital of Switzerland, and all are larger than the actual capital, Bern; they are also delightful in their differences. **Geneva**, situated around the far southwest of both Lake Geneva (Lac Léman) and the country, is heavily French in history and culture. But it has also made itself home to the United Nations European HQ, the Red Cross and numerous other international organizations, and consequently has a cosmopolitan feel not found anywhere else. **Zürich**, in the north of the country and situated on the smaller Lake Zürich, is Switzerland's largest city and the financial centre, but it is also a vibrant, lively place, belying any reputation it may have had as being boring. **Basel**, bisected by the mighty Rhine and in the far northeast, nestled against both France and Germany, has a more serious ambiance. It is home to the country's oldest university, is an important base for the pharmaceutical industry and is endowed with more than 30 museums – far more than any other city.

There are four more **important destinations** – Bern, Lugano, Luzern and Sion – which you may be considering as the centre or starting point of your stay. **Bern**, the capital, has a fabulous medieval heart and is famous for its bears, after which it is named. **Luzern**, in central Switzerland, also has delightful architectural assets, and these are combined with cultural institutions and lovely scenery around the lake it borders to make it a very popular city. Both of these are within an hour or so by train from Zürich and Basel, and less than three from Geneva. **Lugano** is the enchanting lakeside capital of the Italian-speaking canton of Ticino (Tessin in French and German) and, geographically at least, has a remote location in the far south of Switzerland below the Alps. It is connected by international flights via Geneva or Zürich, and by train connections taking about 6 hours from the former and half that from the latter. **Sion** is the anomaly amongst these other cities; far smaller, although with an historic centre, it sometimes receives direct flights from the UK during the winter months as it is the natural gateway to many of the skiing resorts in the Valais. Train connections vary in time from 2½ hours from Zürich to over 5½ hours from Lugano.

Day Trips, Overnighters and Multi-nighters

Organized by region, the next chapter of the guide describes **day trips, overnighters and multi-night trips** that can be taken from many, if not all, of the main and secondary destinations. These 31 places range from important cities like Lausanne to the historically important St Gallen, mountain resorts, remote valleys, curious villages like Gruyères and even international destinations like Vaduz in Liechtenstein and Nauders in the Austrian Tyrol that both adjoin Switzerland. To help you decide which can be visited from your starting point, a **table** at the end of each direct flight and secondary main destination details how long the minimum journey to each would be, and how many changes of transport the journey would involve by train (T), bus (B) or funicular (F). Obviously some are much closer to certain main and secondary destinations than others – so, as well as the journey times, the maps within the **Day Trips, Overnighters and Multi-nighters** chapter, and the grouping of the trips into regions, will help you pick the trips you can manage, depending on how much time you have to spare. If the table identifies a place as a day trip, but it is three hours away, this tells you that you can see everything of interest in that place in less than a day, but clearly you will still need to stay overnight somewhere nearby.

Tours

For those with at least a week to spend, who would like to travel and see as much of the country as possible, we have designed six **regional tours** to fit the geographical constraints of Switzerland. These could mostly be started and ended from any of the direct flight and secondary main destinations, though there are obvious choices from one or two each time. The Bernese Oberland tour, full of mountaintop experiences, most easily fits this format, with only those visitors starting from Lugano having any real travel problems. The Zürich tour, featuring an eclectic selection of stops, also fits that pattern. Travel times from anywhere to the start of the Valais tour of special valleys are, by definition, usually a little longer. The Eastern Graubünden (Grisons)

What to Go For...

	Mountain Scenery	Lakes	Museums	Gastronomy	Architecture	Shopping
Basel			●	●	●	
Bern	●		●		●	
Geneva	●	●	●	●		●
Lugano	●	●		●	●	
Luzern	●	●	●		●	●
Zürich		●	●	●	●	●

tour, on the other hand, presents special problems owing to its isolation in the far southeast of the country, and the fact that there isn't really a nearby town or city with an airport. Consequently, those travellers starting from Zürich have the easiest trip, closely followed by those coming from Basel, Bern and Luzern. A start from Lugano involves a long bus trip initially alongside the Italian lakes, and it is a full day's train journey from Geneva. In many of the tours an integral part of the adventure is the travelling between destinations, and you won't need a car: they are all constructed featuring public transport, from trains, buses and funicular railways to lake steamers and cable cars.

Switzerland awaits your visit; wherever you decide to go, and however you decide to do it, you will leave with many marvellous memories.

Travel

02

Who Goes Where?

	Page	easyJet	bmiBaby	Jet2	FlyBe	British Airways	Swiss	Air Canada	American Airlines	Continental	Delta	Lufthansa	Swiss	Eurostar (via Paris)
Geneva	50	•	•	•	•	•	•	•				•	•	•
Zürich	69	•				•	•	•	•	•	•	•	•	•
Basel	32	•				•	•							•
Sion*	123						•							
Lugano**	99						•							

Winter (ski season) only, Sat only. **not direct, change at Zürich or Geneva*

Getting There

By Air

From both the UK and the USA/Canada, many major scheduled national airlines, such as British Airways and Swiss, can whizz you straight to Geneva, Zürich and Basel. But in addition in the last few years the airline industry has undergone a revolution. Inspired by the success of Stelios Haji-Ioannou's 'upstart' easyJet company, many other 'budget' airlines flocked to join him in breaking the conventions of air travel to offer fares at rock-bottom prices, and in the case of Switzerland these are competing for the same major routes. Because of the constantly changing competition, it is important to note that **no-frills airlines are not always the cheapest**, above all on the very popular routes at peak times. One of the benefits of the no-frills revolution that is not always appreciated is not as much in their own prices as in the concessions they have forced on the older, mainstream carriers (British Airways, Swiss). It is **always** worth comparing no-frills prices with those of the main airlines.

No Frills, No Thrills

Whereas in their first years no-frills airlines had an undoubted 'backpackerish' feel, this has become an increasingly mainstream way to travel. New airlines are still starting up all the time with an eye on expanding the no-frills cake, and national airlines have got in on the act, copying some of the more attractive aspects of budget travel, such as Internet booking with discounts and one-way fares.

The ways in which low prices are achieved sometimes have a negative effect on the experience of travellers, but can sometimes be a bonus, too. First, these airlines often use **smaller regional airports**, where landing fees and tarmac-time charges are at a minimum. In the UK this means you may be able to find a flight from nearer your home town: easyJet flies out of Luton as well as Gatwick, bmiBaby from East Midlands, FlyBe from Southampton, and so on. The **planes** tend to be all one-class only and with the maximum seating configuration.

Fares are one-way – so there is no need to stay over on a Saturday night to qualify for the lowest fares – and can vary enormously on the same route, according to when you travel and how far in advance you book: the most widely advertised, rock-bottom deals are generally for seats on very early-morning, early-in-the-week flights; on the most popular routes, while you might get a price of £40 for a 6am Monday flight, the same route can cost you £140 on a Friday evening.

No-frills airline tickets are only sold direct, by phone or online, not through travel agents. To get the lowest prices you must book

Airlines

From the UK
bmiBaby, t 0870 264 2229, *www.bmibaby.com*.
From Cardiff and East Midlands on Sunday,
Manchester daily and Teeside on Saturday,
between mid-December and late March.
British Airways, t 0845 77 333 77, *www.ba.com*.
From Heathrow, Birmingham and
Manchester to Geneva and Zürich, and from
Heathrow to Basel, daily.
easyJet, t 0870 600 0000, *www.easyjet.com*.
From Gatwick and Luton, daily, to Geneva
and Zürich; from Liverpool and East Midlands
to Geneva; from London Stansted to Basel.
Flybe, t 0871 700 0535, *www.flybe.com*. From
Southampton to Geneva, daily.
Jet2, *www.jet2.com*. From Leeds Bradford three
times weekly to Geneva.
Swiss, t 0845 601 0956, *www.swiss.com*. From
Heathrow, Birmingham and Manchester to
Geneva and Zürich, and from Heathrow to
Basel and from London (City Airport) to
Zürich, daily. Also once a week (Saturdays) in
winter direct to Sion from Heathrow.

From North America
Air Canada, *www.aircanada.ca*, operate a daily
flight from Toronto (Canada) to Zürich.
American Airlines, *www.aa.com*, and **Swiss**,
www.swiss.com, co-share a daily flight from
New York (JFK) to Geneva, and American
Airlines operate a daily flight from New York
(JFK) and Dallas/Fort Worth to Zürich.
Continental Airlines, *www.continental.com*,
operate a daily flight from New York
(Newark) to Zürich.
Delta, *www.delta.com*, operate a daily flight
from Atlanta to Zürich.
Lufthansa, *www.lufthansa-usa.com*, operate
daily flights from Boston, Chicago, Denver/
Detroit, Los Angeles, San Francisco, Toronto,
Vancouver and Washington D.C. via
Frankfurt to Basel, Geneva and Zürich.
Swiss, *www.swiss.com*, operate daily flights
from Boston, Chicago, Los Angeles, Miami,
Montreal (Canada), New York (Newark) and
Washington D.C. to Zürich and from Miami
and New York (Newark) to Geneva.

online, not by phone. You will not be issued
with an actual **ticket** when you book, but
given a reference number to show with your

ID at check-in (some form of photographic ID,
such as a driving licence, is now required
even for UK domestic flights where no passport is needed). There are no refunds if you
miss your flight for any reason, although some
of the airlines will allow you to **change** your
destination, date of travel or the named traveller for a fee of around £15. There are also
charges for any **excess baggage**.

Fly Rail Baggage and Check-In at the Train Station
Fly Rail Baggage greatly simplifies your
journey into Switzerland. Your luggage can be
registered from each airport worldwide,
regardless of the carrier, to your destination in
Switzerland. On the return journey, you can
check-in your luggage at your train station of
departure and pick it up again at the destination. What's more, over 35 train stations in
Switzerland issue boarding passes.

By Train

The Eurostar and TGV Trains from Paris
All of the direct flight destinations, Basel,
Geneva and Zürich, and one of the secondary
main destinations, Bern, can also be reached
by first taking the **Eurostar**, *www.eurostar.com*,
train from London Waterloo to Paris Gare du
Nord. From there Bern, Geneva and Zürich can
be reached on a **TGV** service, *www.sncf.fr*, from
Paris Gare de Lyon; from Paris Gare de l'Est
trains go to Basel. The minimum travelling
times from London (2004) are Basel 9 hours 11
mins; Bern 8 hours 36 mins; Geneva 7 hours 23
mins; and Zürich 9 hours 49 mins.
Tickets in the UK can be purchased from **Rail
Europe**, 178 Piccadilly, London, W1, t 08705
848848, *reservations@raileurope.co.uk*, *www.
raileurope.co.uk* (open Mon–Fri 10–6, Sat 10–5).
Tickets in North America can be purchased
from **Rail Europe**, t 1 877 257-2887 or t 1 800 4
EURAIL in the USA and t 1 800 361-RAIL in
Canada, *www.raileurope.com*.

By Coach
National Express, *www.nationalexpress.com*,
operate the Eurolines long-distance bus
services from the UK to Europe. In 2004 it

Budget Flights via London from North America

While there are lots of options for direct scheduled flights to Geneva and Zürich from many US and Canadian cities (see p.11), it is also possible for North Americans to take advantage of the explosion of cheap inter-European flights by taking a charter to London and booking a UK–Switzerland cheap flight in advance on the budget airline's website (see p.11). This will need careful planning: you're looking at an 8hr flight followed by a 3hr journey across London and another 1½–2½hr hop to Switzerland; it can certainly be done, especially if you are a person who is able to sleep on a night flight, but you may prefer to spend a night or two in London.

Start by finding a cheap charter flight or discounted scheduled flight to London: try the main airlines above, but also check the Sunday paper travel sections for the latest deals, and if possible research your fare initially on some of the US cheap-flight websites: www.priceline.com (bid for tickets), www.expedia.com, www.hotwire.com, www.bestfares.com, www.eurovacations.com, www.cheaptrips.com, www.orbitz.com, www.cheaptickets.com or www.onetravel.com.

When you have the availability and arrival times for London flights, match up a convenient flight time on the website of the budget airline that flies to your chosen Swiss city. Be careful to choose only flights from the airports near London: Luton, Gatwick, Heathrow, London City and Stansted. Regional UK airports such as East Midlands or Liverpool will not be practical options.

You will most likely be arriving at Heathrow terminals 3 or 4 (possibly Gatwick), and may be flying out from Stansted, Luton or Gatwick, all of which are in different directions and will mean travelling through central London. Add together the journey times and prices for Heathrow into central London and back out again to your departure airport. You could mix and match – the Underground (Tube) to Victoria and the Gatwick Express, or a taxi from Heathrow to King's Cross Thameslink and a train to Luton – but don't even think of using a bus or taxi at rush hours (7–10am and 4–7pm); train and/or Tube are the only sensible choices. Always add on waiting times and delays in London's creaky transport system; and finally, since the cheapest airline fares are early morning and late at night, make sure your chosen transport is still operating.

Airport to Airport Taxis

A taxi directly between airports might avoid central London, but is an expensive option: Heathrow–Gatwick: 1hr 30mins, £85–£100. Heathrow–Stansted: 2hrs 15mins, £140–£160. Heathrow–Luton: 1hr 15mins, £80–£90.

Heathrow

Heathrow is about 15 miles west of the centre. **Airport information: t** 0870 0000 123.
By Tube: Heathrow is on the Piccadilly Line. Tube trains depart every 5–9 minutes from 6am to midnight and the journey time to the centre is 55mins. A single fare into the city centre costs £3.80.
By bus: the Airbus A2 (**t** 08705 80 80 80, www.nationalexpress.com) departs from all terminals every 30mins and makes several stops before terminating at King's Cross or Russell Square; the National Express 403 or 500 terminates at Victoria. Tickets cost £10 single. It's a long ride: at least 1hr 45mins.

operated three services a week, on Monday, Wednesday and Friday, from the London (Victoria) coach station to Basel and Zürich. These depart at 3pm on the first leg of the trip to Brussels; the next bus departs 15 minutes later, arriving in Basel at 8am and Zürich at 9.15am, with journey times of 17 hours and 18 hours 15 minutes respectively.

Entry Formalities

Passports and Visas

For citizens of Europe, the American continent, Australia, New Zealand and Japan visas are not necessary (exceptions may apply) for visits of less than three months.

A valid passport is required, and it must be valid for three months past travelling dates.

By train: the Heathrow Express is the fastest option: trains every 15mins between 5.10am and 11.40pm to Paddington Station, which is on the Tube's Bakerloo, Circle and District Lines, taking 15mins. Tickets cost £13 single.
By taxi: There are taxi ranks at all terminals. Fares into central London are about £35–£50.

Gatwick

Gatwick is about 20 miles south of London. There are two terminals, North and South, linked by a shuttle service. Airport information: t 0870 000 2468.
By train: the fastest service is the Gatwick Express (t 08457 48 49 50), which runs from Victoria Station to the South Terminal every 15 minutes and takes about 30mins. Tickets cost £11 for a single. There are two other slower train services: another from Victoria and one from London Bridge.
By taxi: fares from central London with a black cab are about £40–£60.

Luton

30 miles north of London. Airport information: t (01582) 405 100.
By bus: Greenline bus 757 (t 0870 608 7261) runs roughly every half-hour between Luton Airport and stop 6 in Buckingham Palace Road, Victoria, via Baker Street and Marble Arch. Tickets cost £8.50 single. The journey takes 1hr 15mins.
By train: between 8am and 10pm, Thameslink (t 08457 48 49 50) runs frequent trains from King's Cross Thameslink Station (10mins' walk from the King's Cross Station), via Blackfriars, London Bridge and Farringdon, to Luton Airport Parkway. Tickets cost £10.40 single. At Luton a free shuttle bus takes you on to the airport; the journey takes 55mins.

By taxi: a black cab will cost you around £40–£60 from central London.

Stansted

Stansted is the furthest from London, about 35 miles to the northeast. Airport information: t 0870 000 0303.
By bus: Airbus A6 (t 08705 757 747) runs every 30mins from Victoria Station, Marble Arch and Hyde Park Corner, taking 1hr 30mins or more in traffic. There are less frequent services all night. Tickets cost £10 single.
By train: the Stansted Express (t 08457 48 49 50) runs every 30mins (15mins during peak times) between 5am and 11pm to and from Liverpool Street Station, in the City, taking 45mins. Tickets cost £13.80 single.
By taxi: a black cab from central London will cost £45–£65.

Sample Journeys

Heathrow–Luton: get to Heathrow Express from terminal 15mins; wait for train 10mins; journey 15mins; go from Paddington Station down into Tube 10mins; Tube to Farringdon 15mins; go up and buy Thameslink ticket 10mins including queueing; train and shuttle to Luton 55mins. Total journey time 2hrs 10mins, plus 45mins for delays and hitches, so 3hrs would be safest.
Heathrow–Stansted: get to Tube station from terminal 10mins, wait for Tube 5mins, Piccadilly Line to King's Cross 1hr 10mins, change to Circle Line and continue to Liverpool Street Tube Station 15mins, up into main line station and buy Stansted Express ticket 10mins, wait for train 20mins, train journey 45mins. Total journey time 2hrs 55mins, plus 45mins for delays and hitches, so 3hrs 40mins would be safest.

Customs

Alcohol allowances:

	Europe	Outside Europe
Up to 15% vol	2 litres	2 litres
Over 15% vol	1 litre	1 litre

Tobacco allowances:

Cigarettes	200g	400g
Cigars	50g	100g
Pipe tobacco	250g	500g

Getting Around

Getting to Secondary Destinations

Switzerland is such a small country, and the train system is so comprehensive and fast, that there will be few instances when travellers will feel the need to fly to secondary destinations. However, there are valid occasions where flying is worth such consideration.

Swiss, *www.swiss.com*, has one direct (late night) flight between Basel and Lugano and two flights involving a change at Zürich; there are six flights directly from Zürich to Lugano and one to Sion and three flights daily between Geneva and Lugano.

There are also ten daily 50-minute flights between Geneva and Zürich, but, overall, as the train takes just three hours there may not be much, if any, time saving involved.

Getting from Direct Flight and Secondary Destinations to Day Trips/Overnighters

The rationale used in this guide is that day trips/overnighters should be able to be reached on public transport from direct flight cities (Zürich, Basel and Geneva) and secondary destinations (Bern, Luzern, Lugano and Sion) within (more or less) 2 hours and with just (usually) one change. A table listing the daytrips/overnighters that fit this pattern is shown at the end of each direct flight and secondary destination section.

The Swiss Travel System (STS)

This is a thoroughly integrated system that includes **train services**, the famed **post bus system** and a series of **boat services** on the beautiful Swiss lakes which are all immaculately clean and punctual – regardless of weather conditions. The trains run every hour, or even half hour, and connections are easy and, usually, only require a few minutes of changing time. More impressively, in this, the densest public transport system in the world, timetables are even coordinated to allow changes from one form of transport to another with the least possible delays. The **Swiss Federal Railways** (Schweizerische Bundesbahnen, SBB), *www.sbb.ch*, has a marvellous website that allows you to plan trips – on trains, buses and even boats – confidently, and even sometimes tells you what platform you need to be on.

Train Passes Available in Europe

The **Interrail** pass allows European travellers to travel in up to 28 European countries. The Interrail pass is available only to European citizens or those who have lived in Europe for at least six months. You can select the countries available to you using your Interrail pass, with countries grouped together into 8 zones. Switzerland is grouped with Austria, Denmark and Germany in Zone C, and prices (2004) for this zone are as follows: for 12 days' travel, £199 (adult), £135 (under-26); for 22 days' travel, £235 (adult), £165 (under-26). You can also buy tickets that combine two, three or all zones.

The **Eurodomino** pass allows you to choose which country/ies you want to travel in and offers unlimited travel on 3, 4, 5, 6, 7 or 8 days within one month. It is available in 1st or 2nd class for adults and children (4–12) and 2nd class for people under 26 years of age. Certain high-speed trains require a supplement.

2004 Prices for Switzerland (£ sterling)

Period	Adult 1st	Adult 2nd	Youth 2nd
3 days	112	75	57
4 days	124	84	63
5 days	136	92	70
6 days	148	100	76
7 days	160	109	82
8 days	172	117	89

Passes Available in Europe and North America

Anyone who is neither a permanent resident of Switzerland nor the Principality of Liechtenstein is eligible to buy any of the tickets below. No photo is needed, but you must present a passport.

Swiss Pass

Explore the entire country with a Swiss Pass. The passes are good for unlimited usage for 4, 8, 15 or 22 days, or 1 month. The 2004 prices, 1st/2nd class and in GBP/US$ are, respectively, £165/$260–£110/$170; £233/$360–£156/$240; £281/$440–£188/$290; £327/$500–£217/$335; £361/$560–£240/$375. The passes are valid on the legendary scenic routes and are also good on the public transportation systems of 37 Swiss cities. Swiss Pass holders also receive many discounts on mountain-top excursions and other services.

Swiss Saver Pass

Saver formula: if two or more persons travel together, each one receives a 15% discount on the above rates.

Where to Buy Your Pass

Passes that can only be purchased in Europe can be obtained through **Rail Europe**, 178 Piccadilly, London, W1, t 08705 848848, *reservations@raileurope.co.uk*, *www. raileurope.co.uk (open Mon–Fri 10–6, Sat 10–5)*; the **Switzerland Travel Centre**, Swiss Centre, 10 Wardour Street, 10th Floor, London, W1D 6QF, t freephone 0800 100 200 30 or t (020) 7292 1550 *(open Mon–Fri 9–5)*; or, if you have an address in the UK, through the UK version of *www.myswitzerland.com*.

Passes that can only be purchased in North America are available through either **Rail Europe**, t 1 877 257 2887 or 1 800 4 EURAIL in the USA and 1 800 361 RAIL in Canada, *www. raileurope.com*, or through the *www. myswitzerland.com* website.

Swiss Youth Pass

Young people up to 26 years old can obtain the Swiss Youth Pass at a 25% discount on the above fares. Exactly the same advantages are offered as in the Swiss Pass. The Swiss Youth Pass cannot be bought in conjunction with the Saver Pass discount, and it is not available as a Flexi Pass.

Swiss Flexi Pass

This ticket is ideal for people who do not plan on travelling every day. The Swiss Flexi Pass is valid for the amount of days you have purchased within one month (3, 4, 5, 6 or 8 days that do not need to be consecutive). The 2004 prices, 1st/2nd class and in GBP/US$, are, respectively: £158/$250–£105/$166; £192/$294 –£128/$196; £220/$338–£146/$226; £247/$386– £165/$256; £288/$450–£192/$300. On the days you choose to activate your Swiss Flexi Pass, you will enjoy the same advantages as a Swiss Pass holder.

Swiss Saver Flexi Pass

Saver formula: if two or more persons travel together, each one receives a 15% discount on the above rates.

Swiss Transfer Ticket

If you plan on visiting only one destination in Switzerland, the Swiss Transfer Ticket is the way to go. It is also recommended for persons who visit Switzerland for a skiing vacation.

This ticket includes one free round trip to anywhere in Switzerland. The trip must start and end at the Swiss border or at any Swiss airport. It is valid for one month. Each trip needs to be completed by the end of the day and has to be as direct as possible. The 2004 prices, 1st/2nd class and in GBP/US$ are, respectively, £83/$128–£54/$85. Swiss Transfer tickets cannot be obtained in Switzerland.

Swiss Card

Visitors who plan to stay mainly in one region of Switzerland should opt for the Swiss Card. Not only does it include the transfers from the border or airport to one's destination and back, it also offers a 50% discount on all trips effected by train, boat, post bus and most mountain trains and cable cars between the first and second transfer day. The Swiss Card has a maximum validity of one month. The first and last transfers must be completed by the end of the day, and each transfer has to be as direct as possible. The 2004 prices, 1st/2nd class and in GBP/US$ are, respectively, £111/$166–£78/$124. Swiss Cards are sold in Switzerland only at border or airport train stations.

Swiss Travel System Family Card/ Children's Rates

If you have children, be sure to ask for a free Swiss Travel System Family Card, as it will entitle your children up to 16 years of age to free travel, as long as at least one parent is accompanying them. Non-family members between the age of 6 and 16 receive a 50% discount on all Swiss Travel System tickets.

Swiss Half Fare Card

With the Swiss Half Fare Card you can travel at half the fare. You buy ordinary individual tickets for the journey you wish to make, and, producing the Swiss Half Fare Card, you only pay half the fare. The Swiss Half Fare Card is valid for one month and is appropriate for shorter journeys within Switzerland. It can be purchased upon arrival at any train station in Switzerland for CHF 99, or £46 in the UK.

Passes Available in North America

The tickets mentioned below are available to citizens and permanent residents of North America. If you are planning on travelling in other countries as well as Switzerland, consider the Eurailpass family of ticket plans. Although not as comprehensive in Switzerland as the Swisspass family of tickets, they give you unlimited train travel in 17 countries through the extensive 100,000-mile rail network of Europe. Countries included in the Eurail Network are: Austria, Belgium, Denmark, Finland, France, Germany, Greece, Holland, Hungary, Italy, Luxembourg, Norway, Portugal, Republic of Ireland, Spain, Sweden and Switzerland.

The **Eurailpass** is valid for consecutive-day 1st-class travel for 15 days, 21 days, 1 month, 2 months or 3 months, at prices (in 2004) of US$588, 762, 946, 1,338 and 1,654 respectively.

The **EurailpassFlexi** gives you 1st-class travel for any 10 days or any 15 days in a 2-month period, at prices (in 2004) of US$694 and 914 respectively.

The **EurailpassSaver** is a special pass for two or more people travelling together; consecutive-day, 1st-class travel for 15 days, 21 days, 1 month, 2 months or 3 months, at prices (in 2004) of US$498, 648, 804, 1,138 and 1,408 respectively.

The **EurailpassSaverFlexi** is a special pass for two or more people travelling together in 1st class for any 10 days or any 15 days in a 2-month period, at prices (in 2004) of US$592 and 778 respectively.

The **EurailpassYouth** offers a great bargain for those under 26 years of age; consecutive-day, 2nd-class travel for 15 days, 21 days, 1 month, 2 months or 3 months, at prices (in 2004) of US$414, 534, 664, 938 and 1,160 respectively.

The **EurailpassYouthFlexi** is another great deal for those under 26 years of age; 2nd class in any 10 days or any 15 days in a 2-month period, at prices (in 2004) of US$ 488 and 642 respectively.

The **EurailSelectpass** family of tickets offers unlimited travel on the national rail networks of any 3, 4 or 5 adjoining Eurail countries that are connected by train or ship, for a period of 5, 6, 8, 10 or 15 days of rail travel within any two-month period. Travel days, 1st class, can be used consecutively or non-consecutively.

The **EurailSelectpass** costs for 3/4/5 countries US$356/398/438, US$394/436/476, US$470/512/552 and US$542/584/624 for 5, 6, 8 and 10 days respectively, and US$794 for 15 days in 5 countries.

The **EurailSelectpassSaver** is a special pass for two or more people travelling together, and costs for 3/4/5 countries US$304/340/374, US$336/372/406, US$400/436/470 and US$460/496/530 for 5, 6, 8 and 10 days respectively, and US$674 for 15 days in 5 countries.

The **EurailSelectpassYouth** is a special pass for those under 26, and costs for 3/4/5 countries US$249/279/307, US$276/306/334, US$329/359/387 and US$379/409/437 for 5, 6, 8 and 10 days respectively, and US$556 for 15 days in 5 countries.

Specialist Tour Operators

From the UK

Bridge, t 0870 191 7270, *www.bridgetravel.co.uk*. Summer tours of lakes and mountains, as well as skiing holidays.

Crystal, t 0870 160 6040, *www.crystalski.co.uk*. Skiing holidays all over Switzerland for all levels of skier.

HolidaysGo.com, t 0870 013 0499, *www. holidaysgo.com*. Winter holidays from the UK's leading tour operators.

Inghams, t 020 8780 4400, *www.inghams.com*. Skiing holidays to the Valais and Graubünden.

Powder Byrne, t 020 8246 5300, *www.powder byrne.com*. Skiing holidays to Arosa, Flims, Grindelwald, Klosters and Zermatt.

Swisstravelnet for Switzerland, *www. swisstravelnet.com*. Specialist tour operator to Switzerland, offering flights, tours, city packages, car rental and bus tours.

From the USA and Canada

For a full list of US tour operators operating in Switzerland, visit *www.twcrossroads. com/planners/switzerland2004/index.html*.

Mercator Tours, New York, **t** 800 294 1650, *www.mercatortours.com*. A specialist operator to Switzerland with a variety of tours.

Continental Journeys, Sherman Oaks CA, **t** 800 601 4343, *www.continentaljourneys.com*. Feature several escorted tours.

Prime Travel, 1852 Marine Drive, W. Vancouver, BC, V7V 1J6, **t** 604 925 1212, *www.prime-travel.com*. 'Discover Switzerland' tours.

Practical A–Z

Calendar of Events

Late January Cartier Polo World Cup on Snow, St Moritz, *www.polostmoritz.com*. The top polo teams from four continents battle it out on the frozen lake at glittering St Moritz.

February/March Carnival in Basel, Luzern and Zürich. A time when the Swiss become distinctly un-Swiss; strange and fantastic masks and costumes complement carnival musicians (*Guggenmusigen*) making as much noise as they can while people dance away the winter.

Late March to early April Luzern Festival Ostern, *www.lucernefestival.ch*. A festival of sacred and concert music, with events held in the city's beautiful churches and the Concert Hall of the new Culture and Convention Centre.

Mid-June Art 34 Basel, *www.artbasel.com*. In its 4th decade, this is considered one of the leading art events in the world, with galleries from Europe, America, Asia and Australia presenting art from the 20th and 21st centuries.

Late June to early July New Orleans Jazz Ascona, *www.jazzascona.ch*. Reaching its second decade, this is one of Switzerland's most famous jazz festivals. It features the world's top artists and takes over the beautiful lake front of this lovely town.

Early July Allianz Suisse Open, *www.swissopengstaad.com*. A top event on the ATP tennis tour, in a beautiful location in Gstaad.

Early to mid-July Montreux Jazz Festival, *www.montreuxjazz.com*. Soon reaching its 4th decade, this annual festival mixes jazz, blues, rock, reggae and soul with Brazilian and African sounds, including 300 free concerts.

Early to mid-August Festival Internazionale del Film Locarno, *www.pardo.ch*. The latest productions are screened on the largest screen in Europe – 85ft (26m) by 46ft (14m) – located in an open-air setting in the Piazza Grande and watched by 7,000 spectators.

Mid-August to mid-September Luzern Festival, *www.lucernefestival.ch*. Nearing its 70th year, this is a festival of classical music that features the world's most famous orchestras, conductors and soloists.

Early September Omega European Masters, Crans-Montana, *www.golf-european masters.com*. One of the major tournaments on the PGA European Tour, this golf event takes place at 4,921ft (1,500m) with views of Mont Blanc and the Matterhorn.

Mid-September Knabenschiessen, Zürich, *www.knabenschiessen.ch*. One of Zürich's oldest festivals and Switzerland's largest fair: a shooting competition on the Albisgütli for 12- to 17-year-old boys and girls.

Climate and When to Go

For such a small country, Switzerland has an extremely diverse climate. In July it might reach 96°F (36°C) at low levels of altitude yet be snowing at 10,000ft (3,000m); equally, in early October it might be snowing heavily in Graubünden yet be quite pleasant in Basel at the other end of the country. Surprisingly, too, it can be warm and pleasant in cities like Zürich as early in the year as March.

Quite simply, whenever and wherever you go in Switzerland you are likely to encounter many climate changes. That said, in the summer months at lower altitudes it is likely to be pretty warm during the day; in the skiing resorts you can expect a good covering of snow and ice through to the end of March.

Weather forecasts can be checked on *www.meteoswiss.ch*, the Swiss weather organization.

Clothing

With such a variable climate, you need to be well prepared. During spring, summer and autumn it is best to take a mix of clothes, including a warm jacket for excursions to the tops of mountains. In winter, much warmer attire is required, especially a waterproof jacket and warm trousers. At any time of the year you will need good walking shoes, preferably hiking boots. A backpack is useful, too; as with hiking boots, the selection in Switzerland is far better than elsewhere.

Consulates and Embassies

In Switzerland
Australia: Chemin des Fins 2, t 022 799 91 00, f 022 799 91 78, *consulate-geneva@dfat. gov.au, www.australia.ch/eng.*

Canada: Kirchenfeldstrasse 88, 3005 Bern, t 031 357 3200, f 031 357 3210, *bern-ag@dfait-maeci. gc.ca, www.canada- ambassade.ch.*

Republic of Ireland: Kirchenfeldstrasse 68, 3006 Bern, t 031 352 14 42, f 031 352 14 55.

UK: Thunsstrasse 50, 3000, Bern 15, t 031 359 7741, f 031 359 7701, *www.britain-in-switzerland.ch.*

USA: Jubiläumsstrasse 93, 3001, Bern, t 031 357 7011, f 031 357 7336, *www.us-embassy.ch.*

Canadian Consular Services
Canadian Permanent Mission to the UN, Consular Section, 5 avenue de l'Ariana, 1202 Geneva, t 022 919 9200, f 022 919 9233, *genev-cs@dfait-maeci.gc.ca.*

UK Consulates General
37–9 rue de Vermont, 1211 Geneva 20, t 022 918 2400, f 022 918 2322.

UK Vice Consulates
Dr Alan Chalmers, Gewerbestrasse 14, Innovation Centre, 4123 Allschwil, Basel, t/f 061 483 0977, *achalmers@british-vice-consulate.ch.*

Mrs Sandra Darra MBE, Montreux-Vevey, t/f 021 943 3263.

Mr John Takield OBE, Via Sorengo 22, 3rd Floor, PO Box 184, 6903 Lugano, t 091 950 0606, f 091 950 0609, *jtakield@british-vice-consulate.ch.*

Mr Andrew Bushnell, rue des Fontaines, 3974 Mollens, Valais, t 027 480 3210, f 027 480 3211, *abushnell@british-vice-consulate.ch.*

Mr Antony McCammon, Hegibachstrasse 47, 8032 Zürich, t 01 383 6560, f 01 383 6561, *amccammon@british-vice-consulate.ch.*

US Consulates General and Agencies
US Consular Agency, c/o US Mission, 11 rte de Prégny, 1292 Chambésy, Geneva, t 022 840 5160, f 022 840 5162, *consulate.us@ties.itu.int.*
US Consular Agency, Dufourstrasse 101, Zürich, t 01 422 2566, f 01 383 9814.

In the UK
Swiss Embassy, 16–18 Montagu Place, London W1H 2BQ, t (020) 7616 6000, f (020) 7724 7001, *swissembassy@lon.rep.admin.ch, www.eda. admin.ch/londonemb.*

Consulates General
Portland Tower, Portland Street, Manchester M1 3LD, t (0161) 236 2933, f (0161) 236 4689, *vertretung@mch.rep.admin.ch.*
66 Hanover Street, Edinburgh EH2 1HH, t (0131) 226 5660, f (0131) 226 5332.
8 The Horse Park, Boneybefore, Carrickfergus, Co. Antrim BT38 7ED, t 2890 32 16 26, f 2890 24 81 96.
PO Box 368, Helvetia Court, South Esplanade, St Peter Port, Guernsey, t 1481 710267, f 1481 710275.

In the USA
Swiss Embassy, 2900 Cathedral Avenue NW, Washington, D.C. 20008-3499, t (202) 745 7900, f (202) 387 2564, *vertretung@ was.rep.admin.ch, www.swissemb.org.*

Consulates General
1275 Peachtree Street NE, Suite 425, Atlanta, Georgia 30309-3555, t (404) 870 2000, f (404) 870 2011, *vertretung@atl.rep.admin.ch.*
737 N. Michigan Avenue, Suite 2301, Olympia Center, Chicago, Illinois 60611-2615, t (312) 915 0061, f (312) 915 0388, *vertretung@chi.rep. admin.ch.*
Wells Fargo Plaza, 1000 Louisiana, Suite 5670, Houston, Texas 77002-5013, t (713) 650 0000, f (713) 650 1321, *vertretung@hou.rep.admin.ch.*
11766 Wilshire Boulevard, Suite 1400, Los Angeles, California 90025, t (310) 575 1145, f (310) 575 1982, *vertretung@los.rep.admin.ch.*
633 Third Avenue, 30th Floor, New York, New York 10017-6706, t (212) 599 5700, f (212) 599 4266, *vertretung@nyc.rep.admin.ch.*
456 Montgomery Street, Suite 1500, San Francisco, California 94104, t (415) 788 2272, f (415) 788 1402, *vertretung@sfr.rep.admin.ch.*

In Canada
Swiss Embassy, 5 Marlborough Avenue, Ottawa, Ontario K1N 8E6, t (613) 235 1837, f (613) 563 1394, *vertretung@ott.rep.admin. ch, www.eda-admin.ch/canada.*

Consulates General

1572 Dr Penfield, Montreal, Quebec H3G 1C4, **t** (514) 932 7181, **f** (514) 932 9028, *vertretung@mon.rep.admin.ch.*

154 University Avenue, Suite 601, Toronto, Ontario M5H 3Y9, **t** (416) 593 5371, **f** (416) 593 5083, *vertretung@tor.rep.admin.ch.*

790–999 Canada Place, Vancouver, British Columbia V6C 3E1, **t** (604) 684 2231, **f** (604) 684 2806, *vertretung@van.rep.admin.ch.*

Crime and the Police

Crime is not really an important issue for visitors to Switzerland, especially outside the large cities. In the event of an emergency contact the police (*Polizei*), *www.swisspolice. ch*, on the emergency number **t** 117.

Disabled Travellers

Switzerland is very user-friendly for disabled visitors. Stations and trains are always being improved to include lifts (elevators), ramps and wheelchair-accessible toilets (restrooms), and wheelchair-bound passengers can use the trains if the wheelchair is not larger than 2.3ft (70cm) wide, 3.93ft (120cm) long and 3.6ft (109cm) high. On all Intercity and most EuroCity and fast trains special wheelchair compartments are now available in 2nd class; on older trains space will be available in the luggage carriage.

If you give notice at least 1 hour before the train leaves (call toll-free **t** 0800 00 71 02 and be present on the designated platform at least 10 minutes before departure), the wheelchair will be raised into the train by a Mobilift, which are available at more than 150 stations. Seeing Eye dogs travel free.

Hotels and certain **restaurants** with special features for the disabled are marked with a wheelchair symbol in the Swiss Hotel Guide, which is available from the Swiss tourist authorities. Alternatively, check *www.swisshotels.ch*, and then click on 'hotels' in the navigation bar and then 'hotel guide'. By checking the field 'suitable for wheelchairs', the system will then list all suitable properties.

Useful Contacts

Access Ability, *www.access-ability.co.uk.* Information on travel agencies catering specifically for disabled people.

Access Travel, 6 The Hillock, Astley, Lancashire M29 7GW, **t** (01942) 888844, *info@access-travel.co.uk, www.access-travel.co.uk.* Travel agent for disabled people: special air fares and car hire.

Alternative Leisure Co, 165 Middlesex Turnpike, Suite 206, Bedford, MA 01730, **t** (718) 275 0023, **f** 275 2305, *www.alctrips.com.* Vacations abroad for disabled people.

COMPAGNA – Reisebegleitung, Eschenstrasse 1, 9000 St Gallen, **t** 071 220 1607, **f** 071 220 1609, *compagnareisebegleitung@ bluewin. ch.* A volunteer organization that will, for reasonable rates, pick up passengers at stations and accompany them if required.

Disabled Drivers' Motor Club Ltd, Cottingham Way, Thrapston NN14 4PL, **t** 01832 734 724, **f** 01832 733 816, *info@ddmc.org.uk, www.ddmc.org.uk.* Assistance for those travelling by car from the UK.

Emerging Horizons, *www.emerginghorizons. com.* International on-line travel newsletter for people with disabilities.

Mobility International USA, PO Box 10767, Eugene, OR 97440, USA, **t/TTY** (541) 343 1284, **f** 343 6812, *www.miusa.org.* Information on international educational exchange programmes and volunteer service overseas.

RADAR (Royal Association for Disability and Rehabilitation), 12 City Forum, 250 City Road, London EC1V 8AF, **t** (020) 7250 3222, **f** 7250 0212, Minicom **t** (020) 7250 4119, *www.radar. org.uk; radar@radar.org.uk.* Information and books on travel.

SATH (Society for Accessible Travel and Hospitality), 347 5th Avenue, Suite 610, New York, NY 10016, **t** (212) 447 7284, **f** 725 8253, *www.sath.org, sathtravel@aol.com.* Travel and access information; also details other access resources on the web.

Schweizerische Paraplegiker Vereinigung (Swiss Paraplegic Association), Kantonsstrasse 40, 6207 Nottwill, Switzerland, **t** 041 939 5400, **f** 041 939 5439. Offers advice about car hire for the handicapped.

Eating Out

See box above for price categories in this book. For information on Swiss food and wine specialities, dining out and a menu decoder, see **Food and Drink**, pp.25–30.

Electricity

The current used in Switzerland is 220 volts (50 cycles), and most power sockets are designed for three-pin round plugs. However, the standard continental-type plug with two round pins is attached to most small appliances. Those from North America will need a travel converter if their small appliances cannot be adjusted between 110 and 220 volts.

Gay and Lesbian Scene

Switzerland Tourism has a brochure called *It's Only Natural* about the gay and lesbian scene in Switzerland, and their website *http://uk.myswitzerland.com* offers advice about bars, clubs, restaurants and events.

Health and Emergencies

At this time, there are no vaccination and inoculation requirements for visitors to Switzerland from European and western hemisphere countries.

As there is not a state medical health service in Switzerland, medical treatment must be paid for – and it is expensive. Therefore, it is highly advisable to take out insurance cover against personal accident and sickness (you may be asked for proof of it before treatment) – as well as loss or damage to luggage and personal effects and cancellation costs.

Internet Facilities

In all the main cities and towns there are Internet cafés, with varying rates; a minimum of CHF 5 for about 15 minutes is common. In most of the MANOR department stores, often in the electrical department, there are computers with Internet facilities – although you have to stand – offering better rates.

Many hotels also have an Internet Corner or Small Office facilities, but be sure to check first what rates they charge as they can sometimes be excessive.

Language

Switzerland has four national languages. German, spoken in a variety of dialects but written in high German, is used in the north, central and eastern areas; French is spoken in western Switzerland; Italian is the language of Ticino in the south of the country; and Romansch – a derivative of Latin – is spoken in the southeastern region of Graubünden (Grisons). English is widely spoken in all the major cities and towns, and much of the country.

For tips on pronunciation and lists of useful words and phrases, see **Language**, p.246.

Media

Swiss News, the national English journal, *www.swissnews.ch*, is a monthly newspaper costing CHF 5.80, giving a wide range of news about Switzerland in English.

World Radio Geneva, *www.wrgfm.com*, WRG-FM 88.4, is a leading English-speaking radio station.

Almost all hotels now have satellite TV that features CNN, SKY News, BBC Prime and other similar programmes. English newspapers and the *Herald Tribune* are widely available at airports, train stations and other places, on the same day as publication in the largest cities and the next day in other, smaller, places.

The Swiss government has a news agency, *www.swissinfo.ch*, informing visitors in English, German, French, Italian, Spanish and Arabic about current events in both the country and the world in the form of text, photos and radio broadcasts – Swiss Radio International (SRI).

Money

Switzerland is not a member of the European Union, and the Swiss franc (CHF) is the official currency, with 100 *centimes* equalling one franc. Notes (bills) come in denominations of CHF 10, 20, 50, 100, 200 and 1,000. Coins come in denominations of 5, 10, 20 and 50 *centimes* (half-franc) and CHF 1, 2 and 5.

Banks are usually open Mon–Fri 8.30–4.30, but once a week they usually extend these hours. Traveller's cheques and Eurocheques are widely accepted in Switzerland, credit cards are accepted more or less everywhere and ATM machines are prevalent throughout the country.

Post

Post offices, in general, are open Mon–Fri 8–12 and 2–5. However, in large cities they can also open on Saturday 8.30–12, and those located in shopping centres are usually open the same hours as the centre.

Shopping

In the large cities and towns shops are usually open Mon–Fri 8.30–6 approximately, with some closing slightly earlier on Saturday. In smaller towns and villages it is still the custom to close between midday and 2pm. On Sunday the only places you are guaranteed to find a selection of shops open are at Geneva and Zürich Airports and railway stations, and the railway stations at Bern and Luzern. With a very few, although growing, number of exceptions, no shops will be open elsewhere.

Tax free shopping: in Switzerland there is 7.6% VAT (sales tax) on goods that is included in the price, and foreign visitors are entitled to a refund of VAT on goods of a value of CHF 400 or more through the Global Refund system, *www.globalrefund.com*. Shops participating in this scheme prominently display the TAX FREE SHOPPING sign.

Public Holidays

1 January New Year's Day
2 January (regional)
March/April Good Friday and Easter Monday
1 May Labour Day (regional)
May Ascension Day
May Whit Monday
May/June Corpus Christi (regional)
1 August Swiss National Day
25 December Christmas Day
26 December Boxing Day

Switzerland is famous for many products, but perhaps none more so than Swiss **watches** with names like Rolex, Tag Heuer, Omega, Patek Philippe and Audemars Piguet, as well as Swatch at the other end of the market. The Federation of the Swiss Watch Industry (Fédération de l'Industrie Horlogère Suisse, 6 rue d'Argent, 2501-Bienne, **t** 032 328 0828, **f** 032 328 0880, *www.fhs.ch*) is the regulatory body for the industry, and links to every Swiss watchmaker are found on its website. Obviously, there are numerous retail outlets for Swiss watches, but the most famous such company in Switzerland is Bucherer, *www.bucherer.com*, which has branches in Basel, Bern, Geneva, Interlaken, Lausanne, Luzern, Lugano, St Gallen, St Moritz, Zermatt and Zürich – all places mentioned in this guide.

Swiss **knives** are also world-famous, and the Victorinox, *www.victorinox.ch*, name is seen everywhere in Switzerland. Knives, though, aren't their only products; these days they also produce such innovations as the SwissFlame and Altimeter – knives with a built-in flame and altimeter respectively – and, of course, its range of Swiss Army watches. Wenger, *www.wenger-knife.ch*, also produces official Swiss army knives, and recently has come out with its nifty Swiss Business Tool.

Cuckoo clocks, too, are synonymous with Switzerland and the attractive chalet-style ones that you see in all the main souvenir shops are almost certainly hand-carved at the Lötscher, *www.loetscher.ch*, premises in Brienz (*see* p.142). Brienz is famous for its wood carvers and Huggler, *www.huggler-wood carvings.ch*, produces most of the beautiful pieces on display in the souvenir shops.

Schweizer Heimatwerk, *www.heimatwerk.ch*, is a good alternative source for souvenirs as it offers the best design in contemporary Swiss handicrafts in the form of household items, home decor accessories, jewellery, clothes and toys. They have eleven shops, four in the city centre of Zürich and two at the airport, and are represented in Basel and at Geneva airport.

Turning to food, Swiss **cheese**, too, is internationally famous and comes in many tasty guises. The Switzerland Cheese Marketing organization, *www.switzerland-cheese.com*, leaves no holes uncovered in its interesting coverage of the topic on its website. Who can resist, either, Swiss chocolate made by such famous companies as Lindt, *www.lindt.com*, and Suchard?

Sports and Activities

In the winter Switzerland is, of course, famous for its **skiing** and other winter sports activities, and details about these have been given in the appropriate chapters. In the summer **hiking** and **mountain biking** are particularly popular, and **swimming** in the lakes is a refreshing experience.

As for professional sports, **football** (soccer) is well supported, especially in the larger cities; Basel, in particular, has been successful in European competitions recently. **Ice hockey**, too, has plenty of enthusiasts, and Switzerland plays host to major events on the European professional **golf** and **tennis** circuits. (Tennis player Roger Federer, the 2003 Wimbledon champion, comes from Basel.) And, rather incongruously, Switzerland, a country far away from the world's oceans, actually won the 2003 America's Cup yacht race.

Telephones

Dialling from the UK: international access code 00 and country code 41 plus the area code (excluding the leading 0) and then the number.

Dialling from the USA or Canada: international access code 011 and country code 41 plus the area code (excluding the leading 0) and then the number.

Dialling from Switzerland: for the UK dial the country code 0044 followed by the area code (excluding the leading 0) and then the number; for the USA and Canada country code 001 followed by area code and number.

Dialling inside Switzerland: the full area code (including the leading 0) must precede the number.

Most Swiss public payphones can only be used with a Swiss **phone card**, the PTT-Taxcard, which comes in denominations of CHF 5, 10 and 20 and is available at post offices, newsagents and railway stations, etc.

Anglo-Phone, t 157-5014, *www.anglolake.com*, at CHF 2.13 per minute from anywhere in Switzerland, is a 24-hour English-speaking information and talk line that can answer all your questions about current events, excursions and activities and much more.

There is usually a very heavy surcharge for telephone calls made from your **hotel room**, especially for international calls. It is much more economical to use your personal long-distance calling cards such as AT&T and MCI (but remember to get the respective number before leaving home as it is not always readily available in Switzerland), or use a PTT-Taxcard at a public payphone.

Other useful numbers: t 114 international operator; t 1141 international phone rates.

Time

Switzerland operates on a time system one hour ahead of the United Kingdom, and six hours ahead of Eastern Standard Time, USA.

Tipping

Tips are automatically included in all hotel and restaurant bills, although it is customary to give a small tip (10–12%) for special services, such as luggage handling, and to taxi drivers.

Toilets (Restrooms)

Anywhere in Switzerland, these will be immaculately clean and well maintained.

Tourist Information

Switzerland Tourism, *www.myswitzerland. com*, operates the following offices.

In the UK and Ireland

Switzerland Tourism, Swiss Centre, 10 Wardour Street, London W1D 6QF, t (020) 7851 1710, f (020) 7851 1720.

In the USA

Swiss Center, 608 Fifth Avenue, New York, New York 10020-2303, t (212) 757-5944 (toll free in USA 1 877 794 8037), f (212) 262 6116, *info.usa@switzerlandtourism.com*.
501 Santa Monica Boulevard, Suite 607, Santa Monica, California 90401, t (310) 260 2421, f (310) 260 2923.

In Canada

926 The East Mall, Toronto, Ontario M9B 6K1, t (416) 695 2090, f (416) 695 2774, *info.caen@ switzerland.com*.

Where to Stay

Most Swiss hotels are members of the **Swiss Hotel Association**, which issues a Swiss Hotel Guide in book form, or you can check their *www.swisshotels.ch* website. Their hotel ratings are deluxe (*****), first class (****), tourist class (***), standard (**) and basic (*). Prices are set for single and double rooms according to the star rating and season, with the latter being rather variable, and with a continental breakfast usually included in the

Accommodation Price Ranges

Prices are for a double room with bathroom in high season.

luxury over CHF 450
expensive CHF 250–450
moderate CHF 150–250
inexpensive CHF 100–150
cheap under CHF 100

price. There are several organizations of groups of hotels such as **Alpine Classics**, *www.alpineclassic.ch*; **Swiss Budget Hotels**, *www.rooms.ch*; **Idyll Hotels**, *www.idyllhotels. com*; **Hotels Selection Suisse**, *www.selection-suisse.ch*; **Swiss International Hotels**, *www. sin.ch*; and **Swiss Deluxe Hotels**, *www. swissdeluxehotels.com*, all of which are worth looking at.

There are also other organizations, generally at a lower standard than hotels, which are well worthy of consideration. **Bed and Breakfast Switzerland**, *info@bnb.ch*, *www.bnb.ch*, speaks for itself; **Tourism Rural**, *info@tourisme-rural.ch*, *www.tourisme-rural.ch*, offers accommodation in farmhouses and rural homes between the Jura and the Alps; information about youth hostels can be found at **Swiss Youth Hostels**, Schaffhauser-strasse 14, 8042 Zürich, t 01 360 1414, f 01 360 1460, *marketing@youthhostel.ch*, *www.youth hostel.ch*; and the **Swiss Backpacker News**, Eisengasse 34, 5600 Lenzburg, t 062 892 2676, f 062 892 2675, *info@backpacker.ch*, *www. backpacker.ch*, issues a magazine with information about less expensive accommodation.

Food and Drink

04

Eating Out

Switzerland, again with the exception of Ticino, more or less follows the eating habits of other northern European countries. Hotels usually serve breakfast – often in sumptuous buffet form – from around 7am to 10am; lunch is taken between midday and 2pm and dinner starts early, often at 6.30pm. That meal is usually a starter, main course and dessert – with the latter offering a choice between a trolley of mouth-watering desserts or amazing cheese selections.

Restaurants come in all shapes and sizes, from serious Michelin-starred ones down to mountain huts that only open between March and October. At the top of the range, few countries can better Switzerland, and such restaurants, either independent or as an integral part of hotels, offer opulence, service that is second to none and the most beautifully prepared and presented dishes. All of this, though, comes at a price. There are organizations, such as Les Grandes Tables de Suisse, *www.grandestables.ch*, and Relais & Châteaux, *www.relaischateaux.ch*, that promote such restaurants. Switzerland has produced some world-famous chefs, such as Anton Mosimann, and the country also attracts young chefs anxious to make their mark in their own particular culinary styles; these can be found on the Jeunes Restaurateurs d'Europe website, *www.jre.net*.

Besides these, you can find almost any type of restaurant in the major cosmopolitan cities of Basel, Geneva, Zürich and Luzern, with a wide range recommended in the respective chapters. In other places the selection will be much more limited, with regional specialities, lake fish such as perch and the usual cheese dishes being the order of the day. On the other hand, the mountain restaurants (*Bergrestaurants*) usually don't have any competition, and the dishes are more than likely to be fondue, raclette and *rösti*, with the occasional plate of dried meat as a worthy and tasty alternative. The smallest types of restaurant are the 'mountain huts', charming places full of ambience that are usually only open outside the winter months and only locally known. Although the menu is invariably limited, the dishes are wholesome, home-cooked and delightful. Two fine examples of these are described in the Lötschental and Centovalli sections (*see* pp.196 and 188).

As usual, things are different in Ticino, the Italian-speaking canton south of the Alps. The cuisine is heavily influenced by the northern Italian regions of Lombardy and Piedmont, with dinner being an appetizer (*antipasto*), followed by a first course (*primo*), most often pasta, and a second course (*secondo*), usually a meat dish. The meal culminates with cheese then a dessert, possibly *torta di pane* (a bread cake) or *torta della nonna* (a sugar tart), often ending with a *grappa* or *nocino*, a walnut-based liqueur.

The local restaurants are rather different, too, with *osterie*, *canvetti* and grottos being popular. All are simple restaurants with the last usually consisting of a simple kitchen and a small dining room, often with tables outside in the garden, featuring local produce.

Swiss Specialities

Owing to its native French, German and Italian influences – not to mention the cultural influx from around the world in places like Zürich and Geneva – Switzerland has a wide and interesting range of gastronomic tastes.

Menu Decoder

English	German	French	Italian
Breakfast			
Bacon	Speck	Bacon	Bacon
Cereals	Getreideflocken	Céréales	Fiocchi di ceriali
Eggs	Eier	Oeufs	Uova
Fried eggs	Setzeier	Oeufs poêlés	Uova al tegame
Jam	Konfitüre	Confiture	Confettura
Sugar	Zucker	Sucre	Zucchero
Salads			
Caesar salad	Cäsarsalat	Salade César	Insalata alla Cesare
Green salad	Grüner Salat	Salade verte	Insalata verde
Mixed salad	Gemischter Salat	Salade mêlée	Insalata mista
Meats			
Chicken	Huhn	Poulet	Pollo
Duck	Ente	Canard	Anitra
Ham	Schinken	Jambon	Prosciutto
Sirloin steak	Entrecote	Entrecôte	Costata di manzo
Fillet steak	Filetsteak	Filet grillé	Bistecca di filetto
Rabbit	Kaninchen	Lapin	Coniglio
Roast beef	Ochsenbraten	Rôti de bœuf	Arrosto di manzo
Roast lamb	Lammbraten	Rôti d'agneau	Arrosta d'agnello
Roast pork	Schweinsbraten	Rôti de porc	Arrosto di maiale
Turkey	Truthahn	Dinde	Tacchino
Veal cutlet	Kalbskotelett	Côte de veau	Costoletta di vitello
Venison	Rehkotelett	Chevreuil	Capriolo
Fish and Shellfish			
Calamari	Kalmare	Calmars	Calamari
Cod	Kabeljau	Cabillaud	Merluzzo
Crab	Taschenkrebs	Tourteau	Granciporro
Fillet of sole	Seezungenfilets	Filets de sole	Filetti di sogliola
Lobster	Hummer	Homard	Astice
Mussels	Miesmuscheln	Moules	Cozze
Octopus	Krake	Poulpe	Polpo
Oysters	Austern	Huîtres	Ostriche
Plaice	Scholle	Carrelet	Platessa
Prawns	Hummerkrabben	Crevettes	Gamberi imperiale
Salmon	Lachs	Saumon	Salmone
Scallops	Jakobsmuscheln	Coquilles StJacques	Conchiglie dei pellegrini
Seafood	Meeresfrüchte	Fruits de mer	Frutti di mare

In most places, outside Ticino, fondue and raclette melted cheese dishes are popular, as is *rösti* – the Swiss version of hash brown potatoes often found in combination with sausages or the like. Certain regions also have their own favourites: fillet of perch and lake trout around Geneva; local sausage on a bed of leeks and potatoes in Lausanne; in Bern look for smoked pork, sausage and *sauerkraut*; minced veal in cream

English	German	French	Italian
Shrimps	*Garnelen*	*Crevettes*	*Gamberetti*
Sole	*Seezunge*	*Sole*	*Sogliola*
Swordfish	*Schwertfisch*	*Espadon*	*Pesce spada*
Trout	*Forelle*	*Truite*	*Trota*
Tuna	*Thunfisch*	*Thon*	*Tonno*
Turbot	*Steinbutt*	*Turbot*	*Rombo*

Vegetables

Asparagus	*Spargel*	*Asperges*	*Asparagi*
Assorted vegetables	*Gemüseplatte*	*Légumes variés*	*Verdure assortite*
Boiled potatoes	*Salzkartoffein*	*Pommes à l'anglaise*	*Patate lesse*
Broccoli	*Brokkoli*	*Brocolis*	*Broccoli*
Carrots	*Karotten*	*Carottes*	*Carote*
Cucumbers	*Gurken*	*Concombres*	*Cetrioli*
Green peas	*Erbsen*	*Petits pois*	*Piselli*
Lettuce	*Kopfsalat*	*Laitue*	*Lattughe*
Mixed vegetables	*Mischgemüse*	*Macédoine de légumes*	*Macedonia di legumi*
Mushrooms	*Kaiserlinge*	*Oronges/cèpes*	*Ovoli*
New potatoes	*Neue Kartoffein*	*Pommes nouvelles*	*Patate novelle*
Onions	*Zweiben*	*Oignons*	*Cipolle*
Roast potatoes	*Geröstete*	*Pommes rôties*	*Patate arrosto*
Spinach	*Spinat*	*Épinards*	*Spinaci*
Tomatoes	*Tomaten*	*Tomates*	*Pomodori*

Desserts

Apple pie	*Apfelpie*	*Tarte aux pommes*	*Torta di mele*
Apple strudel	*Apfelstrudel*	*Strudel aux pommes*	*Srudel di mele*
Assorted pastries	*Auswahl an Backwerk*	*Pâtisserie assortie*	*Pasticceria assortita*
Cake	*Torte*	*Gâteau*	*Torta*
Fruit Salad	*Obstsalat*	*Fruits rafraîchis*	*Macedonia di frutta*
Ice Cream	*Sahneeis*	*Glace à la crème*	*gelato de crema*
Rice Pudding	*Reisauflauf*	*Gâteau de riz*	*Dolce di riso*
Rum baba	*Baba mit rum*	*Baba au rhum*	*Babà al rum*
Vanilla ice cream	*Vanille-Eis*	*Glace à la vanille*	*Gelato di vaniglia*

Fruit

Apple	*Apfel*	*Pomme*	*Mela*
Apricot	*Aprikose*	*Abricot*	*Albicocca*
Banana	*Banane*	*Banane*	*Banana*
Grapefruit	*Grapefruit*	*Pamplemousse*	*Pompelmo*
Grapes	*Trauben*	*Raisins*	*Uva*
Lemon	*Zitrone*	*Citron*	*Limone*
Orange	*Apfelsine*	*Orange*	*Arancia*

sauce and *rösti* is a favourite in Zürich; and the Italian-style cuisine of polenta, risotto and pasta can be found in Ticino. In the larger cities Spanish restaurants are surprisingly popular. It should not come as a surprise, either, that the presence of the United Nations and other international organizations in Geneva has benefited that city with numerous restaurants offering cuisine from around the world.

English	German	French	Italian
Peach	*Pfirsich*	*Pêche*	*Pesca*
Pear	*Williams Christbine*	*Poire Williams*	*Pere William*
Pineapple	*Ananas*	*Ananas*	*Ananas*
Strawberry	*Erdbeere*	*Fraise*	*Fragola*
Watermelon	*Wassermelone*	*Melon d'eau*	*Cocomero*

Bread-related

Cheese sandwich	*Käsebrot*	*Sandwich au fromage*	*Panino al formaggio*
Ham sandwich	*Schinkenbrot*	*Sandwich au jambon*	*Panino al prosciutto*
Roll	*Semmel*	*Petit pain*	*Panino*
Rye bread	*Roggenbrot*	*Pain de seigle*	*Pane di segale*
Sandwich	*Sandwich*	*Sandwich*	*Panino*
Slice of bread	*Brotschnitte*	*Tranche de pain*	*Fetta di pane*
Toast	*Röstbrot*	*Toast*	*Pane tostato*

Alcoholic Drinks

Beer	*Bier*	*Bière*	*Birra*
Bottled beer	*Flaschenbier*	*Bière en bouteille*	*Birra in bottiglia*
Liqueur	*Likör*	*Liquer*	*Liquore*
Local wine	*Landwein*	*Vin de Pays*	*Vino nostrano*
Red wine	*Rotwein*	*Vin rouge*	*Vino rosso*
Table wine	*Tischwein*	*Vin de table*	*Vino da pasto*
White wine	*Weisseweine*	*Vin blanc*	*Vino bianco*

Non-alcoholic Drinks

Cappuccino	*Cappuccino*	*Cappuccino*	*Cappuccino*
Coffee (black)	*Kaffee Schwarzer*	*Café noir*	*Cafè nero*
Coffee (milk)	*Milchkaffee*	*Café au lait*	*Caffelatte*
Fruit juice	*Fruchtsaft*	*Jus de fruits*	*Succo di frutta*
Ice	*Eis*	*Glace*	*Ghiaccio*
Lemonade	*Limonade*	*Citronnade*	*Limonata*
Milk	*Milch*	*Lait*	*Latte*
Mineral water	*Mineralwasser*	*Eau minérale*	*Acqua minerale*
Tea	*Tee*	*Thé*	*Tè*
Water	*Wasser*	*Eau*	*Acqua*

General Terms

Bill (check)	*Rechnung*	*Addition*	*Conto*
Breakfast	*Frühstück*	*Petit déjeuner*	*Prima colazione*
Dining room	*Speisesaal*	*Salle à manger*	*Sala da pranzo*
Dinner	*Abendessen*	*Dîner*	*Pranzo*
Glass	*Glas*	*Verre*	*Bichiere*
Lunch	*Mittagessen*	*Déjeuner*	*Colazione*

In the mountains, food tends to be filling – cheese fondue, raclette, macaroni cheese with bacon, sausages and *sauerkraut*, *Mostbröckli* (cured beef) and *Zungenwurst* (tongue sausage).

Breads are varied and tempting: rye-based loaves in Graubünden and the Valais, with walnuts in the latter; plaited loaves, crusty white French-style breads, *brioches*, etc. And Swiss pastries and desserts, let alone the cheeses, are world-famous.

The Swiss, of course, invented muesli, and you should try a bowlful of the original home-made kind, a world away from the packet version you'll be used to.

In December, you may see *Weihnachtsguetzli*, special Christmas biscuits, and gingerbread; New Year, Easter and just before Lent is the time to sample other seasonal specialities.

Drinks

Wine is one of Switzerland's best-kept secrets (see *www.swisswine.ch*), and it's not surprising, as it is estimated that 95 per cent of the production is consumed in the country itself.

The long, narrow Valais, with over 13,000 acres (5,250 ha) and 20,000 growers and 700 winemakers, is the most productive region, producing a third of the country's output. It has a diverse range of grapes, with the red Dôle and white Fendant being the most popular. Humagne is one of the more classic red wines; it also comes in a very tasty white vintage, and the white Petite Arvine is particularly fine. The area around Geneva is home to a variety of both red and white wines, in about equal quantities. Its neighbour to the north, the Neuchâtel and three lakes region, produces Pinot Noir reds, a tasty rosé and the most well-known white wines from the Chasselas grapes. The Vaud, between Geneva and the Valais, produces a quarter of Switzerland's wines and has 26 different appellations of origin including the famous Dézaley, dating back to the medieval Cistercian monks. Ticino and the more popular Aigle vintages, in the south, have 90 per cent of their vineyards planted with Merlot, but be sure to try the increasingly popular Merlot Blanco. German Switzerland, roughly speaking from Basel, Zürich, Schaffhausen, St Gallen and across to Graubünden, grows 75 per cent Pinot Noir grapes, with the whites mainly Riesling-Sylvaner.

Swiss beer, generally, is of the lager variety. Feldschlösschen, now owned by Carlsberg, is the largest brewer with its own name brand, and is far and away the leading selling beer with a quarter of the market. The company also owns Cardinal and other regional brands such as Gurten, Hürlimann and Valaisanne. Regionally, Appenzeller lays claim to an ever-growing number of less commercial tastes. In the larger cities brewery-pubs are now making a showing, with their own esoteric beers.

Those wanting something more potent should try the famous liqueurs such as Marc, Kirsch, Pflümli and Williamine, some of which are used to strengthen fondues.

Direct Flight Destinations

Basel

Basel (Bâle in French, Basilea in Italian, and often anglicized to Basle), Switzerland's second largest city, is a lively and progressive place with a population of some 200,000. Situated at the border of three countries – France, Germany and Switzerland – it is home port to more than 500 river-going vessels, serves as one of Europe's largest railroad junctions, and is recognized as an important financial and industrial centre. It is also headquarters to some of the world's major pharmaceutical companies, and is the base for the Bank of International Settlements (BIZ), where representatives of all industrialized countries routinely meet to discuss the world economy. The Church Council held five centuries ago was only the start of Basel's vocation as a centre for worldwide conventions and trade fairs. In 1917, the first Swiss Industries Fair took place here, and it is now the largest fair and congress organizer in the country, responsible, in its own right, for over one million visitors to the city.

Art and culture also play a major role in the life of Basel. Approximately thirty museums, ranging from the more traditional and world-renowned Kunstmuseum (Fine Arts Museum) to the less conventional Paper and Cinema Museums, not to mention numerous other galleries, concert halls and theatres, call the city their home. The most popular cultural event, however, is the colourful and wild **Basel Fasnacht** carnival. The festivities begin in January with the appearance of three mythological figures who appear to chase winter away. The Monday after Ash Wednesday, at the unearthly hour of 4am, the Carnival breaks loose with a morning parade. What follows are three days of unbroken revelry complete with traditional feasts and a procession of elaborate floats, brass bands and a motley collection of followers in outrageous costumes that have to be seen to be believed.

History

Basel's strategic location, in the centre of Europe and at the point where the mighty **River Rhine** (Rhein) takes a dramatic ninety-degree turn to the north, ensured from the outset that this city would play a significant role in the history of Europe and, indeed, the world. Although the origins of the city can be traced back to Celtic times, it was in 44 BC that the Roman general, Lucius Munatius Plancus, founded the settlement of *Augusta Raurica* (Augst). And it was in AD 374 that the name of *Basilea* was first documented, during a visit by Emperor Valentinian I to the city. In the 7th century, the Bishop's seat was transferred from Augst to Basel. Three hundred years later Basel was overrun and destroyed by Hungarians, who then destroyed the settlement. In 1006, the civil power of the Bishop was established by decree of Emperor Henry II who, thirteen years later, inaugurated the Münster (cathedral). The same century saw the first fortifications of the city that, in 1185, were burned down by a great fire. Early the next century, in 1226, the city's recovery continued as Bishop Henry of Thun organized the construction of the first bridge across the Rhine. The 14th century wasn't so kind to Basel. During the period around 1340 the 'Black Death' plague raged throughout the city and, just sixteen years later, most of the city was destroyed by the earthquake of 18 October 1356. During the reconstruction, the second town wall was

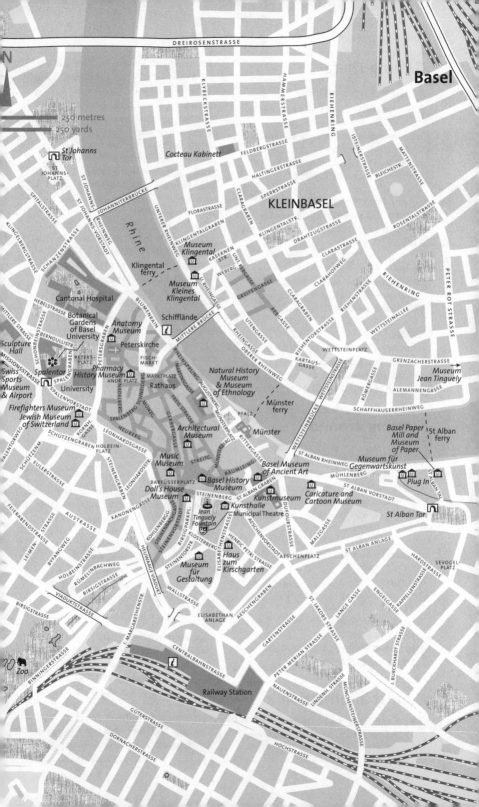

Getting There

By Air

British Airways, www.ba.com, operate a daily service from London (Heathrow).

Swiss, www.swiss.com, operate a daily service from London (Heathrow).

easyJet, www.easyjet.com, operate a daily service from London Stansted.

Getting from the Airport

The No. 50 bus takes 15 minutes to the French/Swiss train station, four times an hour. A taxi costs CHF 20/25.

By Train

Eurostar, www.eurostar.com, from London (Waterloo) to Paris (Gare du Nord) and then from Paris (Gare de l'Est) to Basel.

By Bus

National Express, www.nationalexpress.com, operates the Eurolines bus service, on Monday, Wednesday and Friday, from London (Victoria Coach Station) to Basel.

Getting Around

Public transport in and around Basel on trams and buses is fast, clean and efficient. Tickets must be purchased from ticket vending machines, ticket offices or the tourist office prior to each trip and are available for a singe trip or, more advantageously, for an Unlimited Day Pass. The latter, for 2nd class, costs CHF 7.40 for the City of Basel and CHF 23.40 for the expanded metropolitan area.

Car Hire

Avis, Aeschengraben 31, t 061 206 95 45; airport, t 061 325 28 40.

Europcar, St Alban-Anlage 72, t 061 378 99 66; airport, t 061 325 29 03.

Hertz, Nauenstrasse 33, t 061 205 92 22; airport, t 061 325 27 80.

Tourist Information

Basel: Basel Tourismus, Schifflände 5, t 061 268 68 68, f 061 268 68 70, office@baseltourismus.

ch, www.baseltourismus.ch (open Mon–Fri 8.30–6.30, Sat 10–5, Sun and holidays 10–4).

A Basel city **information and hotel reservation office** is located in the train station (Bahnhof) SSB, t 061 271 36 84, f 061 272 93 42, hotel@messebasel.ch (open Mon–Fri 8.30–6.30, Sat and Sun 9–2, closed holidays).

A Basel **hotel reservation service** is also located in the station, Messeplatz, t 061 206 26 30, f 061 206 21 84, hotel@messe.ch, www.messe.ch (open Mon–Fri 9–12 and 1–5).

The **Weekend-Break**, run by Basel Tourismus, is valid Fri–Mon, for a maximum of three nights, for selected hotels. The rates, for 2004, range from CHF 75 per person in a double room and CHF 99 in a single room for a 2-star hotel to CHF 140pp in a single room and CHF 213 in a single room for a 5-star hotel. This includes breakfast, Mobility Ticket for use during your stay and taxes, except for CHF 3.20pp per night City Tax.

Basel Tourismus also provides a **Gay Life Package** valid Fri–Mon for a maximum stay of three nights. It is available for as little as CHF 93pp per night for a double room in a 2-star hotel up to CHF 223pp per night for a 5-star hotel. This includes breakfast, a BaselCard, a Gay Card (available only with this package), Mobility Ticket and taxes and services, excluding a City Tax of CHF 3.20pp per night.

BaselCard gives free admission to 35 museums, a free city sightseeing tour, free ferryboat rides and reductions for theatre and musical tickets, restaurants and some shops. It is available for periods of 24 hours at CHF 25, 48 hours at CHF 33 and 72 hours at CHF 45; buy it in hotels or from Basel Tourismus.

Mobility Ticket: everyone who spends a night at a city hotel automatically receives a Mobility Ticket allowing free use of public transport for the duration of their stay.

Guided Tours

A walking tour through the **old city** is conducted by Basel Tourismus. It departs from the Welcome Desk there between early May and mid-Oct daily at 2.30pm and at other times of the year on Sat at 2.30pm. It takes 2 hours and a ticket costs CHF 15. Likewise, it has tours of the town hall (Rathaus) every Thurs.

Similarly, Basel Tourismus operates a guided tour of *Augusta Raurica*, an old Roman town just 6 miles (10km) upriver from Basel. This departs from the entrance of the Römer-museum (a 10min walk from the Kaiseraugst train station) between early May and mid-Oct on Sun at 2.30, taking about 1½ hours; CHF 12.

Panoramic tour on board tram No.15 or 16: every Sun at 10.30am a vintage streetcar departs from the train station on a 1-hour guided roundtrip tour of Basel; tickets CHF 20.

Disabled Facilities

A city map for wheelchair users showing accessible buildings, public WCs, car parks for disabled people and useful telephone numbers is available from the tourist office.

Transport for disabled people: IVB, t 061 426 98 00 or 22er-Taxi, t 061 271 22 22, is available, but must be ordered 24 hours in advance.

Lost Property

City and BVB, St Johanns-Vorstadt 51, t 061 267 70 34.
Bahnhof SBB, t 0512 29 24 67.

Market Days

Fruit and vegetables: Marktplatz, Tues, Thurs and Sat 6–1.30; Mon, Wed and Fri 6am–7pm.
Flea market: Petersplatz and Kserne, Sat 7.30–4; Barfüsserplatz, every 2nd and 4th Wed 7–7.

Medical Emergencies

Dentist, doctor and pharmacy: t 061 261 15 15.

Exhibitions and Festivals

Late Jan: Vogel Gryff – a local custom that is Kleinbasel's major festival.
Feb: Fasnacht – begins after Ash Wednesday.
May: Basel Summer Festival.
Aug: Theatre Festival Basel.
Sept: Basler Begge Brotmärt – about 35 Basel bakers sell over 150 types of bread at Barfüsserplatz on a Tues in mid month.
Oct: Swiss Indoors – the largest international tennis tournament in Switzerland.
Late Oct to mid-Nov: Basler Herbstmesse (autumn fair).
End Nov to before Christmas: Weihnachts-markt (Christmas market) – 150 stalls at Barfüsserplatz selling all kinds of goodies.
New Year's Eve: Silvester – a New Year celebra-tion starting at Münsterplatz at 11.30pm.

Shopping

If you are in need of basic supplies on a Sunday, there are a couple of small grocery stores open in the concourse under the railway station. A supermarket directly across from the station is open as well.

Where to Stay

★★★★★Drei Könige am Rhein, Blumenrain 8, t 061 260 50 50, f 061 260 50 60, www.drei-koenige-basel.ch (luxury). Considered the oldest hotel in Europe, its name 'Three Kings' dates from 1032, when a royal delegation met here to settle questions over the succession of the royal line among three kings. The hotel has played host to all manner of kings and royalty, politicians and artists, from Bonaparte to Picasso. It sits on a fantastic riverside site, very near to the city centre and the Middle Bridge. Some of the 140 rooms directly overlook the Rhine. First-class service, an elegantly traditional ambience and all modern comforts.

★★★★Sorat Hotel im Messeturm, Messeplatz 12, t 061 560 40 00, f 061 560 55 55, www.sorat-hotels.com (luxury). This occupies the 5th to 14th floors of the 31-storey Messe-turm, Switzerland's tallest building. Its 230 rooms – some wheelchair accessible and non-smoking – are minimalist; select yellow, orange, red, green or pink walls.

★★★★Drachen, Aeschenvorstadt 24, t 061 270 23 23, f 061 270 23 24, www.drachen.ch (luxury). In a quiet area between the theatre and Kunstmuseum, this will appeal to those seeking the intimacy of a smaller hotel. Each of the 67 rooms is elegant; the restaurant, with wonderful murals, serves health food.

★★★Der Teufelhof, Leonhardsgraben 47–49, t 061 261 10 10, f 061 261 10 04, www.teufelhof.com (expensive). This, the most eclectic hotel in Basel, offers a tempting combination of art, haute cuisine and even theatre. The Art Hotel, featuring 8 rooms and a suite – TVs available on request – was created in July/August 2002 with an overall Träume (dream) theme. Three designers, one Swiss and two Italians, have designed the 20 rooms, 3 suites and a junior suite in the Gallery Hotel. The restaurants are superb.

****St Gotthard**, Centralbahnstrasse 13, **t** 061 225 13 13, **f** 061 225 13 14, *www.st-gotthard.ch* (*expensive*). Opposite the Central Station and originally built in 1882. Owned ever since by the Geyer family, all the 104 rooms have been renovated to very high standards.

****Merian am Rhein**, Rheingasse 2, **t** 061 685 11 11, **f** 061 685 11 01, *www.merian-hotel.ch* (*expensive*). On the north bank of the river just across the Middle Bridge is a charming, medium-sized hotel. The rooms are bright and attractive; many have Rhine views.

Balade, Klingental 8, **t** 061 699 19 00, **f** 061 699 19 20, *www.hotel-balade.ch* (*moderate*). An unusual, red, rectangular building close to the Klingental Monastery. Twenty-four very bright and artistic double rooms, along with similar style restaurant, bistro and bar.

Royal, Scwarzwaldallee 179, **t** 061 686 55 55, **f** 061 686 55 99, *www.royal-hotel.ch* (*moderate*). A small, individualistic hotel behind the Messeplatz near the German train station, designed with Feng Shui in mind. It has 15 rooms, all very different.

***Rheinfelderhof**, Hammerstrasse 61, **t** 061 699 11 11, **f** 061 699 11 00, *www.rheinfelder hof.ch* (*moderate*). This occupies an impressive corner site on the north side of the Rhine, and is an amalgamation of a beer hall and another hotel. There are 35 modern and spacious rooms, some of which have views across the river to the cathedral.

***Basilisk**, Klingentalstrasse 1, **t** 061 686 96 66, **f** 061 686 96 67, *www.hotel-basilisk.ch* (*moderate*). Near the old Klingental Monastery, this has 56 quite large and modern rooms; the restaurant has a garden terrace.

Resslirytti, Theodorsgraben 42, **t** 061 691 66 41, **f** 061 691 45 90 (*moderate*). Named the 'Merry-Go-Round' after the merry-go-round in the Italian restaurant, this has 30 very nice, large rooms decorated in warm tints of pink and blue and with all modern comforts. Located in a quiet area, north of the river.

***Rochat**, Petersgraben 23, **t** 061261 81 40, **f** 061 261 64 92, *www.hotelrochat.ch* (*moderate*). A classical 1899 building in a quiet location not too far from the Botanic Gardens. Its 50 rooms have a modern, unfussy decor with Internet connection and a safe.

Stadthof, Gerbergasse 84, **t** 061 261 87 1, **f** 061 261 25 84, *www.stadthof.ch* (*inexpensive*).

Off Barfüsserplatz, this small hotel, first recorded in 1295, has 3 singles and 6 doubles.

Bed & Breakfast Agency, Sonnenweg 3, **t** 061 702 21 51, mobile **t** 079 356 39 78, **f** 061 703 96 76, *www.bbbasel.ch* (*inexpensive*). Has contacts with more than 150 places to stay, some providing meals or cooking facilities.

Jugendherberge Basel, St Alban-Kirchrain 10, **t** 061 272 05 72, **f** 061 272 08 33, *www. youthhostel.ch/basel* (*inexpensive*). The usual range of rooms and facilities, all simple, basic and clean, and rates are inclusive of breakfast and sheets.

Basel Back Pack, Dornacherstrasse 192, **t** 061 333 00 37, **f** 061 333 00 39, *www.baselback pack.ch* (*cheap*). Some blocks south of the Central Station. A real mix of accommodation: double beds, 3 beds and 5 dorms here, along with a house bar and lounge, shop corner, community kitchen and dining area.

Eating Out

Bruderholz, Bruderholzallee 42, **t** 061 361 82 22, **f** 061 361 82 03, *www.stucki-bruderholz.ch* (*very expensive*). With two Michelin stars, the Bruderholz is situated above the city and ranks equally high above most other Basel restaurants. Set in an elegant mansion with lovely gardens and classical salons, the gourmet creations of French cuisine are presented in such an elegant manner that they are almost too beautiful to be eaten.

Bel Etage, Leonhardsgraben 49, **t** 061 261 10 10 (*very expensive*). The gourmet restaurant of the Hotel Teufelhof (*see* p.35), with one Michelin star. Like the hotel, it is self-indulgent in art and cuisine with new, market-fresh dishes daily. The wine list contains more than 450 selections, some rare.

Café Spitz, Greifengasse/Rheingasse, **t** 061 685 11 11, **f** 061 685 11 01, *www.merian-hotel.ch* (*expensive*). Known as the fish restaurant, and with good reason as it is undoubtedly the finest of its genre in Basel, having won the Goldener Fisch award. Sitting on the terrace with views of the Rhine and Münster, the only problem is what to select as the menu is full of innovative dishes featuring many unusual species.

Charon, Schützengraben 62, **t** 061 261 99 80, **f** 061 261 99 09 (*expensive*). This small Art

Nouveau restaurant serves such dishes as spicy fish soup with shrimps, whole fried sole in bay caper sauce and *crème brûlée*.

Kunsthalle, Steinenberg 7, t 061 272 42 33 (*expensive*). A very traditional, beautiful restaurant popular with Basel high society. Inside, there are two great rooms with impressive murals, and in the summer it has tables in the beautiful central garden, with a summer bar, next to the Tinguely fountain. The cuisine is classic French, Italian and Swiss; leave room for desserts.

Rollerhof, Münsterplatz 20, t 061 263 04 84, f 061 263 04 85, *www.rollerhof.ch* (*expensive*). Part of the Museum of Culture, this stylish restaurant is in one of Basel's most famous houses. In a wooden galleried inner courtyard, dine on fresh Mediterranean and seasonal food. The Bistro, open all day, features salads, fish and veal sausage.

Bodega zum Strasse, Barfüsserplatz 16, t 061 261 22 72 (*expensive*). A charming little Italian restaurant, with a small dining room decorated with modern paintings and photographs. It offers an enticing seasonal menu with fine pasta and fish on Friday. A meeting place for the arty set and football fans.

Safran Zunft, Gerbergasse 11, t 061 269 94 94, f 061 264 94 99, *www.safran-zunft.ch* (*expensive*). This spice guild was first mentioned in the 14th century. The original building was demolished and this replacement dates from 1902. A favourite at Fasnacht time, it specializes in typical Swiss cuisine. Famous for Fondue Bacchus where you cook tender, thinly sliced pieces of veal in a heated, spicy rosé wine broth.

Spillmann, Basel Eisengasse 1, t 061 261 17 60, f 061 261 16 72, *www.restaurant-spillmann.ch* (*expensive*). Situated next to the Middle Bridge, this is one of the few restaurants to have an open terrace right over the Rhine. It offers cold plates, a small fish selection and meat and vegetarian dishes.

Fischerstube, Rheingasse 45, t 061 692 66 35, f 061 692 74 04 (*moderate*). In Kleinbasel just a block from the Rhine, this is famous for its home-brewed Ueli beer and Weizenbier (wheat beer).The menu slants towards barley with soup and Uelibier sausage.

Bierstube zum Stadtkeller, Marktgasse 11, t 061 261 72 51, f 061 261 31 95, *www.stadtkeller* basel.ch (*moderate*). A colourful, traditional Basel pub with its walls full of photos and Fasnacht medals. A local favourite, with typical pub food.

Schlüsselzunft, Freie Strasse 25, t 061 261 20 46, f 061 261 20 56, *www.schluesselzunft.ch* (*moderate*). An historical guild house famous for Samuel Buri's mural and its covered courtyard. It serves Swiss specialities like sliced veal.

Brasserie zum Braunen Mutz, Barfüsserplatz 10, t 061 261 33 69, *www.brauner-mutz-basel.ch* (*moderate*). Basel's only real traditional beer hall – and delightful it is, too – offering authentic dishes like veal sausages and *sauerkraut*. It has daily lunch specials for less than CHF 20.

Hasenburg Château Lapin, Schneidergasse 20, t 061 261 32 58 (*moderate*). Behind Marktplatz, this quaint, typical pub is very popular during Fasnacht; it has a varied menu, and a reasonable set meal, with a nice *rösti*.

Café Restaurant Spalenborg, Spalenberg 16, t 061 261 32 05 (*inexpensive*). Near the Spalentor; has dozens of types of pizzas, pastas and other similar dishes.

Café Pfalz, Münsterberg 11, t 061 272 65 11, f 061 272 63 38 (*inexpensive*). Located opposite the main door of the Münster; a good little salad bar also serving home-made pies, etc.

Nightlife

Music lovers might head for the **Bird's Eye Jazz Club**, Kohlenberg 20, t 061 263 33 41, *www.birdseye.ch*, or the **Caram Bar**, St Johanns-Vorstadt 13, t 061 382 47 07, housed in a former bowling alley and featuring a variety of music styles. Basel is not short on dance clubs and discos, with **Mayday Dance Club**, Steinenvorstadt 55, t 061 281 88 55, open Thurs, Fri and Sat, the current trendy favourite. **Mad Max**, Steinentorstrasse 35, t 061 281 88 55, Fri and Sat, has a futuristic design; with two floors and five bars, it is also Basel's largest – but you have to be smartly dressed and over 28 to gain entry. **Route 66**, Freie Strasse 52 (in the passage), t 061 261 79 75, caters to a mixed bunch and has an American focus. While **Isola**, Gempenstrasse 60, Fri and Sat, behind the Central Station, is a discreet gay club with a tasteful interior design.

completed; parts of this and some of the gates are preserved to this day. Yet another fire struck Basel in 1417, and in 1444 the city once again felt the scourge of war when the Battle of St Jacob, between the Swiss Confederates and the French Dauphin and his allies, took place close to Basel.

It was Basel's geographic position that encouraged leaders of the Church to hold their council in the city between 1431 and 1448, during which Amadeus VIII of Savoy was elected Pope (taking the name Felix V), an event that would have far reaching cultural and intellectual consequences. Aaneas Silvius Piccolomini, later to become Pope Pius II, familiar with the city from his attendance at the Ecumenical Council, the last Church Council of the Middle Ages, thereafter founded the University of Basel, which was the first university of the Swiss Confederation. Basel, in turn, became an educational base and a centre for humanism and the arts. Many great scholars, such as Erasmus of Rotterdam (who published the first edition of the New Testament in the original Greek text in 1416), the physician Paracelsus, mathematicians Euler and Bernoullis, philosopher Friedrich Nietzsche and the historian Jakob Burckhardt, were attracted to the city. Trade, naturally, blossomed and in 1471 Basel obtained permission to hold two fairs annually. Monuments to the resulting wealth are still visible in the array of elaborate medieval buildings, most notably in the highly decorative and very unusual town hall (Rathaus), which dates from 1504; the equally impressive, but rather more austere, Romanesque/Gothic cathedral; and the imposing Spalentor, which dates from when Basel was last walled in during the 14th century.

In 1501, Basel joined the Swiss Confederation, and 1529 saw the Reformation accepted by the city. Since 1833 the canton of Basel has been divided into two half-cantons, Basel Town and Basel Country. Travel between the city and other parts of Switzerland was made considerably easier when the first railway reached the city in 1844, and maritime connections were enhanced by the opening of the port of Basel in 1906.

The Old Town: Between Middle Bridge, Marktplatz and the Münster

For the sake of convenience, the description of sights below follows a roughly anti-clockwise direction from the bridge.

The Schifflände boat landing and an equestrian statue of Karl Burckhardt (1878–1923) are situated between the tourist office and the famous **Middle Bridge** (Mittlere Brücke). The first bridge was built here in 1226 by the bishop-prince Heinrich von Thun to cross the mighty perpetually rushing waters of the Rhine that are 870ft (265m) wide here. To protect the bridge, von Thun established the fortified town of Kleinbasel on the north bank of the river. Later, in 1392, the city parliament of Grossbasel, on the south side, bought Kleinbasel from Bishop Friedrich von Blankenheim for an astounding price of 29,800 guilders, thus joining the two cities. The bridge had its more sinister uses, too, as in the Middle Ages women accused of infidelity or infanti-cide were bound and thrown into the Rhine; for the lucky ones, it was taken as a sign of their innocence if the swift currents deposited them on the riverbanks. In the middle of the bridge there was a chapel where merchants and seamen could offer up prayers; the **Käppelijoch** you see today is just a replica. Tradition says, though, that walking around it three times will cure a toothache! A fortified gate once protected the Grossbasel end of the bridge, and in 1640 a strange mechanical head, the **Lällekönig** (*Lälli* being the Basel word for tongue), was mounted on the Rhine façade. It came across its name because the copper-beaten head, adorned with a many-pointed crown, was connected to a clockwork mechanism that made the figure roll its eyes and stick out a long red tongue towards the Kleinbasel side of the city. Again, what you see today – on the façade of the Churrasco restaurant – is a replica; the original is in the Basel History Museum (*see* p.40).

People may be surprised to learn, especially as there is no physical evidence of it, that the river here is a confluence of the Rhine and one of its tributaries. At one time, the Birsig river flowed openly from the Fischmarkt to here, but the residents of the houses on either side had the unhealthy habit of dumping their rubbish into it. As a consequence, it was diverted through an underground channel into the Rhine.

Just south is the traffic circle of **Fischmarkt**, and this is dominated by what was originally a late Gothic 36ft (11m) fountain, dating from the late 14th century and created by the master stonemason Parler. Richly decorated, either with paintings or gilt, the three principal figures are the Virgin Mary with child and sceptre, the Apostle Peter with a key and John the Evangelist grasping a chalice and a book. There are numerous smaller angels, holding either musical instruments or the Basel coat-of-arms, with more saints on the baldachin, and on the finial, at the very top, stands another angel clasping a palm leaf. Again, the original is in the Basel History Museum (*see* p.40); this is just an early 20th-century copy.

The Rhine and its tributaries were rich in fish, and this played an important role in most people's diets in the Middle Ages, especially during Lent. On market days, fish merchants would keep their wares fresh by placing baskets of live 'green' fish in the basin of the fountain.

Immediately behind are a series of steep steps whose walls are covered with the unfortunately all-too-common scourge of graffiti. These lead up to an area near the Botanical Gardens, *see* p.45.

To the southwest of Fischmarkt is the **Pharmacy History Museum of Basel University** (Pharmazie-Historisches Museum der Universität Basel; *Totengässlein 3, t 061 264 91 11, f 061 264 91 12, www.pharmaziemuseum.ch; open Tues–Fri 10–6, Sat 10–5; adm*). Here, around old buildings in a neat courtyard, is one of the world's largest museums of this type, including apothecary shops and an historic drugstore – Herbarium – in a former pharmacy.

Marktplatz, next door, is not just, as the name implies, the past and present site of Basel's daily open-air market. It is also home to the city's magnificent **Rathaus** (town hall). In 1501, it was the influence of the craftsmen, who organized themselves into fifteen guilds, which persuaded the city of Basel to join the Swiss Confederation. To celebrate this, in the early 16th century a new red town hall was built with a frescoed façade, although it has been recently renovated. It dominates the square, as does its impressive tower, added retroactively early in the 20th century, and both are roofed with the colourful tiles so popular in Basel. Look, also, for the coats-of-arms of the twelve cantons that formed the Swiss Confederation in 1501 on the battlements. On

Walks from Marktplatz

Basel makes extreme efforts to assist its visitors. You will find evidence of this on the side of the plaza opposite the town hall, where the authorities have erected a metal signpost directing you to five different walks around the city. These all begin here, last between 30 and 90 minutes and are named after a prominent personality of Basel – Erasmus, Thomas Platter, Jakob Burckhardt, Paracelsus or Hans Holbein. To keep you on course, signs are posted along each route displaying a portrait of the respective person. An information brochure to accompany the walks is available from the tourist office.

the right-hand side of the central arcade is an unusual plaque: the **Birsig mark** (Birsigmarke) indicates the levels the Birsig river flooded to in 1529 and 1530. These days it is home to the government of the canton of Basel City.

Freie Strasse, running southeast from Marktplatz, is the main shopping street these days, and is lined with buildings of differing architectural styles. In the 3rd and 4th centuries it was a main Roman military and trade route, and became a main city thoroughfare in the Middle Ages; then in the 19th century many ancient guild houses along here were demolished, and replaced by buildings in the Historicist and Jugendstil style. Look, especially, across from the post office at the blue and white façade of the **Haus zum Schlüssel**, the only guild house to retain its original character. This belonged to the Merchant's Guild (Zunft der Kaufleute), the most important of the four senior guilds and consequently known as the Key Guild (Schlüsselzunft). The impressive **post office**, dating from 1853, replaced the city merchants' hall of 1376–78 that, itself, had been renovated in 1580.

Barfüsserplatz, just to the south, is another important and busy square – a transport hub with an important and always busy tram station. There are some old houses here, dating from the late 17th century, and some good restaurants both here and in the **Stadt Casino** just across the road.

Incidentally, the name Barfüsser originates from the bare-footed Franciscan monks who once occupied the imposing, sharply sloping-roofed church. If you take a moment to look around the back you will discover, under a wooden protective roof, carved sandstone exhibits with coats-of-arms, house signs, inscriptions and border stones moved from their original locations. Constructed in the mid-13th century, the **Barfüsserkirche** – a major example of mendicant religious orders north of the Alps – now functions as the **Basel History Museum** (Historiches Museum Basel; *Steinenberg 4, t 061 205 86 00, www.historischesmuseumbasel.ch; open Wed–Mon 10–5; adm*), considered the most important cultural museum on the Upper Rhine. Notable exhibits include the Amerbach Cabinet, the Basel cathedral treasury containing unique examples of the medieval goldsmith's art, Basel's *Dance of Death*, Gothic tapestry carpets and late Gothic and Renaissance glass painting, ecclesiastical art and furniture. Barfüsserplatz was also once used as a cattle market, thus its dialect name, **Seibi** (Swine Square).

Other museums around Barfüsserplatz include, just north, the **Architectural Museum** (Architekturmuseum; *Pfluggässlein 3, t 061 261 14 13, f 061 261 14 28,* *www.architekturmuseum.ch; open Tues–Fri 1–6, Sat 10–4, Sun 1–4; adm).* Suitably, this is housed on four floors of the most unusual example of 1950s architecture in Basel. Founded in 1984, the museum has an exhibition programme centred around three principles: Swiss architecture of the classical modern period; contemporary architecture in the international field; and various themes from the architectural periphery. Just to the south, and in a renowned building on Barfüsserplatz that has been remodelled and has disabled access, is Europe's largest **Doll's House Museum** (Puppenhausmuseum; *Steinenvorstadt 1, t 061 225 95 95, f 061 225 95 96, www.puppenhaus museum.ch; open daily 11–5; adm).* On four floors, each one with a modern interactive information system, there are over 6,000 exhibits including teddy bears, dolls, doll's houses, carousels and many more items that will take you back to your, or your children's, childhood.

To the west, now, and along Steinenberg, on the right a combination of different level squares, just outside the Municipal Theatre, provide a popular gathering place for young and old alike. The favourite attraction by far, though, and set in the midst of a large water basin that used to be the stage of the old City Theatre, is the highly imaginative **Jean Tinguely Fountain** (Tinguelybrunnen). A native of Basel, Tinguely (1925–91) had, to understate the obvious, quite a creative mind. Any attempt to describe this unbelievably outlandish fountain, opened in 1977, would never do it justice. Suffice it to say that the numerous components are made from parts of old machines, etc. connected by other pieces of metal, and you never know where to look next for the fine sprays of water they emit. The best comparison that might be made is with the wondrous inventions of Salvador Dalí, an analogy that will be reinforced if you are curious enough to visit the recently opened Museum Jean Tinguely (*see p.47).*

At the eastern end of the street is an interesting art museum, the **Kunsthalle Basel** (*Steinenberg 7, t 061 206 99 00, f 061 206 99 19, www.kunsthallebasel.ch; open Tues and Thurs–Sun 11–5, Wed 11–8.30; adm).* It held its first exhibition in 1872 and since then has put on numerous important modern art exhibitions.

You can find more art, albeit in two differing forms, just to the northeast on St Alban-Graben. Housed in two classical town houses is the unusual **Basel Museum of Ancient Art** (Antikenmuseum Basel; *St Alban-Graben 5, t 061 271 22 02, f 061 272 18 61, www.antikenmuseumbasel.ch; open Tues–Sun 10–5, Wed till 9pm; adm).* Opened in 1966, it is the only one of its kind in Switzerland solely devoted to the ancient civilizations of the Mediterranean area. Ranging from the 4th millennium BC to the 7th century AD, the permanent exhibition displays ancient art from the Egyptian, Greek, Etruscan and Roman cultures, as well as some examples from the Ancient Near East and Cyprus.

On the other side of the street is the **Fine Arts Museum** (Kunstmuseum; *St Alban-Graben 16, t 061 206 62 62, f 061 206 62 52, www.kunstmuseumbasel.ch).* In fact, the Basel Public Art Collection (Öffentliche Kunstsammlung Basel) has three sections: the Kunstmuseum and the **Copper Etchings Gallery** (Kupferstichkabinett), housed in this building (*open Tues–Sun 10–5),* and the Museum für Gegenwartskunst (*see p.47),* to the east by the Rhine (*adm for both houses, but free first Sun of month).* Opened in

A Fountain Tale

For over 600 years, from the mid-13th century until the first pumped water supply to Basel's municipal buildings in 1866, the city's demands for water were met by fountains. Today, although having long lost their original function, they are still operated by the Industrielle Werke Basel and much loved by children who use them as summer paddling pools. There are over 150 in the city.

1661, the highly regarded Kunstmuseum was not only the first museum open to the public in Basel, but claims to be the world's first public art collection. Its main specialities are paintings and drawings of the Upper Rhine region and the Netherlands between 1400 and 1600, and 19th- and 20th-century art. Not only does it have the world's largest collection by the Holbein family, but its Renaissance collections include important works by Witz, Schongauer, Cranach the Elder, Grünewald and others. More up-to-date works by Arnold Böcklin, the Basel artist, feature in the 19th-century collection. Cubism works by Picasso, Braque and Léger, and German Abstract and American art since 1950 form part of the impressive collection of 20th-century paintings.

Due north, the tall spires and coloured tiled roof of the **Münster** or cathedral (*www.muensterbasel.ch; open Mon–Fri 10–5, Sat 10–12 and 2–4, Sun and hols 1–5; free but the tower visit is CHF 4*), beckon. The forecourt was at one time gated in and this space, **Münsterplatz**, is now rather charming. As well as *boules* courts, there is the notable **Pisoni Fountain** (Pisonibrunnen), sitting under horse chestnut trees. Created in 1784 by Paolo Antonio Pisoni, it is considered a particularly attractive example, not just in Switzerland, but also in southern Germany, of a so-called Braid Fountain (Zopfbrunnen). This motif was popular during the transition from rococo to classicism during the Age of Enlightenment. Ceremonial processions, festivals, tournaments and parades for royal and imperial visitors were held here, as well as markets. And many of the buildings around the square were built in the late Gothic style for senior clerics. After the reformation, however, in 1529, the bishop and his acolytes were forced to leave and the mansions were left empty. Quickly, though, wealthy merchants saw the opportunity to buy them up and, usually, altered them to late Baroque and classical styles during the 18th century. A perfect example is the large **Rollerhof**, which was altered in 1758 by the silk ribbon merchant Martin Bachofen and today plays host to a restaurant on its ground floor.

This area of Basel has been inhabited for 2,000 years, and a variety of churches and cathedrals have existed on this site. The first recorded one dates back to the Carolingian period, but it was destroyed in 917 at the hands of the Hungarians. It is recorded that, in 1019, a cathedral was consecrated here in the presence of Emperor Henry II, heir of the last Burgundian king. Construction of the present structure was begun at the end of the 12th century, in the late Romanesque style. But by the time it had been completed, it had gained Gothic additions – and, of course, it has seen many more additions and renovations throughout the centuries.

Turning to the façade of the Münster, the 221ft (67.3m) George Tower (Georgturm) was rebuilt in the Gothic style after the 1356 earthquake, except three yellow sandstone levels which date from the 11th century. It was named after the prominent equestrian statue of St George slaying a dragon, dating from 1372. Other ornamentation includes, on the Martins Tower (Martinsturm), an equestrian statue of St Martin in the act of sharing his cloak.

Still outside, the small Gothic **cloister** on the Rhine side of the Great Hall dates from 1467–87 and is worth investigating. And don't overlook the small garden where, incongruously, modern sculptures stand in restless harmony with the ancient gravestones and sepulchres. Look at the back of the cathedral, too, where you will find the **Pfalz**. The word derives from 'palatium' meaning palace, and is so-called because the bishop's residence was very close by. This little square directly overlooks the Rhine, and steep steps lead down to the Münsterfähre ferry (*see* box, below).

From the river and opposite bank, Basel can be seen from a different perspective. The opposite bank is delightful, with tall houses, no two the same, adorning the tree-lined river front and embellished by all manner of flowers and plants sprouting from their window boxes. Cafés, too, add to the atmosphere. In the warm summer months you will come across the sight of sunbathers completely covering the gently sloping quayside. In the direct background are the beginnings of the Black Forest of southern Germany, and towards the west are the French Vosges mountains.

Back outside the cathedral, take a look at the tracery in the round window of the south transept that depicts a Star of David, an ancient symbol for the intermingling of the visible (material) and the invisible (spiritual) worlds. The grand door, Gallus Gate (Galluspforte), of the northern portal dates from the late 12th century and is named after the nearest altar; on it are splendid depictions of the *Last Judgement*.

The comparatively plain interior is highlighted by stained-glass windows, a simple altar, elaborately carved choir stalls and, particularly, a dragon sculpted into the floor of the nave that is thought to date from around 1170. The ambitious and energetic may want to consider climbing over 200 steps to the top of the St George Tower. The reward is a splendid panoramic view over the city.

The Rhine Ferryboats

Since the late 19th century, the cheapest and most efficient way of crossing the Rhine has been by way of one of four ferryboats, and these are quite unusual. Small, wooden and only half covered, they would have no hope whatsoever of succeeding against the swift-flowing currents under their power alone. To solve the problem, therefore, a strong cable was stretched from bank to bank, with a much smaller one attached from that to the ferry itself. The undertow keeps the smaller cable stretched to its limit, and it is this that determines the position of the landing pier. Watch closely and you will notice how the ferryman skilfully holds the boat to the pier solely by the pressure of his wooden pole. These boats are quite an experience, as well as an unparalleled opportunity to see a parade of diverse vessels on the river. And the price is just CHF 1.20.

Basel Basilisks

Omnipresent in Basel, basilisks have over the centuries been depicted in a variety of different forms of mythical beasts, and since the first half of the 15th century have featured on Basel's coat-of-arms. A competition was held in 1884 for the design of cast-iron basilisk fountains, and today there are about 30 green basilisk fountains throughout the city.

Just to the east of the cathedral, along Rittergasse, is a charming house and garden protected by beautifully crafted wrought-iron railings. Almost directly across from the larger house is the small **Archaeological Park** (Archäologischen Park) which has illuminated panels set in the ground revealing ancient walls, and even some bones, encased in glass to protect them from the elements. This is a reminder that, over 2,000 years ago, the Celts from the Rauriker tribe settled here.

Back to the northwest of the cathedral, in Augustinergasse, you will come to the **Augustiner Fountain** (Augustinerbrunnen) which has a basilisk (see box, above) sitting atop a column, dating from 1530, grasping in its talons the Basel coat-of-arms.

Almost across from it is a building incorporating two museums, built in 1844–49 by Melchior Berri (1801–54) to replace the Augustinian Monastery with a multipurpose building that was to become one of the earliest museum buildings in Switzerland. A figurative frieze by the sculptor Johann Jakob Oechslin adorns the façade, as does the basilea, embodying the city of Basel – holding the coat-of-arms and a cornucopia, and wearing a crown. The two museums are the **Natural History Museum** (Naturhistorisches Museum Basel; www.nmb.bs.ch), where you can see animals through the millennia and around the world, as well as live animals in the terrarium; and the **Museum of Ethnology** (Museum der Kulturen; www.mkb.bs.ch), where exhibits from European and non-European cultures, such as the cult house of the Abelam of Papua New Guinea, wooden copies of two Mayan temples and ghost masks from Cameroon, feature in Switzerland's largest such museum (both museums at Augustinergasse 2, t 061 266 55 00, f 061 266 55 46; open Tues–Sun 10–5; adm).

Along the opposite side of Augustinergasse, which changes its name to **Rheinsprung** as it goes down the hill, nicely restored private Gothic and Baroque houses have a unique view directly over the Rhine. Rheinsprung is a particularly historic street. On the Rhine side stands the college building of the Old University that opened in 1460 and is the oldest in Switzerland. The Haus zum Kranichstreit, with a Gothic window and decorated, as was common in the Renaissance era, with shell patterns, dates from 1563. Much more modern is the mural on the windowless extension. Created by Samuel Buri in 1935, the **Gänseliesel** shows, behind scaffolding that the painter 'used' to execute it, a goose maiden.

Nearby are two late Baroque houses – dating from the 1760s – built for brothers and replacing earlier Gothic residences on Augustinergasse. Lukas and Jakob Sarasin were very affluent silk merchants and their houses, the Blue and White (Blaue and Weisse), with large courtyards to their rear, are named after their coloured plaster. Today they are the seat of the Justice Department. Take a look at the pale stone in the cobbled street in front of the White House, as it gave rise to a Basel legend. Supposedly, in

November 1797 the Guild Director Ochs took a stroll along Rheinsprung, as far as this stone, with Napoleon. Look, also, for a series of delightful half-timbered houses, two of which date from 1438 and 1573.

West of the Old Town

The area here is quite high above the Old Town, and is best reached on foot either by the steps next to the Fischmarkt or by leaving Barfüsserplatz by way of the steep hill to the more even street of LeonhardsGraben.

The most important attraction up here is one of Basel's splendours from the past. Dating from the 14th century, when the city was last walled in, the **Spalentor** gate was reinforced a century later and is magnificent indeed. Twin turrets, joined by fortifications topped by another colourful tiled tower, protect a portcullis and an obviously ancient wooden gate. There is also the obligatory moat.

Immediately to its north, even non-gardeners will be impressed with the **Botanical Gardens of Basel University** (*Schönbeinstrasse 6, t 061 267 35 19, f 061 267 29 83, www.unibas.ch/botgarten; open daily April–Oct 8–6; Nov–Mar 8–5, greenhouses open 9–5*), but green-fingered visitors will be positively envious. The gardens themselves, originally founded in 1589 and here since 1898, are pleasing enough, but the huge glass houses – often with a central pond, and home to tremendous cacti and a variety of other flora (more than 8,000 species) as well as tropical birds, butterflies and frogs – are an absolute delight. The church immediately east is that of the rather austere **Peterskirche**; it is thought that there was a church here as early as the 9th century.

This area is not short of museums, either, with three to both the north and southeast of Spalentor. Starting with the north, the one farthest away is the **Anatomy Museum** (Anatomisches Museum; *Pestalozzistrasse 20, t 061 267 35 35; open Mon and Wed–Fri 2–5, Thurs 2–9, Sun 10–4; adm*). If body parts are your thing, this is your place. The museum shows many dissections of human body parts, organs and tissues, explains pre-natal development of the body and exhibits an immense number of important specimens. It also has the oldest preserved skeleton in existence, that of Jacob Karrer dating from 1543.

The two museums closest to Spalentor are in adjacent streets. The **Sculpture Hall** (Skulpturhalle; *Mittlere Strasse 17, t 061 261 52 45, f 061 261 50 42, www.skulpturhalle. ch; open Tues–Sun 10–5; free*) has one of the largest collections of ancient sculptures including, uniquely, a reconstruction of Athens' Parthenon. The other is the **Swiss Sports Museum** (Schweizer Sportmuseum; *Missionsstrasse 28, t 061 261 12 21, www.swiss-sports-museum.ch; open Mon–Fri 10–12 and 2–5, Sat 1–5, Sun 11–5; adm*), with a cross-section of sports and games covering three centuries.

Now heading southeast, back towards Barfüsserplatz, there are two museums just around the corner from each other. The one on the busiest street, the **Firefighters' Museum** (Schweizerisches Feuerwehrmuseum; *Spalenvorstadt 11, t 061 268 14 00, www.berufsfeuerwehr-basel.ch; open Sun 2–5; free*), will only appeal to a few. However, of more interest culturally but with equally strange opening hours is the **Jewish Museum of Switzerland** (Jüdisches Museum der Schweiz; *Kornhausgasse 8, t 061 261 95 14; open Mon and Wed 2–5, Sun 11–5; free*). There are tombstones from the Middle

Ages, Hebrew prints and documents relating to Jewish history in Basel and to Judaism generally, as well as exhibits detailing day-to-day aspects of Jewish life.

The last museum up here has many interesting aspects. The **Music Museum** (Musikmuseum; *Im Lohnhof 9, t 061 205 86 00, f 061 205 86 01, www.historisches-museumbasel.ch/mumu; open Tues, Wed and Fri 2–7, Thurs 2–8, Sun 11–4; adm; guided tours at 6.15pm on the first Thurs of the month*) has sections dating back to around 1070, when it was a monastery for Augustine canons. Later, it was given the name of Lohnhof after the employers Lohnherren, who worked here after 1669. From 1835 to 1995 it served as a prison, and twenty-four of the cells on three floors are now exhibition cabinets. On the ground floor you will see instruments in their musical and social context in a 'Music in Basel' exhibition; the first floor concentrates on concerto, chorale and dance instruments, whilst on the upper floor are those involved in parades, celebrations and signals.

South and East of the Old Town

There are two museums south of the Old Town, close to the Central Station. Closest to the station, and rather strange, is the **Museum für Gestaltung** (*Klosterberg 11, t 061 273 35 95, www.museum-gestaltung-basel.ch; open Tues–Sun 12–5; free*), where you can discover things about everyday culture and question perceptions. The other will be of more interest to most visitors: the **Haus zum Kirschgarten** (*Elisabethenstrasse 27–29, t 061 205 86 78; open Tues, Thurs, Fri and Sun 10–5, Wed 10–8, Sat 1–5; adm*) is a magnificent mansion that was built between 1775 and 1780 as a home and office for a Basel silk ribbon manufacturer. The two floors of historical rooms depict the culture of the 18th and 19th centuries; this is one of Switzerland's most important such museums. Look especially for the Pauls-Eisenbeiss Foundation's porcelain collection, as well as the Nathan-Rupp and Dr Eugen Gschwind watch and clock collections.

Directly east of the Kunstmuseum is a museum that has nothing to do with Leonardo da Vinci. The **Caricature and Cartoon Museum** (Karikatur und Cartoon Museum; *St Alban-Vorstadt 28, t 061 271 13 36, f 061 274 03 36, www.cartoonmuseum.ch; open Wed–Sat 2–5, Sun 10–5; adm*) has ever-changing exhibitions of original works by international artists of the 20th and 21st centuries.

Three more very diverse and eclectic museums are grouped together close to the river, near the St Alban ferry. The closest to it is the very interesting **Basel Paper Mill and Museum of Paper** (Basler Papiermühle; *St Alban-Tal 37, t 061 272 96 52, www.papiermuseum.ch; open Tues–Sun 2–5; adm*). During the 12th century the Cluniac monastery of St Alban built a canal to provide waterpower by means of waterwheels for twelve mills. Later, during the Middle Ages, ten of these were converted to paper mills, and for no less than 446 years – until 1924 – paper was still produced in two of them. Since 1980 a museum has been housed in the Stegreif and Gallician mills; in 1983 it was recognized by the government as a rehabilitation centre for the employment of handicapped people and it became the Swiss Paper Museum two years later. The affluence that this business produced for the Gallician family can be clearly seen on the first two floors, but this really is a working museum focusing on paper, writing and printing. So much so, you can even try your hand working the old, but still functioning, machines and other equipment.

A little west is a most unusual museum, the **Plug In** (*St Alban-Rheinweg 64, t 061 283 60 50, f 061 283 60 51, www.weallplugin.org; open Wed, Fri and Sat 2–6, Thurs 2–6 and 8pm–10pm; free*), which invites you into its public living room to see how there can be artistic interaction with new media. Next door is the third part of the Public Art Collection (Öffentliche Kunstammlung Basel; *see* p.41), the **Museum für Gegenwartskunst** (*St Alban-Rheinweg 60, t 061 206 62 62, f 061 206 62 53, www. mgkbasel.ch; open Tues–Sun 10–5; adm combined with the Kunstmuseum*). This displays work from the 1960s to the present day: minimal and conceptual art to the German Neuen Wilden (New Wild Ones) and neo-expressionist painters. It is housed in a 19th-century factory building that has been converted specifically to combine, harmoniously, the old structure with modern art.

The North Side of the Rhine

Three more museums are easily reached as they are just north of the Mittlere Brücke. Going in that direction, the first is the **Museum Klingental** (*Ausstellungsraum Klingental, Kasernenstrasse 23, t 061 681 66 98; open Tues–Fri 3–5, Sat and Sun 11–4; free*), which exhibits the current creative work of artists from Basel and its surroundings. Next, located in the former Klingental Dominican Convent, is the **Museum Kleines Klingental** (*Unterer Rheinweg 26, t 061 303 00 82, f 267 66 44, www.kleines-klingental.ch; open Wed and Sat 2–5, Sun 10–5; free*), featuring original medieval sculptures from Basel cathedral. Go, also, to see a 17th-century model of the city and an exhibition devoted to the history of the convent. A few blocks away, or take the No.8 tram, is a specialist museum that has the most minimal of opening hours. The **Cocteau Kabinett** (*Feldbergstrasse 57, t 061 692 52 85; open Sat 3–6; adm*) is devoted to Jean Cocteau (1889–1963), who was a versatile representative of the avant-garde movement. Expect to find books, autographs, drawings, glass and ceramics belonging to this lyricist, novelist, dramatist, essayist, illustrator and filmmaker.

Unfortunately the best museum, and greatest attraction, this side of the Rhine is rather less accessible as it is far to the east by the river and almost next to the railway bridge over it. It's too far to walk, so hop on either a No.31 or 36 bus, and get off when you see a large, square building whose exterior walls are different from each other – a feature added by the Ticino architect Mario Botta to establish a differing spatial relationship to the surroundings. The extraordinary **Museum Jean Tinguely** (*Paul Sacher-Anlage 1, t 061 681 93 20, f 061 681 93 21, www.tinguely.ch; open Tues–Sun 11–7, adm*) is dedicated to the life and amazingly intricate post-war kinetic art of Jean Tinguely (1925–91). Growing up in Basel, he tinkered with experiments making constructions that moved and made noises. Moving to Paris in 1953, he created unique artistic machines using randomly driven mechanical movement with optical-spatial and acoustic changeability components. They were later to become known as Méta-mécaniques, and four years later he evolved into Méta-Matics – machines that a user can operate to create abstract works of art. In 1960 his sensational 'Homage to New York' was placed in the gardens of the Museum of Modern Art in that city.

Always innovating, he decided to paint everything black in 1963, and then started using ball bearings to create shaking, circling and rotating movements in Bascule and Eos sculptures. Following up earlier ideas, he then delved into the idea of large sound-mixing machines that came to be known as Méta-Harmonies. Towards the end of his life, in 1987, he created the Grosse Méta Maxi-Maxi Utopia, his vision of a walk-in, poetically utopian dream world made from everyday, but widely diverse, materials. The interior is as creative as the exterior, and within large open-plan galleries you will find examples of all of his ultra-imaginative work.

Greater Basel

North of the Rhine

The **Fondation Beyeler** (*Baselstrasse 101, t 061 645 97 00, f 061 645 97 19, www. beyeler.ch; open Thurs–Tues 10–6, Wed 10–8; adm exp*), surrounded by a 19th-century English landscape garden, is situated in the northwest suburb of Riehen and can be reached by a No.6 tram from the city centre to Riehen Dorf. For a period of 50 years Hildy and Ernst Beyeler built up a particularly fine collection of 20th-century modern masters, whilst working as gallery owners. Transferred to a foundation in 1982, it was first shown as a full collection in Madrid's Centro de Arte Reina Sofia in 1989. The Genovese architect Renzo Piano specifically designed this building for the requirements of this art form, and the 200 current works are by such artists as Cézanne, Van Gogh, Monet, Picasso, Bacon and Warhol, along with a small selection of tribal art from Africa, Oceania and Alaska.

Close to the Fondation Beyeler, in the former offices of the patrician house Berowergut, is the **Kunst Raum Riehen** (*Baselstrasse 71, t 061 641 20 29; open Wed–Fri 1–6, Sat and Sun 11–6; free*), which has temporary exhibitions of all forms of contemporary art.

Another place that is well worth the effort to get to (take a no.55 bus from Basel Claraplatz) is the **Vitra Design Museum** (*Charles-Eames-Strasse 1, t (49) 7621 702 32 00, www.design-museum.de; open Tues–Sun and German public holidays 11–6; adm; bring your passport*) in Germany. Itself housed in a spectacular building designed by the American Frank O. Gehry, this is one of the world's leading industrial furniture design and architecture museums. As well as ever-changing exhibitions it offers, on Tues–Sun and German public holidays at midday and 2pm, architectural tours of nearby buildings such as the Conference Pavilion and Fire Station, both dating from 1993. These take place even when the museum itself is closed to prepare for new exhibitions.

South of the Rhine

The **Fondation Herzog** (*Oslostrasse 8, Dreispitz Gate 13, t 061 333 11 85, www. fondation-herzog.ch; open Tues, Wed, Fri 2–6.30, Sat 1.30–5, adm*) has over 300,000 photographs depicting the history of photography and industrial society (take a no.10 or 11 tram).

Kunsthaus Baselland (*St Jacob-Strasse 170, t 061 312 83 88, f 061 312 83 89, www.kunsthausbaselland.ch; open Tues and Thurs–Sun 11–5, Wed 2–8; adm*) is in a

Excursions from Basel

Destination	Journey Time (hours.mins)	Recommended Length of Trip	Connections
Zürich	0.54	D/T – O/N – M/N	T
Solothurn	1.05	D/T	T/T
Luzern (1)	1.08	D/T – O/N – M/N	T
Bern	1.09	D/T – O/N – M/N	T
Neuchâtel	1.27	D/T	T
Schaffhausen and Rhine Falls	1.28	D/T	T/T
Thun	1.35	D/T	T
Rapperswil	1.48	D/T	T/T
Lausanne	2.09	D/T – O/N	T/T
Stein am Rhein	2.11	D/T	T/T/T
St Gallen	2.12	D/T	T/T
Interlaken	2.14	D/T	T
Engelberg	2.20	D/T – O/N	T/T
Montreux and Vevey	2.34	D/T	T/T/T
Brienz	2.47	D/T	T/T
Geneva	2.48	D/T – O/N – M/N	T
Vaduz, Liechtenstein	3.02	D/T – O/N	T/B
Lötschental	3.04	O/N – M/N	T/B
Sion	3.04	D/T	T/T
Grindelwald (2)	3.07	M/N	T
Gruyères	3.12	D/T	T/T/B/T/B
Wengen (2)	3.14	M/N	T/T/T
Mürren and Schilthorn 007	3.28	M/N	T/T/T/F/T
Les Diablerets	3.56	D/T – O/N	T/T/T
Lugano	3.56	D/T – O/N – M/N	T
Leukerbad	4.13	O/N – M/N	T/T/T/B
Ascona	4.13	O/N – M/N	T/T/B
Scuol	4.14	O/N – M/N	T/T
Crans Montana	4.19	D/T – O/N	T/T/T/B
Saas-Fee	4.23	M/N	T/T/B
Centovalli	4.24	D/T – O/N	T/T/T
Val d'Anniviers	4.40	O/N – M/N	T/T/B/B
Zermatt	4.43	M/N	T/T/T
Nauders, Austria	5.01	O/N – M/N	T/T/T/B

(1) The starting point for the Pilatus trip.
(2) The starting points for the Jungfraujoch and Männlichen trips.
T: train; B: bus; F: funicular.
D/T: day trip; O/N: overnighter; M/N: multi-nighter.
*Journey time is one-way, and the minimum possible. See **Introduction** p.7.*

strange, rectangular-shaped building and holds exhibitions of international and regional contemporary art (take a no.14 tram to the Schänzli stop).

Three Countries Corner (Dreiländereck)

This is an interesting diversion from the history and culture of the city centre. Cross the Middle Bridge (Mittlere Brücke) and continue straight to the junction of Greifengasse and Rebgasse to take a tram No.14 to the end of the line. Alighting, follow the signs directing you towards your destination, Three Countries Corner (Dreiländereck). This journey winds you through the docks, passing the **Shipping Museum** (Verkehrsdrehscheibe Schweiz; *Westquaistrasse 2, t 061 631 42 61, www.verkehrsdrehscheiber.ch; open Mar–Nov Tues–Sun 10–5; Dec–Feb Tues, Sat and Sun 10–5; adm*). It's a small museum with many models of ships etc., but not many descriptions in English. Within a short distance you will reach the banks of the Rhine and a riverside walk that snakes around to the right. Small marinas are on one side, docks on the other and, across the Rhine, it will be immediately apparent from the architectural styles where Switzerland and France meet. After a few hundred yards the land narrows dramatically to a point, and you come to the **Three Countries Corner** (Dreiländereck) itself, with Germany and its rolling hills forming a backdrop straight ahead. Of course, some entrepreneur could not resist the temptation to open the futuristic Dreiländereck bar/restaurant here, where waiters dress in sailor's outfits and move around on in-line skates.

Geneva

Geneva – Genève in French and Genf in German – has a marvellous location at the southwestern end of Lake Geneva (known locally as Lac Léman) surrounded by mountains, particularly the grand but elusive Mont Blanc, and is blessed with a genial climate. It also has a history of welcoming foreigners. It is no wonder, then, that politicians, ambassadors and royalty, not to mention affluent businessmen – a group never prone to self-denial – found themselves attracted by the city's charms. As far back as 1864 Geneva initiated its role in international diplomacy by becoming the home of the International Red Cross, founded by the Swiss Henri Dunant. This role was extended greatly after the First World War, when the city was chosen as the site for the headquarters of the League of Nations, and later, after the Second World War, as the European headquarters of the new United Nations organization. These days it is home to over 200 international organizations, and one-third of the population – of 180,000 – emanates from 157 different nations. Consequently, Geneva is far and away the most cosmopolitan city in Switzerland, and an interesting side product is the abundance of restaurants offering a wide range of international cuisine. The downside for tourists is that with such a community of super-rich international diplomats, civil servants and tax exiles, there is a demand for expensive hotels, restaurants and shops. As a consequence, the city has a reputation for being somewhat expensive. However, in return, it has gained affluence and a cosmopolitan ambience –

Geneva

Getting There

By Air

From the UK

Bmibaby, www.bmibaby.com, operate flights from Cardiff and East Midlands on Sun, Manchester daily and Teesside on Sat, between mid-Dec to late-Mar.

easyJet, www.easyjet.com, operate flights from London (Gatwick and Luton), Liverpool and East Midlands.

Flybe, www.flybe.com, operate flights from Southampton, on a daily basis.

Jet2, www.jet2.com, operate flights from Leeds Bradford three times a week.

British Airways, www.ba.com, and **Swiss**, www.swiss.com, operate daily flights from London (Heathrow), Birmingham and Manchester.

From North America

American Airlines, www.aa.com, and **Swiss** co-share a daily flight from New York (JFK).

Lufthansa, www.lufthansa-usa.com, operate daily flights from Boston, Chicago, Denver/Detroit, Los Angeles, San Francisco, Toronto (Canada), Vancouver (Canada) and Washington DC via Frankfurt.

Swiss, www.swiss.com, operate daily flights from Miami and New York (Newark).

Getting from the Airport

Cointrin International Airport, t 022 717 71 11, **f** 022 798 43 77, www.gva.ch, is located just over three miles (5km) from the city. **Trains** run every 10 minutes and take just 6 minutes; fare CHF 5. **Bus** no. 10 runs to the Cornavin train station; fare CHF 2.20. **Taxis** take between 15 to 20 minutes, depending upon traffic; fare usually CHF 28–33.

By Train

Eurostar, www.eurostar.com, from London (Waterloo) to Paris (Gare du Nord) and then a TGV, www.sncf.fr, from Paris (Gare de Lyon).

Getting Around

Public transport in and around Geneva on trams, buses and ferry boats is clean and efficient. Tickets must be purchased from ticket vending machines, ticket offices or the tourist office before each trip and are available for single trips or, more advantageously, as an Unlimited Day Pass. A single trip costs CHF 2.20 for one hour on the city network, and CHF 5 for a day pass.

Car Hire

Avis, Cointrin Airport, **t** 022 929 03 30; rue de Lausanne 44, **t** 022 731 90 00.

Europcar, Cointrin Airport, **t** 022 798 11 10; rue de Lausanne 37, **t** 022 909 69 00.

Hertz, Cointrin Airport, **t** 022 798 22 02; rue de Berne 60, **t** 022 731 12 00

Rent A Car, rue Hoffman 1, **t** 022 733 50 53.

Bike Hire

Genev'Roule is a bike loan and rental organization run by the Geneva Red Cross. Between May to Oct bikes can be rented daily 7.30am– 9.30pm at either place de Montbrillant 17 (behind the train station), Bains des Pâquis and Plaine de Plainpalais: **t/f** 022 740 13 43, genevroule@croix-rouge-ge.ch. You must produce valid ID, a guarantee of CHF 50, take care of the bike by locking it with the provided padlock and return it by 9.30pm. In the winter (Nov–April), bikes can be rented Mon–Fri 8–6 at arcade Montbrillant 17 for CHF 5 for 24hrs.

Tourist Information

Geneva: Geneva Tourism has two main offices: rue du Mont-Blanc 18, **t** 022 909 70 00, **f** 909 70 11 (*open Mon–Sat 9–6, Sun (in summer) 9–6*), and Pont de la Machine 1, **t** 022 311 98 27, **f** 022 311 80 52 (*open Mon 1–6, Thurs–Fri 9–6, Sat 10–5*); both with e-mail info@ geneva-tourism. ch and website www. geneva-tourism.ch. Additional offices are located at the train station, Cornavin (*only open during the summer*), and at Cointrin Airport (*open daily, year-round, 9am–10pm*).

Geneva Tourism offers special weekend **hotel package rates** (Forfait Week-end) that include accommodation in a double or single room with bath or shower (but only in hotels that participate in the plan), with breakfast, a 2-hour guided city tour and voucher booklets offering certain privileges and reductions. These range in price from CHF 89pp at a 2-star hotel to CHF 183pp at a 5-star hotel, and bookings can be made online.

Guided Trips and Tours

Geneva Tourism sponsors a series of **walks** that, in 2003, included the Old Town, a thematic visit to Carouge and 'Geneva: History and Legends'. These all depart from the Geneva Tourism office on the Pont de la Machine, and cost CHF 8.

Key Tours, rue des Alpes 7, **t** 022 731 41 40, **f** 022 732 27 07, *www.keytours.ch*, operate a city bus tour, and a number of other trips to destinations farther away.

No chapter about Geneva would be complete if it did not include information about **boat trips** that can be taken on Lake Geneva (Lac Léman). Beware, though, there is only a limited service between November and March. **Mouettes Genevoises Navigation**, quai du Mont-Blanc 8, **t** 022 732 29 44, **f** 022 738 79 88, operate both the popular mouette taxi service across the inner bay and several other trips both on the lake and the River Rhône. **Compagnie Générale de Navigation sur le Lac Léman** (CGN), *www.cgn.ch*, operates services to cities and towns in both Switzerland and France up and down the whole length of the lake, and they set sail from the quai du Mont-Blanc.

Yvoire, a delightful French village (*see* p.69), can be reached on a CGN lake steamer.

Market Days

Crafts: Thurs at place de la Fusterie
Flower market: daily at place du Molard
Flea market: Wed and Sat at Plaine de Plainpalais
Fruit and vegetables: Tues and Fri morning at Plaine de Plainpalais

Medical Emergencies

Chemist/pharmacy emergency service, **t** 022 420 64 80.
Dental emergency service, chemin Malombre 5, **t** 022 346 64 44, **f** 022 346 64 46 (*Mon–Fri 8am–8pm, Sat, Sun and holidays 8–5*).
Doctor's emergency service, **t** 022 748 49 50.

Exhibitions and Festivals

Early Mar: Motor Show.
Early April: International Exhibition of Inventions.
Late April: International fair for books.
Late April: Europ'Art, international art fair.
Mid-June: Bol d'Or Regatta on the lake.
4 July: one of the largest celebrations of American Independence outside the USA.
End of July/middle of Aug: Fêtes de Genève, the Geneva festival, fairs and fireworks.
1 Aug: Swiss National Day.
Last week Aug/first week Sept: La Bâtie Festival, a music and theatre festival.
Early Oct: International Fair of Minerals, Fossils and Gems.
11 and 12 Dec: the Escalade, commemorating the attempt by the Duke of Savoy to invade Geneva in 1602.

Shopping

On the right bank the area of rue du Rhône and rues de la Confédération, du Marché and de la Croix-d'Or (these last three known as the rues Basses) is the fashionable shopping district. Also on the right bank, many antique shops, art galleries and boutiques etc. can be found in the Old Town. On the left bank, most of the shops are between the train station, Cornavin, and the quai du Mont-Blanc – particularly along the rue du Mont-Blanc.

Main train station: the shops here open daily 8am–8pm.
Airport, Les Galeries de l'Aéroport, Centre Commercial: 60 shops open daily 8am–8pm, bars and restaurants open daily 6am–11pm.
Swiss Corner, rue des Alpes 7, **t/f** 022 731 06 84, open daily. The widest array of souvenirs in Geneva, with a great selection of cuckoo clocks, T-shirts, watches, knives, etc.
Pastor Frères, rue du Mont-Blanc 7, **t** 022 731 45 19, **f** 022 738 82 28. The finest selection of Swiss Army knives, knives, scissors, etc.
Schweizer Heimatwerk, Geneva Airport, **t** 022 788 33 00, *www.heimatwerk.ch*. Sells contemporary Swiss handicrafts: household items, home decor accessories, jewellery, clothes and toys.

Where to Stay

★★★★★**Hôtel des Bergues**, quai des Bergues 33, **t** 022 908 70 00, **f** 022 908 70 97, *www.hotel desbergues.com* (*luxury*). Founded in 1834, the oldest of Geneva's hotels is housed in a magnificent neoclassical building with a great location. Its guests have included any number of world statesmen, royalty and famous celebrities. Like them you can enjoy, in any of the 96 rooms or 26 suites, original Directoire and Louis Philippe 19th-century furnishings, the latest hi-tech amenities and even a pair of goldfish to keep you company.

★★★★★Beau-Rivage, quai du Mont-Blanc 13, t 022 716 66 66, f 022 716 60 60, *www. beau-rivage.ch (luxury–expensive)*. Founded in 1865, this is the last privately owned 5-star hotel in Geneva, and is still run by the Mayer family. The location is superb, overlooking both the Brunswick Memorial and the lake, and the style is purely classical. This is reflected in the 5-storey atrium in the lobby, where a recent restoration has revealed fragments of the Pompeian frescoes dating from the opening. Seventy-nine very spacious rooms and 14 suites, whose private balconies offer spectacular views.

★★★★Le Warwick, rue de Lausanne 14, t 022 716 80 00, f 022 716 80 01 *(expensive)*. Located diagonally to the left of the train station, this is the most impressive hotel in the area. Its 167 spacious rooms have been renovated to the highest standards. Two floors are non-smoking, and on the seventh floor there are different-size suites with their own terraces.

★★★★★Hôtel de la Cigogne, place Longemalle 17, t 022 818 40 40, f 022 818 40 50 *(expensive)*. The elegant façade here tells you there is something special waiting inside – and you won't be disappointed. The lobby is full of antiques, wooden beams and elaborate decor, and the 43 rooms and 9 suites in this boutique hotel are each distinct in style – some go back in time with four-poster beds.

★★★★Ambassador, quai des Bergues 21, t 022 908 05 30, f 022 738 90 80 *(expensive)*. This is the only 4-star hotel on the right bank of the Rhône. Privately owned, it overlooks a little square. All of its 82 rooms were renovated five years ago and are modern in style with the latest technical amenities.

★★★★Hôtel du Midi, place Chevelu 4, t 022 544 15 00, f 022 544 15 20 *(expensive)*. This 8-storey building is in a quiet location near the Rhône. It has 90 well-equipped and fairly spacious rooms, and the 1st floor has

recently been renovated to include two business rooms.

★★Touring-Balance, place Longemalle 13, t 022 818 62 62, f 022 818 62 61 *(moderate)*. Situated on the left bank in the shopping area close to the Flower Clock, this hotel has some style. The classically unique façade dates from 1905, and much attention has been paid to giving the 58 good-sized rooms an individual identity.

★★★Suisse, place Cornavin 10, t 022 732 66 30, f 022 732 62 39 *(moderate)*. Opened in 1890 and in a central location opposite the train station, this hotel has 57 rooms, 3 mini suites and 2 connecting rooms (with some non-smoking rooms) that have all been carefully designed to make the best use of the space available. It is modern in style and facilities, with a private safe and same-day laundry and dry cleaning service.

Résidence Mont-Blanc, rue Thalberg 4, t 022 716 40 00, f 022 738 87 61, *www.residence-montblanc.ch (moderate)*. A fine location just a minute or so away from the lake. Modern studios and apartments offer an alternative to hotel accommodation. The in-house pool and fitness centre is a bonus.

★★★Astoria, place Cornavin 6, t 022 544 52 52, f 022 544 52 54, *www.astoria-geneve.ch (moderate)*. Very central, opposite the train station – and the hotel will take care of your bags for CHF 2.50pp. All of the 63 rooms have been recently renovated, and they offer modern facilities as well as a modem plug, safe and soundproofing.

★★★Montana, rue des Alpes 23, t 022 732 08 40, f 022 738 25 11 *(moderate)*. Just down from the train station, this is another of the mid-size, 40-room hotels that are to be found in this neighbourhood. Modern decor, good facilities and soundproofed windows.

★★★Excelsior, rue Rousseau 34, t 022 732 09 45, f 022 738 43 69 *(moderate)*. In a central but less busy area, the 60 rooms in this hotel have a charming old-fashioned ambience along with modern facilities like fax-modem.

★★★At Home, rue de Fribourg 16, t 022 906 19 00, f 022 738 44 30 *(moderate–inexpensive)*. A block away from the station on a street full of good restaurants and Internet cafés. Just 22 rooms – with singles, doubles, triples as well as studios, suites and apartments –

but they all have a shower or bath, and are nicely furnished and equipped. Special prices for students under 26.

Tor, rue Lévrier 3, t 022 909 88 20, f 022 909 88 21 (*moderate–inexpensive*). This small B&B hotel, just 22 rooms – some for three and four people – has an excellent location just off the rue du Mont-Blanc and just three blocks from the lake.

Bel'Espérance, rue de la Vallée 1, t 022 818 37 37, f 022 818 37 73 (*moderate–inexpensive*). Situated on the slopes of the Old Town, this has 40 comfortable and very nice rooms. Single, double, triple and family rooms and studios, owned and managed by the Salvation Army, so don't expect any alcohol.

Hôtel des Tourelles, boulevard James-Fazy 2, t 022 732 44 23, f 022 732 76 20, www.destourelles.ch (*moderate–inexpensive*). In a charming 19th-century building, this is the only hotel of its class that overlooks the Rhône. Its 23 comfortable, but sometimes small, rooms combine a flavour of the past with modern comforts.

Rio, place Isaac-Mercier 1, t 022 732 32 64, f 022 732 82 64 (*moderate–inexpensive*). This very elegant piece-of-cheese-shaped building is just 3 minutes' walk, directly to the right, away from the train station. Take an old-fashioned French-style lift to the hotel itself, and find 30 rather old-fashioned but comfortable rooms in varying combinations, with or without a shower, and a pleasant lounge by the reception.

*Hôtel de la Cloche**, rue de la Cloche 6, t 022 732 94 81, f 022 738 16 12 (*inexpensive*). This has a surprisingly good location, in an old house in one of the side streets just off the quai du Mont-Blanc. A B&B hotel with just 8 rooms.

City Hostel Geneva, rue Ferrier 2, t 022 901 15 00, f 022 901 15 60 (*inexpensive*). Geneva's backpacker hotel, located just 5 minutes' walk from the train station. Single and double rooms as well as dormitory accommodation for 2, 3 and 4 people, with toilets, showers and lockers on each floor.

Geneva Youth Hostel, rue Rothschild 30, t 022 732 62 60, f 022 738 39 87, www.yh-geneva.ch (*cheap*). Not far from the train station, this has 350 places available in combinations of 2 to 6 beds, some with showers and toilets, as well as dormitories and facilities for the disabled. Amenities include washing machines and dryers, cooking facilities, leisure room with TV/games, and Internet.

Home St Pierre Petershöfli, cours St Pierre 4, t 022 310 37 07, f 022 310 17 27, www.homest-pierre.ch (*cheap*). In the heart of the Old Town, this building is immersed in history and owned and supported by the German Lutheran Church and the Swiss-German Reformed Church of Geneva. It was founded in 1874 to provide a refuge for German and Swiss-German women who came to the city to improve their French. Still catering only to women, it has single and double rooms and two dormitories.

Eating Out

L'Amphitryon, quai des Bergues 33, t 022 908 70 40 (*very expensive*). Set in what resembles a traditional dining room, albeit looking over the kitchen, this is the small and intimate gourmet restaurant of the Hotel des Bergues. The chef, David Félisaz, specializes in creative and refined cuisine based on the availability of seasonal produce. An example is the skate fish from La Rochelle, with buttered watercress and fried bacon and celery cooked in milk gratinéed with Reblochon cheese. *Closed Sat, Sun, July, Aug.*

Le Chat-Botté, quai du Mont-Blanc 13, t 022 716 66 66 (*very expensive*). An unusual name – Puss in Boots – for a gourmet restaurant located within the Hotel Beau-Rivage that has a decor resembling a country house library. The young chef has learnt to combine tradition and creativity by using the freshest produce. The wine list here is exceptional, as is the *sommelier*, Jean-Christophe Ollivier, who will diplomatically advise you to try wines that otherwise you may never have heard of. *Open daily.*

Le Pavillon, quai des Bergues 33, t 022 908 70 60 (*expensive*). On the ground floor of the Hotel des Bergues, and with a covered terrace overlooking the water, this brasserie-style restaurant has daily specials and *à la carte* dishes of French and Swiss specialities. Afternoon tea on the terrace is popular. *Open daily.*

Café du Centre, place du Molard 5, **t** 022 311 85 86 (*expensive*). With its window full of tempting fish and shellfish, this is a fish lover's paradise, and those who simply can't resist such temptations will opt for the special dishes, *Brasserie, Centre, Mareyeur* and *Royal*, that range from CHF 71 to 260. *Open daily*.

Au Pied de Cochon, place du Bourg-de-Four 4, **t** 022 310 47 97 (*expensive*). As the name implies, this is the place to make a pig of yourself, especially if you like pig's trotters. But don't let that put you off; there are plenty of other tasty selections available, to be eaten in the old and characterful dining room or on the terrace. *Open daily*.

Hung Wan, quai du Mont-Blanc 7, **t** 022 731 73 30 (*expensive*). With a prominent position alongside the lake, this is a classical and authentic Chinese restaurant with the highest standards of cuisine and service. *Open daily*.

Le Lacustre, quai Général-Guisan, **t** 022 312 21 13, *www.restaurant-lacustre.ch* (*expensive*). Designed like the interior of an old ship, and with a great location overlooking the water by the Molard Pier. The speciality is perch (although they don't come from the lake), and Swiss and international dishes. A wonderful lakeside terrace, too. *Open daily*.

Edelweiss, place de la Navigation 2, **t** 022 544 51 51 (*moderate*). In the hotel of the same name, this really does look, and feel, like a typical Swiss chalet. There's fondue in all its varieties – including chocolate – and plenty of other tasty choices like country pâté, air-dried meats, perch, a range of meats, chicken and duck. *Open daily*.

Swiss Cottage, rue Barton 6, **t** 022 732 40 00 (*moderate*). The main dining room on the upper level is a real attraction. The walls are embellished with very imaginative murals of typical Swiss scenes, and prove a perfect backdrop to an equally imaginative array of fondues, raclette, fish and meat. *Open daily*.

Chez Uchino, rue de Zürich 66, **t** 022 755 10 32, 66 (*moderate*). Expect a good ambience in this very small Japanese restaurant. Reasonably priced, and located next door to a Japanese store. *Closed Sat and Sun*.

El Ruedo, rue de Fribourg 5, **t** 022 732 65 08 (*moderate*). Named The Ring, this has the traditional bullfight and Real Madrid decor common in Spanish restaurants. Fish and seafood, along with grandmother's cooking (*Cocina Abuela*) featuring Galician-style cod and octopus (*pulpo*), are the specialities – as are *paella valenciana* and an enticing array of tapas and good wines. *Open daily*.

Khmer Angkor Restaurant Cambodgien, rue du Môle 31, **t** 022 732 38 43, 31 (*moderate*). A little difficult to find, but well worth the bother. It seems that all resident or visiting Cambodians congregate here to sample the exotically prepared dishes, many with shrimps. *Closed Sat lunch and Sun*.

Manora, rue Cornavin 6, **t** 022 909 44 10 (*moderate*). This has an unlikely location in the Placette department store, but shouldn't be missed. The food is self-served from innovatively arranged separate areas that each specialize in a different type of food.

La Grappe d'Or, rue des Pâquis 19, **t** 022 732 75 16 (*moderate*). This unpretentious place, with a café in the front, restaurant at the back and six tables outside, is open all day long and has a surprisingly inventive menu: perch fillets, steak, chicken and lamb, salads, pasta dishes, small and large plates of cold and mixed meats, as well as fondues. *Open daily*.

Lord Nelson Pub, place du Molard 9, **t** 022 311 11 00 (*moderate*). Not really a good imitation of an English pub, but they do brew some tasty beer and it does have a good location in this popular square. Expect a good mix of dishes, along with the usual pub sandwiches and daily specials. *Open daily*.

Shahi Restaurant, place de Cornavin 2, **t** 022 738 44 36 (*moderate*). Located on the first floor of a building diagonally opposite the railway station, this serves spicy Indian and Pakistani dishes, and offers an impressive hot buffet at lunchtimes. You can order takeaways, too. *Closed Sat and Sun lunch*.

Nightlife

The Velvet Club, rue Jeu de L'Arc 7, **t** 022 735 00 00. Non-stop cabaret revue. *Open daily 10pm–5am with free admission*.

Le Prétexte, rue du Prince 9, **t** 022 310 14 28. A gay nightclub featuring male striptease. *Open daily 10pm–5am, adm CHF 20 inc drink*.

a fascinating combination considerably enhanced by a decidedly Gallic flair. Art and culture flourish here, too; Geneva hosts thirty museums exhibiting a variety of prestigious collections, and is justly proud of its musical conservatories and opera.

As it is the place where the lake – the largest freshwater one in western Europe – flows speedily into the Rhône, the city is effectively cut into two parts. The left bank of Geneva is dominated by the Old Town and its cathedral topping the hill, and is also home to many museums, an upmarket shopping area and the Jardins Anglais and the Jet d'Eau, both set alongside the lake. The right bank is home to the Cornavin train station, and between that and the lake it has its own shopping areas as well as the majority of the city's hotels and ethnic restaurants. Alongside the lake, there are numerous five-star hotels, piers for lake steamers and, slightly farther away, wonderful parks that lead to the botanic gardens and the United Nations complex, and a couple of museums.

Owing to its geographical location, squeezed into a tight corner of Switzerland and rather surrounded by France, there aren't many opportunities for trips outside Geneva, other than to Yvoire (*see* p.69). That doesn't present a problem, however, as there is more than enough to see and do in this delightful and interesting city to keep anyone occupied for at least three days, or even more. What's more, most places can easily be reached on foot or by using the excellent public transport system, making a car superfluous.

History

The geographical location of Geneva, set in the far southwestern corner of Lac Léman where the fast-flowing River Rhône leaves the lake and continues its meandering way to the Mediterranean, has made it a strategically important site for thousands of years. There is evidence of human occupancy around the shores of Lake Geneva, as the locals prefer to call it, dating back to around 3,000 BC. It is likely, though, that it wasn't until nearly 500 BC that the Celtic *Allobroges* clan settled in the area, and built a stockade on the hill that is now the Old Town of Geneva.

Between 122 and 120 BC the Romans defeated the *Allobroges*, making the settlement a major stronghold. In 58 BC Julius Caesar destroyed its bridge to prevent the Helvetic people, who later gave their name to the country, from escaping from the invading Barbarians and fleeing into the Roman Empire. In fact, his account of the event in *Comments on the Gallic Wars*, penned six years later, contains the first known written reference to Geneva. The town thrived under Roman rule, and shortly before AD 400 it was awarded the status of a bishopric, at the centre of a huge diocese. The Roman influence is still in evidence today: Geneva's oldest square, Bourg-de-Four, was formerly a Roman forum, and there are extensive, well-restored remains underneath the Cathedral of St Pierre.

The Germanic Burgundian tribe displaced the Romans in AD 443 and, for the next six hundred years, control of the city passed from one faction to another. From the 11th century to the Reformation, Geneva was part of the Holy Roman Empire, yet was governed by its bishops as their own seigneury. Although Geneva didn't gain any real importance until the 15th century, when its trade fairs placed it on the world's map, it was continually under threat from the neighbouring House of Savoy. The attacks were particularly strong during the first three decades of the 16th century, when reinforcements from the cantons of Fribourg and Bern were necessary to preserve the city's autonomy.

The year 1536 saw the triumph of the Reformation, and Geneva attained the political status of a republic. A year later Jean Calvin arrived to live in the city and, under his leadership, the Republic was elevated to 'Mother of the Protestant Church'. From that time forward large numbers of Protestants, many fleeing persecution in neighbouring countries, found their way to Geneva, establishing it as a city of faith and learning. These influences led, in 1559, to Calvin founding the Academy, the predecessor of the current university.

The night of 11 December is the anniversary of an event that is still commemorated in Geneva to this day. On this date in 1602, forces led by Charles-Emmanuel, Duke of Savoy, tried unsuccessfully to storm the city. The French term *Escalade* makes reference to this ill-fated attempt to scale Geneva's walls, and is the name given to the three-day festival weekend held annually in mid-December to celebrate the event.

The 18th and 19th centuries were periods of prosperity for Geneva, as it blossomed into an important centre for industry – particularly watchmaking, commerce, banking, arts, medicine and science. Among its more prominent citizens of that era were Jean-Jacques Rousseau, Voltaire and the biologist Charles Bonnet. In 1798 French troops entered, and annexed, Geneva (where Napoleon stopped for one night on 9 May 1800) and it remained a part of France until the defeat of the French forces resulted in its freedom on 31 December 1813. Determining the time to be right, Geneva joined the Swiss Confederation and became a canton on 19 May 1815. Yet another, and the last to date, revolution took place in 1846, when James Fazy overturned the government of the Restoration; the new constitution forged from that conflict is still in use today.

The Old Town (Vieille Ville)

The Old Town in Geneva is full of character, and there are numerous attractions amongst the many boutiques, antique shops, restaurants and bars. The most important is the **Cathedral of St Pierre** (*cours St-Pierre; open Jan, Feb, Nov and Dec 9–12 and 2–5; Mar, April, May and Oct 9–12 and 2–6; June, July, Aug and Sept 9–12. Mass is held on Sun at 10am; during July and Aug there is a bell concert at 5pm and between June and Sept there is organ music for an hour at 6pm*). The cathedral was built between 1160 and 1232 and is somewhat of an architectural hybrid, with elements of Romanesque, Gothic and Graeco-Roman styles. Although of grand proportions, it reflects the effects of the Reformation, like most churches in Switzerland, and is rather austere inside. Enlightened by beautiful stained-glass windows, the main attractions are the amazingly intricate tomb of the Duke of Rohan, leader of the French Protestants who died in 1638, the cleverly sculptured stone choir and Calvin's chair. The tower, with its 157 steps, affords a marvellous view of Geneva. Visitors wanting to investigate the art from the cathedral more fully should visit the Art and History Museum (*see p.62*).

Do not leave, however, before exploring underneath the cathedral, where you will find one of the largest European **subterranean archaeological sites** open to the public (*t 022 311 75 75; open June–Sept Tues–Fri 11–5, Sat and Sun 11–5.30; Oct–May Tues–Fri 2–5, Sat and Sun 1.30–5.30; adm*). The size and array of exhibits is most impressive, and includes the portal of the old Romanesque cathedral dating from 1000 and other items dating back as far as AD 350.

The rather austere, but not unattractive, building on the corner of the place de la Taconnerie, just across from the cathedral, is worth some attention. This is the historic **Auditoire de Calvin** (*t 022 819 88 19; open Mon–Sat 10.30–12.30 and 2–5*). There used to be a 5th-century church here that was built over the Roman walls, but that burnt down in the 11th century. It was replaced in the 13th century by a parish church – of which some traces can be seen in the present nave – which, in turn, was replaced by this small, Gothic-style chapel that dates from the 15th century. At the beginning of the Reformation the building was deprived of its name, and even its use as a church. However, reformers and reformed exiles from many other European countries didn't just gather here to pray in their own language – as some, like the Church of Scotland and the Dutch and Italian Reformed Churches do today – but also listened to prominent reformers such as Calvin, Knox and de Bèze. Between 1556 and 1559 British refugees led by John Knox printed a new English translation of the Bible here – the first with explanatory notes – known as the Geneva or Breeches Bible, which was largely used in the preparation of the King James Authorized Bible. The Auditoire was also the heart of the university; John Calvin and his successors lectured here for 200 years, hence its name, meaning Calvin's Lecture Theatre.

Just around the corner is the **Hôtel de Ville** (town hall), originally constructed in the 15th century – the Tour Badet is the only remnant from that era – but with substantial additions over the next two centuries. It is the administrative seat of Geneva's government, and boasts international connections, too. In 1864 the First Geneva Convention on the Red Cross met here. Eight years later the international arbitration between the USA and Great Britain to resolve their 'Alabama' dispute was held in what is now known as the 'Alabama Room', and on 15 November 1920 the initial assembly of the League of Nations met here. Note the unusual square ramp of the staircase that enabled horsemen to ride the three floors without dismounting, and provided access for sedan chairs and their like.

Back outside, and actually more striking, is the building directly across from the town hall. On the open ground-floor area stand five original cannon, three with wheels and two without, that date from the 17th and 18th centuries. Once part of Geneva's artillery, they give a strong clue as to one of the building's former uses. Though built as a granary in the 15th century, it was converted for use as an armoury in 1720 and was used for that purpose until 1877, hence the name **Arsenal**. The three mosaics adorning the walls behind the cannons, by Alexandre Cingria in 1949, depict the arrival of Julius Caesar in Geneva, Middle Ages fairs at the Bourg-de-Four and the arrival of Huguenot refugees in the city. The rooms above the wooden-beamed ceiling serve as the state archives. If you happen to be in Geneva during the *Escalade* festivities in December, make a point of coming here and buying some vegetable soup, which is sold in commemorative bowls.

Just a short walk from the cathedral are two interesting museums, the first of which is the **Maison Tavel** (*rue du Puits-Saint-Pierre 6*, **t** *022 418 37 00; open daily 10–5; free, but CHF 2.50 for temporary exhibitions*). This was originally constructed by the Tavel family as their private residence during the 12th century, and is the oldest private house in Geneva. With the exception of the cellars, however, it was destroyed by a fire in 1334 and rebuilt by the Tavels, who proceeded to make it a combination of fortified mansion and urban palace. Subsequently owned by eminent local families over the centuries, it was acquired by the City of Geneva in 1963. Tastefully restored from the cellars to the attic, it is now devoted – by way of objects, drawings, photographs, furniture and other such exhibits – to demonstrating the daily life of urban Geneva from the Middle Ages to the early 20th century. One of the highlights is the Magnin Model, a huge scale model that reconstructs how Geneva looked, including the fortifications, before the 1850s.

In the next street is the **Barbier-Mueller Museum** (*rue Jean Calvin 10*, **t** *022 312 02 70; open daily 11–5; adm*), which has over 7,000 colourful, esoteric – and sometimes erotic – items from Africa, Oceania and the southeast Asian islands. Josef Mueller started the collection in 1907, and since then two generations of the Barbier-Mueller family have continued to complete it, and opened this museum in 1977. Just beyond the museum, a plaque on one of the houses honours George Eliot, revealing that the celebrated English author lived there between October 1849 and March 1850.

Don't leave the Old Town, though, before taking a break in the **place du Bourg-de-Four**. This square has traditionally been one of the city's main meeting places, starting in the Roman era, carrying on through the Middle Ages fairs and into the present day. A strange bronze statue of a nymph welcomes you on arrival. Take a seat at one of the many cafés to soak up the atmosphere, and admire, too, marvellous examples of 16th-, 17th- and 18th-century architecture, the façade of the Palais de Justice and the 18th-century fountain. As a bonus, you may get a sighting of the towering waters of the Jet d'Eau fountain, if you happen to look down rue Verdaine.

Place Neuve, Promenade des Bastions and Surrounding Museums

Place Neuve is best reached from the Old Town by way of the rampe de la Treille, dating from the 16th century. Yes, *rampe* does mean 'ramp', and it is quite steep, too; but the chestnut trees offer considerable shade and the architectural characteristics of the houses to the right provide an interesting diversion. The long, rectangular promenade at the top, embellished with a statue of the diplomat Pictet de Rochemont (1755–1824), instrumental in the Treaty of Paris in 1814 and the Congress of Vienna in 1815, offers an ideal vantage point from which to gain a better perspective of the place Neuve and Promenade des Bastions below, and the surrounding hills in the distance. This should give a clue to its earlier use as an observation and artillery post for the defence of Geneva. Interestingly, one of the trees is Geneva's 'official' chestnut tree, and tradition dictates that its first blossoming marks the arrival of spring.

The **place Neuve** is a square new in name but older in character. Located just outside the city walls, it is surrounded by some memorable buildings and has become something of a focal point of Genevese culture. The **Rath Museum** (*place Neuve 1, t 022 418 33 40; open Tues, Thurs, Fri, Sat and Sun 10–5 and Wed 12– 9; adm varies according to exhibitions*), inaugurated in 1826, is considered to be the first building in Switzerland dedicated to exhibiting the fine arts. It was donated as a gift to the people of Geneva by two sisters, Jeanne-Françoise and Henrietta Rath, and is housed in an impressive building combining French taste and Italian style. There are no permanent exhibitions, as this museum specializes in temporary exhibitions of international and Swiss art. To its right are two other delightful buildings. First is the **Grand Théâtre** (*t 022 418 30 00*), Geneva's opera house inspired by the Paris Garnier Opéra and inaugurated in 1879. In 1951 it was destroyed by fire, but after a 10-year restoration it re-opened grander than ever. Then comes the **Geneva Conservatory** (Conservatoire de Musique de Genève; *boulevard Saint-Georges 36, t 022 329 67 22*), a delightful, Byzantine-style building decorated with muses and antique divinities that was constructed between 1856 and 1858. In the centre of the square stands an equestrian statue of the Genevese **Général Henri Dufour**, a national hero and cartographer of the first geographical map of Switzerland.

Take a few moments, now, to explore the **Promenade des Bastions**, chosen in 1816 as the site of Geneva's first botanical gardens. Although that garden is now officially housed elsewhere, lovely plants and trees remain as testimony to its former role. However, the most important thing here is built into the ramparts of the Old Town. Construction of the 492ft (150m) **Reformation Wall** (Mur dés Réformateurs) began in 1909 to mark the 400th anniversary of the birth of Jean Calvin and the 350th anniversary of the foundation of the Academy of Geneva. At its centre, at a height of 16.5ft (5m) each, are statues of the four great figures of the Reformation: **Guillaume Farel** (1489–1565), one of the first to preach the Reformation in Geneva; **Jean Calvin** (1509–64) the leader of the Reformers; **Théodore de Bèze** (1513–1605), the first rector of the Academy of Geneva, and **John Knox** (1513–72), the founder of Presbyterianism in Scotland. Behind them you will read the motto of both the Reformation and Geneva, *Post Tenebras Lux* – After the Darkness, the Light: 'darkness' referring to the times before the Reformation and 'light' to those after, when they believed the Bible was finally understood. To each side, there are further statues and reliefs of important Protestant figures of the many Calvinist countries, and crucial moments in the development of the Reformation.

The impressive building to the south, the **Palais Eynard**, has been put to a variety of uses but is now a part of the university. If you are really interested in the Reformation, visit the **Musée Historique de la Réformation, Musée Jean-Jacques Rousseau** (*Promenade des Bastions, t 022 418 28 00; open Mon–Fri 9–12 and 2–5, Sat 9–12; free*). Here you will find manuscripts and portraits of both Genevese personalities and people linked with Geneva covering four centuries of history, and documents of all kinds relating to the international Reformation movement.

The rue des Vieux-Grenadiers, just across the nearby Plaine de Plainpalais, is home to two museums. The **Patek Philippe Museum** (*t 022 807 09 10, www.patekmuseum.*

com; open Tues–Fri 2–5, Sat 10–5; adm) was opened in 1999 and is housed in an interesting early 20th-century building. Here, you will find a collection of antique timepieces from the 16th to 19th centuries, the famed Patek Philippe collection dating from 1839 to the present and exhibits of the crafts of watchmaking. The **Museum of Modern and Contemporary Art (MAMCO)** (*t 022 320 61 22, f 022 781 56 81, www.mamco.ch; open Wed–Sun 12–6, Tues 12–9; adm*), opened in 1994, is housed in a former factory. The open-plan environment allows it to exhibit its wide range of videos, paintings, photos and sculptures dating from the early 1960s to the present day in a flexible and innovative manner.

Back around the Promenade des Bastions, on the other side of the Old Town, are several more museums and one other more eclectic attraction.

First is the **Petit Palais, Modern Art Museum** (*terrasse St-Victor 2, t 022 346 14 33, f 022 346 53 15; closed for repairs and renovations, reopening date unknown*). This is a beautiful small palace built in 1862 in the Second Empire style, and it exhibits paintings, drawings and sculpture that trace the history of modern art between 1870 and 1930. There are more than 300 items from all the major schools that influenced French art for more than half a century, including works by Cézanne, Renoir and Gauguin, amongst others.

Behind that is the **Art and History Museum** (Musée d'Art et d'Histoire; *rue Charles-Galland 2, t 022 418 26 00; open daily 10–5; free*). This is everything you would expect of a museum: a grand, very classical façade, elegant staircases and a marvellous inner patio – and that's just the building. Built between 1903 and 1910, this structure was donated by Charles Galland (1806–1901), a benefactor of the city. It also happens to be Switzerland's only museum whose exhibits, numbering in excess of 1,000,000 – and organized in three sections comprising archaeology, fine arts and applied arts – relate to the entire span of Western culture from its origins to date. Not-to-be-missed exhibits are the 15th-century altarpiece by Konrad Wilz and stained-glass windows that were originally in the cathedral.

A right turn out of the museum will take you across another bridge and into an area of elegant houses. Your curiosity will soon be aroused by the sight, down one of the turnings to the left, of a genuine **Russian Orthodox Church** (*rue Toepffer 9, t 022 346 47 09; open Tues–Fri 9–12, Sat 2–8*). In 1859 the many Orthodox Russians living in Geneva were given permission to build a church, and were lucky in that another resident, the Grand Duchess Anna Feodorovna, sister-in-law of Tsar Alexander I and aunt of Queen Victoria, became their patron. The site granted them was once the home of an ancient Benedictine priory, which had been destroyed in the 16th century. The Byzantine Muscovite-style edifice that replaced it in 1866 is easily identifiable by the golden, glittering cupolas, and don't miss the experience of going inside. It's very small, domed, dark and ornate with brown walls adorned by inlaid crosses, modern stained-glass windows, the aroma of incense and, of course, numerous candles. If you want a souvenir they will gladly sell you a CD or tape of Russian Orthodox music.

Not too far away, up a slight hill to route de Malagnou, are two more museums. The **Natural History Museum** (Musée d'Histoire Naturelle; *route de Malagnou 1, t 022 418 63 00; open daily 9.30–5; free*), inaugurated in 1965, is one of the more modern of its genre in Europe and one of the most visited museums in Geneva. It offers a wide array of exhibits, including many animals preserved by the works of taxidermy, which are innovatively displayed. A little behind, and set further back from the road within pretty grounds in the Palladian-style Villa Bryn Bella, you will find – and what could be more appropriate in Switzerland? – the **Clock and Watch Museum** (Musée d'Horlogerie et d'Emaillerie; *route de Malagnou 15, t 022 418 64 70; open daily 10–5; free*). Modern-minded visitors might wrongly assume from its French name that it has some connection with e-mail. Expect, however, to see watches, clocks, clock-making tools and snuffboxes, etc., most of which were manufactured in Geneva. There are also showcases devoted to the Geneva group of enamel workers and the jewellery class of the School of Decorative Arts.

The Bay of Geneva and the Jet d'Eau

Essentially, this section covers the attractions on both sides of the lake closest to the city itself, in the area where the lake siphons into the River Rhône.

Among the first things you will notice along the attractive quai du Mont-Blanc are the steamers moored on the lake, indicative of the many trips originating from here. But your attention, most certainly, will soon be drawn to the unusual monument in a little park, the place des Alpes. The elaborate **Brunswick Monument** is actually the tomb of Charles d'Este-Guelph, Duke of Brunswick. Born in 1804, he was a fine linguist, horseman and musician, but in 1830 this also paranoid and eccentric man was chased into Parisian exile. Establishing himself as a talented investor he accumulated a large fortune and spent the last three years of his life in Geneva, where he died in 1873. He bequeathed a large part of his fortune to the City of Geneva, but specified that it should establish an eminent and worthy location and commission the finest artists of the era to create an exact replica of the Scaligeri Mausoleum in Verona, where his remains would be interred. This elaborate and well-placed monument should see him rest in peace.

In this immediate area you will notice several five-star hotels, only a few of Geneva's impressive tally of fourteen such establishments. However, the dominant feature of the Bay of Geneva, the towering the **Jet d'Eau**, lies on the other bank with – on fine days – a backdrop of the Alps. And in summer you do not have to walk all the way around the bay to get there. Between March and October, simply head for the nearby Pâquis Pier and for a mere CHF 2.20 you can take one of the popular little *Mouette* ferry boats that cross every 10 minutes to the Gustave-Ador Pier, right next to the Jetée des Eaux-Vives that leads to the fountain (but beware of the spray).

You will by now be in no doubt, even if you were previously unaware of the fact, that the massive fountain of water emitting from the Jet d'Eau is the symbol of this city. Surprisingly, what is now a picturesque scene familiar to people throughout the world was conceived as a matter of practicality. Towards the end of the last century the turbine house on the Rhône had excess water on days when industrial demand was light. A quick-thinking engineer, Butticaz by name, designed a way to divert this excess water to a fountain, reaching a height of 98ft (30m), outside the plant. In 1891 the first solely decorative fountain, reaching a height of 295ft (90m), was created in its present position on the lake. This was raised in several stages, and today it gushes 132 gallons (500 litres) a second at a speed of 124 miles (200km) per hour at the nozzle, through an independent pump to an elevation of 459ft (140m). But don't expect to see it year-round. It is turned on to celebrate the coming of spring, usually to coincide with the Motor Show at the beginning of March, and operates, high winds permitting, until the second Sunday in October. Beginning on the week of Ascension Thursday in May, until closing, it is illuminated each night with eight 13,500-watt projection lights.

Follow the lakeside back towards the city centre. In the summer months the surrounding quays are delightful places to sunbathe, or just pass the time of day, while swans, ducks, small boats and lake steamers cavort over the glistening waters. In those waters, though, are two blocks of stone that could easily be overlooked. Named **Neiton** and **Neptune**, these 'Niton' rocks emerged at the end of the Ice Age, and were even used during the Bronze Age for celebrations of rites and sacrifices. More recently, the largest was represented by General Henri Dufour (whose equestrian statue is in the place Neuve) as the basis, at 1,225ft (373.6m) above sea level, for his land survey and his famous 1:100,000 map of Switzerland in 1864.

Soon after, the **English Garden** (Jardin Anglais), dating from 1854, offers a variety of attractions. The most spectacular, without doubt, is the **Flower Clock** (Horloge Fleurie), installed in 1955 to commemorate Geneva's long and illustrious watch-making tradition. With a diameter of 16.4ft (5m), a circumference of 51.5ft (15.7m) and a second hand measuring 8.2ft (2.5m), it took no small technical expertise to get the second hand to travel 10.6 inches (27cm) each second to compensate for the speed of rotation varying between the rising and descending phases of this inclined clock. The floral decoration changes as well, with as many as 6,500 plants of varying varieties that change with the season, comprising each setting of eight concentric circles. The Jardin Anglais also features a statue of Gustav Ador (1845–1928), with an inscription telling you he was president of just about every organization going, and the nearby Four Season's Fountain, featuring Neptune with ladies below and children at the top.

Between the gardens and the Mont-Blanc bridge is where the **National Monument** has stood since its inauguration in 1869. It features two young ladies, carrying double-edged swords and with their arms encircling each other's waist. The one with the crenellated headwear represents the Republic of Geneva and the other is Helvetia (Switzerland). The symbolism is the date, 12 September 1814, when Geneva joined the Swiss Confederation.

Just away from the left bank of the lake is one of the most important shopping areas in Geneva, especially along the rue du Rhône and the Rues Basses. But hidden in there is the **place Molard**, the modern city's answer to the place du Bourg-de-Four, which is just a few hundred feet away up the hill. Lined with outdoor cafés, the square is graced by an octagonal fountain with a marble obelisk dating from 1771 and the Tour du Molard that originates from the 14th century when it was part of the surrounding wall. The Tour was rebuilt in 1591, restored several times later, and has a painted frieze showing the coats-of-arms of the main medieval figures and the Reformation, and a tablet indicating 'Geneva, City of Refuge'.

In the middle of the Pont des Bergues there is a most unusual little island. The **Ile Rousseau** was created in 1583 as a defensive fortification, and in 1628 it became a shipyard. An island until as late as 1832, when the footbridge the Pont des Bergues was built, it was then that it was named after one of Geneva's most illustrious citizens, the philosopher/writer Jean-Jacques Rousseau, whose statue you will find in the grounds. These days the little park is a haven for ducks and swans, and from here it is interesting to note just how fast the waters flow away from the lake into the river.

The United Nations, Red Cross, Botanic Gardens and Lakeside Parks

Between March and October it is fun to take the **Paqui-Express Mini-Train** (*t 022 781 04 04, www.wwsa.ch/stt*) that steams off from the Mont-Blanc Rotunda on the quai du Mont-Blanc every 45 minutes between 10am and dusk, on a 35-minute return journey with a fare of CHF 7.90. As it rolls on its way, the quai du Mont-Blanc transforms itself into the quai Wilson by the **Pâquis Baths**, a feature of life here since 1932 – now featuring a sauna, massage and Turkish baths. All along the quai are huge luxury hotels, the casino and the imposing Palais Wilson. Soon there begins a whole series of delightful parks, whose imminent arrival is announced by a graceful bronze of *The Youth and the Horse* (*L'Adolescent et le Cheval*). These days the parks are continuous and, in fact, have no discernible boundaries. Still, each has its own separate identity and intriguing history, and most include a structure, or structures, of not inconsiderable architectural interest. The history of each park is lengthy and complicated, and very well documented by a multilingual commentary (and sign-boards along the way). One interesting note, though, is that two of the properties, the Moynier and Perle du Lac, were purchased by the League of Nations in 1926. But, unable to acquire enough land for their needs, they subsequently deeded these to the city in exchange for a portion of the Barembé estate (*see* p.66). History aside, these parks are a delight. Competing for your attention are a wealth of beautiful buildings, statues, fountains and arrays of trees, plants and shrubs, along with all the activity on the lake.

Cheat a little, though, and get off at the stop for the **Botanic Gardens and Conservatory** (Conservatoire et Jardin Botanique; *chemin de L'Impératrice 1, t 022 418 51 00; open daily April–Sept 8–7.30, Oct and Mar 9.30–5; free*). These have clearly thrived since being moved from the Promenade des Bastions in 1904 and, as delightful as the nearby parks are, the gardens are more so. As well as the abundant plantlife (more than 16,000 species), you will find deer, flamingoes, aviaries, ponds, fountains, statues, a 19th-century mansion (Le Chêne), a special conservatory for the herbarium (La Console) and a variety of greenhouses, including a beautiful domed one. There is even a 'scent and touch garden' for visually impaired visitors. It is home, too, to a botanical library and a world-famous scientific institute. This is a quiet place to relax in before moving on to the United Nations complex, and more museums.

Take the exit from the gardens on the city side and farthest away from the lake, turn right on to avenue de la Paix and follow it to the oversize 39ft-high (12m) chair with a broken left leg. The symbolism here, as conceived by the humanitarian organization Handicap International, is to encourage all nations to sign up to the Ottawa landmine ban treaty. This, the place des Nations, is also the main entrance to the United Nations complex. However, this is not the entrance for ordinary visitors; that is farther up and around the hill, and along the way a special treat awaits in the **Ariana Park** to the right.

This, once, consisted of a surface area of 62 acres (25.1 hectares) forming part of the Barembé estate, which was the property of Gustav Revilliod, a prominent Genevese. Extensively travelled, he represented the Swiss Federation at such events as the inauguration of the Suez Canal in 1869. Revilliod also had an inveterate passion for collecting, and he amassed a phenomenal number of objects on his journeys. In 1877 he decided to build the Italian Renaissance-style **Ariana Museum** in the grounds to house his treasures, naming it Ariana after his mother, Arine de la Rive, a member of one of Geneva's oldest families. Upon his death, in 1890, the property and CHF 1,000,000 for its upkeep were bequeathed to the city. Fourteen years later, in 1904, the Botanical Gardens were established in the lower part of the grounds, below the railway lines. The remainder of the estate, with the exception of the museum and the immediate land around it, were given to the League of Nations in 1928 in exchange for the two lakeside properties, as described on p.65.

This acquisition enabled the organization to build its headquarters, but at the cost of the Revilliod family home, which was demolished along with various outbuildings and a small zoo. Fortunately, someone had the good sense to preserve the museum, and in 1954 the city opened an International Ceramic Academy in the building. And the **Swiss Museum of Ceramics and Glass** (Musée Suisse de la Céramique et du Verre; *avenue de la Paix 10, t 022 418 54 50; open daily 10–5; free*) really is a gem! The classical lines of the domed exterior, attractive in their own right, enclose an interior that is as beautiful as it is unusual. Its design is deceptive as well; from the outside there is no indication that the main two-storey hall is oval in shape. Enter now, stepping on to the brown marble floor of the ground level, the perimeter of which is encircled by attractive marble pillars of similar colouring, which support the lone upper floor. But, as your attention is drawn upwards, your surroundings pale somewhat into insignificance in comparison with the intricate beauty above you. Around the second floor, elegant wrought-iron railings connect eighteen marble pillars, each sculpted in a unique, but complementary, helicoidal design. Crowning this majestic display is a ring of stained-glass windows, with one set into the light blue dome above each archway between the columns. The only museum of its kind in Switzerland, and one of the most important in Europe, it has over 20,000 objects covering a span of seven centuries of ceramics. Capitalizing on this delightful scene, the authorities have had the insight to create a small café/bar on the higher level where you can sit on the terrace overlooking the UN complex.

Just outside the building you will find a majestic Japanese bell, which has an interesting story in its own right. The original bell, dating from 1657 and the property of a temple in Shinagawa, was lost during the troubled period of Japanese history preceding the fall of the feudal regime around 1867. In 1873, unaware of its origin, Revilliod rescued the bell from a meltdown and placed it in the museum. In 1930 it was returned home to Japan, and a grateful Shinagawa offered Geneva a consecrated replica that was installed in 1991.

Security, as you might expect, is stringent at the Portail Pregny Gate entrance to the **United Nations** (*avenue de la Paix 14, t 022 917 48 96, www.unog.ch; open July–Aug daily 10–5; Sept–June Mon–Fri 10–12 and 2–4; adm. It is best to confirm before visiting, however, as these times, and the itineraries, are subject to change according to the demands of the conference programme*). Expect a request for identification, which will be held by security until you exit. Once approved, you may pass through and walk down to the visitors' service area located in the main building. Among the highlights of what you will learn during the hour-long guided tour, conducted in any one of eighteen languages, are the following. The League of Nations was founded by President Woodrow Wilson in 1920 and this complex, completed in 1936, has a larger surface area than the Palace of Versailles, just outside Paris. After the Second World War the League of Nations was succeeded by the United Nations, whose responsibilities are divided between New York (where the political decisions are made) and Geneva (where all humanitarian facets are considered). Note, also, that materials for the construction and furnishings of the old Palais des Nations were donated by different countries around the world. You will see an introductory film, the Grand Assembly Hall with its bronze doors, the Salle des Pas Perdus (the main foyer of the Assembly Hall), conference rooms in the new building, and some gifts donated by various countries to the UN in Geneva. A tapestry from China will almost certainly catch your eye, with its optical illusion that a door, no matter what the angle from which it is surveyed, appears always to be facing you. All in all this is a very informative tour; before leaving you may want to sign the Golden Book for Peace, demonstrating your support for the United Nations' never-ending crusade for peace.

Philatelists will enjoy the UN also. In 1962 the **United Nations Philatelic Museum** was opened to house the Charles Mistelli collection. This Genevese doctor began collecting postage stamps, envelopes, etc. relating to the League of Nations in 1919, and those relating to the United Nations and its specialized agencies in 1951. His collection was purchased using funds raised by the sale of a special stamp issued by the Swiss Post Office and sold on premises provided by the United Nations Organization. The exhibition is now enhanced by audiovisual presentations, a 'readers corner' with philatelic publications from around the world, and various temporary displays.

Almost directly across from the United Nations is the **International Red Cross and Red Crescent Museum** (Musée de la Croix-Rouge et du Croissant-Rouge; *avenue de la Paix 17, t 022 748 95 25, www.micr.ch; open Wed–Mon 10–5*). This modern museum uses state-of-the-art audiovisual demonstrations to showcase the organizations' activities over their 130-year history.

To get back to the town centre just walk back down avenue de la Paix, passing the impressive white walls and metal gates of the Federation of Russia to place des Nations, and catch a bus back to the Gare de Cornavin.

Excursions from Geneva

Destination	Journey Time (hours.mins)	Recommended Length of Trip	Connections
Lausanne	0.34	D/T – O/N	T
Montreux and Vevey	0.49	D/T	T
Neuchâtel	1.14	D/T	T
Sion	1.23	D/T	T
Bern	1.43	D/T – O/N – M/N	T
Solothurn	2.00	D/T	T
Les Diablerets	2.02	D/T – O/N	T/T
Thun	2.11	D/T	T/T
Crans Montana	2.37	D/T – O/N	T/B
Gruyères	2.38	D/T	T/T/B
Interlaken	2.44	D/T	T/T
Basel	2.47	D/T – O/N – M/N	T
Leukerbad	2.55	O/N – M/N	T/B
Zürich	2.56	D/T – O/N – M/N	T
Val d'Anniviers	3.05	O/N – M/N	T/B/B
Luzern (1)	3.17	D/T – O/N – M/N	T/T/T
Brienz	3.17	D/T	T/T/T
Saas-Fee	3.18	M/N	T/B
Zermatt	3.25	M/N	T/T
Lötschental	3.34	O/N – M/N	T/T/B
Grindelwald (2)	3.39	M/N	T/T/T
Wengen (2)	3.44	M/N	T/T/T/T
Rapperswil	3.52	D/T	T/T
Mürren and Schilthorn 007	4.00	M/N	T/T/T/F/T
Schaffhausen and Rhine Falls	4.07	D/T	T/T
Centovalli	4.07	D/T – O/N	T/T/T
Stein am Rhein	4.22	D/T	T/T
St Gallen	4.23	D/T	T
Engelberg	4.28	D/T – O/N	T/T/T
Ascona	4.45	O/N – M/N	T/T/B
Vaduz, Liechtenstein	5.16	D/T – O/N	T/T/B
Lugano	5.43	D/T – O/N – M/N	T/T/T/T
Scuol	6.34	O/N – M/N	T/T/T
Nauders, Austria	7.33	O/N – M/N	T/T/T/B

(1) The starting point for the Pilatus trip.
(2) The starting points for the Jungfraujoch and Männlichen trips.
T: train; B: bus; F: funicular.
D/T: day trip; O/N: overnighter; M/N: multi-nighter.
Journey times are one-way, and the minimum possible. See **Introduction***, p.7.*

Yvoire

The charming village of Yvoire across on the French side of the lake is well worth a special trip (*see* 'Guided Trips and Tours', p.53). The voyage by boat is itself pleasant enough, especially on the weekend when the lake seems to come alive with the sails of hundreds of yachts fluttering in the breeze, and the shores are dotted with sunbathers in the pretty villages. Yvoire, though, is something special. A fortified medieval town, with an interesting castle as well, its narrow lanes are crowded with wooden and stone buildings that are literally covered with the brightest and most colourful flowers you are ever likely to see. Browse or shop in delightful craft boutiques, and dine in one of the many, many restaurants, most of which specialize in lake perch fillets. Yvoire's charms have not gone unnoticed, however, and this small village often gets just a little too crowded for comfort. Even so, it is a charming place that merits a visit, and you will come away with delightful memories.

Zürich

Zürich used to have a reputation for being a somewhat dull city, possibly because of its historical role as leader of the Reformation in Switzerland and its modern role as the country's financial capital. Present-day visitors will quickly realize, however, that this is no longer the case.

The city boasts a great geographical location. Situated in the centre-north of the country, at the far north end of the lake that shares its name and with snow-capped mountains looming in the east, scenically beautiful Zürich enjoys a fine climate for most of the year.

With a population of over 360,000, it is also Switzerland's largest city. You might expect such a business-minded place to be constrained and bland, but culturally conscious Zürich is neither. It enjoys an international reputation as an art-dealing centre, with many notable auction houses based in the city. Museums, art galleries, theatres, music and clubs abound, along with an outdoor environment of pavement cafés and bars that make for a lively atmosphere. Shoppers will not be disappointed, either, with every world-famous brand on show along the one-and-a-quarter-mile length of the Bahnhofstrasse, Switzerland's most famous street. The charming Old Town is home to a variety of art galleries and antique dealers, not to mention any number of stylish boutiques in the area between the Bahnhofstrasse and the River Limmat. On the opposite side of the Limmat, the pedestrian area known as Dörfli offers an array of more shops, bars, nightclubs and discos. Take a look, too, under the train station at Shopville, the only place in Zürich where you will find stores open on Sundays. Hotels are of the highest standard and the restaurants have a decidedly international flavour, though prices can be quite high.

Within more or less an hour of Zürich, by train, there are a handful of interesting places to explore. Rapperswil is the closest, and lunch on a lake steamer on the way back is a delightful experience; Schaffhausen, an attractive place in itself, is enhanced by the nearby Rhine Falls; and Stein am Rhein, a fascinating medieval city, is just a

river cruise away when continuing on from Schaffhausen or a short train trip from Zürich. Slightly farther away, but worth a visit for its famous library and cathedral, is St Gallen.

Given all of this, it isn't surprising that, in 2003 and for the second year running, a study conducted by the consulting firm William M. Mercer and based upon 39 criteria in 215 major worldwide cities named Zürich as having the best quality of life in the world.

History

Although the Romans built a customs post at Lindenhof as early as 15 BC, thereby founding *Turicum*, Zürich was first recorded as a town in official documents in AD 929. It subsequently acquired the status of Free Imperial Town in 1218. A little over a century later, in 1336, local artisans, organized in guilds and led by Rudolf Brun, successfully conspired to overthrow the city council, instituting a new constitution that, naturally, gave domination to the guilds. These days, however, things have changed. The guilds appear in public only once a year, on the third Monday in April, during the Zürich Spring Festival of *Sechseläuten*. Members don traditional guild costume and march throughout the city before reaching their destination, Sechseläuten Square, in early evening.

In 1351, Zürich joined the Swiss Confederation. That same century saw the construction of walls to fortify the city centre. And strong they were, lasting well into the 19th century and standing, preserved and intact, in the Old Town to this day. During the early 16th century, in 1519, Huldrych Zwingli brought the Reformation to Zürich.

In the 19th century Zürich metamorphosed into the financial and economic centre of Switzerland. And with the opening of the Zürich Stock Exchange in 1877, it became a major player in international financial and trade markets as well. In fact, today Zürich is home to what is considered the world's fourth most important stock exchange, is the world's largest gold trading centre and hosts a variety of thriving industries that provide a total of over 350,000 jobs.

West of the Limmat: Bahnhofstrasse and the Old Town

The main railway station, **Hauptbahnhof**, is a place virtually every visitor to Zürich will pass through at one time or another. Opened in 1872, this station superficially looks just like a station. But don't be deceived. Delve deeper and you will find beneath it a comprehensive shopping complex of over 170 stores. This is important because it is the only place in Zürich where you will find shops open on a Sunday, besides the airport. In addition, the station forecourt is the best place to find foreign newspapers.

Immediately behind the station, the large, castle-like structure – dating from 1898 and with a tower replicating the town gate of Baden – houses the **Swiss National Museum** (Schweiz Landesmuseum; *Museumstrasse 1, t 01 218 65 11, www.musee-suisse.ch; open Tues–Sun 10.30–5; adm*). Enter through a huge courtyard, passing cannons and a small cafeteria, to investigate three floors and a basement filled with exhibits, grouped together in tours taking you from prehistory to the 20th century, giving an interesting and innovative insight into Swiss cultural history. Once a year

Getting There

By Air

From the UK

easyJet, www.easyjet.com, operate daily flights from London (Gatwick and Luton).

British Airways, www.ba.com, and **Swiss**, www.swiss.com, operate daily flights from London (Heathrow), Birmingham and Manchester and Swiss also operate daily flights from London (City Airport).

From North America

Air Canada, www.aircanada.ca, operate a daily flight from Toronto.

American Airlines, wwwaa.com, operate daily flights from New York (JFK) and Dallas/Fort Worth.

Continental, www.continental.com, operate a daily flight from New York (Newark).

Delta, www.delta.com, operate a daily flight from Atlanta.

Lufthansa, www.lufthansa-usa.com, operate daily flights from Boston, Chicago, Denver/Detroit, Los Angeles, San Francisco, Toronto (Canada), Vancouver (Canada) and Washington DC via Frankfurt.

Swiss, www.swiss.com, operate daily flights from Boston, Chicago, Los Angeles, Miami, Montreal (Canada), New York (Newark) and Washington DC.

Getting from the Airport

Zürich Kloten Airport, reservations and information, **t** 0848 800 700, is about 8 miles (12km) from the city centre.

Take the **airport train, which will take you to the centre in 10 minutes**. Departures are scheduled every 10–15 minutes and the fare is CHF 5.40. After purchase, all tickets must be validated, either in the bottom left-hand corner of the ticket machine or in one of the orange-coloured machines on the platforms.

Alternatively, **taxis** from the airport to the centre of Zürich cost about CHF 50.

Many hotels operate their own **shuttle bus service** to and from the airport; check before you leave.

By Train

Eurostar, www.eurostar.com, from London (Waterloo) to Paris (Gare du Nord), then a TGV, www.sncf.fr, from Paris (Gare de Lyon) to Zürich.

By Bus

National Express, www.nationalexpress.com, operate the Eurolines bus service, on Monday, Wednesday and Friday, from London (Victoria Coach Station) to Zürich.

Getting Around

Public transport in and around Zürich, on any combination of trams, buses, boats, the S-Bahn (a rapid suburban train) and some railways, is fast, clean and efficient and operated by Zürcher Verkehrsverbund, www.zvv.ch. Tickets must be purchased from ticket-vending machines, ticket offices or the tourist office before each trip and are available for single trips or, more advantageously, as an Unlimited Day Pass. The latter, for 2nd class, cost CHF 7.20 for the city of Zürich.

The main train station is the **Hauptbahnhof**. All the long-distance trains start from this terminal, as do local ones, and around it are a series of important tram stop hubs. Long-distance trains, **SBB**, information, **t** 157 33 33 (Mon–Fri 8–5.30).

Car Hire

Avis, Kloten Airport, **t** 01 800 77 33; Gartenhofstrasse 17, **t** 01 296 87 87.

Europcar, Kloten Airport, **t** 01 813 20 44; Lindenstrasse 33, **t** 01 383 17 47.

Hertz, Kloten Airport, **t** 01 816 32 55; Morgortenstrasse 5, **t** 01 242 84 84.

Rent a Car, Hardstrasse 8, **t** 043 499 02 02.

Bike Hire

Three hundred city bikes are available free daily, between 7.30am and 9.30pm, from Usteristrasse/Globus (near the main railway station), Theaterplatz (near Stadelhofen), Tessinerplatz (near Enge station/Hotel Ascot) and Marktplatz Oerlikon (near Oerlikon Station/Swissôtel). Take a valid form of ID and a deposit of CHF 20.

Tourist Information

Zürich: the Zürich Tourismus office, Haupt-bahnhof, **t** 01 215 40 00, **f** 01 215 40 44, information@ zurichtourism.ch, www.zurich-tourism.ch, is located on the ground floor concourse at the main railway station (*open Nov–Mar Mon–Fri 8.30–7, Sat–Sun 9–6.30; April–Oct Mon–Sat 8am–8.30pm, Sun 8.30–6.30*).

ZürichCARD is available from the tourist office in the main station, at Zürich Airport and at some hotels. It is valid on all forms of transport, gives free admission to 43 museums, a complimentary welcome drink in 24 restaurants and a number of other discounts; CHF 15 for 24hrs or CHF 30 for 72hrs.

Zürich **hotel reservation** service, **t** 01 215 40 00, **f** 01 215 40 44 or hotel@zurichtourismus.ch (*open Mon–Sat 8–6.30 and Sun 8–12 and 1–6*), offers an on-line booking service, www. zurich tourismus.ch, and you will also find special offers from selected hotels at this site.

Guided Walks and Tours

Stroll through the Old Town: departs April–Oct from the tourist office in the train station on Mon, Tues and Thurs at 3pm and other days at 11am and 3pm. The commentary is in English and German, it takes 2 hours and the ticket costs CHF 20.

Great Tour of Zürich: leaves daily year-round from the Sihlquai bus station and shows you some of the Old Town before carrying on around the lake to the charming town of Rapperswil, known as the 'City of Roses', before returning on a lake steamer. This trip take about 4½ hours and has a commentary in English and German; a ticket costs CHF 45.

Classic Trolley Sightseeing: a 2-hour trip which takes place April–Oct and takes you all around town, with a choice of commentary in eight languages via state-of-the-art headsets. This trolley, the first of its kind in Switzerland, is built to a traditional design but boasts modern amenities, and departs from the Sihlquai bus station at 9.45am, midday and 2pm, with tickets costing CHF 32.

Zürichsee Schiffahrtsgesellschaft, **t** 01 487 13 13, **f** 01 487 13 20, www.zsg.ch, offers a variety of **boat trips** on Lake Zürich throughout the year, but with a much expanded schedule April–Oct. Some of these are evening trips featuring music and dancing and even fondue cruises. However, your best bet may be a short round-trip lasting 1½ hours and departing from Bürkiplatz (on the southwest side of where the Limmat meets the lake) at 1.05pm and 2.35pm and costing CHF 5.40.

Internet Cafés

Internet Café, Uraniastrasse 3, **t** 01 210 33 11 (*open Mon–Sat 9am–midnight, Sun 11am–11pm*); just CHF.25 a minute.

Lost Property and Police

City Police and Public Transportation, Werdmühlestrasse 10, **t** 01 216 51 11 (*open Mon–Fri 7.30–5.30*).
City Police, Bahnhofquai 3, **t** 01 216 71 11 (*Sat and Sun*).
Railway (SBB) Lost Property Office, **t** 01 157 22 22, at the main station (*open daily 6am–10pm*).

Market Days

Vegetable and flower market: Tues and Fri at Bürkiplatz and Wed at Helvetiaplatz 6–11am.
Flea market: Sat at Bürkiplatz, Mar–Oct 6.15–3.30.
Speciality market: Wed at the main railway station, Feb–mid-June and mid-Aug–mid-Nov 11–8.

Medical Emergencies

Chemist/pharmacy emergency service, **t** 01 266 62 22.
Dental, SOS-Zahnärzte, Theaterstrasse 14, **t** 01 262 11 11 (24-hours), www.sos.ch, for an appointment.
Doctors, Bellevuepraxis, Theaterstrasse 14, **t** 01 262 44 44 (*7.30am–8.30pm*).

Exhibitions and Festivals

Late Jan: CSI Zürich, a major international equestrian event.

Early Feb–late Mar: International Country Music Festival which, lasting 6½ weeks, is the longest in the world.

Late Feb/early Mar: Carnival.

Mid-April: Zürich Sechseläuten, the city's traditional spring festival.

Mid-June: Festival Tropical Caliente, considered to be the largest Latin event in Switzerland and in Europe.

Late June–mid-July: The **Zürich Festival**, with theatre, opera, music and other exhibitions.

1 Aug: Swiss National Day, celebrations and fireworks.

Late to end Aug: Zürich Theatre Spectacle and international theatre festival.

Mid-Sept: Knabenschiessen, Switzerland's largest fair where boys and girls aged 12 to 17 compete in a shooting competition, and the winners are crowned.

Early Nov: Expovina, a wine exhibition on boats on the lake, with restaurants participating.

Shopping

Undoubtedly, the best place to start shopping in Zürich is **Bahnhofstrasse**, where you can find almost everything from designer name merchandise to souvenirs. It is well worth, too, venturing off to explore the shops and boutiques in the pretty, old area between Bahnhofstrasse and the Limmat. The other side of Bahnhofstrasse is more modern, and you will find department stores and other larger shops.

Main railway station: Shopville, Mon–Sun 8–8, chemist/pharmacy 7am–midnight.

Airport: Mon–Sun 8–8.

Meng Cutlery, www.wengcutlery.ch. Has two shops close to Bahnhofstrasse. The one at Rennweg 31 has a fine collection of souvenirs, whilst the other at Poststrasse 4 has a wide range of knives, cutlery, etc.

Schweizer Heimatwerk, www.heimatwerk.ch. Offers a good alternative to souvenirs – superb design in contemporary Swiss handicrafts in the form of household items, home furnishing accessories, jewellery, clothes and toys. Their shops are easily found as they are located at Rudolf Brun-Brücke, Bahnhofstrasse 2, Rennweg 14, the Central Station main hall and at the airport in Transit Hall A behind passport control in the basement.

Drinks of the World, Halle Landesmuseum – in Shopville under the train station, t 01 211 10 50 (open Mon–Sat 9am–9.30pm and Sun 9–8). Not only has the widest array of beers you can find anywhere, but it is also the only place in Zürich where you can buy beer, and other alcohol, to take away on Sun.

Confiserie Sprüngli, Paradeplatz, t 01 224 47 11, www.confiserie-spruengli.ch. This shop has been in business since 1836. One glance at the shop window will tell you instantly why – this is the most famous address for the most exquisite Swiss chocolate, confectionery and cake specialities.

Where to Stay

★★★★★**Widder**, Rennweg 7, t 01 224 25 26, f 01 224 24 24, www.widderhotel.ch (luxury). Located in the Augustiner quarter, just off Bahnhofstrasse, this refined, private and luxurious hotel is the result of a very detailed restoration of 8 historic townhouses. The 42 rooms and 7 suites are exceptional in that in total design – floor plan, furnishings, fittings and ambience – they are unique creations. Many decades before the hotel, the Widder Bar was famous for its jazz performances, and this tradition has been revived in the current Widder Bar.

★★★★★**Savoy Baur en Ville Zürich**, Am Paradeplatz, t 01 215 25 25, f 01 215 25 00, www.savoy-baurenville.ch (luxury). This is housed in a traditional building at the junction of Bahnhofstrasse and Paradeplatz in the centre of the city. A luxurious hotel which fits like a glove into its elegant, stylish surroundings, and offers a high level of comfort and service.

★★★★**Splügenschloss**, Splügenstrasse 2/Genferstrasse, t 289 99 99, f 289 99 98, www.splugenscloss.ch (expensive). This particularly gracious and charming hotel in a classic turn-of-the-century building is in a quiet suburb near the lake, but just a few minutes from the city centre. It is famous for its personal service and attention, and each of the 50 rooms (and 2 suites) has a delightful ambience, a sitting area and a desk with computer, fax connections and voice mail.

★★★★**Glärnischhof**, Claridenstrasse 30, **t** 01 286 22 22, **f** 01 286 22 86, *www.glaernischhof.com* (*expensive*). Tucked away just a few minutes off Bahnhofstrasse in a quiet location, this hotel has 62 very modern rooms with state-of-the-art facilities. Also on offer are two restaurants – including the highly rated Le Poisson – and complimentary access to the Luxor squash and fitness club next door.

★★★★**Ambassador**, Falkenstrasse 6, **t** 01 258 98 98, **f** 01 258 98 00, *www.ambassadorhotel.ch* (*expensive*). The location here is a little different, as it is tucked away behind the Opera House close to the lake. The 45 rooms are fair-sized and modern, with a safe for a laptop and modem connection (some rooms have an ISDN connection), as well as soundproofed windows. There's a good bar, too.

★★★**Scheuble**, Mühlegasse 17, **t** 01 268 48 00, **f** 01 268 48 01, *www.scheuble.ch* (*expensive–moderate*). Behind an attractive 19th-century façade, and the Florist Diel, is a hotel of some charm. In 1991 it was completely renovated by the architect Pia Schmid, who has brought a bright modern ambience with a blend of European and Asian accents to the 65 rooms. The location, too, is a real plus.

★★★★**Rigihof**, Universitätstrasse 101, **t** 01 361 16 85, **f** 01 361 16 17, *www.hotel-rigihof.ch* (*moderate*). Built in 1931, this is a fine example of the Bauhaus style. All of its 66 rooms – modern, with high-tech facilities – are dedicated, by way of wall paintings and documentation, to celebrities who lived in Zürich and invented something that benefited many people. There is also a library and the Bauhaus Restaurant. Take tram 10 from the station to the Winkelriedstrasse stop.

★★★**Franziskaner**, Niederdorfstrasse 1, **t** 01 250 53 00, **f** 01 250 53 01, *www.hotel-franziskaner.ch* (*moderate*). Another hotel with a good location, near the Limmat Quai between the railway station and the Grossmünster. The 19 rooms have a mix of styles – some are themed rooms – and modern facilities. It has a Jugendstil bar and summer terrace.

★★★**Rütli–Garni**, Zähringerstrasse 43, **t** 01 254 58 00, **f** 01 254 58 01, *www.rutli.ch* (*moderate*). This is a good choice for its central location and its 66 modern rooms with modem/fax connection and voice mail. Other amenities include a free Internet terminal in the lobby and a hotel bus to and from the airport.

Lady's First, Mainaustrasse 24, **t** 01 380 80 10, **f** 01 380 80 20, *www.ladysfirst* (*moderate*). An unusual hotel in many respects; men are now allowed in, but not on the top two floors or in the spa. There are 28 high-ceilinged and parquet-floored modern and stylish rooms – as would be expected of those designed by Pia Schmid (*see* Hotel Scheuble) – in this 19th-century house. Take the No. 4 tram from the railway station, in the Tiefenbrunnen direction.

★★★**Altstadt**, Kirchgasse 4, **t** 01 250 53 53, **f** 01 250 53 54, *www.hotel-altstadt.ch* (*moderate*). Located in a quiet sloping street just behind the Grossmünster, this is a small, 23-room Old Town hotel. Although not necessarily large, the rooms have been decorated with artistic flair. Modern facilities and a nice bar.

★★★**City Hotel**, Löwenstrasse 34, **t** 01 217 17 17, **f** 01 217 18 18, *www.hotelcity.ch* (*moderate*). This hotel is just off Bahnhofstrasse, surrounded by department stores and boutiques. Its 72 individually designed rooms are stylish and come with every facility, including access to the Internet. A pleasant roof terrace, too.

★★★**Hôtel du Théâtre**, Seilergraben 69, **t** 01 267 26 70, **f** 01 267 26 71, *www.hotel-du-theatre.ch* (*moderate*). This once was an important German-speaking theatre in the 1950s. These days it is an interesting B&B hotel with 50 rooms innovatively designed, technically up-to-date and with sound-proofed windows. Forget bedtime reading, there are dozens of audio books awaiting your attention. Breakfast buffet CHF 15pp.

***Leoneck**, Leonhardstrasse 1, **t** 01 254 22 22, **f** 01 254 22 00, *www.leoneck.ch* (*moderate*). Less than a 6min walk from the train station, at the tram stop 'Haldenegg', on lines 6, 7, 10 and 15. Its 65 very clean and comfortable rooms each have an often amusing Swiss ethno-style mural depicting a traditional Swiss scene behind the bed. Buffet breakfast, at CHF 16pp, is in the highly whimsical 'Crazy Cow' restaurant.

****Limmathof**, Limmatquai 142, **t** 01 261 42 20 or **f** 01 262 02 17 (*moderate*). Centrally located directly across the Limmat river from the railway station. The 62 comfortable, well-equipped rooms are within an historic house in the old part of town.

Zic-Zac Rock-Hotel, Marktgasse 17, **t** 01 261 21 81, **f** 01 261 21 71, *www.ziczac.ch* (*moderate*). Carrying on the same theme as the restaurant below it, every room here – and they come in varying sizes with shower in the room or in the hallway – is named after a pop star. It also offers 24-hour check-in, a bus service to and from the airport and tea/coffee and croissants (CHF 5) in the morning.

Villette, Kruggasse 4, **t** 01 251 23 36, **f** 01 251 23 39 (*inexpensive*). Located in an old house in one of the narrow streets behind the Grossmünster and close to the Quai Brücke, its rooms are clean and comfortable. Continental breakfast included.

***Martahaus–Garni**, Zähringerstrasse 36, **t** 01 251 45 50, **f** 01 251 45 40, *www.martahaus.ch* (*inexpensive*). Centrally located, this offers a wide variety of accommodation: single, double, treble or 4-bedded rooms, studios and even dormitories. To economize, choose rooms with toilet and shower on the floor.

Hotel Biber–City Backpacker, Niederdorfstrasse 5, **t** 01 251 90 15, **f** 01 251 90 24, *sleep@city-backpacker.ch* (*cheap*). In the Old Town; this has kitchen and washing facilities, Internet station, a rooftop terrace and lockers, and offers dormitory accommodation for CHF 29.

Hotel Formule 1, Heidi-Abel-Weg 7, **t** 01 307 48 00, **f** 01 307 48 48 (*very cheap*). Out by the airport, this has modern, innovatively designed rooms with shower and toilet facilities out in the hallway. All you can eat breakfast buffet CHF 8pp.

Youth Hostel Zürich, Mutscellenstrasse 114, **t** 01 482 35 44, **f** 01 480 17 27, *zuerich@youthhostel.ch* (*very cheap*). A combination of 4- and 6-bedded rooms, as well as a games/TV room, washing and drying machines and an Internet corner. Take tram 4 from the railway station to the Morgental stop.

Eating Out

Widder, Rennweg 7, **t** 01 224 25 26, **f** 01 224 24 24, *www.widderhotel.ch* (*very expensive*). Like everything about this hotel, the restaurant is exemplary and very, very classy. In fact, it is not just one restaurant but two – one for non-smokers and one for smokers – and both are small, refined and intimate in their decor. Choose from the *Menu Table d'Hôtes*, with 3, 4 or the whole 7-course menu costing CHF 88, 9 and 130 respectively. On this, and the main menu, you will find an enticing array of original Swiss fish and meat dishes, all beautifully prepared and presented. And you can visit the Wytresor (wine strongroom), where bottles from its magnificent collection of Swiss and European wines can cost up to CHF 1,850! *Open daily*.

Sukhothai, Erlachstrasse 46, **t** 01 462 66 22, **f** 01 462 66 54, *www.sukhothai.ch* (*very expensive*). A Michelin-star restaurant that is not only Switzerland's premier Thai restaurant, but was also voted the best Thai restaurant in Europe by *Guide Bleu Switzerland 2002*. In a dining area combining Western style and Thai art forms, you will be enchanted by Wanphen Heymann Sukphan's exquisitely thought-out and tastefully harmonized dishes, that may include exotic fish especially flown in from Thailand. *Closed Sun and Mon*.

Haus zum Rüden, Limmatquai 42, **t** 01 261 95 66, **f** 01 261 18 04, *www.hauszumrueden.ch* (*expensive*). This building, beside the river, was first mentioned in 1295, and the first-floor restaurant has a genuine Gothic atmosphere. The classical Zürich specialities and the very fine wine list – try the unusual white Humagne du Valais – are equally impressive. The *menu gastronomique*, CHF 138pp without wine, is for those with fine palates and deep pockets. *Open daily*.

Le Poisson, Claridenstrasse 30, **t** 01 286 22 22 (*expensive*). This award-winning restaurant is in the Hotel Glärnischof. Obviously, fish is the speciality, and it comes in many enticing combinations – including several dishes of gilt head bream, a local favourite. Leave room for the tasty, often alcohol-flavoured desserts, and from the smallish wine list select the rather unusual white Merlot. *Open daily*.

Le Dézaley, Restaurant Vaudois, Römergasse 7 + 9, **t** 01 251 61 29, **f** 01 252 27 02, *www.le-dezaley.ch* (*expensive*). This restaurant, under the shadow of the Grossmünster and in a 13th-century house, serves up a wide selection of traditional delights: Swiss cheese fondues, meat and Chinese fondues, sausages, *rösti* with liver, Zürich-style veal, local snails and crisp fried bread with all kinds of additions. *Closed Sun*.

Vis à Vis Bistrot Bar, Talstrasse 40, **t** 01 211 73 10 (*moderate*). This is a modern version of a typical French bistro and bar. The bar, to the right, is a great place for a snack and a drink, whilst the bistro, to the left, serves superb classical French cuisine. Look for the reasonably priced *menu du jour* and monthly market suggestions, all complemented by French wines that are sold by the glass. *Closed Sat and Sun*.

Bodega Española, Münstergasse 15, **t** 01 251 23 10 (*moderate*). In a circa 1874 building of much character, this is as good and as authentic a Spanish restaurant as you will find. A formal restaurant is located upstairs, with a bodega-style bar on the ground floor, where mouthwatering tapas and robust wine are served at bench tables. *Open daily*.

Turm, Tony Navarro Restaurant, Obere Zäune 19, **t** 01 262 52 00 (*moderate*). The inside is nothing less than a tropical forest, enhanced with brightly covered chairs and tablecloths. Dishes are based on Mexican/Spanish cuisine – with a touch of Caribbean thrown in for good measure – and include such

unusual, and debatable, delicacies as kangaroo and alligator fillets. *Open daily*.

Raclette Stube, Zähringerstrasse 16, **t** 01 251 41 30 (*moderate*). A small, typical Swiss restaurant of a style found more often in the countryside. Cheese specialities such as fondue and raclette, at reasonable prices, are the order of the day. *Open eves daily*.

Restaurant Zeughauskeller, Bahnhofstrasse 28a, **t** 01 211 26 90 (*moderate*). Built in 1487 as the ancient arsenal of Zürich, this enormous restaurant abounds with character. The original wooden beams and walls have been retained, and various tools of battle, from a modern cannon to bows and arrows, are on display. Enjoy hearty traditional Swiss dishes, many featuring pork and sausage, served on huge bench tables. *Open daily 11.30am–11pm*.

Zic Zac Rock-Garden, Marktgasse 17, **t** 01 261 21 81, **f** 01 261 21 75, *www.ziczac.ch* (*moderate*). This is Switzerland's equivalent to those other more well-known rock cafés, although it is a lot less plush. It does, however, offer meals from breakfast to dinner with a wide range of dishes at quite reasonable prices. Look, too, for an equally wide range of tempting drinks and cocktails. *Open daily*.

Lions Pub, Uraniastrasse 9, **t** 01 211 11 55 (*moderate*). As good an imitation of an English pub as you are likely to find – in fact it is the meeting place of the English Speaking Club. Typical pub food – with the exception of the mussels – Walkers crisps and, of course, English football and rugby via satellite. *Open daily*.

Brasserie Federal, Bahnhof, **t** 01 217 15 15 (*moderate*). Conveniently, this is in the main railway station, right next to the tourist office. The daily lunch menu is very reasonably priced, or you might want to select from over 100 Swiss beers whilst mulling over your tourist information. *Open daily*.

Jules Verne Panorama Bar, Uraniastrasse 9, **t** 01 211 11 55 (*inexpensive*). This is not a restaurant in the strict sense of the word, but it should not be overlooked, if only for its spectacular views of the city and the Alps. The entrance is through the Brasserie

Lipp, where a lift will whisk you up to the 12th-floor bar. Once there, treat yourself to one, or more, of an enticing selection of tapas and pâtisseries, and wash them down with champagne or a cocktail. *Open daily*.

Sushi Bar, Bleicherweg 19, **t** 01 202 02 32, *www.japfood.ch* (*inexpensive*). A nice, small restaurant located close to Paradeplatz. The sushi dishes circulate around an uneven shaped bar on a carousel; you choose what you want and pay according to the colour of the plate (from CHF 5.80 to 8.50). Wash it down with saké or Japanese beer. *Closed Sun*.

Tibits, Seefeld-strasse 2, **t** 01 260 32 22, **f** 01 260 32 23, *www.tibits.ch* (*inexpensive*). A modern vegetarian restaurant that offers a unique salad bar with hot snacks and two hot menus, freshly squeezed fruit juices, alcoholic drinks made with fruit juices, an array of fine coffees and good wines. There is also a takeaway section. *Open daily*.

Restaurant Rheinfelder Bierhalle, Niederdorf-strasse 15 (*inexpensive*). This is exactly what its name says it is – half restaurant, half beer hall – very informal, no privacy, but as cheap as you'll get. *Hauptbahnhof rösti, würste* and spaghetti Bolognese for as little as CHF 13. *Open daily*.

Conditorei Café Schober, Napfgasse 4, **t** 01 251 80 60. Although not strictly a restaurant, this should not be missed. It has the most tempting array of cakes, cookies, chocolates and other goodies, along with all kinds of flavoured – including alcohol – teas, coffees and chocolates, juices and even aperitifs that you are ever likely to see. These can be taken in the lavishly decorated rooms or in a pleasant little outside patio. *Open daily*.

Entertainment and Nightlife

There is plenty of choice for opera, theatre and classical music lovers.

The **Zürich Opera House** (Opernhaus), Falkenstrasse 1, **t** 01 268 64 00, *www.opern-haus.ch*, is a gracious, Baroque-style building, where famous stars like Cecilia Bartoli and Ruggero Raimondi perform.

The **Tonhalle**, Claridenstrasse 7, **t** 01 206 34 34, *www.tonhalle.ch*, was built in 1895; the present conductor of this world-famous orchestra is David Zinnan.

Schauspielhaus, Schiffbaustrasse 4, **t** 01 265 58 58, *www.schauspielhaus.ch*, is the city's largest theatre, and the current artistic director, Christoph Marthaler, is known for his innovative productions.

Hellenstadion, Wallisellenstrasse, 45, **t** 01 316 77 77, *www.hellenstadion.ch*, is Zürich's largest indoor arens and, as such, hosts a wide variety of events from theatre productions to ice hockey games.

There is certainly no shortage of **nightlife** in Zürich. The club scene changes frequently as trends come and go, but up-to-date information is freely available in *City Guide Zürich*, *www.hellovisitors.com*, which has pages of current details. Similarly, *Zürich News*, *www.zuerich.ch*, a bi-weekly brochure, has more such information.

Jazz enthusiasts might head for the **Blue Note**, Stockerstrasse 45, **t** 01 202 17 17, *www.bluenote.ch*, which stays open until 2am on Fri and Sat, or try the famous **Widder Bar**, Widdergasse 6, **t** 01 224 25 26, *www.widderhotel.ch/de/bar*, that closes an hour earlier.

The Nelson Pub, Beatengasse 11, **t** 01 212 60 16, is a typical British pub and you can expect international beers and music here until 2am or 3am during weekdays and as late (or early) as 5am on Fri and Sat. Fans of alternative and modern rock will like **Abart**, Manessastrasse 170, **t** 01 201 82 45, which has Fri parties and discos on Sat that go on very late. **Rote Fabrik**, Seestrasse 395, **t** 01 481 91 43, *www.rotefabrik.ch*, is found at Wollishofen out by Lake Zürich and there you can find everything from concerts, theatre, literature parties and films to good food and drink.

The **gay and lesbian** scene is quite open in Zürich. The *City Guide Zürich*, *www.hellovisi-tors.com*, has up-to-date information and the Zürich Tourist Office website, *www.zurich-tourism.ch*, offers some relevant websites.

Labyrinth, Pfingstweidstrasse 70, **t** 01 440 59 80, has an open-ended time limit on Fri and Sat nights; with its wild dance music, it is popular with gays, and straights, too.

the courtyard becomes the stage for 'Live at Sunset' concerts featuring international music stars.

Back outside, on the station's opposite side stands a statue of Alfred Escher (1819–82), founder of the Swiss railway system. Immediately behind him is the famous **Bahnhofstrasse**. Along its 1¼-mile (2km) length you will find an eclectic variety of fine stores, banks, hotels and restaurants; the cost of property here is astronomically high. A pleasant, seemingly incongruous little park hides a dark secret. At one time it was the public execution site – hence the reason no one was anxious to build on it. The statue in the park's centre is of **Jo Heinrich Pestalozzi**, who acted upon his opposition to private education by founding the city's public school system.

Take a look, now, at the small fountain at the end of the park alongside Bahnhofstrasse. Actually, as fountains go in Zürich – and there are more than 1,200 of them in all shapes and sizes – this may seem like nothing extraordinary. It is elegant, and interesting in that it was donated by the city of Paris to Zürich in 1870 to initiate the World Convention of Water Experts. The four nymphs – one set on each corner – personify simplicity, purity, sobriety and charity, and are meant to symbolize international cooperation. Don't be frightened to take a drink either, as the water flowing from the city's fountains is considered to be of better quality than that running to the taps of local residences.

If you are here on or around the hour, make a point of looking above the door of the Kurz shop, diagonally across Bahnhofstrasse, where you will see a delightful musical clock featuring a parade of characters in Swiss national costumes.

The nearby Brasserie Lipp may look like an ordinary restaurant, but a real treat unfolds when you take the lift to the **Jules Verne Bar** located on the 12th floor of this unusual, octagonal-shaped tower. Apart from the chance to have a drink and a rest, it offers a fantastic bird's-eye view of the city and a breathtaking panorama of the surrounding countryside.

Just behind here and to the south, **Kaminfegergasse** is an interesting, tiny, cobblestoned street. Lining the way are ancient houses, one of which dates from 1401 and is thought to be the oldest brick home in Zürich. Note, also, the pulleys in the gables which are ingeniously used, as in many houses in Amsterdam, to haul furniture and other unwieldy objects by crane to the upper floors.

Further on, and closer to the river, **Lindenhof** is an area set up for open-air chess, with game sets and seats around the edge of what is a popular little park. Although it may look insignificant, this has a story to tell – and the statue, dating from 1292, of a woman dressed in military uniform, gives a clue. On one occasion, the Hapsburgs were attacking the city from below, while the men of Zürich were away battling at Winterthur. The women of the city, determined to defend their homes, devised a clever plan that foiled the advancing troops. Dressed in military uniforms, they stood in lines along the walls of Lindenhof. The Hapsburgs, convinced the city was formidably protected, retreated. A more peaceful place these days, it affords wonderful views over the Limmat river, with the old town hall in the foreground and the two towers of the cathedral on the hill behind, and provides a delightful atmosphere in which people simply come to relax.

Leaving Lindenhof from its south side, you are confronted with quite an unusual perspective. Directly ahead, with one almost directly behind the other, are two contrasting spires, each adorned with a striking clock. The nearest, belonging to St Peter's church and looming at 28.5ft (8.7m), boasts the largest clockface in Europe – beating Big Ben in London by an inch or so (just a few centimetres). The latter embellishes the Fraumünster, home to Chagall's famous stained-glass windows (*see* p.81).

St Peter's (*open weekdays 8–6*), the oldest of Zürich's medieval churches, was first mentioned in documents in 857. Although remnants of four earlier constructions remain, the current structure dates from 1705–6 and was the first of the churches built after the Reformation in Zürich. In the tower, used as a fire watch as late as 1911, there are five bells, with the largest, an A-flat, weighing 6 tons (6,203kg). It has a charming small plaza outside.

Pay close attention now because, even though it's easy to miss, you need to descend down along narrow **Thermengasse**, the name of which offers a clue to its attraction. Metal grille steps offer a view of the ruins that lie beneath, and diagrams and other documentation verify that in Roman times this was a thermal spring. What you see is only a small part of what once was, and quite impressive it must have been.

Weinplatz, an attractive little square with a wonderfully ornate wrought-metal fountain, is situated right next to the Limmat river. It is also home to Zum Storchen, the hotel with the finest river views in Zürich. A footpath runs alongside it and the Limmat towards the next bridge, with a good view of the ancient town hall across the crystalline swift-flowing waters of the Limmat. South, near the next bridge, Münsterbrücke, is a uniquely elegant building with an ornate gold wrought-iron balcony. It becomes apparent just what a fine house this is when its main façade reveals itself in Münsterhof square. As previously explained, guilds have played an important part in Zürich's history, and the Wine Guild is one of the grandest of them all. Obviously not wishing to skimp on any luxury for themselves, the members constructed this guild house (zur Meise) as their headquarters in 1750. It is now a branch of the **National Museum** (*Münsterhof 20, t 01 221 28 07; open Tues–Sun 10.30–5; adm*), featuring an amazing collection of porcelain and glazed pottery, with notable examples from the Schooren factory near Zürich and Nyon. Note also the memorial in honour of Sir Winston Churchill (1874–1965), who made his famous 'Europe Arise' speech from here on 19 September 1946.

A short walk west along Poststrasse, through Paradeplatz (now a part of Bahnhofstrasse), takes you to Bärengasse 20–22. Here, incongruously surrounded by modern buildings, you will find Weltkugel and Schanzenhof, two wooden-framed, white-painted buildings dating from the Baroque period. Together, these form the **Museum Bärengasse** (*t 01 211 17 16, www.musee-suisse.ch; open Tues–Sun 10.30–5; adm*). This is comprised of several elements, but of most interest is the permanent exhibition, 'Mind and Passion – Zürich from 1750 to 1800', dedicated to things important to men and women during an era when Zürich was an intellectual centre. Also, on the ground floor there is the **Sasha Morgenthaler Doll Museum**. Sasha (1893–1975) began her craft by making toys for her own children, and her enchanting life-like creations have been seen around the world.

Churches abound in Zürich. There are over 100 in the city – 60 per cent Protestant and 30 per cent Catholic. Back on Münsterhof, the **Fraumünster** (*open May–Sept 9–12 and 2–6; Oct–Feb 10–12 and 2–5; Mar–April 10–12 and 2–4*) is easily identifiable by its elegant spire and four large clockfaces. As the name denotes, this is the Women's Cathedral, and it has a truly ancient history. Legend, of course, plays its part, but it is documented that, as far back as AD 853, the German King Ludwig donated an existing convent to his daughter, Hildegard. It was she who, soon after, commissioned the construction of a new church that has been perpetually enlarged, renovated or recon-structed over the ensuing centuries. As intriguing as this history is, it is not the primary reason people from around the world come to visit the Fraumünster. That honour goes to its innovatively interpretive stained-glass windows. The most famous of these are by the Russian emigré Marc Chagall (1887–1985), who was commissioned by the church in the 1960s. His five-part biblical stained-glass cycle was installed in the choir in 1970 and in the south transept in 1980. Not to be overlooked, either, is the work of the Swiss artist Augusto Giacometti (1877–1947), whose creation *Heavenly Paradise* was installed following the Second World War.

Outside, an equestrian statue guarding the Münsterbrucke is of a past mayor.

The East Side of the Limmat

Almost directly across from the Fraumünster is the picturesque **Kirchgasse**, dating from the 11th and 12th centuries. The different-styled houses that line it, a bit younger, were built during the 13th–18th centuries. It is, however, the twin round-topped towers (not the originals) of the **Grossmünster** (*open mid-Mar–Oct 9–6; Nov–mid-Mar 10–5*) which dominate this area. Walking around the plaza to the main entrance, note on the exterior the representation of a horse and rider, and a figure of Charlemagne. The former, c. 1180, is considered the earliest portrayal of a horseman in the northern Alps. The latter is just a copy; exposure to weather was damaging the 15th-century original, which can now be seen in the Romanesque crypt. According to a rather intricate legend, Charlemagne founded the Grossmünster. As the story goes, Feliz and Regula, city and cathedral patrons and members of the Christian Thebaic Legion that had been decimated in the Valais in the 3rd century, escaped to Zürich only to meet martyrs' deaths. Afterwards, they reportedly picked up their own decapi-tated heads and ascended to a location where they wished to be buried. Later during a hunting excursion, Charlemagne was pursuing a stag from Aachen, Germany to Zürich. There, his steed stumbled over the graves of Feliz and Regula, which Charlemagne then designated as the site for the Grossmünster.

Construction commenced on this Romanesque-type structure at the beginning of the 12th century, though it was not completed for another hundred years. The interior, with the exception of the stained-glass windows by Augusto Giacometti and the Bronze Doors by Otto Münch, is rather austere, but that is not without reason. This, the parish church of Zürich, was at the epicentre of the Swiss Reformation move-ment, led by Huldrych Zwingli (1484–1531) and Heinrich Bullinger (1504–75). One of the first initiatives of these leaders was to remove, in 1519, all artwork, altars and other physical embellishments – even the organ. It is Heinrich Bullinger, an elected pastor of the Grossmünster, who can be thanked for the Reformed Church seen today. In 1566, he wrote the Second Helvetic Confession that, even now, belongs to the Book of Confessions of the United Presbyterian Church in the USA.

Interestingly, Zwingli's and Bullinger's work managed to transcend pure theology – becoming the basis of Swiss democracy and social policies and instrumental in the economic and industrial growth of Zürich. Rather than a hierarchical organization, they envisioned the church as a meeting place for parishioners to worship as equals. This movement paved the way for national referenda that placed special emphasis on improving the lot of the weak and persecuted, and saw Zürich become a model system for providing for the poor. A new work ethic emphasized law and discipline both in public and personal spheres. And, as citizens were required to study the Bible in German, a majority of the population learned to read and write. This, in turn, contributed to industrial and economic growth in the city.

Just a few blocks north is the **Museum of Fine Arts** (Kunsthaus; *Heimplatz 1, t 01 253 84 84, www.kunsthaus.ch; open Tues–Thurs 10–9, Fri–Sun 10–5; adm*), one of the most important art museums in Switzerland. Its wide and varied collection includes many Old Masters, Swiss art from the 19th and 20th centuries, a unique collection of Alberto Giacometti's work, the largest Munch collection outside Norway, some of Monet's French impressionistic art, 18 Picassos and much, much more.

North from the Grossmünster runs Münstergasse, where you can leave thoughts of art and austerity behind and instead see just how cosmopolitan Zürich can be. This area is known as the **Dörfli**, Zürich's pedestrian zone. Among the trendy shops, art galleries and interesting restaurants, there are two places that merit special atten-tion: the **Bodega Española** and **Conditorei Café Schober**, both described in 'Eating Out' (*see* pp.77 and 78).

Back outside, and further down Münstergasse, a warrior stands at a safe distance – atop another fountain. This, the **Stüssihofstatt Fountain**, dates from 1574, although the original water receptacle was replaced in 1811. From here Niederdorfstrasse slopes gently down to Central, just across the Limmat from the Hauptbahnhof. In truth this is less salubrious, and expect it to get somewhat seedier along the way. A shop selling condoms, a Condomeria, indicates the presence of sex shows, and cheaper restau-rants (sometimes no more than shop fronts) and of course the irrepressible McDonalds predominate. The area is, however, by no means threatening. You may even find a craft market open near the Hotel Biban, and enjoy the entertainment of street artists along your way.

Two Other Museums Just Outside the City Centre

There are two other interesting, if rather eclectic, museums just a short distance outside the city centre. The closest of these is on the east side of the lake, and involves a short and rather pleasant walk along the embankment, or a short tram trip on either number 2 or 4. It will be certain to appeal to those of you who are addicted to Starbuck's; pay attention, though, to the rather unusual opening hours. The **Johan Jacobs Museum** (*Seefeldquai 17, t 01 388 61 51, f 01 388 61 37, www.johann-jacobs-museum.ch; open Fri 2–7, Sat 2–5 and Sun 10–5; adm*) was founded in 1984 and has a

Excursions from Zürich

Destination	Journey Time (hours.mins)	Recommended Length of Trip	Connections
Rapperswil	0.35	D/T	T
Schaffhausen and Rhine Falls	0.38	D/T	T
Luzern (1)	0.48	D/T – O/N – M/N	T
Basel	0.50	D/T – O/N – M/N	T
Solothurn	0.56	D/T	T
Stein am Rhein	1.04	D/T	T
St Gallen	1.06	D/T	T
Bern	1.09	D/T – O/N – M/N	T
Thun	1.37	D/T	T
Vaduz, Liechtenstein	1.46	D/T – O/N	T/B
Neuchâtel	1.47	D/T	T
Engelberg	2.08	D/T – O/N	T/T
Interlaken	2.10	D/T	T
Lausanne	2.20	D/T – O/N	T
Brienz	2.36	D/T	T/T
Montreux and Vevey	2.45	D/T	T/T
Scuol	2.45	O/N – M/N	T/T
Lugano	2.53	D/T – O/N – M/N	T
Geneva	2.56	D/T – O/N – M/N	T
Lötschental	3.00	O/N – M/N	T/T/B
Grindelwald (2)	3.05	M/N	T/T
Gruyères	3.08	D/T	T/T/B/T/B
Wengen (2)	3.10	M/N	T/T/T
Ascona	3.13	O/N – M/N	T/B
Centovalli	3.21	D/T – O/N	T/T
Sion	3.26	D/T	T/T
Mürren and Schilthorn 007	3.26	M/N	T/T/F/T
Les Diablerets	3.46	D/T – O/N	T/T/T
Nauders, Austria	3.48	O/N – M/N	T/T/B
Saas-Fee	4.08	M/N	T/T/B
Leukerbad	4.09	O/N – M/N	T/T/B
Crans Montana	4.15	D/T-O/N	T/T/B
Zermatt	4.39	M/N	T/T
Val d'Anniviers	4.49	O/N – M/N	T/T/B/B

(1) The starting point for the Pilatus trip.
(2) The starting points for the Jungfraujoch and Männlichen trips.
T: train; B: bus; F: funicular.
D/T: day trip; O/N: overnighter; M/N: multi-nighter.
*Journey time is one-way, and the minimum possible. See **Introduction**, p.7.*

large collection of paintings, prints, porcelain and silver of its own. It organizes annually changing exhibitions, based on its own collections, highlighting the cultural history of coffee.

On the other side of the lake, and reached by way of tram No. 7, is the attractive Rieter Park. And that is where you will find the **Museum Rietberg** (*Gablerstrasse 15, t 01 206 31 31, f 01 206 31 32, www.rietberg.ch*), showing an eclectic and spectacular collection of Asian, African, Oceanian and American art. The **Villa Wesendonck** (*open Tues and Thurs–Sun 10–5 and Wed 10–8*), where Richard Wagner lived for a short period in 1857, holds the main collection, which is formed around the nucleus of the famous sculptures donated to Zürich by Eduard Baron von der Heydt in 1952. Two smaller houses, the **Park-Villa Rieter** and the **Haus zum Kiel** (*open Tues–Sat 1–5, Sun 10–5*), hold, respectively, exhibitions of Indian, Chinese and Japanese paintings and special exhibitions of non-European art.

Secondary Main Destinations

06

Bern

Bern, or Berne in French, is the administrative capital of Switzerland and has a dramatic location on an elevated promontory surrounded by the River Aare. Running on a west to east axis, it offers (weather permitting) spectacular views of the Bernese Oberland, and specifically the peaks of the Eiger, Mönch and Jungfrau, dominating the southwestern horizon.

History and fate have combined, equally spectacularly, to leave the city a special heritage. With its attractive sandstone buildings, colourful and historic water fountains, intricate towers and an extensive labyrinth of arcades (3¾miles/6km of them) lining the long and comparatively narrow streets, its appearance has remained unchanged for many centuries. As a consequence, Bern is actually one of the finest examples of medieval civic architecture in Europe and, as such, has been placed on the UNESCO list of World Heritage Sites. It's impossible not to mention, either, the Bear Pits (der Bärengraben); Bern was named after a bear, and this symbol of the city has been here since 1480.

The population of Bern only totals about 127,000, or 300,000 including the metropolitan area, but it has all the attributes of a much larger city. Museums are plentiful; one of them has the world's largest collection of Paul Klee's works, whilst another shows how Einstein lived here while he was developing his theory of relativity. Even Tobler created the world-famous Toblerone chocolate here. There are interesting theatres, even one as part of a hotel, and the nightlife is vibrant. Hotels are plentiful, although in general they lack the character found in other cities, but that is not reflected in the diverse and interesting restaurant scene. Shoppers will be delighted with Bern, especially as many of the shops are found under those famous arcades. On Tuesdays and Saturdays there are also very lively and colourful fresh vegetable, fruit and flower markets in the city centre.

If you can tear yourself away, day trips can be taken to Thun, Neuchâtel and Solothurn, and the Bernese Oberland is less than two hours away.

History

Drawn by Bern's strategic location, on a long promontory surrounded by the River Aare, Berchtold V, Duke of Zähringen, founded the first settlement here in 1191. Emperor Lothar III of Upper Burgundy had bestowed this title upon Berchtold, and Bern subsequently became a part of that region. Tradition has it that Bern came by its name in a curious manner. The surrounding areas were covered with forest and the Duke, reportedly, was determined to name his new town after the first animal he killed while hunting there. This just happened to be a bear, the German name for which is *Bär*. The legend is somewhat corroborated by the local dialect pronunciation of Bern – *Bärn*. In 1224 the oldest version of the city's well-known coat-of-arms, featuring a bear and the name *ob Berne*, first appeared. And high on the list of the city's main tourist attractions are the Bear Pits – *Bärengraben* – in which bears, known affectionately as *Mutze* by the local population, have been living since 1480.

Getting There

Although Bern has an airport (Bern-Belp), there are no direct flights from either the UK or USA at present. Nor does Swiss airlines operate any internal flights from other cities.

The nearest **airports** are at Zürich, Basel and Geneva, respectively 1 hour 9 minutes, 1 hour 7 minutes and 1 hour 45 minutes away by train.

Bern is easily reached by **train** from most other cities and towns in Switzerland.

Getting Around

Public transport in and around Bern, on a combination of trams and buses, is fast, clean and efficient. A Visitors' Card offering un-limited travel on all tram and bus routes costs CHF 7 for 24 hours, CHF 11 for 48 hours and CHF 15 for 72 hours; it is available from the tourist centre at the railway station and most hotels. Remember to validate it at the ticket machine by each stop before the first trip.

Car Hire
Avis, Wabernstrasse 41, **t** 031 378 15 15.
Europcar, Laupenstrasse 22, **t** 031 381 75 75.
Hertz, Kochergasse 1, **t** 031 318 21 60.

Tourist Information

Bern: Bern Tourismus, at the railway station, **t** 031 328 12 12, **f** 031 312 12 33, *info-res@ bernetourism.ch, www.bernetourism. ch (open June–Sept Mon–Sun 9–8.30; Oct–May Mon–Sat 9–6.30, Sun 10–5)*. There is another tourist centre at the **Bear Pits** *(open Mar–May and Oct Mon–Sun 10–4, June–Sept Mon–Sun 9–6, Nov–Feb Fri–Sun 11–4)*. During these same hours they offer, free every 20mins, a fascinating and very clever multi-media show, over a model of the city.

Bern Tourismus also operates **Bern à la Carte**, an accommodation package for those planning to stay for a period of 2 to 4 nights.

Basically, charges are based on two seasons: low season is Nov–April, high season May–Oct. Separate lists are available for each season with the prices ranging from 2 nights in the low season at a tourist standard hotel for CHF 139 to 4 nights in the high season at a 5-star hotel for CHF 641. Quotes are per person, based on double occupancy. This package also includes a 'Bern Pass' voucher booklet with free offers and price reductions, a ticket for a city sightseeing tour in summer, a 24-hour Visitors' Card for the city public transport network in winter, an Old Town booklet guide, detailed information on Bern, its surroundings, and service and taxes.

Guided Trips and Tours
Stroll through the Old Town: leaves the tourist office June–Sept daily at 11am; it takes about 1½ hours and costs CHF 14.

Tours of the Clock Tower, organized by Bern Tourismus, are held 1 May–30 June and Oct at 4.30pm, and 1 July–30 Sept at 11.30am and 4.30pm. These start on the east side of the clock tower, last 45mins and cost CHF 8.

City tour by coach: leaves from the tourist office at 2pm on Sat Nov–Mar and daily April–Oct, taking 1½ hours; tickets cost CHF 24.

Alpar AG, t 031 960 22 22: operating out of Bern-Belp Airport, Alpar offer thrilling flights in a light plane over the peaks of the Bernese Oberland, and even as far as Zermatt and the Matterhorn. There are frequent buses to the airport from the railway station forecourt.

Lost Property
City Lost Property Office (Städtisches Fundbüro), Predigergasse 5, **t** 031 321 50 50 *(open Mon–Fri 10–4 and until 6pm Thurs)*.
Railways Lost Property Office (Schweizerische Bundesbahnen SBB), **t** 051 220 23 37, Bern station *(open Mon–Fri 8–12 and 2–6)*.

Medical Emergencies
Chemist emergency service: after 9pm call **t** 031 311 22 11.

Berchtold entrusted the construction of the city to Cuno of Bubenberg. Among his achievements was the clearing of the surrounding oak forests, the wood from which was used to construct houses. Around the initial settlement, situated at the end of the promontory, Cuno built the first city wall that was dominated in the centre by a

Market Days

General market: Tues/Sat, Waisenhausplatz.
Vegetable, fruit and flower market: Tues and
Sat mornings all year on Bundesplatz,
Bärenplatz and adjacent streets, and daily
on Bärenplatz May–Oct.

Exhibitions and Festivals

Early Mar: Bern Carnival, **Bärner Fasnacht**.
May: International Jazz Festival and **Bern
Geranium Market**.
July: Gurten Open-Air Rock and Pop Festival.
Aug: Circus Knie – Swiss National Circus.
Sept: Bern International Dance Festival.
Nov: Onion Market (4th Mon).
Dec: Christmas Market.

Shopping

Under the arcades along Spitalgasse and
Marktgasse you will find the latest in high
fashion; Münstergasse and Junkerngasse offer
more avant-garde fashion; on Kramgasse,
Postgasse and Gerechtigkeitsgasse you are
more likely to find a wider variety of shops,
including some selling antiques.
Rail City, *www.railcity.ch*, a complex above the
railway station. Supermarkets and food
shops open daily, including Sun, 6am–9pm.
Swiss Plaza, Kramgasse 75, **t** 031 311 56 16. Has a
fine selection of souvenirs and offers a free
engraving service for Victorinox and Wenger
Swiss Army knives.
Schweizer Heimatwerk, Kramgasse 61, **t** 031 311
30 00, *www.heimatwerk.ch*. A company that
specializes in genuine Swiss handicrafts
such as home decor accessories, jewellery,
clothes and toys.
Drinks of the World Bern, Bahnhofplatz 10 (in
Rail City over the train station), **t** 031 311 51 10,
open daily 9–9. Not only has the widest
range of beers you can find anywhere, but it
is the only place in Bern where you can buy
beer, and other alcohol, to take away on Sun.

Where to Stay

★★★★★**Bellevue Palace**, Kochergasse 3–5, **t** 031
320 45 45, **f** 031 311 47 43, *www.bellevue-
palace.ch* (*luxury*). This, the largest and most
impressive hotel in Bern, is adjacent to the
Swiss Parliament building and is used as the
official residence of visiting dignitaries and
parliamentarians. The rooms are tastefully
decorated in a variety of styles, and are
furnished with every modern facility. The
terrace and some rooms offer marvellous
views over the River Aare and to the Alps.
★★★★★**Schweizerhof Bern**, Bahnhofplatz 11,
t 031 326 80 80, **f** 031 326 80 90, *www.
schweizerhof-bern.ch* (*luxury*). A very central
location just outside the railway station –
and even free porter service to and from
your platform. First opened in 1859, and
extensively renovated in 1997, it is a
boutique hotel with its own private
collection of art and antiques and a reputation for personal service. The 84 rooms are
spacious, well-appointed and with all
modern facilities.
★★★★**Belle Epoque**, Gerechtigkeitsgasse 18,
t 031 311 43 36, **f** 031 311 39 36, *www.belle-
epoque.ch* (*expensive*). Situated on one of the
most distinguished streets in the quieter
part of the Old Town (near the Bear Pits),
the style of this small, well-designed hotel
fully lives up to its name. Each of the 17
rooms, and the public areas, are furnished
with original furniture and art from the
Belle Epoque era at the turn of the 20th
century.
★★★★**Bern**, Zeughausgasse 9, **t** 031 329 22 22,
f 031 329 22 99, *www.hotelbern.ch*
(*expensive*). In the heart of the city, this hotel
has a most unusual exterior reflecting its
prior use as a fire station. Inside, its 100
rooms are tasteful and thoroughly modern;
it has a choice of restaurants including the
gourmet Kurierstube and a small terrace.
★★★★**Bären**, Schauplatzgasse 4, **t** 031 311 33 67,
f 031 311 69 83, *www.baerenbern.ch*

huge clock tower. This also served as the main gate, giving access to and from the city.
Bern was expanded in the 13th century when, under the protectorate of Count Peter
of Savoy, the walls were extended westwards along the promontory. The main
gateway then became the prison tower – Käfigturm – which was subsequently

(*expensive*). A 57-room modern Best Western hotel that is located just around the corner from the parliament building. Investigate the famous display of bear paintings in the Bären Bar; relax in the sauna and solarium or take out a free bike for a ride around Bern.

★★★★**Savoy–Garni**, Neuengasse 26, **t** 031 311 44 05, **f** 031 312 19 78, *www.zghotels.ch* (*moderate*). Close to the railway station, this is a very pleasant hotel – wheelchair accessible, too – that has nice rooms with soundproofed windows and adjustable heating.

★★★**Continental-Garni**, Zeughausgasse 27, **t** 031 329 21 21, **f** 031 329 21 99, *www.hotelcontinental* (*moderate*). Very conveniently located in the centre of the city, but still just a few minutes walk from the railway station. The 40 rooms are very clean and comfortable. There's an open terrace, too.

★★★**Kreuz**, Zeughausgasse 41, **t** 031 329 95 95, **f** 031 329 95 96, *www.hotelkreuz-bern.ch* (*moderate*). One of a few hotels on this street, it is easily identified by the flower boxes outside its windows. The 100 rooms – making it the second largest hotel in Bern – are modern in style, but not overly large.

★★★**Metropole**, Zeughausgasse 26, **t** 031 311 50 21, **f** 031 312 11 53, *www.hotelmetropole.ch* (*moderate*). Situated on a corner, this hotel has medium-sized and nicely furnished rooms.

★★★**Zum Goldenen Adler**, Gerechtigeitsgasse 7, **t** 031 311 17 25, **f** 031 311 37 61, *www.goldenen-adler-bern.ch* (*moderate*). In the less busy part of the Old Town, this hotel has a long history and the public areas are pleasantly old-fashioned. It has 40 rooms that are reasonably sized and comfortable.

★★★**City Am Bahnhof**, Bahnhofplatz, **t** 031 311 53 77, **f** 031 311 06 36, *www.fhotels.ch* (*moderate*). Part of the small Fassbind chain, this is not just very pleasant, but also good value. Situated opposite the railway station, expect 58 modern rooms with such perks as parquet floors, translucent partitions between the living and bathroom areas and videos free of charge 24hrs a day.

★★**Goldener Schlüssel**, Rathausgasse 72, **t** 031 311 56 88, **f** 031 311 012 16, *www.goldener-schluessel.ch* (*moderate*). A small hotel with much character and enjoying a central but quiet location. The 29 rooms are comfy, but on the small side.

★★**National Am Hirschengraben**, Hirschengraben 24, **t** 031 381 19 88, **f** 031 381 68 78, *www.nationalbern.ch* (*moderate–inexpensive*). A couple of blocks from the railway station, and slightly away from the Old Town. This distinguished building – that also includes a theatre – dates from 1908, and the wooden lift introduces you to its comfortable, old-fashioned style. Rooms, in various styles and sizes, are comfy and fairly basic.

★★★**Jardin**, Militärstrasse 38, **t** 031 333 01 17, **f** 031 333 09 43, *www.hotel-jardin.ch* (*moderate–inexpensive*). Just 10mins from the railway station, on the number 9 tram, this small 17-room hotel offers an alternative for those wanting to be outside the centre.

Pension Marthahaus, Wytennbachstrasse 22a, **t** 031 332 41 35, **f** 031 333 33 86, *www.marthahaus.ch* (*inexpensive*). Outside the town centre. Rooms with 1–5 beds, garden terrace, free Internet and bikes, and cooking and washing facilities. Take the bus number 20 to the second stop (Gewerbe Schule), and the pension is at the end of the first street to the right.

Bern Backpackers – Hotel Glocke, Rathausgasse 75, **t** 031 311 37 71, **f** 031 332 69 04, *www.bernbackpackers.com* (*inexpensive*). In the heart of old Bern, close to the clock tower, this offers basic accommodation and dorms, and has kitchen facilities, a common room with TV, video and Internet.

Swiss Youth Hostels, Weihergasse 4, **t** 031 311 63 16, **f** 031 312 52 40, *www.youthhostel.ch* (*cheap*). Simple, basic and clean accommodation with 2-, 4-, 5- and 6-bedded rooms, as well as 2 dormitories.

reconstructed in the 17th century. The additions that took place during the 14th century saw the city walls, dismantled only 100 years ago, reaching where the railway station stands today.

Eating Out

La Terrasse, Kochergasse 3-5, **t** 031 320 45 45, **f** 031 31 47 43 (*very expensive–expensive*). In the summer this is *the* place in Bern to eat. The Terrace of the Bellevue Palace hotel sparkles with crystal glasses full of fine wines, exquisite culinary creations and unparalleled views over the River Aare to the snow-covered peaks of the Alps.

Le Chariot, Gerechtigkeitsgasse 18, **t** 031 311 43 36 (*expensive*). Like the hotel it is part of (the Belle Epoque), this restaurant has some style. And so does the cuisine. At lunch look for *paninis* and fresh salads; in the evening the chef offers one of his specialities.

Gourmanderje Moléson, Aarbergergasse 24, **t** 031 311 44 63, **f** 031 312 01 45, *www.moleson-bern.ch* (*expensive*). Founded in 1865, this typical bistro has a logo of two piglets' heads poking out of a lidded pot. The speciality here is Alsatian pies and extravagant desserts, prepared with ecologically grown products. *Closed Sun.*

Le Beaujolais, Aarbergergasse 50/52, **t** 031 311 48 86 (*expensive*). The front room is rather plain and café-like. A small bar stands in the middle, and a more formal dining room is at the rear. The cuisine is French, with house specialities being duck, pork, veal and lamb fillets, and fried perch. Leave room for the tempting desserts. *Closed Sat and Sun lunch.*

Brasserie Bärengraben, Muristalden 1, **t** 031 331 42 18, **f** 031 331 25 60 (*expensive–moderate*). Housed in one of the 200-year-old customs houses on the Nydeggbrücke, close to the Bear Pits. Eat inside, or out on the terrace, and enjoy a delightful mix of French-orientated dishes. *Open all day.*

Altes Tramdepot Brauerei & Restaurant, Gr. Muristalden 6, **t** 031 368 14 15, **f** 031 368 14 16, *www.altestramdepot.ch* (*moderate*). A delightful combination of microbrewery and restaurant in a converted old tram shed next to the famous Bear Pits. Watch the beer being brewed, taste it here or back at your hotel. The cuisine is varied, and includes meat, fish, vegetarian and wok dishes.

Ringgenberg, Kornhausplatz 19, **t** 031 311 25 40, **f** 031 311 97 97 (*moderate*). Opposite the grand theatre, this has earned itself a fine reputation. The cuisine is French Mediterranean, and the decor is similarly light: plain cream walls, benches and kitchen chairs with blackboards detailing the menus and special wine deals. It's equally acceptable to pop in here for a glass of wine or a beer.

Harmonie, Hotelgasse 3, **t** 031 313 11 41 (*moderate*). Step through the doors and step back in time into this charmingly old-fashioned restaurant that has been family-owned since 1915. Although there are other choices, those in the know will order the famous cheese fondue or other traditional Swiss specialities. *Closed Sat and Sun.*

Klötzlikeller, Gerechtigkeitsgasse 62, **t** 031 311 74 56 (*moderate*). A very typical restaurant in the oldest cellar in Bern, dating from 1635. Under the stone arched ceiling you can eat pasta, meat and a few fish selections, all at reasonable prices. *Open Tues–Sat 4pm–12am.*

Bar & Bistro Boomerang's, Sternengässchen 5, **t** 031 311 32 71 (*moderate*). A strange combination of Australian-orientated and Czech cuisine and, yes, they certainly do want you to come back. Look for Aussie pies and even crocodile steaks, and a Czech Corner (in Czech) on the menu. The array of Aussie cocktails are, if you are not careful, sure to send you 'Down Under'. *Closed Sun.*

Le Mazot, Bärenplatz 5, **t** 031 311 70 88 (*moderate*). Sit inside, or at tables outside, and enjoy the best of Valais (Walliser) specialities: a tempting range of fondue, raclette and *rösti* dishes as well as traditional sausage and cheese plates. Those with large appetites can try the Walliser Menu 'Le Mazot', combining raclette, air-dried meat and fondue.

Times were not all peaceful, however, and Bern often had to defend itself against attackers. The most significant of the battles occurred in 1339 when Bern fought successfully against the combined troops of the nobility of Burgundy and the city of

Swiss Chalet Restaurant, Rathausgasse 75, **t** 031 311 10 08 (*moderate*). A very typical Swiss country restaurant right in the middle of Bern, with an ambience of authenticity created by wooden beams, cowbells, horns and a Swiss musical show. These complement a very Swiss menu that highlights a selection of home-made fondues.

Tibits, Bahnhofplatz 10, **t** 031 312 91 11, **f** 031 312 91 20, *www.tibits.ch* (*moderate*). A vegetarian food chain that has a very modern style, and features restaurants, bars with specialist drinks and takeaway sections. This one is in the railway station. *Closed Sun.*

Brasserie Anker, Schmiedenplatz 1 and Kornhausplatz 16, **t** 031 311 11 13, *www.roeschti.ch* (*moderate*). If you like *rösti*, or want to try more variations of it, this is the place to come. Advertising itself as the land of *rösti*, it offers numerous variations on the theme.

Entertainment and Nightlife

The **Municipal Theatre** (Stadttheater Bern), Kornhausplatz, **t** 031 329 51 51, *www.stadttheaterbern.ch*, is housed in a magnificent building in the heart of the city, and hosts opera and ballet productions as well as plays. The **DAS-Theater an der Effingerstrasse**, Effingerstrasse 14, **t** 031 382 72 72, is a smaller, more intimate, theatre. Of the other theatres in Bern, perhaps the most interesting is the **Berner Puppen-Theater**, Gerechtigkeitsgasse 31, *www.berner-puppentheater.ch*, with its puppet productions.

The **Allegro Grand Casino Bern**, Kursaal, **t** 031 339 55 55, *www.grandcasino-bern.ch*, open Sun–Wed until 2am and Thurs–Sat until 4am, adm CHF 10, has a 19th-century-style decor, and you can try your luck at 10 different games tables and 250 machines.

The **Bar Club Messy**, Neuengasse 17, **t** 031 311 30 58, and **Chikito Club of Clubs**, Neuengasse 47, **t** 031 333 14 09 (the latter established since 1928 and considered the most popular in Bern), both offer cabaret shows and are open 5pm–3.30am, whilst **Mocambo**, Genfergasse 10, **t** 031 311 50 41, has a striptease show and has similar hours.

Marian's Jazzroom, Engestrasse 54, **t** 031 309 61 11, *www.mariansjazzroom.ch*, is found in the Hotel Inner Enge and, having hosted numerous international stars, is considered one of the most famous jazz clubs in Europe. **Mahogany Hall**, Klösterlistutz 18, **t** 031 328 52 00, *www.mahogany.ch*, has a special club atmosphere and is popular with a wide range of artists.

Those who fancy a dance have plenty of opportunities in Bern, amongst them: **Gaskessel**, Sandrainstrasse 25, **t** 031 372 49 00, open on Fri and Sat to 3.30am, a mix of a cultural centre in an old industrial building. **Guayas** bar & club, Parkterrasse 16, **t** 031 318 70 75, *www.guayas.ch*, has two dance floors and a wide mix of music, and is well known for its after-hours (after 5am) Sun morning shows. **Tonis the Club**, Aabergergasse 35, **t** 031 0900 575 150, *www.tonis.ch*, is open until 3.30am and offers music to most people's tastes on its two floors, along with specialized cocktails.

There is no shortage of late-night bars, either. **Mr Pickwick Pub**, Wallgasse, **t** 031 311 28 62, a 'typical' English pub, opens until 12.30am early in the week and an hour later Thurs–Sat. **Pery Bar**, Schmiedenplatz 3, **t** 031 311 59 08, has a cocktail bar on the ground floor and a DJ presents 1960s to '90s music until 1.30am, 2.30am or 3.30am, getting later as the week gets older. **The Art Café**, Gurtengasse 3, **t** 031 311 42 64, *www.artcafe.ch*, has a very elegant bar with DJs playing until 3.30am on Thurs, Fri and Sat. **The Eclipse-Bar**, Gurtengasse 6, **t** 031 318 47 00, *www.eclipsebar.ch*, is ultra-modern in style and has a large aquarium in the lounge. DJs play music from the 1960s onwards and the house cocktails are good – open until 3.30am Thurs–Sat.

Fribourg, which had been founded by the father of Berchtold V. This victory not only guaranteed the future independence of the city, but also initiated an expansion of its powers. Soon after, in 1353, Bern joined the Swiss Confederation, and the succeeding centuries saw its power base widen considerably.

An unwelcome change that befell Bern, this one fundamentally altering the city's appearance, occurred in 1405. In that year a fire destroyed a great number of the timber buildings. Most of the houses were rebuilt on their original foundations, this time using sandstone from local quarries instead of wood. Many of these were rebuilt for a second time in the 16th and 17th centuries, and the consequent harmony of appearance and elaborate detail still delight visitors today. Also, in the mid-16th century the famous historic fountains that adorn the streets of Bern were built, mostly to replace the wooden ones of earlier centuries. These are guarded, more often than not, by an elaborate and vividly coloured figure standing proudly atop a column.

Between 1536 and 1798 Bern gained, mostly at the expense of the House of Savoy, large tracts of territory along Lake Geneva. And it is mainly because of these Bernese efforts that much of the French area of Switzerland is a part of the Swiss Confederation today. The French invasion of 1798, and the new Switzerland that emerged like a phoenix in 1815 from the ruins left by Napoleon, destroyed Bern's dominance. It was forced to cede nearly half its land, which was used to form the new cantons of Aargau and Waadt. The city even lost control of the canton of Bern. By way of compensation, however, it became the cantonal capital and, in 1848, was chosen by the first Swiss Parliament as capital of the Swiss Confederation.

Western Old Town

The modern railway station – **Hauptbahnhof** – marks the western edge of the promontory, but don't expect to see the trains; they are hidden away on the lower levels. It is also the home to the main tourist information centre of **Bern Tourismus**, and the starting point for some interesting walking tours which they organize (*see* p.88). In front of the station's main exit is the busy Bahnhofplatz, where many trams and buses start from, and which is dominated by the impressive **Church of the Holy Ghost** (Heiliggeistkirche). This Protestant church was built between 1726 and 1729 in the Swiss-Baroque style.

A few minutes' walk northeast of the station takes you to the **Fine Arts Museum** (Kunstmuseum; *Hodlerstrasse 8-12, t 031 328 09 44, f 031 328 09 55, www.kunstmuseumbern.ch; open Tues 10–9, Wed–Sun 10–5; adm*). The classical-style building, enhanced by statues and engravings, includes amongst its exhibits some 3,000 paintings and sculptures and nearly 55,000 drawings, with art from the Italian *trecento* by Duccio and Fra Angelico; Swiss art from the 15th century including the work of Niklaus Manuel, Albert Anker, Ferdinand Hodler and Cuno Amiet; and international art from the 19th and early 20th centuries. In the latter category are works by Wassily Kandinsky and Pablo Picasso, as well as the world's largest collection of works by the Swiss artist Paul Klee (1879–1940); this museum has almost half of all Klee's output, with 200 pictures, sculptures and puppets on display. Adolf Wölfli (1864–1930), the writer, poet, draftsman and composer, is another native Swiss whose work is on display here. This, though, is in the form of texts, drawings, collages and musical compositions that together form a 25,000-page illustrated narrative of his childhood and mythological future.

On 20 June 2002 the foundation stone was laid for what will become, some time in 2005/06, the **Paul Klee Centre**, which will also include a Children's Museum. This will have a core collection of 4,000 pieces, making it unique in the world in having such a high proportion of the complete works of any one artist, while making the collection accessible to the public.

A left out of the museum will bring you to **Waisenhausplatz** and an attractive old house. Constructed between 1782 and 1786, this once served as the **Boy's Orphanage** (Knabenwaisenhaus) but, since 1941, it has housed the police headquarters. Across the road is a rather bland fountain – a rarity in Bern. Waisenhausplatz hosts a general market on Tuesdays and Saturdays.

Zeughausgasse, to the left, has some shops and hotels, but it is the two buildings near the end that will attract your attention. The first of these, the **French Church** (Französische Kirche; *t 031 311 37 32; open Mon-Sat 9–11 and 2–5*), is the oldest house of worship in the city. Originally constructed in the late 13th century as the church of the Dominican monastery, it has had many uses over the years. It was the seat of the Town Council, and sometimes used by the Inquisition Tribunal in the 14th century. After the Reformation, in 1528, it was converted into a hospital, and the Chancel was even used as a granary. The 17th century saw the beginnings of a French-speaking reformed community, which was enlarged after the Nantes Edict in 1685, when Huguenot refugees flooded into the city. In the 19th century the Roman Catholic parish used sections of the church, and in 1875 it became the property of the General Reformed parish of Bern. Next you will come to the **Cornhouse** (Kornhaus) and, underneath its arches, the impressive **Municipal Theatre** (Stadttheater) to the left, just before the bridge that carries traffic high over the Aare.

Eastern Old Town

An interesting street named **Rathausgasse** runs directly to the end of the promontory; it is parallel to, but much quieter than, Kramgasse just to the south. Arcades line either side, populated with quaint shops, hotels and restaurants. But remember to look up. Near the tops of the houses the windows of the small rooms are often adorned with colourful, pretty flower boxes.

At the end of the street is the building after which the street is named. The **Rathaus** (town hall), built between 1406 and 1416, has a most distinct façade, but it was completely restored between 1939 and 1942. Directly across the road stands the **Venner Fountain** (Vennerbrunnen), over which a knight, holding the flag of Bern in one hand and brandishing a sword in the other, stands vigil.

The street changes name here – as all the streets running towards the end of the promontory do at cross roads – and becomes Postgasse. The architecture continues much as before, if a little bit older, but do pay some attention to the **Antonite House** (Antonierhaus) at number 62. Noticeably different in style to its neighbours, particularly with its curved arches, it was built at the end of the 15th century as the church of the Order of Antonites. Rebuilt in 1939 it has, over its history, been used as a granary, coach-house and even an antiques hall.

At the end of Postgasse you will be able to see clearly how the River Aare doubles around on itself, in the process forming the promontory upon which sits the city of Bern. The church in front of you is the **Nydegg Church** (Nydeggkirche), which was originally built in the mid-14th century over the foundations of the old Nydegg fortress destroyed nearly a century before. It was completely renovated, though, in the 1950s, and very little of the original remains.

Across the Aare by way of the Nydeggbrücke is the highlight for most visitors to Bern, the **Bear Pits** (Bärengraben; *open summer 8–5.30, winter 9–4*). As described in the introduction, bears have been associated with Bern since its foundation. But it was not until 1513, when Bernese troops returned victoriously home accompanied by a bear, that they were formally kept in the city. And they have been there ever since, except for a brief period when French troops confiscated them. The present pits – there are two – have provided a permanent home for the bears since 1857, but have been expanded and restored since then. The bears are well cared for, and are still perfectly willing to do all sorts of tricks to get you to throw them extra treats. Easter is a particularly popular time at the pits, as it is then that the new cubs make their first public appearances. Whilst here, make a point of seeing the innovative Bern-Show with a complex set of movies, slides and interactive models, operated by the Tourist Centre on site, and maybe enjoy a freshly brewed beer at the open-plan Altes Tramdepot Brauerei & Restaurant.

Look back at the city from the old **Nydeggbrücke**. The views are fantastic: the city directly ahead with the Münster (cathedral) spire dominating to the left, the river below and the rolling green hills behind. Notice, also, the row of old buildings on the city side, and to the right of the bridge. The strange one, with no ground floor and steps leading to the river, is the Ländtetor. Dating from the late 13th century, it served as the entrance to the landing stage for boats crossing the Aare.

The main street through the centre of the narrow promontory is **Gerechtigkeits-gasse**, though it changes its name four times before finally reaching the railway station. Colonnaded and arched along the entirety of its length, it is particularly pretty here where commercialization isn't so predominant. Antique shops, specialist stores, bars, restaurants and even a hotel or two co-exist in complete harmony and peace. And, this being Bern, you will not be surprised to find another of those colourful water fountains-cum-statues – this time, the **Justice Fountain** (Gerechtigkeitsbrunnen) that originates from 1543.

Bern's **Münster** (cathedral; *t 031 312 04 62; open summer Tues–Sat 10–5, Sun 11.30–5; winter Tues–Fri 10–12 and 2–4, on Sat it closes an hour later and on Sun 11.30–4*) occupies a prime position in a wonderful square near the southern edge of the promontory, where you can stop for a drink at the café, maybe, and then stroll to the edge and enjoy the vistas. Immediately below is a patchwork of picturesque rooftops and then the Aare flowing forcefully through its locks. The way the surrounding countryside wraps itself around the promontory shows clearly what an unusual city Bern is. And, of course, you cannot fail to be enchanted by the immense snow-capped peaks of the Bernese Oberland in the distance. Although it is believed that, from

Bern's very founding, a chapel has stood on this site, construction of the present cathedral was not initiated until 1421. The 328ft (100m) spire was not added to this, the largest church in Switzerland, until 1893. The interior, as the effects of the Reformation dictated more often than not in Switzerland, is rather bland. Look, though, for the sculptured main portal featuring the *Last Judgement*, stained-glass windows from the period 1421–50 and carved choir stalls from 1523. The adventurous and fit may attempt the 344 steps to the second tower platform (*open up to 30mins before the church closes*), where the rewards are unsurpassed views of the city.

Outside the main entrance, the **Moses Fountain** (Mosesbrunnen) was erected in 1790 on the site of an earlier one from 1544. A narrow alleyway, Münstergassen, leads to Kramgasse, an extension of Gerechtigkeitsgasse. Immediately, you will notice an increase in activity, as we are now very near to the centre of Bern.

The **Einstein House Museum** (Einstein Haus; *Kramgasse 49, t 031 312 00 91; open Tues–Fri 10–5, Sat 10–4; closed Jan–Feb*) is in the second-floor flat where Einstein lived between 1903 and 1905. In fact the genius retained close ties with Bern, and it was here that he wrote his first treatise on the special theory of relativity. The Albert Einstein Society has overseen the restoration of the original furnishings and these, together with other documents and writings, are on display.

The museum is sandwiched outside between two fountains. To the east is the **Samson Fountain** (Samsonbrunnen) that dates from 1527, but most visitors' sights will, by now, be riveted to the left. To the west, the **Zähringer Fountain** (Zähringer-brunnen), commemorating the city's founder Berchtold V since 1535, is very elaborate with a Bern bear and Zähringer coat-of-arms.

It is, though, overshadowed, in every sense, by the **Clock Tower** (Zeitglockentuem) directly behind it. This ranks alongside the bears as the city's emblem. The original 12th-century tower, some parts of which still stand, formed the boundary to the first extension of the city. Following the devastation of a fire in 1405 the structure was rebuilt in stone and a tower bell installed. At that time, when the clock chimes had to be struck by hand each hour, it showed the official time and all other clocks were set by it. This practice continued until the advent of more modern communications. It was not until 1530 that the Astronomical Clock and humorous figure play were added. And it is the latter, which commences playing four minutes before the hour, which attracts so many people these days. Less known is the fact that all road distances in Switzerland are measured from this point.

Helvetiaplatz Museums

From the Clock Tower and Casinoplatz, Kirchenfeldbrücke heads south, high over the Aare, to Helvetiaplatz. On a clear day you will have an unobstructed view to the mesmerizing peaks of the Eiger, Mönch and Jungfrau, shimmering on the horizon. The opposite bank of the Aare differs dramatically from the city side. Less densely populated and with large houses, some of which are embassies, there are several museums and the Swiss National Library in the space of a few blocks.

Of these, the grand **Bern Historical Museum** (Historiches Museum Bern; *Helvetiaplatz 5, t 031 350 77 11, www.bhm.ch; open Tues–Sun 10–5, Wed until 8; adm*) is impressive – inside and out. It was originally built to house the Swiss National Museum (Landesmuseum) in 1894, but that was eventually housed in Zürich and this subsequently became the second largest historical museum in the country. It has over 250,000 objects covering prehistory to the present; the Burgundian tapestries from the 15th and 16th centuries and the 6th-century BC Graechwil Hydria Greek bronze vessel are some of the most important.

Also in the plaza is a museum of topographical interest, the **Swiss Alpine Museum** (Schweizerisches Alpines Museum; *Helvetiaplatz 4, t 031 351 04 34, www.alpines museum.ch; open Mon 2–5, Tues–Sun 10–5; adm*). This gives you a real insight into those magical mountains that attract people from all over the world to Switzerland.

The other museum in the plaza is the **Kunsthalle Bern**, (*Helvetiaplatz 1, t 031 351 00 31, f 031 352 53 85, www.kunsthallebern.ch; open Tues 10–7, Wed–Sun 10–5; adm*). Opened in 1918, it has gained a world-renowned reputation for presenting a wide array of Bernese, national and international art in the form of solo special exhibitions of the works of, amongst others, Klee, Giacometti, Moore, Johns and Nauman, along with special thematic exhibitions.

Other smaller, specialist-interest museums around Helvetiaplatz include the **Swiss Rifle Museum**, the **Natural History Museum** and the **Museum for Communication**.

Bundesplatz and Bärenplatz

Back on the promontory, dominating the bank left of the Kirchenfeldbrücke are four buildings that form an elongated façade accentuated by a central dome. The building to the far right and nearest to the bridge is the very grand **Bellevue Palace Hotel** (a good refreshment stop with fine service and views to match). The others, and there are three, form the Swiss **House of Parliament** (Schweizerische Parlament, *www.parlament.ch*). Erected between 1851 and 1902, there is very little difference in style between the east and west wings, but the central parliament building, home to the Federal Council and Federal Assembly, truly is architecturally impressive. To get a closer view, turn left at the end of the bridge and walk along the terrace that runs in front of it.

Just past the domed section of the parliament building, climb the steps that bring you out into Bundesplatz. This square, in conjunction with Bärenplatz – which leads out of it – and Waisenhausplatz, mentioned earlier, serve as the sites for Bern's famous markets. Every morning after mid-May there is a colourful geranium market in Bundesplatz. On Tuesday and Saturday mornings the vegetable, fruit and flower markets occupy Bundesplatz, Bärenplatz and their surrounding streets. Between May and October they are in Bärenplatz daily.

In the middle of Bärenplatz, between Marktgasse and Spitalgasse, is the **Prison Tower** (Käfigturm), which was actually used as such until 1897. This was constructed on the site of the second west gate, *c.* 1256, in 1690.

Just down Spitalgasse in the direction of the train station are two more marvellous water fountains-cum-statues. You will also see, if the weather's fine, people just sitting and enjoying each other's company on the steps leading to the arcades.

Excursions from Bern

Destination	Journey Time (hours.mins)	Recommended Length of Trip	Connections
Thun	0.19	D/T	T
Neuchâtel	0.39	D/T	T
Solothurn	0.43	D/T	T
Interlaken	0.48	D/T	T
Basel	1.07	D/T – O/N – M/N	T
Lausanne	1.07	D/T – O/N	T
Zürich	1.09	D/T – O/N – M/N	T
Brienz	1.21	D/T	T/T
Luzern (1)	1.26	D/T – O/N – M/N	T
Montreux and Vevey	1.32	D/T	T/T
Grindelwald (2)	1.35	M/N	T/T
Wengen (2)	1.40	M/N	T/T/T
Lötschental	1.42	O/N – M/N	T/B
Geneva	1.43	D/T – O/N – M/N	T
Gruyères	1.47	D/T	T/B/T/B
Mürren and Schilthorn 007	1.56	M/N	T/T/F/T
Schaffhausen and Rhine Falls	2.03	D/T	T/T
Rapperswil	2.05	D/T	T/T
Sion	2.13	D/T	T/T
Leukerbad	2.16	O/N – M/N	T/T/B
St Gallen	2.19	D/T	T/T
Engelberg	2.30	D/T – O/N	T/T
Les Diablerets	2.33	D/T – O/N	T/T/T
Saas-Fee	2.35	M/N	T/B
Stein am Rhein	2.35	D/T	T/T
Crans Montana	2.56	D/T – O/N	T/T/B
Vaduz, Liechtenstein	3.02	D/T – O/N	T/T/B
Zermatt	3.09	M/N	T/T
Val d'Anniviers	3.24	O/N – M/N	T/T/B/B
Centovalli	3.38	D/T – O/N	T/T
Ascona	4.16	O/N – M/N	T/T/T/B
Lugano	4.16	D/T – O/N – M/N	T/T
Scuol	4.31	O/N – M/N	T/T/T
Nauders, Austria	5.34	O/N – M/N	T/T/T/B

(1) The starting point for the Pilatus trip.
(2) The starting points for the Jungfraujoch and Männlichen trips.
T: train; B: bus; F: funicular.
D/T: day trip; O/N: overnighter; M/N: multi-nighter.
*Journey time is one-way, and the minimum possible. See **Introduction**, p.7.*

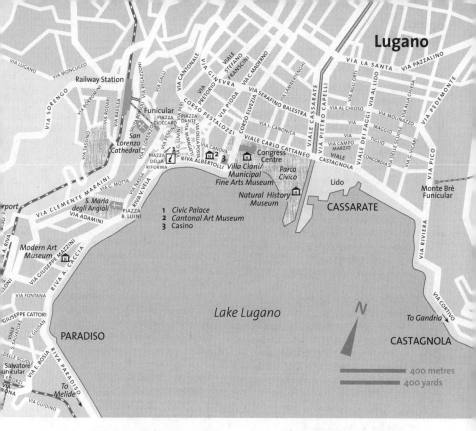

Map legend:
1 Civic Palace
2 Cantonal Art Museum
3 Casino

Lugano

Perhaps because of its relatively remote location and small size, Lugano is often overlooked by visitors to Switzerland – a mistake if you consider its fabulous location surrounded by mountains and nestled against the lake.

Culturally, like the canton it is part of (Ticino), this delightful city is far closer to Italy than the rest of the country. And this, along with a pleasantly benign climate that delivers about 2,300 hours of sunshine annually, gives the city a decidedly Mediterranean feel. Spring comes early here, usually by mid-March, and with it a burst of colour that contrasts sharply with the surrounding snowcapped mountains.

Besides the interesting museums and churches, it is a delight to wander through the narrow streets of the Old Town, or simply sit at an outdoor café, watching the animated conversation and Mediterranean style of the Italian-orientated Swiss. Another major attraction is the places nearby that can be visited by lake steamer, especially between April and October.

As tourism has been important here since the mid-19th century, there is a wide range of hotels to choose from, including one or two really special 5-star ones. You won't go hungry, either, with many Italian restaurants to choose from.

Getting There

Although Lugano has an airport, *see* below, there are no direct scheduled international flights from the UK and USA, and within Switzerland Swiss airlines only operate scheduled flights to and from Zürich.

The nearest airports are at Zürich, Basel and Geneva, respectively 2hrs 51mins, 3hrs 53mins and 5hrs 43mins away by train.

Lugano's geographical location, south of the Alps and close to Italy and Milan, makes for long, and often difficult, train connections with other Swiss cities and towns.

Lugano Comunicazione e Servizi Turistici, t 091 605 12 26, f 091 605 13 36, offer a range of services and are open daily 8–8.

Getting from the Airport

Shuttle Bus, t 079 221 42 43, *www.shuttle-bus.com*, departs from Agno Airport after all passengers have left the departure lounge and will take you either to the railway station (CHF 8 one-way or CHF 15 return) or to the Piazza Manzoni (CHF 10 one-way or CHF 18 return).

Getting Around

The **train station** is located in Piazzale della Stazione in an elevated position slightly above the town centre; the quickest – and cheapest – way down is on the **funicular** to the Piazza Cioccaro in the heart of the Old Town.

Lugano is quite small enough for you not to need to worry too much about public transport. In fact, the only **bus** that anyone will need to take is the No. 1 that runs around the lakeside and through the city centre, from Paradiso to Castagnola.

Lugano Regional Pass: available from hotels and respective transport and tourist offices for either 3 days for CHF 72 or 7 days for CHF 96. It offers 100% free local transport on buses, lake steamers, the Monte Brè and San Salvatore funiculars and some other places. Expect, also, 50% reductions on other attractions and transport, including the airport shuttle bus, as well as 25% off the Monte Generoso trip.

Car Hire

Avis, Agno Airport, t 091 605 54 59; Via Clemente Maraini 8, t 091 913 41 51.

Europcar, Agno Airport, t 091 605 12 11; railway station, t 091 971 01 01.

Hertz, Agno Airport, t 091 605 58 93; Via San Gottardo 13, t 091 923 46 75.

Sixt, Via G. Guisan 10, t 091 994 23 15.

Tourist Information

Lugano: Lugano Turismo, Riva Albertolli – Palazzo Civico, t 091 913 32 32, f 091 922 76 53, *info@lugano-tourism.ch*, *www. lugano-tourism.ch* (*open April–Oct Mon–Fri 9–6.30, Sat 9–12.30 and 1.30–5, Sun 10–3; Nov– Mar Mon–Fri 9–12.30 and 1.30–5.30, public hols 10–12.30 and 1.30–4, closed Sat and Sun*).

Although politically Swiss, 84% of the people in Ticino are Italian-speaking; this may occasionally cause some communication difficulties, but many *Ticinesi* understand English.

Guided Trips and Tours

Guided city walk: May–Oct on Mon at 9.30am, meeting point at Sta. Maria degli Angioli, Piazza Luini, free of charge. Call t 091 913 32 32 to reserve your place.

Lost Property

Polizia Comunale, Piazza Riforma, t 800 80 65, open Mon–Fri 7.30–12 and 1.30–5.

Market Days

Flowers, fruit and vegetables: Tues and Fri mornings at Piazza Riforma.

Antiques and flea market: all day Sat in the Canova quarter.

Medical Emergencies

Dental, Via delle Scuole 46, Pregassona, Mon–Fri 8–4, Sat 9–3.

Exhibitions and Festivals

Late Mar: **Camellia and Magnolia** exhibition.
Easter Week: traditional processions.
April: start of the 3-month **Lugano Classic Music Festival**.
July: **Estival Jazz Festival** through the streets.
Late Aug: **Blues to Bop Festival**.

Shopping

Shops are usually open Mon–Fri 8–12 and 1.30–6.30 – although some extend their hours until 9pm on Thurs – and Sat 8–12 and 1.30–5. Department stores have longer hours, usually Mon–Fri 8–6.30, and close a little earlier on Sat.

The main shopping area is along the Via Nassa up through the Piazza Dante and in the surrounding side streets. Fashion, particularly of the Italian style, is king around here, especially in the numerous small boutiques and other clothing stores.

An interesting area to check out is the Quartiere Maghetti, in the streets just off the piazza of the same name. This older part of Lugano has been completely renovated and has now become the equivalent of a shopping mall – although outdoors. There are all kinds of shops, restaurants and bars here.

Where to Stay

★★★★★Principe Leopoldo & Residence, Via Montalbano, **t** 091 985 88 55, **f** 091 985 88 25, *www.leopoldohotel.com* (*luxury*). This is one of the few hotels in the world to combine history with magnificent views. It is an 18th-century neoclassical-style mansion constructed by a prince and cavalry general of the German Hohenzollern dynasty, with wonderful views over Lugano and the lake from its position on Golden Hill (Collina d'Oro). The hotel exudes discretion and an enchanting ambience, in no small part due to the urbane and charming presence of general manager Maurice Urech. The 70 rooms and suites are beautifully equipped, and an outdoor pool, sauna, jacuzzi, and exquisite restaurants complete the package.

★★★★★Grand Hotel Villa Castagnola, Viale Castagnola 31, **t** 091 973 25 5, **f** 091 973 25 50, *www.slh.com/villcast* (*luxury*). This started life as the home of a noble Russian family, but was transformed into a hotel in 1885. Just across the main road from the lake, and fronted by large luscious gardens, it is now a gracious hotel in the style of a country estate. Its 75 rooms and 18 suites are all uniquely different in décor, but all offer breathtaking views. Also a beauty and health centre, indoor heated pool, sauna, solarium and even indoor golf.

★★★★Romantik Hotel Ticino, Piazza Cioccaro 1, **t** 091 922 77 72, **f** 091 923 62 78, *www.romantikhotels.com/lugano* (*expensive*). This is housed within a charming 400-year-old Ticino house that is notable for its flower-filled patio and for the beautiful art collection on display in the public areas and restaurant. Slap in the centre of Old Town Lugano, it offers 23 tastefully decorated rooms with all modern comforts.

★★★Art-Deco Hotel del Lago, Lungolago Motta 9, **t** 091 649 70 41, **f** 091 649 89 15, *www.hotel-dellago.ch* (*expensive*). Situated in Melide, just a few minutes south of Lugano by train or bus, and even easily reached by boat, this is a pleasant alternative to staying in the city. Right on the lake, it has 8 Art Deco-style rooms or suites and 7 elegantly classical rooms.

★★★★Lido Seegarten, Viale Castagnola 24, **t** 091 973 63 63, **f** 091 973 62 62, *www.hotel lido-lugano.com* (*expensive*). Architecturally impressive, and even more impressive as the only hotel in Lugano with a lakeside location. It has 64 large and modern rooms; the best are those that overlook the outdoor restaurant and pool, with the latter having a ramp down to the lake itself and a floating deck a few yards offshore.

★★★Excelsior, Riva V. Vela 4, **t** 091 922 86 61, **f** 091 922 81 89, *info@excelsior.ch* (*moderate*). This has a fine central location on the main street next to the lake. Its 80 rooms all have TV, private bath/shower, radio and telephone – ask for one with a lakeside balcony. One- or two-room apartments also available.

★★★International Au Lac, Via Nassa 68, **t** 091 922 75 41, **f** 091 922 75 44, *www.hotel-international.ch* (*moderate*). A hotel with classical style, on the corner of Via Nassa and next to the Sta. Maria degli Angioli church. Dating from 1906, it has 78 very nice rooms, especially those facing the lake. Most unusually, there is a garden with a pool and a sun terrace. *Only open Easter–end Oct.*

★★★Cassarate Lago, Viale Castagnola 21, **t** 091 972 24 12, **f** 091 972 79 62, *www.hotelcas arate-lago.com* (*moderate*). Just 50yds from the lake, this hotel has a large shopping centre at street level. Its 84 modern rooms often have a large photograph/painting of a local scene above the headboard. Outdoor swimming pool on the 1st floor.

***La Residenza Garni**, Pzza. della Riscossa 16, **t** 091 973 35 00, **f** 091 973 35 01, *laresidenza@ ticino.com* (*moderate*). In a quiet part of town, not far from the Monte Brè funicular, this hotel is in a rather bland-looking building. All the 40 rooms, on one floor, are modern in style and have an in-room safe.

Moosmann Ca del Lago, Gandria, **t** 091 971 72 61, **f** 091 972 71 32, *www.hotel-moosmann-gandria.ch* (*moderate*). Gandria is a car-free oasis of a village clinging to the hills and directly on the lake, just a short distance from Lugano. This hotel, with 20 rooms, is actually on the lakeside and is a charming escape from the city. *Open early April–Oct.*

***Nassa**, Via Nassa 60/62, **t** 091 910 70 60, **f** 091 910 70 61 (*moderate*). Despite its Nassa Street address, this hotel fronts the Piazza C. Battaglini and some of the 21 rooms, all with a modern decor, directly overlook the lake.

***Walter Garni**, Piazza Rezzonico 7, **t** 091 922 74 25, **f** 091 923 42 33, *www.walteraulac.ch* (*moderate*). This hotel, with the lake directly in front of it and the pedestrian area of the Old Town directly behind it, has been a Lugano tradition since 1888. All of the 42 rooms have a lake view, and they are a pleasant blend of old and new, with facilities like an in-room safe.

Albergo Pestalozzi, Piazza Indipendenza 9, **t** 091 921 46 46, **f** 091 922 20 45, *pestalo@ bluewin* (*moderate*). Located in a distin-guished-looking building in the town centre, this classifies itself as an Art Nouveau non-alcoholic hotel and restaurant. The decor of the 56 rooms matches that style, and you can choose rooms with running water, running water and WC, shower and WC without TV, and shower or bath with WC and TV, as well as facilities for a third or fourth person.

Albergo Rosa, Via Landriani 2/4, **t** 091 922 92 86, **f** 091 923 42 70, *rosa.hotel@ticino.com* (*moderate*). Across from the Parco Civico, in an attractive building. Choose from 28 basi-cally furnished rooms; those with just run-ning water are CHF 50 less than those with private shower and WC. Nice outside patio.

San Carlo Garni, Via Nassa 28, **t** 091 922 71 07, **f** 091 922 80 22, *sancarlo@ticino.com* (*moderate*). This small 22-room hotel is in the pedestrian zone that is Via Nassa, and has a nice modern ambience. All rooms have a pleasing decor, a shower or bath, TV and telephone.

***Zurigo**, Corso Pestalozzi 13, **t** 091 923 43 43, **f** 091 923 92 68, *www.hotelzurigo.ch* (*moderate*). Just on the edge of the Old Town and near the shops, this hotel has 40 rooms (with a modern minimalist flavour) split between standard and superior, with the latter having air conditioning.

***Acquarello**, Piazza Cioccaro 9, **t** 091 911 68 68, **f** 091 911 68 69, *www.acquarello.ch* (*moderate*). This has an excellent location in the very heart of the Old Town, and right next to the funicular to and from the train station. Quite a nice style, too; its 59 rooms were all totally renovated in 2002 and now feature ISDN connections.

Atlantico Garni, Via Concordia 12, **t** 091 971 29 21, **f** 091 29 22, *info@atlanticolugano.ch* (*moderate*). Located in a modern block in the quieter eastern part of town, this has a similar style. 17 rooms altogether, but those with a shower/WC on the floor are a little cheaper.

Eating Out

Dining out in Lugano follows the Italian tradition (*see* **Food and Drink**, p.26).

Principe Leopoldo, Via Montalbano, **t** 091 985 88 55, **f** 091 985 88 25 (*very expensive*). This is the gourmet restaurant of the hotel of the same name, and besides being awarded three red forks by Michelin, the executive chef, Dario Ranza, was nominated Swiss Chef of the Year for 2002/3. His speciality is Swiss-Italian cuisine with Mediterranean flavours. The risotto is excellent, the seafood very tempting, and for meat you can select from duck, veal, pigeon, duck and lamb, as well as the usual beef. The wine list is exten-sive – there are even 2½ pages of champagnes and *spumantis* – but don't overlook the white merlots. If the weather's fine, take a seat at one of the outdoor gazebos looking directly down on the lake.

Al Portone, Viale Cassarate 3, **t** 091 923 55 11, **f** 091 971 65 05, *www.ristorantealportone.ch* (*very expensive*). Just north of the Parco Civico, this could easily be overlooked from the exterior. It is, however, without any doubt the best non-hotel restaurant in Lugano. Run by Roberto and Doris Galizzi and their son Silvio, it serves up some of the finest and most beautifully presented examples of Swiss-Italian cuisine with all the subtle flavours of the Mediterranean. There are two *degustazione* menus, at CHF 120 and CHF 150, or you can select what you fancy from the menu. The wine list specializes in the finest Ticino vintages. *Closed Sun and Mon, mid-July–mid-Aug and the 1st week of Jan.*

Le Relais, Viale Castagnola 31, **t** 091 973 25 55 (*very expensive–expensive*). Full of pastel colours, large plants and little private areas, this is the gourmet restaurant of the Grand Hotel Villa Castagnola. An extra delight, in the summer, is having dinner on the panoramic terrace whilst being serenaded by a pianist. Beautifully crafted, light Mediterranean cuisine is presented by chef de cuisine René Nagy. Try the 4-course fish menu for CHF 86, the *degustazione* menu of 5 courses (with wine from CHF 138 or without CHF 98) or choose from the wide-ranging menu. Leave room for a delicious dessert. *Open eves only.*

Orologio, Via Nizzola 2, **t** 091 923 23 38, **f** 091 923 12 10 (*very expensive–expensive*). Opened in 1907, this has traditionally been one of the city's finest restaurants. Now, completely renovated and furnished in a minimalist style, it continues to serve classic Mediterranean cuisine. The 5-course gastronomic menu costs CHF 72, while the 3-course daily menu is just CHF 43. Look, too, for interesting specials. *Closed Sun.*

Arté, Piazza Emilio Bossi 7, **t** 091 973 48 00 (*expensive*). Although technically a part of the Grand Hotel Villa Castagnola, just 100 yards away, this is much more modern in style. As you step down into the dining room it gives the optical illusion that you are about to walk directly into the lake just the other side of the large windows. The *chef de cuisine* here, Frank Oerthle, specializes in innovative gourmet cuisine including many fish dishes. *Closed Sun and Mon.*

Art-Deco Hotel del Lago, Lungolago Motta 9, **t** 091 649 70 41, **f** 091 649 89 15, *www.hotel-dellago.ch* (*expensive*). This hotel restaurant (*see* p.103 for directions) specializes in excellent fusion seafood cuisine. It offers three set meals: a tasting menu, surprise gourmet menu and a special seafood platter for two, ranging from CHF 59 to CHF 75. On the main menu there are many sushi-type choices, and other Asian-influenced dishes.

Lungolago, Via Nassa 11, **t/f** 091 923 12 33 (*expensive*). Although it has a Nassa address, this is one of many restaurants along here that also share a front onto the Riva V. Vela lining the lake. There are many outside tables here, and it is not unusual to see couples sharing champagne – sold by the flute – whilst trying to make selections from a large and varied menu (translated into four languages – including Russian!). It's trendy, too.

Trani, Via Cattedrale 12, **t** 091 922 05 05, **f** 091 922 73 83, *www.trani.ch* (*expensive*). At the top of a steep pedestrian street is this fascinating complex of restaurant, wine bar and wine shop. The name originates from an Italian town famous for its wine production; producers from there have set up 'Trani' shops in northern Italy that have become a cultural institution. In the curved brick-ceilinged dining room you'll find a small but interesting menu, which may include seasonal specialities like asparagus or artichoke. At the wine bar try the Tavolozza, a method of trying six different quality wines and keeping notes on them – then buy the ones you like at the shop. *Closed Sun and hols.*

Grand Café al Porto, Via Pessina 3, **t** 091 910 51 30, **f** 091 910 51 33 (*moderate*). Do not be put off by the couple or so chairs and tables outside – the inside is quite magnificent and full of surprises. One half of the front room is covered with a grand, wooden-beamed ceiling, with chandeliers and mirrors, while the other part has a fireplace dated 1803 and a counter full of the most delicate pastries, cookies, etc; there are other side rooms, too. The menu is rather limited. *Closed Sun.*

Bottegone del Vino, Via Magatti 3, **t** 091 922 76 89 (*moderate*). Rather a delightful cross between a brasserie and a wine bar, close to the Piazza della Riforma. Expect wine bottles everywhere (it advertises how many prizes it has won), communal tables and a menu that changes daily which is chalked up on the walls. *Closed Sun and hols.*

Cyrano, Corso Pestalozzi 27, **t** 091 922 21 82, **f** 091 922 22 82 (*moderate*). This is a little difficult to find, as it is in an ochre-coloured building just off the main street. But it's worth it for the innovative Italian/Mediterranean menu served in two quite different dining rooms, separated by a nice bar. *Closed Sat and Sun.*

La Tinera, Via dei Gorini 2, **t** 091 923 52 19 (*moderate*). In the basement of a building just off Piazza della Riforma, this has a typical Ticinese ambience with wooden-beamed ceilings, pots and pans and wine around the walls, and wooden tables and chairs. The menu offers an array of set meals, Ticinese- and Lombard-influenced, as well as daily specials.

Café Ars, Riva Albertolli 5, **t** 091 921 18 76 (*moderate*). In the arcade just along from the Arcobaleno (*see* right), this has a modern and fairly sparse decor. There's a good selection of *antipasti*, spaghetti, Caesar salad and more, along with a daily menu for between CHF 16 and CHF 22. *Closed Sat lunch and Sun.*

Birreria della Posta, Piazza Manzoni, **t** 091 923 36 26 (*moderate–inexpensive*). Very centrally located, this is a place of three different characters. The main room is full of wood and old-fashioned in ambience, the next is a glassed-in patio and the last a real patio. Look for all kinds of fare here: tasty salads, hamburgers, sandwiches, dumplings, pasta and some good-looking fish dishes.

Caffè Federale, Piazza della Riforma, **t** 091 923 91 75, **f** 091 921 43 40 (*moderate–inexpensive*). Established in Lugano's main square since 1855, the Federale is a great place to sit outside and be entertained by passers-by. There's a small but varied menu, with daily suggestions for around CHF 20 and a wide selection of drinks.

Caffè Caruso, Piazza Rezzonico 7, **t** 091 922 20 60, **f** 091 922 22 43 (*moderate–inexpensive*). This tiny but attractive Italian bar has a couple of outdoor tables and stands just off the Piazza della Riforma. Expect spaghetti, of course, but also such delights as fish paella Naples-style.

Bar Vela, Riva Vela 10, **t** 091 922 04 66 (*inexpensive*). This is a trendy little bar that sits on the main lakeside street near Piazza B. Luini. There are a couple of outside tables, protected by glass partitioning from the lake and road, and not that many more inside. A small range of hot and cold dishes is on offer, as well as sandwiches with either hot or cold bread.

Arcobaleno, Riva Albertolli/Via Mericoni 2, **t** 091 922 62 18 (*inexpensive*). This is the place to treat yourself to a fantastic selection of ice cream, ice cream and fruit, ice cream and alcohol, fruit drinks and cocktails and the like. And if you are hungry they have a nice range of toasted sandwiches. Sit inside, or on the arcade, protected from the lake winds and road noise by glass panels.

Entertainment and Nightlife

Lugano isn't famed for its nightlife. However, jazz lovers may wish to try out the **Mamy Jazz Club**, Piazza Indipendenza 1, **t** 091 921 39 70, *www.mamyjazzclub.ch*.

Gamblers, though, have two choices of where to win – or lose – money. The **Casinò Lugano**, Via Stauffacher 1, **t** 091 973 71 11, *www.casinolugano.ch*, is open Sun–Thurs 12pm–3am, Fri and Sat 12pm–4am. This has all the usual games, plus a novelty virtual horserace game, located on the 1st floor, where 12 players can play simultaneously. On the other side of the lake, in the Italian enclave of Campione d'Italia, is the **Casinò di Campione**, Piazza le Milano, **t** (39) 640 1111, **f** (39) 640 1112, *www.casinocampione.it*, open Sun–Mon 12pm–5am, Fri and Sat 12pm–6am. Besides all the expected games of chance, there is every opportunity of seeing a spectacular show.

History

Ticino makes up seven per cent of Switzerland's land territory, and is located across the 46th parallel, equidistant from the North Pole and the Equator. It also has the distinction of being the only one of the country's twenty-six cantons situated entirely south of the Alps.

There are indications that a rural borough existed here as long ago as the 10th century, and up until the late 13th century it was the property of Como. However, from then and until the very beginning of the 16th century, control alternated between Como and the Duchy of Milan. During the last period of control by the latter, however, from 1434 to 1501 it actually had its own Counts of Lugano. From 1513 to 1798 it became part of the Bellinzona district of Switzerland. In 1798 the Ticino area asked to remain within the Helvetic Republic, rather than becoming a part of Napoleon's Cisalpinian Republic that emerged in 1803. Lugano than became part of the free and independent Swiss canton of Ticino. During the 18th century Lugano played a large part in the struggle for a united Italy. Prominent citizens like the Ciani brothers organized networks of Italian refugees escaping from Austrian repression, and the Villa Ciani became the centre of that activity.

Ticino and its people, the *Ticinesi*, have been inextricably linked with the Italian regions of Lombardy and Piedmont, and this is reflected in the fact that the official language is Italian, spoken by 84 per cent of the population. Today, Ticino has only around 300,000 inhabitants, just over four per cent of the country's total, with the bulk of the population, 100,000, around the community of Lugano. The city itself, though, has a population of just 30,000.

In the second half of the 19th century tourists began to discover the delights of Lugano, and tourism has now become an integral part of the city's vibrant economy. The opening of the Gotthard railway line at the end of the 19th century played a large part, too, in opening up what was, up to that time, mainly a rural community. These days, Lugano, perhaps surprisingly, is the third largest financial market in Switzerland.

Around the City

At each end of the bay on which Lugano sits are two small mountains – San Salvatore to the south and Monte Bré to the northeast – that, by way of a funicular, offer spectacular views not only of the city, but also of the surrounding mountains for many miles around. And because most of the places of interest are located in between them – with the exception of a few places just a block or so away – Lugano is an easy place to explore.

Start, then, at the southern end of the city in the area known as Paradiso and head for the **San Salvatore Funicular** (*t 091 985 28 28, f 091 985 28 39, www.montesansalvatore.ch; open mid-Mar–mid-Nov from 8.30am, and in Mar, Oct and Nov the last one leaves at 5pm; April, May and Sept at 6.30pm; June, July and Aug at 11pm; return ticket CHF 20*). The trip to the 2,992ft (912m) summit takes just 12 minutes, and once there you will find, besides the views, a restaurant, a small chapel and the **San Salvatore Museum** (*open Wed–Sun 10–12 and 1–3*), which rather bizarrely specializes in the

Archfraternity of Good Death and Prayer, with exhibits of objects collected over the centuries. It also has a room dedicated to fossils and minerals found in the region.

Moving north, you will note that beautiful villas are a notable feature of this city and one of them, the **Villa Malpensata**, is just a few moments away. This typically grand 19th-century villa in lovely grounds passed out of private ownership when, in 1893, it and the collection of paintings, sculptures and other pieces of art it contained were bequeathed to the city by Antonio Caccia, a writer and art collector. There was a proviso, however. The income from the estate was to be used to found a fine arts museum bearing the name of the donor, Antonio Caccia. Such a museum was opened in 1912 but, just 21 years later, it was relocated to the Villa Ciani (*see below*, p.108). From that point forward, the Villa Malpensata has been utilized in a variety of ways and now houses the **Modern Art Museum** (*Museo d'Arte Moderna, Riva A. Caccia 5, t 091 994 43 70, f 091 800 74 97, www.mdam.ch; open Tues–Sun 9–7; adm*). You will find works of art from the 20th century only, with the emphasis on expressionism; the museum particularly favours artists who focus their work on elements of humanitarianism. While there is a permanent collection on display, the museum's fame arises from its reputation as a host for major touring exhibitions that have recently included the likes of Chagall, Kirchner, Modigliani, Munch and their peers.

Walking back towards town, it would be entirely possible to overlook the church of **Santa Maria degli Angioli** (*Piazza Luini 3, t 091 922 01 12*), but that would be a mistake. Completed in 1500 and consecrated 15 years later, this is one of Lugano's most important buildings. Initially it was aligned with the St Francis Rule Fathers Franciscan monastery, but after 1602 it changed to the Reformed Fathers from Milan. Most notable here is the wall separating the nave from the chancel, which is entirely overlaid with an immense fresco. Created by Bernardino Luini in 1529, this gloriously depicts the *Passion and Crucifixion of Christ*. However, two other works by the same artist, *The Last Supper* and *The Madonna with Child*, are considered more important.

Via Nassa diverges from the lakeside here, and runs almost parallel to it. In the old days this was where fishermen used to hang their nets to dry, but not so now. Expect to find, instead, upmarket jewellers, boutiques, supermarkets and a host of bars and restaurants on this pedestrian and part-arcaded street. At its end, and almost surrounded by outdoor restaurants and bars, is the **Piazza della Riforma**, Lugano's main square. The large impressive building on its lakeside is the **Civic Palace** that dates from 1844, and was built to provide a home for the cantonal government. The 1814 constitution allowed for Lugano, Locarno and Bellinzona to alternate every six years as the capital of the canton, and when it wasn't used for that purpose it became a hotel. Eventually Bellinzona became the permanent capital, and in 1890 this became home for the Municipal Assembly, Town Council and the respective administrative offices. Look at the four statues adorning the pediment: created by the renowned 19th-century Lombardian artist Francesco Somaini (1795–1855), they represent, from left to right, *Religion, Concord, Strength* and *Freedom*. Take a peek inside, too, and admire Vincenzo Vela's (1820–91) powerful statue of Spartacus. The tourist office is in a corner of the building facing the lake, and the embarkation pier for the **Società Navigazione del Lago di Lugano** lake steamers is just across the road. Also, next to it, in the Piazza A. Manzoni (near the Burger King), you will find the **tourist train** (*Trenini Turistici*, *t 091 940 29 40*), that departs every half-hour between 10am and 5.30pm for a 20/25min trip covering three miles (5km) and costing CHF 5.

The side streets and alleys of the Old Town around here are full of charm, and not far away is the **Sant'Antonio Abate** church, Piazza Dante; although it opened in 1651 it wasn't entirely completed until the early 18th century. The Somaschi boarding school was attached to the church, until it became the cantonal high school in 1852 before being demolished in 1908. And it is that connection, despite a portrait of St Antonio on the vault of the choir, that it is most known for, as it is a place of memorial to the famed Italian writer, Alessandro Manzoni, who studied at the school. The **San Lorenzo Cathedral**, Via Cattedrale, atop a nearby hill, has a history dating back over 1,000 years as it is thought a church existed here as long ago as 875. What you see, on the outside, is a Renaissance façade dating from 1517, with 15th-century vaults replacing the original wooden ceiling. Some parts of the original construction can still be identified inside.

Before heading back to the lakeside, cross Via della Posta into the Canova quarter to find the **Cantonal Art Museum** (Museo Cantonale d'Arte; *Via Canova 10, t 091 910 47 80, f 091 910 47 89; open Tues 2–5, Wed–Sun 10–5; adm*). Housed in a group of buildings that date from the Middle Ages and are noteworthy in their own right, this museum boasts a collection of works by Swiss-Italian and Italian artists of the late 18th, 19th and 20th centuries. There is also an emphasis on contemporary art, with works by such impressionists as Turner, Rosso, Hodler and Righini, as well as photography by Swiss and international artists. It is in the streets around here that you will find the antiques and flea market each Saturday.

Nearby is another church to explore – one with a fascinating history. **San Rocco**, in Piazza San Rocco, was originally built in 1349 and was then dedicated to St Biagio. In 1512–27 and then again in 1528 Lugano, little more than a large village at the time, suffered two devastating plagues. Its citizens asked that the church be rebuilt, and the new church was re-named after St Rocco as he was believed to be able to keep plagues away. Given the previous problems, it was also designed for use as a leprosy hospital. Inside, the frescoes on the nave date from the 17th century, but the neo-Baroque façade is much more modern and has only existed since 1909.

The **San Carlino**, Rivetta Tell, found on the lake just before the Ciani Park, was erected in 1999 and meant to be a temporary attraction. However, this real curiosity has proved so popular that it has now been made permanent. Francesco Borromini built the original San Carlino in Rome, and this museum-piece replica of half the church, designed in turn by the world-renowned Ticinese architect Mario Botta and made of 32,000 pieces of wood and 108ft (33m) tall, commemorates the 400th anniversary of his birth.

Ciani Park is the largest open area on the lake, and the house and its extensive gardens are named after two brothers, Giacomo and Filippo Ciani. Although their family originated from the Ticino, the brothers were born in Milan. As important figures in liberal politics, and very enterprising entrepreneurs, they played a major role in the political and economic development of Lugano, becoming among its most prominent 19th-century citizens. In fact, they founded, in 1844, the first kindergarten in Lugano for children of the working classes. Between 1840 and 1843, they acquired, expanded and refurbished an existing 17th-century home, fashioning it into the **Villa Ciani**, as it is known today. The municipality compulsorily purchased the property in 1912 and initially used it to house the local history museum. In 1933, it metamorphosed into the **Municipal Fine Arts Museum** (Museo Civico di Belle Arti; *Parco Civico, t 091 800 71 96, f 091 800 74 97; open Tues–Fri 10–12 and 2–6; adm*). Today, it exhibits a collection of works by Swiss and other European artists from the 15th to 20th centuries.

Move on east now – on a No. 1 bus, if you prefer, to the ACT Cassarate stop – and then walk behind the impressive Grand Hotel Villa Castagnola to the **Monte Brè Funicular** (*t 091 971 31 71, f 091 972 37 48, www.montebre.ch; return ticket CHF 19*). The first stage of the journey is an automatic service between Cassarate and Suvigliana that takes four minutes; the second stage uses cars that have been restored to their original 1912 style, and takes you to the top, 3,061ft (933m) above sea level. There, the Ristorante Vetta Monte Brè allows you to sit, rest and admire truly wonderful views that, on a clear day, can include the peaks of the Bernese and Valais Alps. The more adventurous can wander the short distance to the local village, that has been restored in typical Ticinese style.

There is one more museum in the eastern suburb of Castagnola (again reached on the No. 1 bus or by boat) that is certainly of interest, the **Museum of Non-European Culture** (Museo delle Culture Extraeurope; *t 091 971 73 53, f 091 800 74 97; open Wed–Sun 10–5; adm*). The pretty old mansion in which it is housed is situated on the lake, and the Brignoni collection of 650 mainly wooden objects and figures from Oceania, Asia and Africa is considered one of the more important collections of its kind in Europe. These, certainly, are significant ethnographically and anthropologically, and they also include much primitivism, surrealism and exoticism.

Not far from here is a gracious mansion that attracted the attention of Baron Thyssen-Bornemisza in 1932. Enchanted with the beauty of the area and, in particular, the magnificent location and design of the **Villa Favorita**, he purchased the home and expanded it to accommodate his large and fabulous collection of fine art, the finest private one in the world. This collection was later augmented by his son Hans Heinrich who, in addition to an interest in the Old and modern Masters, developed an enthusiasm for 19th- and 20th-century artists. A collection of those works was put on permanent display, and in the 1970s and 80s the Villa attracted worldwide attention with a variety of special exhibitions. In 1991, however, many of the major attractions were transferred to the Thyssen-Bornemisza museum in Madrid. The Villa Favorita has now been closed for a while, and the authorities have no idea whether or not it will re-open.

Lake Trips from Lugano

One of the many attractions of Lugano is the fact that there are several places of interest nearby that can be reached by boat (and train or sometimes bus). Between March and the end of October/November many of these trips are run by the **Società**

Navigazione del Lago di Lugano (*Viale Castagnola 12,* **t** *091 971 52 23,* **f** *091 971 27 93, www.lakelugano.ch*).

The closest place is the charming village of **Gandria**, once a fishing village, which is just around the bay about 3 miles (5km) from Lugano (although it is possible to get to and from Gandria by the Porlezza-Lugano bus, stopping by the post office in Castagnola and the Gandria restaurant in Gandria). Sitting at the foot of Monte Brè on the steep mountainside, this community of narrow streets and old-fashioned ambience is a car-free haven. The more active could consider taking the footpath alongside the lake back to Castagnola, a walk of about an hour. This is known as the Olive Tree Path, and new, recently fruiting olive trees have been reintroduced to supplant the ancient ones that used to grow here. Along the way, there are 18 panels explaining everything about olive trees and olive oil that you could possibly want to know. At Castagnola you can hop on the No.1 bus back to the town centre.

Another of these trips, further along the lake in an isolated position near the Italian border, is a very curious museum, the **Swiss Customs Museum** (Museo delle Dogane Svizzere; **t** *091 923 98 43; open April–Oct 1.30–5.30; free*). It is accessible only via a lake steamer that departs from Lugano Giardino at 1pm. The history of this museum revolves around – and this is the curious part – smuggling. Smuggling is an illegal activity that, inevitably, afflicts every border to some degree, and the physical features of this particular coast were certainly conducive to its success. In fact, it was a local way of life that has only recently come to an end. During 1856, in an effort to control the epidemic, the Swiss authorities constructed the first customs house on the steep slopes of Monte Caprino. The present building, which replaced the original in 1904, continued in operation until 1935, when it became a museum that has something for people of every age, including, since 1994, an interactive exhibition.

Two other lakeside attractions are between Lugano and Capolago – although they can't really be managed on the same day. The first of these is the closest: **Swiss-miniatur** (**t** *091 640 10 60,* **f** *091 640 10 69, www.swissminiatur.ch; open mid-Mar–Oct 9–6; adm*), which children of all ages will find fascinating. You can get there by lake steamer, train or bus, getting off at Melide. Here, the entire landscape of Switzerland is replicated in miniature to a scale of 1:25 over an area of 2.7 acres (11,000sq m). This enables you to formulate a mental vision of the country as a whole and to under-stand better either where you are going or where you have been. And model train lovers will certainly be on track: a model railway 1.86 miles (3.5km) long has been constructed, and the whole network is centrally controlled.

The second attraction entails taking a lake steamer or train to Capolago and then boarding an old-fashioned cog wheel steam-powered railway on a 40min trip to Vetta, the summit of **Monte Generoso** (**t** *091 648 11 05,* **f** *091 648 11 07, www. montegeneroso.ch*). This is the highest summit in the region, at 5,591ft (1,704m), and besides having a marvellous perspective of the various branches of the lake it is also possible to see, to the south, the Lombard plain as far as the Apennines and the alpine range including the Eiger, Matterhorn, Jungfrau and Monte Rosa northwards. Relax at one of the cafés or restaurants, or maybe stroll around and try and sight one

Excursions from Lugano

Destination	Journey Time (hours.mins)	Recommended Length of Trip	Connections
Ascona	1.08	O/N – M/N	T/T/B
Centovalli	1.12	D/T – O/N	T/T/T
Luzern (1)	2.29	D/T – O/N – M/N	T/T
Zürich	2.41	D/T – O/N – M/N	T
Rapperswil	2.47	D/T	T/T
Schaffhausen and Rhine Falls	3.38	D/T	T
Basel	3.40	D/T – O/N – M/N	T/T
St. Gallen	3.46	D/T	T/T
Solothurn	3.56	D/T	T/T
Engelberg	4.00	D/T – O/N	T/T/T
Bern	4.01	D/T – O/N – M/N	T/T
Vaduz, Liechtenstein	4.03	D/T – O/N	T/B/T/B
Stein am Rhein	4.12	D/T	T/T
Thun	4.15	D/T	T/T/T/T
Sion	4.21	D/T	T/T/T/T
Leukerbad	4.34	O/N – M/N	T/T/T/T/B
Neuchâtel	4.39	D/T	T/T
Saas-Fee	4.47	M/N	T/T/T/B
Brienz	4.59	D/T	T/T/T
Montreux and Vevey	5.02	D/T	T/T/T/T
Interlaken	5.02	D/T	T/T
Zermatt	5.04	M/N	T/T/T/T/T
Lötschental	5.10	O/N – M/N	T/T/T/T/B
Crans Montana	5.12	D/T – O/N	T/T/T/T/B
Grindelwald (2)	5.12	M/N	T/T/T
Lausanne	5.21	D/T – O/N	T/T
Wengen (2)	5.27	M/N	T/T/T/T
Mürren and Schilthorn 007	5.33	M/N	T/T/T/F/T
Scuol	5.42	O/N – M/N	T/B/T/T
Les Diablerets	5.44	D/T – O/N	T/T/T/T/T
Gruyères	5.46	D/T	T/T/T/B/B
Val d'Anniviers	5.52	O/N – M/N	T/T/T/B/B
Geneva	6.00	D/T – O/N – M/N	T/T/T
Nauders, Austria	6.41	O/N – M/N	T/B/T/T/B

(1) The starting point for the Pilatus trip.
(2) The starting points for the Jungfraujoch and Männlichen trips.
T: train; B: bus; F: funicular.
D/T: day trip; O/N: overnighter; M/N: multi-nighter.
Journey time is one-way, and the minimum possible. See **Introduction**, p.7.

of the rare species of animal and plant life that have survived here since the last Ice Age.

Finally, there is a small but important museum within the Casa Carmuzzi complex in Montagnola, approximately 10 minutes west of Lugano. You can reach it by post bus to Montagnola, departing from the Via Sorengo just 150yds from the train station via the underpass. The **Hermann Hesse Museum** (Museo Hermann Hesse; *Torre Camuzzi,* **t** *091 993 37 70,* **f** *091 993 37 72, www.hessemontagnola.ch; open Mar–Oct Tues–Sun 10–12.30 and 2–6.30; Nov–Feb Sat and Sun the same hours; adm*) was inaugurated on 2 July 1997 on the 120th anniversary of this painter, poet, novelist and Nobel Prize winner's birth. One of four museums in the world dedicated to his memory (this is considered the third most important), it contains memorabilia from the last 43 years of his life until his death in 1962, during which time he lived in Ticino. Expect to find some watercolours and a documentary showing the man at work; recitals of his works can be heard on Sundays.

Luzern

Besides being one of Switzerland's most attractive cities, Luzern (Lucerne in French) is also famous for the arts. It boasts many fascinating museums and an international Festival of Music which was begun in 1938 and today attracts music lovers from all over the world. The arcades and cafés of the Reuss river promenades are a lively meeting place, and visitors can browse or shop to their hearts' content in the Old Town. In fact, both the city government and private donors spent large sums renovating Luzern on the occasion of its 800th birthday in 1978. And, if all this was not enough of an attraction, the town benefits from a beautiful location in the heart of Switzerland, at the northern end of the lake of Luzern (Vierwaldstätter See), with panoramic views of the surrounding Alps.

History

The first mention of Luzern, *Luciaria* as it was known at the time, was made in AD 840. Early on it was christened the 'city of lights', a reference to a miracle in which, legend has it, an angel guided its early citizens with a heavenly light to the place where they were to erect a chapel in honour of St Nicklaus, patron saint of sailors and fishermen. Around 1220, this small fishing and monastery village was catapulted to international importance when the opening of the nearby Gotthard Pass facilitated a lucrative trade between the north and south. From that time on, rich merchants, pilgrims, diplomats and messengers either prepared for their journeys or started one from the city of Luzern that, by 1450, was home to over 400 inns and restaurants. It was the resulting exposure to a wealth of international influences that endowed this city with its adventurous and outward-looking character and led, in turn, in the 18th century to a great emphasis not only on trade, but also on a keen educational awareness of foreign cultures. The 19th-century completion of the European rail network

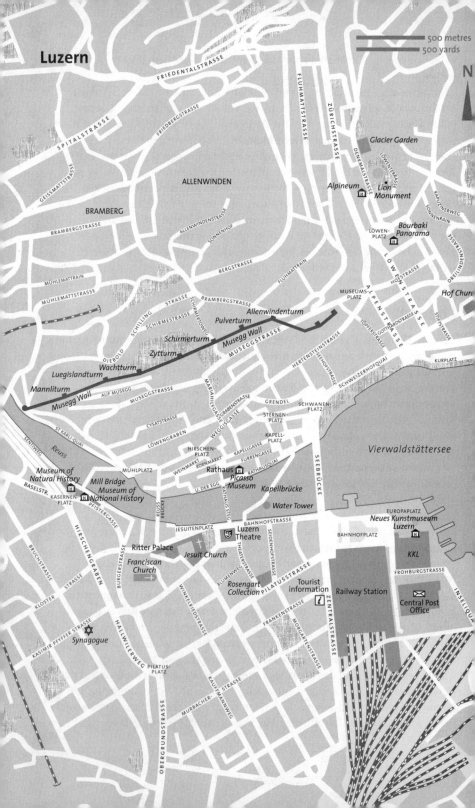

was the key that finally opened the door for travellers from all over the world to discover the charms of Luzern – and many they are.

Late 14th-century walls, with their nine defensive towers, stand defiantly behind the town which is chock-full of wonderfully decorated and frescoed old houses that adorn a maze of small streets, lanes and squares. Among the more prominent of Luzern's many monuments are the 1666 Baroque Jesuit Church, standing as a reminder of the profound influence the Jesuits had over the city from 1574 until their demise in the Sonderbund War of 1847, and the Italian Renaissance **Rathaus** (town hall), built between 1602 and 1606. The city's main focal points, however, are two medieval covered bridges that link the old and new areas of town: most well known is the unique 14th-century wooden covered **Chapel Bridge** (Kapellbrücke), the roof supports of which were embellished during the 17th century with triangular paintings of scenes depicting Swiss history and illustrating the legends of St Leodegar and St Mauritius. At its side is the distinctive 13th-century octagonal water tower – the city's signature landmark. Below the city walls stands the **Mill Bridge** (Spreuerbrücke), built in 1408; its roof is similarly decorated with a series of paintings known as the *Dance of Death*.

Around the City

Given Luzern's geographical situation, with most places of interest being either side of the river, it's best to start at the train station – home of the tourist office – and then take a clockwise circular route, ending up in the Old Town and at the famous Chapel Bridge and Water Tower.

Outside the station itself is a decorative old arch which, in fact, used to be the main entrance to the station. However, there was a major fire in 1971, and the resulting new station, an innovation by the Spanish architect Santiago Calatrava built between 1984 and 1991, was the first of what proved to be an ever-increasing number of modern buildings in Luzern.

The dominant building just behind the station, and bordering the lake, is the new Culture and Congress Centre (KKL), the brainchild of the French architect Jean Nouvel, which was inaugurated in 1998. An integral part of this is the **New Museum of Art Luzern** (Neues Kunstmuseum Luzern; *Europaplatz 1, t 041 226 78 00, f 041 226 78 01, www.kunstmuseumluzern.ch; open Tues and Thurs–Sun 10–5, Wed 10–9; adm*). This is the setting for international contemporary art in the form of dynamic temporary exhibitions. These are complemented by the permanent exhibitions of the Luzern Art Society, founded in 1819, that include Swiss art of the 18th to 20th centuries, together with selected works of expressionist trends, of classical Modernism, and international and Swiss contemporary art from 1960.

Nearby, just a few minutes' walk to the west, is Luzern's newest museum. You can't miss it as it is a distinguished Empire-style neoclassical structure dating from 1924 that was once home to the Swiss National Bank. Since March 2002, however, it has been home to the **Rosengart Collection** (Sammlung Rosengart; *Pilatusstrasse 10, t 041 220 16 60, f 041 220 16 63, www.rosengart.ch; open daily April–Oct 10–6; Nov–Mar 11–5; adm exp; joint adm available with Picasso Museum, and with this and the New*

Getting There

Luzern doesn't have its own **airport**. The nearest ones are at Zürich, Basel and Geneva; these are, respectively, 50mins, 1hr 13mins and 3hrs 17mins away. Being centrally located in Switzerland, Luzern is easily reached by **train** from most other cities and towns.

Car Hire

Avis, Luzernerstrasse 56, **t** 041 318 60 66.
Europcar, Luzernerstrasse 17, **t** 041 444 44 28.
Hertz, Luzernerstrasse 33, **t** 041 420 02 77.
Miecar, Neuweg 8, **t** 041 210 00 44.

Tourist Information

Luzern: tourist information office, Zentral-strasse 5, **t** 041 227 17 17, **f** 041 227 17 18, *www.luzern.org (open April–Oct Mon–Fri 8.30–7.30, Sat and Sun 9–7.30, but mid-June–mid-Sep it has longer hours: Mon–Fri 8.30–8.30, Sat and Sun 9–8.30; in winter Mon–Fri 8.30–6, Sat and Sun 9–6)*.

It also operates a **hotel reservation service**, **t** 041 227 17 27, *www.luzern.org*.

Guided Trips and Tours

Guided city walk: in May–Oct this 2hr walk takes place daily, and in Nov–April just on Wed and Sat. Departs from the tourist information office, Zentralstrasse 5, at 9.45am; tickets CHF 16.

Lost Property

Fundbüro, Hirschengraben 17b, **t** 041 208 78 08 *(open Mon–Fri 8–12 and 1.30–5)*.

Market Days

Fish market: every Tues, Fri and Sat at Unter der Egg.
Flowers, fruit and vegetables: Tues and Sat mornings alongside the Reuss river and Sat mornings at Helvetiaplatz.
Flea market: May–Oct on Sat at Burgerstrasse, Reussteg and Ruessplatz.
Handicraft market: April–Dec every Sat at Weinmarkt.

Medical Emergencies

Chemist/pharmacy: **t** 041 211 33 33.

Credit cards: American Express, **t** 01 659 63 33, **Eurocard**, **t** 01 279 65 56, **Visa**, **t** 0800 892 733.
Doctors: **t** 111.

Exhibitions and Festivals

Jan: Mozart Days Luzern.
Mid-Feb: Carnival.
Late Mar: Honky Tonk Bar and Restaurant Festival, *www.honky-tonk.ch*.
Late Mar–early April: Luzern Festival Ostern.
Early May: FUMETTO, Luzern's Comix-Festival, *www.fumetto.ch*.
June: Corpus Christi Day.
Late June: Old Town Festival.
Mid-July–late Aug: Open-Air Cinema Luzern.
Late July: Blue Balls Festival 03, *www.blueballs.ch*.
Mid-Aug: Lucerne Festival Summer, *www.lucernefestival.ch*.
Mid-Aug: Swiss Outdoor Wrestling and Alpine Festival.
Late Sept: World Band Festival, *www.worldbandfestival.ch*.
Early Nov: Lucerne Blues Festival, *www.bluesfestival.ch*.
Mid-Nov: Comedy Festival.
Late Nov: Lucerne Festival Piano.
Late Nov: GWAND, Fashion events Lucerne, *www.gwand.ch*.
Dec: Barstreet-Festival.
Early Dec: St Nicholas Procession.

Shopping

Swiss Lion, Löwenplatz 11, **t** 041 410 61 81, **f** 041 410 61 80, *www.swisslion.ch*. Suitably close to the Swiss Lion monument and in the same building as the Bourbaki Panorama, has a wide variety of Victorinox knives etc., plus other souvenirs and an extensive selection of fine watches, including AP and Omega.

Where to Stay

★★★★★**Palace Luzern**, Haldenstrasse 10, **t** 041 416 16 16, **f** 041 416 10 00, *www.palace-luzern. com (luxury)*. Located on the shores of the lake, and just 5 minutes' walk from the Old Town. Its 8-storey façade, distinguished by elegant turrets, French windows and balconies, has graced the Luzern skyline since 1906. All of its 168 rooms and suites, whilst still having state-of-the-art technology, radiate an Art Nouveau style with Ionic columns, arched ceilings, intricate tapestries, rich brocades and glittering chandeliers – as do the charming public areas and bars. Its new Jasper restaurant is considered the best in town.

★★★★The Hotel, Sempacherstrasse 14, **t** 041 226 86 86, **f** 041 2226 86 90, *www.the-hotel.ch* (*luxury*). Situated in a pleasant square, close to the train station, this is a most unusual deluxe boutique hotel. Designed by the French star architect, Jean Nouvel, the 25 studios and suites combine elegance and design with a fascinating interplay of nature (wood) and technology (steel). An extra quirk is that film scenes, of 25 movies from Jean Nouvel's personal background, are projected on to the ceilings.

★★★★Art Deco Hotel Montana, Adligenswilerstrasse 22, **t** 041 419 00 00, **f** 041 419 00 01, *www.hotel-montana.ch* (*expensive*). This was one of the last classical hotels built in Luzern (in 1909–10), on a hill just behind the Palace Hotel. Recently, with the help of the acclaimed Zürich architect Pia Schmid, it has been converted into an Art Deco-style building. Its 62 rooms, ranging from standard to the two acclaimed Tower suites, have a decor that plays on stripes, squares and rectangles combined with warm colours and sharp black and white effects.

★★★★Hôtel des Balances, Weinmarkt, **t** 041 418 28 28, **f** 041 418 28 38, *www.balances.ch* (*expensive*). This is located in the former Guildhall, in a distinguished position in the Old Town, and has an attractively painted façade. The 57 rooms are decorated and equipped to the highest standards; the best are those that overlook the Reuss river, Chapel Bridge and Jesuit Church.

★★★★Monopol, Pilatusstrasse 1, **t** 041 226 43 43, **f** 041 226 43 44, *ww.hotel-monopol.com* (*expensive*). First opened in 1899; the current owners have not only redeveloped the interior, but have reinstated the dome topping its classical façade. Directly across from the train station, it has 73 modern, elegant – and sometimes spacious – rooms with all modern facilities.

★★★★Luzernerhof, Alpenstrasse 3, **t** 041 418 47 47, **f** 041 418 47 49, *www.luzernerhof.ch* (*expensive*). Located between the Lion Monument and the lake, this hotel has an extremely modern façade. However, the 63 rooms and public areas have a comfortable traditional decor. The restaurant serves international dishes.

★★★★Rebstock, St Leodegar-Strasse 3, **t** 041 410 35 81, **f** 041 410 39 17, *www.hereweare.ch* (*moderate*). Close to the Hof Church and in the historic Wey district, this has a typical redwood half-timbered façade, and a choice of three restaurants. Surrounded by contemporary art, you will find 30 individually designed and interesting rooms.

★★★★Cascada, Bundesplatz 18, **t** 041 226 80 88, **f** 041 226 80 00, *www.cascada.ch* (*moderate*). A few minutes from the Old Town, parallel to the railway tracks, this is rather an eclectic hotel. True to its name, each of the 65 individually designed rooms and suites have a unique painting, by Heinz Blum, of a Swiss waterfall. It also has disabled facilities and a Spanish restaurant.

★★★Krone, Weinmarkt 12, **t** 041 419 44 00, **f** 041 419 44 90, *www.krone-luzern.ch* (*moderate*). This is a charming hotel with 24 rooms, a great riverside location in the Old Town and two restaurants. It offers a high degree of comfort and reasonable rates.

★★★Gefängishotel Löwengraben, Löwengraben 18, **t** 041 417 12 12, **f** 041 417 12 11, *www.loewengraben.ch* (*moderate*). Dating from 1862, this was actually used as a jail until 1998. Some 50 cells have been transformed into rooms with up to 4 beds and suites – much larger and good value – that were once the visitors' room, the jail warden's office, the prison library and the games room.

★★★Baslertor, Pfistergasse 17, **t** 041 249 22 22, **f** 041 249 22 33, *www.baslertor.ch* (*inexpensive*). Close to the Jesuit Church, this hotel has 30 rooms mixed as singles, twins and doubles; all have Internet connections and some have air conditioning. Unusually, and refreshingly, it has a nice small pool.

Derby, Falkengasse 4, **t** 041 410 26 62, **f** 041 410 42 82 (*inexpensive*). In the heart of the

Old Town, this is a new hotel with just fifteen rooms.

★★★Weinhof, Weystrasse 10, **t** 041 410 12 51, **f** 041 12 56, *www.hotel-weinhof.ch* (*inexpensive*). In the Old Town, close to the Lion Monument, this has 28 modern, if rather small, rooms. It also offers a typical Swiss restaurant and two bowling alleys.

Tourist Hotel Luzern, St Karliquai 12, **t** 041 410 24 74, **f** 041 410 84 14, *www.touristhotel.ch* (*inexpensive*). This fairly basic hotel is located alongside the Reuss river, a short distance behind the town centre. It has 30 rooms in a combination of single, double, 3 and 4 bedrooms as well as a suite for 6. Choose between private or shared bathrooms.

★★Goldener Stern, Burgerstrasse 35, **t** 041 227 50 60, **f** 041 227 50 61, *www.goldener-stern.ch* (*inexpensive*). Located in a traditional old building, just across from the Franciscan church, this is a small, family-run hotel in a fine location with 13 rooms of different sizes.

Pickwick, Rathausquai 6, **t** 041 410 59 27, **f** 041 410 51 08, *www.hotelpickwick.ch* (*inexpensive*). Directly next to the Reuss river, and with its own sun terrace, this is the best located budget hotel in Luzern. Associated with the Pickwick pubs, it has 22 rooms that come with or without a private bathroom.

Rösli, Pfistergasse 12, **t** 041 249 22 77, **f** 041 249 22 88, *www.roesli.ch* (*inexpensive*). Just across the road from – and part of – the Baslertor (it's where you have to check in). Just 6 rooms, and a good economical choice.

Backpackers Lucerne, Alpenquai 42, **t** 041 360 04 20, **f** 041 360 04 42 (*cheap*). About 10 mins from the station, this has double rooms (all with balcony) and dormitory accommodation – as well as free kitchen facilities, laundry and a bar with games and books.

Eating Out

A local speciality to look for is *Kügelipastete*. This creamed, meat-filled shell is made from a recipe imported by mercenary soldiers who fought in Spain.

Jasper, Haldenstrasse 10, **t** 041 416 16 16, **f** 041 416 10 00, *www.palace-luzern.com* (*very expensive*). A new restaurant that has very quickly established itself as the best restaurant in Luzern. With its low-intensity Mediterranean minimalist style, it is quite a contrast to the Palace Hotel, of which it is a part. The cuisine is sublime. Expect starters like *Gröstel* of octopus with spring onions and dried tomatoes, followed by a main course of duck breast with confit of San Marzanno tomatoes and *chantrelles*. The Surprise Menu, for two people, consists of 3–5 courses and costs CHF 75–125 pp.

Rotes Gatter, Weinmarkt, **t** 041 418 28 28, **f** 041 418 28 38, *www.balances.ch* (*expensive*). In the Hotel Des Balances, this restaurant has the very best location in Luzern as it is set on a covered private terrace right next to the Reuss river. Chef Andy Fluri creates interestingly mixed menus to match the ambience. The Rotes Gatter Fondue, with veal, maize poulard, lamb entrecôte, king prawns and fillet strips of red mullet, salmon, pike and perch, is an interesting selection for two people. Leave room for the *tartes flambées*.

Bam Bou & More, Sempacherstrasse 14, **t** 041 226 86 86, **f** 041 2226 86 90, *www.the-hotel. ch* (*expensive*). As eclectic in style and cuisine as the hotel (The Hotel) it is in. With a definite Asian influence, the menu has a selective range of choices. Try the three home-made snacks – Peking duck roll, Indonesian crêpes and Thai spring rolls for a starter. Followed, maybe, by finely sliced duck, marinated Indonesian-style, and served on wok-fried spaghetti with artichokes and roasted red peppers and Joseph's famous Makhanwalla sauce.

Li Tai Pe, Furrengasse 14, **t** 041 410 10 23, **f** 041 410 94 55 (*expensive*). A particularly fine Chinese restaurant, which has established for itself a great and well-deserved reputation. The dishes, well prepared and plentiful, can be ordered à la carte or through a selection of menus. Some specialities, including Peking duck and braised whole carp, must be ordered in advance; reservations recommended.

Don José, Hofstrasse 13, t 041 410 27 30, f 041 41065 07 (*expensive*). As the name implies, a Spanish restaurant – and it seems every large Swiss town has at least one. This has all the familiar favourites: a series of tapas, tortillas, paellas, meat and fish and shellfish, along with daily and summer specials.

Old Swiss House, Löwenplatz 4, t 041 410 61 71, f 041 410 17 38, www.oldswisshouse.ch (*expensive*). Next to the Lion Monument, in a beautiful house with a wood-partitioned façade that dates from 1859, this restaurant, full of antiques – many of which date from the 17th century – is a Luzern landmark. The house speciality, served by staff in original Luzern costumes, is a deluxe Wiener-schnitzel with veal escalopes dipped in a highly secret mixture of beaten egg, Swiss cheese and herbs. *Open 9am–12.30am.*

Helvetia, Waldstätterstrasse 9, t 041 210 44 50, f 041 210 44 60, www.helvetialuzern.ch (*moderate*). Another of the group of restaurants in this part of Luzern, slightly away from the tourist area. Its speciality is home-made pasta cooked daily, along with a fine selection of salads, vegetarian dishes and veal. For dessert they offer some unusual *tartes flambées*. Eat inside or on the square.

Taube, Burgerstrasse 3, t 041 210 07 47, f 041 210 97 47 (*moderate*). In a building over 500 years old that, in 1772, became a restaurant named the Pigeon (*Taube*). Up until 1998, when it reverted to the Pigeon name, it was known as the Pot of Valais (*Walliser Kanne*). These days it specializes in popular regional and seasonal dishes.

Chill's Food Engineering, Waldstätterstrasse 3, t/f 041 210 55 00, www.chills.ch (*moderate*). A delightful little restaurant which specializes in Thai and Asian cuisine. Look for starters like satay and wonton soup, with curries featuring as main dishes, and such things as fried bananas and coconut ice cream for dessert.

Rathaus Brauerei, Unter der Egg 2, t 041 410 52 27, f 041 410 59 57 (*moderate*). A very popular brewery pub right on the banks of the Reuss near the town hall. The usual food is available – salads, sausages, Bratwurst and French fries, along with filled pretzels, cold and vegetarian dishes. The beer is served in various sizes, including 2-litre bottles to take away.

Bourbaki, Löwenplatz 11, t 041 412 16 35, f 041 412 16 36 (*inexpensive*). A combination of modern restaurant, bar, bistro and takeaway that is located underneath the Bourbaki Panorama. It has a variety of daily specials, including a vegetarian menu, ranging from CHF 15 to CHF 21.

Fischerstube, Mühlenplatz 11, t 041 410 99 98 (*inexpensive*). This is a local, apparently working-class, pub, and the favourite of some rather unusual characters. More of a social experience than a gastronomic one.

Café Bar Salu, Am Helvetiagarten, t 041 210 67 77 (*inexpensive*). Another small place on this popular little square that specializes in home-made fresh soups, salads and sandwiches. Make your choices at the bar, and then take them to the outside tables.

Shine, Sempacherstrasse 16, t/f 041 211 26 26, www.shine-bar.ch (*inexpensive*). A delightful bar/café that has nice easy chairs and tables, even outside on the pavement. OK, the food may run in the main to small sandwiches etc., but you won't worry too much when you see the amazing drinks menu. Aperitifs, after and before dinner drinks, *digestifs*, sours, shots, spirits and wines and, of course, beer. And the cocktails are mind-blowing – literally.

Mahlzeit/Barock, Winkelriedstrasse 62, t 041 210 08 83 (*inexpensive*). Very small and a little out-of-the-way, but it offers very good deals on couscous, kebabs and falafel.

Entertainment and Nightlife

The **Grand Casino Luzern**, Haldenstrasse 6 (next to the Palace Hotel), t 041 418 56 56, f 041 418 56 55, www.casinoluzern.ch, open 12pm–4am, minimum age 20, CHF 10 adm from 4pm, has American roulette, blackjack, mini punto banco, stud poker, craps and slot machines, as well as a variety of bars and a restaurant.

Museum of Art Luzern). The connection with the Picasso Museum isn't superficial, either. Angela Rosengart, who was born in Luzern in 1932 and still lives here, started working with her father, an art dealer, at age 16 and eventually became a co-owner of the business in 1957. In 1978 she and her father donated seven paintings and a sculpture by Picasso to the city in honour of its 800th anniversary, and these became the foundation of the Picasso Museum, which has been substantially added to since. This museum, though, displays her own collection of over 200 important works by more than 20 world-famous 19th- and 20th-century masters, including Cézanne, Monet, Picasso, Matisse, Klee, Miró and many more.

Just a block or two north is an area with four more places of interest. The first of these is the **Luzern Theatre** (*Theaterstrasse 2*, **t** *041 210 33 63*, **f** *041 210 33 67*), close to the Chapel Bridge. Luzern has a long theatrical history, with Easter plays being regularly presented in the Weinmarkt as long ago as the 15th century. In later centuries these took place in the Jesuit Theatre, and in 1838–9 one of the first municipal theatres in Switzerland was built on this spot. In 1924 a fire caused much damage, and only the middle section of the façade facing the Reuss is original.

However, it is the tall, elegant, onion-domed façade of the **Jesuit Church** (*Bahnhofstrasse 11a*, **t** *041 210 07 56; open daily 6am–6.30pm*) that will attract your attention most. Constructed between 1666 and 1673 and considered to be the first sacred Baroque structure in Switzerland, it is said to be on the site of the first two collegiate churches in Luzern. The main spires are the creation of H. V. von Segesser and date from 1893. It has a rather complex interior design with a beautiful central ceiling painting of St Francis Xavier, a red marble stucco High Altar dating from 1681, and it has the vestments of the famous Swiss, Brother Klaus.

Directly to the west lies another church with a simpler façade, but a long history. The **Franciscan Church** (Franziskanerkirche; **t** *041 210 14 67*) dates from around 1270 and is considered to be the oldest building in Luzern. Of interest inside is the cycle of flags on the north nave wall and the fresco above the choir arch.

Between that and the river is a rather beautiful building that was modelled after the Renaissance palaces of Italian nobility. The **Ritter Palace** (Ritterscher Palast) dates from 1556–7 and is named after the person who began the construction, Mayor Lux Ritter. Originally, this belonged to the Jesuits, but since 1804 it has been utilized as a government building and is now the seat of the Luzern cantonal government. Its main hall was added in 1841–3, and the three-storied Tuscan patio is also of note.

A little farther along the river it is impossible not to notice the strange **Water Spikes** in the middle. Up until the middle of the 19th century the Reuss Steps channelled the water over the city mills. They were then replaced by these mechanical 'spikes', which are lowered by hand to regulate the water flow. These are connected to another wooden river crossing, the **Mill Bridge** (Spreuerbrücke), altogether less pristine than the Chapel Bridge. Completed in 1408, as part of the city's fortifications, it came by its name from the ruling that only chaffs of wheat were to be thrown into the river from this bridge. It is embellished by 67 paintings depicting the *Dance of Death*, which are the work, between 1626 and 1635, of Kaspar Meglinger, and a shrine stands in the middle of the bridge. Interestingly, neither this nor the Chapel Bridge were built to service pedestrian traffic but, rather, to close the gap over the water in the city's walled fortifications.

Before crossing the bridge, though, there are two museums to be explored nearby. The **Museum of National History** (Historichesmuseum; *Pfistergasse 24, t 041 228 54 24, www.hmluzern.ch; open Tues–Fri 10–12 and 2–5, Sat and Sun 10–5; adm*) is located in the old arsenal and has a wide and interesting range of exhibits detailing the history of Luzern and Switzerland, including a mail shirt of Duke Leopold III from 1386. The **Museum of Natural History** (Naturmuseum; *Kasernenplatz 6, t 041 228 54 11, f 041 228 54 06; open Tues–Sat 10–12 and 2–5, Sat and Sun 10–5; adm*) is a lively, hands-on museum with a variety of live animals and interactive displays.

Across the river, the impressive and remarkably well-preserved city walls of 860 yards (786m) now beckon – and their formidability is awesome. To get a closer perspective, walk away from the city and then ascend the steep steps by the closest, and quite small, tower. These take you behind the **Musegg Wall** (Museggmauer) where you will note, perhaps with some surprise, that the steep adjacent fields leading up to them are occupied by grazing cows. These walls were built between 1350 and 1408 as part of Luzern's medieval fortifications, and of the nine remaining **towers** (*turme*), six are quite different from each other. One of these towers, the **Zytturm**, is the proud host of the oldest clock in Luzern, visible from a great distance. The respect endowed upon it by the city is such that it is this clock's privilege to chime one minute before all the others. This, the Männli and Schirmer towers and some battlements are open to the public, but only in the summer from 8am to 7pm.

Towards the western end of the walls a memorial chapel and a fountain with a strange, water-emitting head greet you before a pathway, Schirmertoweg, leads under an archway, decorated with two lions and a shield, to the city side of the walls. A little farther to the east Löwenplatz, a strange traffic junction with a combination of old and new structures, is home to the **Bourbaki Panorama** (*Löwenstrasse 11, t 041 412 30 30, www.panorama-luzern.ch; open daily 9–6; adm*). This is the largest (1,315.6sq yards / 1,100sq m) round mural in the world and, painted by Edouard Castres, it depicts the retreat and internment of General Bourbaki's French Eastern Army at Les Verrières in Switzerland during the Franco-German War of 1870–1.

The predominance of tourist shops in what is a less than inspiring area of Luzern signal the presence of three most unusual attractions. The **Lion Monument** (Löwendenkmal) was designed by the classicist Danish sculptor, Thorvaldsen, and was carved in 1820–1 from natural sandstone indigenous to this area by a stone-mason from Constance, Ahorn (1789–1856). In addition to agriculture and town crafts, mercenary military service was an important and gainful trade during the era of the old Confederation and, at the beginning of the French Revolution in 1789, about 40,000 Swiss were serving under foreign banners. The Lion Monument is dedicated to the Swiss mercenaries who were either killed during the invasion of the Tuileries in Paris, seat of Louis XIV, on 10 August 1792 or executed by guillotine on 2 and 3 September 1792 for their part in that heroic but unsuccessful revolt. The inscription *helvitorium fidei ac virtuiti* means, 'to the loyalty and bravery of the Swiss'. Measuring

6.6yds (6m) high by 10.9yds (10m) long, it was dedicated on 10 August 1821 and purchased by the town of Luzern in 1882.

Almost next door, the **Glacier Garden** (Gletschgarten; *Denkmalstrasse 4, t 041 410 43 40, f 041 410 43 10, www.glaciergarden.org; open daily April–Oct 9–6; Nov–Mar 10–5; adm*), discovered in 1872, is one of the oldest of natural wonders. Gigantic potholes and rocks carved in the strangest of shapes by the Ice Age, 10,000 years ago, co-exist with fossilized remains from over 20,000,000 years ago when Luzern was a sub-tropical palm beach. Also to be seen on display are the oldest relief map of Switzerland, a historical model of Luzern, a variety of other geological exhibits and, incongruously, a Hall of Mirrors based on a juxtaposition of aspects of the Alhambra in Granada, Spain.

The last of the three attractions is the **Alpineum–3D-Panorama of the Alps** (Alpineum-3D-Alpen-Panorama; *Denkmalstrasse 11, t 041 410 62 66, f 041 410 40 64, www.alpineum.ch; open daily April–Oct 9–12.30 and 1.30–6; adm*). Although most visitors will have seen or will be seeing the Alps for real themselves, this large and panoramic painting from around 1900 gives a surreal 3D glimpse of Switzerland's most famous peaks.

Back down towards the lake front, you can't miss the imposing façade of the **Hof Church** (Hofkirche). A Benedictine monastery was founded here, with the earliest reference being the year 735, and subsequently a collegiate Romanesque church dedicated to St Leodegar and Mauritius was constructed around 1345. However, a fire destroyed most of that in 1633 and only the two distinguished spires – dating from 1504 and 1625 – survived and were incorporated into the new late Renaissance church that was built in 1634–9. In fact, it is the only religious building of late Renaissance times in Switzerland. There is a *Mount of Olives* painting, with late Gothic figures, in a niche on the north tower, and the interior is ornately decorated.

The Old Town itself is not very large, but there is still plenty to see and do. Plenty of shops, too, are situated in this attractive area of compact plazas and brilliantly painted façades. Three squares are of particular note: the **Weinmarkt** is where the citizens of Luzern swore a federal oath with the cantons of Uri, Schwyz and Unterwalden; the **Hirschenplatz** is named after a medieval inn; and the main features of the **Kornmarkt** are the prettily painted Pfistern guildhall and the **Rathaus** (town hall). The latter was built in 1602–6 in the Italian Renaissance style, and has a Bern farmhouse roof; the open façade facing the Reuss still serves today as a weekly marketplace. Right next door in one of the city's most beautiful buildings, the Am-Rhyn house, is the **Picasso Museum** (*Furrengasse 21, t 041 410 35 33; open daily April–Oct 10–6, Nov–Mar 11–1 and 2–4; adm*), containing important works created by the artist in his last twenty years, plus an exhibition of over 200 photos of Picasso by David Douglas Duncan.

Of course, the main attraction in Luzern is the wooden, covered **Chapel Bridge** (Kapellbrücke). Named after the nearby St Peter's Chapel, it was built in the early 14th century as part of the city's fortifications. Take time to admire the unusual paintings that adorn its gabled roof. Dating from the 17th century, they are the creations of

Heinrich Wägmann, and depict representations of Swiss and local history, including the martyrdom of Luzern's two patron saints, Mauritius and Leodegar. Hans Rudolf von Sonnenberg and Renward Cysat wrote the accompanying verses. The **Water Tower** (Wasserturm), dating from the beginning of the 14th century and situated about two-thirds of the way across the bridge, is a formidable 111.5ft/34m-tall octagonal stone tower that was originally part of the city wall. Subsequently utilized as an archive, treasury, prison and torture chamber, these days the base – as might be expected – houses a tourist shop. It is also used as the Guildhall of the Artillery Association. The water tower and the bridge have long been the most photographed monuments in Switzerland. However, being made of wood, the bridge has always been susceptible to the danger of fire. And, tragically, that danger materialized in the early hours of 18 August 1993 when a fire destroyed two-thirds of the bridge and 65 of the 111 gable paintings. Sadly, only 30 of the paintings could be restored, though facsimiles supplied by Ilford, the camera/film maker, and made on fadeless Ilfachrome Classic Deluxe materials have temporarily replaced the originals. The substructure of the bridge was undamaged, however, enabling it to be rebuilt and reopened to the public on 14 April 1994.

Outside Town

There are two more attractions to be found just outside the centre of Luzern, one on the north side of the lake and the other on the south side.

As the one on the north side is closer, and being far more multi-faceted is likely to be of more interest, start with the **Swiss Museum of Transport and Communication** (Verkehrshaus der Schweiz; *Lidostrasse 5, t 041 370 44 44, f 041 375 75 00, www.verkehrs haus.org; open April–Oct 10–6; Nov–Mar 10–5; adm exp; combined adm available with IMAX cinema*). Opened in 1959, this has evolved into the most diverse museum of its kind in Europe, its exhibitions and collections all related to the development and significance of transport and communication – as well as other attractions. It's a fascinating place, with a varied collection of planes, boats and trains as well as cars, model ships, engines, a space station and even a horse-drawn coach that used to operate as the Grimsel Pass mail coach. The **Planetarium** was opened in 1969 by the astronaut John H. Glenn via the Early Bird news satellite, and over 6.7 million visitors have attended shows since then. The **IMAX Filmtheater** has a 82ft x 62ft (25m x 19m) screen – the largest in Switzerland – and uses a 2.75in (70mm) film format; the sound blasts out with 22,000 watt power. The last part of this fascinating museum is perhaps the most unexpected, the **Hans Erni Museum**. Erni, born in 1909, is Switzerland's most popular artist, and made his name in 1939 when he painted *Switzerland, Holiday Land of Nations*, which was exhibited at that year's national exhibition. A dedicated humanist, he has over 300 of his varied works – paintings, graphic art and sculptures – displayed here, with the most prominent being the *Panta Rhei*, a 860sq ft (80sq m) mural in the Auditorium.

Richard Wagner had been to Luzern several times before, but it was in 1866 that he and his then partner Cosima von Bülow (she was at that time still married to the

Excursions from Luzern

Destination	Journey Time (hours.mins)	Recommended Length of Trip	Connections
Zürich	0.47	D/T – O/N – M/N	T
Engelberg	0.58	D/T – O/N	T
Basel	1.14	D/T – O/N – M/N	T
Solothurn	1.14	D/T	T/T
Rapperswil	1.15	D/T	T
Bern	1.21	D/T – O/N – M/N	T/T
Brienz	1.35	D/T	T
Schaffhausen and Rhine Falls	1.40	D/T	T/T
Neuchâtel	1.57	D/T	T/T
Thun	1.59	D/T	T/T
Interlaken	2.03	D/T	T/T
St Gallen	2.06	D/T	T/T
Stein am Rhein	2.14	D/T	T/T/T
Vaduz, Liechtenstein	2.25	D/T – O/N	T/T/B
Grindelwald (2)	2.35	M/N	T/T
Lausanne	2.37	D/T – O/N	T
Lugano	2.39	D/T – O/N – M/N	T
Wengen (2)	2.40	M/N	T/T/T
Ascona	2.56	O/N – M/N	T/T/B
Mürren and Schilthorn 007	2.56	M/N	T/T/F/T
Montreux and Vevey	3.01	D/T	T/T
Lötschental	3.07	O/N – M/N	T/T/T/B
Centovalli	3.09	D/T – O/N	T/T/T
Gruyères	3.15	D/T	T/B/T/B
Geneva	3.18	D/T – O/N – M/N	T/T/T
Scuol	3.43	O/N – M/N	T/T/T
Sion	3.48	D/T	T/T
Leukerbad	4.16	O/N – M/N	T/T/T/T/B
Les Diablerets	4.23	D/T – O/N	T/T/T
Saas-Fee	4.26	M/N	T/T/T/B
Crans Montana	4.33	D/T – O/N	T/T/T/T/B
Zermatt	4.46	M/N	T/T/T/T
Nauders, Austria	4.46	O/N – M/N	T/T/T/B
Val d'Anniviers	5.20	O/N – M/N	T/T/T/B/B

(1) The starting point for the Pilatus trip.
(2) The starting points for the Jungfraujoch and Männlichen trips.
T: train; B: bus; F: funicular.
D/T: day trip; O/N: overnighter; M/N: multi-nighter.
Journey time is one-way, and the minimum possible. See **Introduction**, p.7.

conductor and pianist Hans von Bülow) discovered a charming, although rundown, villa at Tribschen, a headland on the lake southeast of town. After renovating it, they moved in and stayed until 1872, a period he considered the happiest of his life. During these years not only did he complete *Meistersinger* and *Siegfried* and begin composing *Götterdämmerung*, but *Siegfried Idyll* was first performed as a present to Cosima – by then his wife – on the birth of their son, Siegfried. These days it is home to the **Richard Wagner Museum** (*Wagnerwegg 27, t 041 360 23 70; open mid-Mar–Nov Tues–Sun 10–12 and 2–5; adm; no. 6 or 8 bus to the Wartegg stop or by boat in summer from the Bahnhofquai*). Here you will find original manuscripts, scores and paintings as well as other exhibits, and on the upper floor there is a historic collection of rare wind and stringed instruments gathered by Henry Schumacher in the 19th century.

Sion

Sion (Sitten in German) is an impressive sight. In the centre of the wide Rhône valley, it sits at the foot of two isolated, castle-topped hills surrounded on both sides – and for long distances – by majestic snow-capped mountains whose lower slopes are covered with vineyards, producing the fine wines that are one of the area's claims to fame.

These wines, and an interesting history, make Sion an attractive proposition in its own right. However, in the winter time the town is also important as a gateway to the majestic winter sports resorts of the Valais, such as Crans-Montana, Saas-Fee and Zermatt (*see* 'Valais', p.189).

History

After Julius Caesar's campaign, the citizens of *Sedunum* – both locals and Romans – lived at the foot of the twin towers, Valère and Tourbillon. The fledgling city underwent several changes of status, and in 377 was home to the first Christian inscription in Switzerland – praising the magistrate Asclepidotes for replacing an imperial building by an even more sumptuous one. On the main route to Italy, the city remained prosperous until the Barbarian invasions, which caused the bishop of canton Valais to move from Martigny (*Octodurum*) to Sion in 580. King Rudolph III provided the bishops with a regular subsidy from 999, and early in the following century, in 1032, Sion became the Imperial City, with the bishop ruling over the whole of the canton of Valais from Martigny to the Furka. This was reinforced early in the 12th century with the construction of the church of Valère.

However, the proximity and overlapping of territory of the Counts of Savoy – the rulers of the Lower Valais – led to more than one war. Finally, in 1475, after having been overrun by the Savoyards, federal troops retook Sion after the Battle of La Planta, thus reuniting the Valais with Sion as its political and geographical capital. From then until the late 1700s the powers of the bishops were relentlessly watered down in favour of civil power, with the brief exception of 1516–22 when Bishop Mathew Schiner was

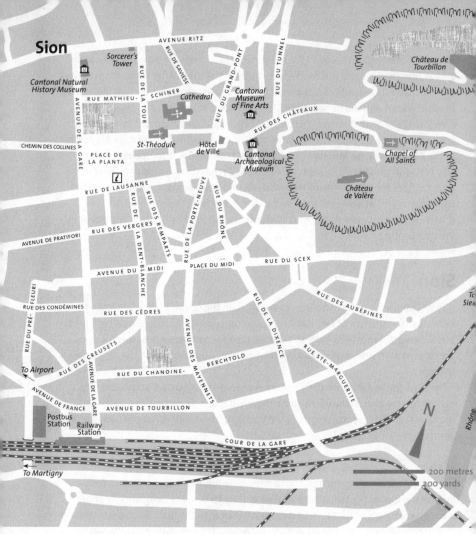

Sion

- AVENUE RITZ
- Sorcerer's Tower
- Cantonal Natural History Museum
- RUE DE SAVIÈSE
- RUE DE LA TOUR
- SCHINER
- RUE MATHIEU-
- Cathedral
- RUE DU GRAND-PONT
- RUE DU TUNNEL
- Château de Tourbillon
- Cantonal Museum of Fine Arts
- RUE DES CHÂTEAUX
- AVENUE DE LA GARE
- CHEMIN DES COLLINES
- St-Théodule
- PLACE DE LA PLANTA
- Hôtel de Ville
- Cantonal Archaeological Museum
- Chapel of All Saints
- Château de Valère
- RUE DE LAUSANNE
- RUE DE
- RUE DES REMPARTS
- RUE DE LA PORTE-NEUVE
- RUE DU RHÔNE
- AVENUE DE PRATIFORI
- RUE DES VERGERS
- RUE DE LA DENT-BLANCHE
- AVENUE DU MIDI
- PLACE DU MIDI
- RUE DU SCEX
- RUE DU PRÉ-FLEURI
- RUE DES CONDÉMINES
- RUE DES CÈDRES
- AVENUE DES MAYENNETS
- RUE DE LA DIXENCE
- RUE DES AUBÉPINES
- To Sie
- RUE DES CREUSETS
- AVENUE DE LA GARE
- RUE DU CHANOINE-
- BERCHTOLD
- RUE STE-MARGUERITE
- To Airport
- AVENUE DE FRANCE
- AVENUE DE TOURBILLON
- Postbus Station
- Railway Station
- COUR DE LA GARE
- Rhône
- To Martigny
- N
- 200 metres
- 200 yards

promoted to Cardinal. However, in 1780 and to great joy, the Valais renewed its alliance with the seven Catholic cantons and the citizens of the Lower Valais claimed Sion and demanded equal rights. Napoleon, seizing upon this and wanting to keep the access to Italy under his control, annexed Valais to France as the 'Simplon Department', and Sion became a prefecture with a mayor.

The emperor was defeated in 1815 when the valley of the Rhône joined the Swiss Confederation, but the Lower Valais claimed its own political rights, with Sion becoming the capital of the French-speaking district and Sierre the capital of the German-speaking people. Nevertheless, problems continued with the Upper Valais being defeated in a civil war in 1840 and a new constitution making Sion the capital. However, the people of the Upper Valais had their revenge, occupying Sion in 1844 – albeit only for three years.

Around the Town

The twin hillsides of Valère and Tourbillon dominate Sion and are therefore the ideal place to start, although it has to be said it is a long hard walk up to them. The avenue des Châteaux – with its fine but much decayed houses – ends at a car park between them, where the Romanesque/Gothic **Chapel of All Saints** (Chapelle de Tous-les-Saints), originally built by Canon Thomas de Blandrate in 1325 but restored in 1964, is worth a visit. The **Château de Valère** (*t 027 606 47 15*), to the south, is actually the better preserved and is home to two separate entities, a church and a museum. The **Valère Church** (*open June–Sept Mon–Sat 10–6, Sun 2–6; Oct–May Tues–Sat 10–5, Sun 2–5; guided tours mid-Mar–mid-Nov at 10.15, 11.15, 12.15, 2.15, 3.15, 4.15 and 5.15; adm, also combined adm with museum*) is the most interesting. It has two distinct architectural styles: Romanesque from the 12th century and Gothic from the 13th century. In the former you will find capitals decorated with the teratological language of that era. Of note in the latter are the painted tomb of Guillaume de Rarogne, bishop from 1437 to 1451; important 15th- and 16th-century frescoes; and a rare 14th-century organ, unique in that it is painted on both sides and is the oldest playable one in the world. The **Cantonal Historical Museum** (Musée Cantonal d'Histoire; *open daily June–Sept 11–6, Oct–May Tues–Sun 11–5; adm*) is one of the most important of its genre in Switzerland. Its most important exhibits are the objects from the excavations of Roman *Octodurum* in Martigny, including the head of a Mithraic bull, and medieval collections featuring a liturgical chest and sculptures.

Another steep climb up the opposite, northern hill brings you to the ruins of the **Château de Tourbillon** (*t 027 606 47 45; open mid-Mar–mid-Nov Tues–Sun 10–6; free*). Originally built by Bishop Boniface de Challant between 1290 and 1308, it was almost completely destroyed by the Patriots of Valais in 1461. The Bishop of Raron, Guillaume VI, rebuilt it in 1477, but a major fire destroyed it once more in 1788.

Back westwards down the hill there are two more museums. The **Cantonal Museum of Fine Arts** (Musée Cantonal des Beaux-Arts; *place de la Majorie 15, t 027 606 46 90; open Tues–Sun June–Sept 1–6; Oct–May 1–5; adm*) is located in two wonderful old houses. The exhibits here are devoted to local and national art from the 17th century to date, with representations of Baroque, romantic and primitivist work and also abstract, kinetic and minimalist works by the likes of Dubuis, Duarte and Zuber. Just to its south is the **Cantonal Archaeological Museum** (Musée Cantonal d'Archéologie; *rue des Châteaux 12, t 027 606 47 00; open Tues–Sun June–Sept 1–6; Oct–May 1–5; adm*). Here you will find extensive collections documenting the occupation of the Valais from 30,000 BC to the end of the Roman era in the 5th century, and important objects from the Bronze Age.

All of the remaining attractions in Sion are found within a small area bounded by the rue du Grand-Pont (to the east), avenue Ritz (to the north), avenue de la Gare (to the west) and rue de Lausanne (to the south).

The **Hôtel de Ville** (town hall; *Grand-Pont 12*) has a façade dating from 1660 that is adorned by an astronomical clock. Inside, in the entrance hall, is the earliest Christian inscription in Switzerland that dates from 377 and praises the munificence of the

Getting There

Although Sion has an **airport**, *see* below, there is a severely restricted service. In fact, this exists only during the winter sports season when there is a single weekly flight from the UK, and also a service to and from Zürich. The nearest major airports are at Geneva, Zürich and Basel and, respectively, they are 1 hour 24 minutes, 3 hours 27 minutes and 3 hours 34 minutes away.

Because of its location in the relatively isolated Valais region in the south of the country, **train** connections (except for most of the west and north of Switzerland) can be rather difficult.

Getting from the Airport

Sion Airport, **t** 027 329 06 00, **f** 027 329 06 16, *www.sionairport.ch*, is located just to the west of the city.

There is an irregular bus service, one each way every 30 to 50mins depending upon the time of day, for CHF 3; a taxi costs around CHF 20.

Tourist Information

Sion: Sion Tourisme, place de la Planta, **t** 027 327 77 27, **f** 027 327 77 28, *www. siontourism. ch (open mid-July–end Aug Mon– Fri 8.30–6, Sat 10–4; rest of the year Mon–Fri 8.30–12 and 2–5.30, Sat 9–12)*.

Guided Tours

The tourist office, on Tues and Thurs between mid-July and end Aug, organizes a tour of the **Old Town, Castle of Valère and wine tasting**. It departs from the tourist office at 9am, lasts 2½hrs and costs CHF 15.

Le P'tit Sédunois, **t** 027 327 34 34, *www.sion.ch*, is one of those little 'trains' offering round trips in the city, Mon–Sat, from the train station via the tourist office to Valère and back, for a fare of CHF 3.

Alpine Tours, Aéroport de Sion, **t/f** 027 323 57 07, *www.gvmsion.ch*, offer, for those who don't mind light aircraft, a choice of six different tours, lasting from 30 to 120mins, that will take you up to and around all the major peaks from the Mont Blanc to the Matterhorn and Eiger. Fares range from CHF 164–542 for two passengers and CHF 206–710 for three passengers.

Where to Stay

Sion

★★★★Europa, rue de l'Envol 19, **t** 027 322 24 23, **f** 027 322 25 35, *www.zghotels.ch (moderate)*. This, the largest hotel in Sion with 65 contemporary rooms, is located on the west side of town towards the airport. It also has 10 'Business Suites' with a small office and fax and modem points. Ask for special airport prices.

magistrate Asclepidotes. Upstairs, behind magnificently wooden carved doors, the Salle de la Bourgeoisie has equally wonderfully carved panels and portraits of two great rivals: George Supersaxo, champion of the French party, and Mathew Schiner, the bishop and cardinal who championed the Empire.

Across the road is another Supersaxo connection, in the form of the **House of Supersaxo** (Maison Supersaxo; *passage Supersaxo*), dating from 1505, which features a Gothic staircase, carved doors and a beautiful carved and painted ceiling by Jacobinus de Malacridis. In this immediate area there are also several other Baroque or classical homes of old aristocratic families. One of the most important, on rue de Lausanne, is the Kalbermatten House – known as 'The Prefecture' – that was the house of the French Ambassador, Chateaubriand.

You will also come across two churches next to each other, the most important being **Sion Cathedral** (Notre-Dame du Glarier; *Cathédrale 13*, **t** 027 322 80 66), whose

★★★**Hôtel du Castel**, Scex 38, **t** 027 322 91 71, **f** 027 322 57 24, *hotelcastel@netplus.ch* (*inexpensive*). Located in a modern block, almost directly under the Valère hill, this has comfortable, well-equipped rooms.

★★★**Hôtel du Rhône**, Scex 10, **t** 027 322 82 91, **f** 027 323 11 88, *www.bestwestern.ch/ durhô-nesion* (*inexpensive*). With 37 doubles and 8 singles – 15 of which are non-smoking; located just outside the Old Town area.

★★**Elite**, avenue du Midi 6, **t** 027 322 03 27, **f** 027 322 23 61, *hotelelite.sion@bluewin.ch* (*inexpensive*). With just 29 rooms, this is the most centrally located hotel in Sion, a few mins from the train/bus stations and the sights.

★★**IBIS**, avenue Grand-Champsec 21, **t** 027 205 71 00, **f** 027 205 71 71, *www.ibishotel.com* (*cheap*). Located somewhat away from the city centre, to the west across the Rhône, this has 71 rooms in the typical IBIS style that offers comfort at a good price.

Auberge de Jeunesse, rue de l'Industrie 2, **t** 027 323 74 70, **f** 027 323 74 38, *www.youthhostel.ch* (*cheap*). Just south of the railway station, this has 20 rooms (some with disabled facilities) each with 2, 3 or 4 beds, with toilets, showers and washrooms on each floor. Also a garden terrace, and billiards, table tennis and table football.

Sierre

★★★**Atlantic**, route de Sion 38, **t** 027 455 25 35, **f** 027 456 16 94, (*inexpensive*). As there isn't much of a selection of hotels in Sion itself, this hotel, just a few miles to the east, is a very good alternative. Besides 37 rooms with modern facilities, it offers a very fine restaurant (with a fantastic shrimp dish) and a large garden with an oversize swimming pool that is overlooked by vineyards.

Eating Out

Le Jardin Gourmand, avenue de la Gare 22, **t** 027 323 23 10, **f** 027 323 23 21 (*very expensive*). An elegant restaurant with a terrace in the city centre. It offers imaginative cuisine and its speciality is the 'Tête à Tête' menu featuring 6 courses and costing CHF 89. It also has other set menus for two people, and an interesting mix on the main menu.

Grotto de La Fontaine, Grand-Pont 21, **t** 027 323 83 77 (*moderate*). A charming, informal – expect long marble tables – restaurant whose specialities are dishes from Ticino and northern Italy: from traditional pizzas to dishes featuring white truffles, quail, rabbit and pigeon ravioli.

La Bergère, avenue de la Gare 30, **t** 027 322 14 81, **f** 027 322 14 36, *www.labergere.com* (*inexpensive*). An informal type of place with much wood in evidence. A pizzeria that serves pizzas, salads, meats, fondues and Valais specialities such as *rösti* and dried meats. Nicely priced daily specials, too.

Romanesque tower indicates that it was started in the first half of the 12th century. However, wars in succeeding centuries meant that it was completed in the late Gothic style by the bishops Supersaxo, Jost de Silenen and Nicholas Schiner between 1457 and 1522. The other church, **St Théodule** (Eglise St-Théodule; *rue St-Théodule 14*), dedicated to the patron saint of the Valais, dates from 1514–16 and was constructed by the Master sculptor Ulrich Ruffiner under the patronage of Mathew Schiner.

The last two attractions are situated in the northwest of this quadrant. The **Cantonal Natural History Museum** (Musée Cantonal d'Histoire Naturelle; *avenue de la Gare 42*, **t** *027 606 47 30; open Tues–Sun June–Sept 1–6; Oct–May 1–5; adm*) exhibits, amongst other things, the last specimens of important species like the bear, wolf and bearded vulture that once inhabited the area. The **Sorcerer's Tower** (Tour des Sorciers; *rue de la Tour*, **t** *027 606 47 35*) is now all that is left of the walls that once encircled the city.

Excursions from Sion

Destination	Journey Time (hours.mins)	Recommended Length of Trip	Connections
Montreux and Vevey	0.39	D/T	T
Crans Montana	0.43	D/T – O/N	B
Lausanne	1.01	D/T – O/N	T
Leukerbad	1.04	O/N – M/N	T/B
Val d'Anniviers	1.19	O/N – M/N	T/B/B
Les Diablerets	1.21	D/T – O/N	T/T
Lötschental	1.25	O/N – M/N	T/T/B
Saas-Fee	1.33	M/N	T/B
Zermatt	1.41	M/N	T/T
Geneva	1.43	D/T – O/N – M/N	T
Neuchâtel	1.53	D/T	T/T
Thun	2.07	D/T	T/T
Bern	2.14	D/T – O/N – M/N	T/T
Interlaken	2.15	D/T	T/T/T
Solothurn	2.34	D/T	T/T
Centovalli	2.39	D/T – O/N	T/T/T
Brienz	2.49	D/T	T/T/T/T
Gruyères	2.58	D/T	T/B/T/B
Grindelwald (2)	3.00	M/N	T/T/T/T
Wengen (2)	3.05	M/N	T/T/T/T/T
Basel	3.21	D/T – O/N – M/N	T/T/T
Ascona	3.21	O/N – M/N	T/T/B
Mürren and Schilthorn 007	3.21	M/N	T/T/T/T/F/T
Zürich	3.27	D/T – O/N – M/N	T/T
Luzern (1)	3.49	D/T	T/T
Lugano	3.54	D/T – O/N – M/N	T/T/T/T
Rapperswil	4.23	D/T	T/T/T
Schaffhausen and Rhine Falls	4.36	D/T	T/T/T
St Gallen	4.54	D/T	T/T
Engelberg	4.58	D/T – O/N	T/T/T
Stein am Rhein	5.00	D/T	T/T/T
Vaduz, Liechtenstein	5.46	D/T – O/N	T/T/T/B
Scuol	7.04	O/N – M/N	T/T/T/T
Nauders, Austria	8.07	O/N – M/N	T/T/T/T/B

(1) The starting point for the Pilatus trip.
(2) The starting points for the Jungfraujoch and Männlichen trips.
T: train; B: bus; F: funicular.
D/T: day trip; O/N: overnighter; M/N: multi-nighter.
Journey time is one-way, and the minimum possible. See **Introduction**, p.7.

Day Trips, Overnighters and Multi-nighters

The Bernese Oberland

Interlaken

As the name implies, Interlaken lies between two lakes, Brienz and Thun, at an altitude of 1,870ft (570m) above sea level. As the natural gateway to the famous trio of mountains – the Eiger, Mönch and Jungfrau – and the pretty villages of Grindelwald, Wengen and Mürren, the town grew rapidly during the last century to meet tourists' demands. The luxury accommodation of large and gracious hotels and the diversion of the casino and other attractions have transformed Interlaken into a celebrated resort. Today, with a population of less than 20,000, it is still far and away the largest town in the area.

The area closest to Interlaken West station is busy and full of souvenir shops, restaurants and bars. On the way to Interlaken Ost (East), by the Victoria-Jungfrau Grand Hotel and Spa, there is much more parkland and open space, and the hotels and buildings become larger and grander. Besides shopping there is not too much else to do in Interlaken, as for most people it will be just a stopping-off point for other destinations.

Mystery Park (*t 033 827 57 57, f 033 827 57 58, www.mysterypark.ch; open daily 10–6; adm exp*) opened early in 2003 and is Interlaken's newest and most unusual attraction. It is located just outside the town centre, and a free shuttle bus takes you there from Interlaken Ost train station. This is a theme park, but a serious one that appeals to all ages; it has seven pavilions exploring the mysteries of the Vimanas Ancient Indians, the Orient, the Maya, Megastones culture, the Nazca Plains of Peru and the challenging question of whether we live alone in the universe.

Jungfraubahnen Pass

Available from 1 May until 31 October from hotels, local travel agencies, tourist offices or train stations of the participating transportation companies, this pass is a necessity for those planning to spend five days in the region between Interlaken, Grindelwald, Mürren and Wengen.

It allows five days of unlimited travel on the following services: AVG, the Grindelwaldbus; BGF, the cable car between Grindelwald and First; BLM, between Lauterbrunnen and Mürren via the funicular to Grütschalp; BOB, from Interlaken Ost to either Lauterbrunnen or Grindelwald; GGM, the gondola car between Grindelwald and Männlichen; HB, from Interlaken to Harder Kulm; LGP, Grindelwald to Pfingstegg; LWM, the cable car between Wengen and Männlichen; SPB, Wilderswil to Schynige Platte; WAB, from either Grindelwald or Lauterbrunnen to Kleine Scheidegg; and the JB, from Kleine Scheidegg to the Eigergletscher station. Very importantly, it also gives you a special rate of CHF 49.50 for the spectacular Eigergletscher to Jungfraujoch trip.

The Jungfraubahnen Pass costs CHF 165; or CHF 120 in conjunction with a Swiss Pass, Swiss Card, children of 6–15, and the Half Fare Card.

William Tell Open Air Theatre (Tell-Freilichtspiele; *Höheweg 37, t 033 822 37 22, f 033 822 57 33, www.tellspiele.ch; tickets CHF 22, CHF 30 and CHF 38*). Friedrich Schiller's William Tell has been performed in the Rugen Woods, very close to Interlaken, every summer since 1912. Set 700 years ago, in an era during which Switzerland was under the tyrannical rule of Austria, it tells of the Swiss people's hardship and suffering and their heroic struggle for freedom. Over 250 actors, dressed in national costume, re-enact the story against a background of authentic 13th-century wooden houses and towering trees. It is performed primarily on Fridays and Saturdays between the end of June and beginning of September, and seats are covered.

Harder Kulm Restaurant sits at an altitude of 4,337ft (1,322m) on the forested mountain behind Interlaken. You can get there in 10 minutes on the rather unusual small red carriage of the Harder Railway, from the valley station opposite Interlaken Ost train station. Opened in 1908, it is actually a funicular which was constructed along a mile-long winding route in order to preserve the integrity of the landscape. There is a human-interest story here as well. Two local women, unbeknownst to their husbands, responded when the landlord, Jungfrau Railways, solicited applicants for the restaurant tenancy. What Rosemarie Feuz and Hilde Zurbrügg started as a bit of a joke has now, with much encouragement and support from the railway, become a resounding success. It is now somewhat of a tradition for the locals to meet there for Sunday morning breakfast, but visitors will enjoy it any time – especially for its breathtaking views across the lakes and over the entire Jungfrau region. An added attraction is the Alpine Wildlife Park with its resident ibex.

To visit the **St Beatus Caves** (Beatushöhlen-Genossenschaft; *t 033 841 16 43, f 033 841 10 64, www.beatushoehlen.ch; open daily mid-April–mid-Oct 10.30–5 with 50min tours every 30mins; adm exp*), take the BLS steamer from Interlaken West along the north side of Lake Thun to either Sundlauenen or Beatenbucht. Thousands of years ago cave

Tourist Information

Interlaken: Interlaken Tourismus, Höheweg 37 (the Metropole Hotel building), **t** 033 826 53 00, **f** 033 826 53 75, *www.interlakentourism. ch* (*open July–mid-Sept Mon–Fri 8–6.30, Sat 8–5, Sun 10–12 and 5–7; mid-Sept–end Sept Mon–Fri 8–6.30, Sat 9–2; May, June and Oct Mon–Fri 8–6, Sat 9–12; Nov–April Mon–Fri 8–12 and 1.30–6, Sat 9–12*).

Where to Stay

*****Victoria-Jungfrau Grand Hotel and Spa, Höheweg 41, **t** 033 828 28 28, **f** 033 828 28 80, *www.victoria-jungfrau.ch* (*luxury*). A very grand, traditional hotel. The 212 rooms and suites have every modern facility and a classically elegant decor. In the spa you will find a fully equipped health, fitness and beauty centre with whirlpools, steam bath, saunas, massage, gymnastic centre and a wonderful Art Deco pool area. La Terrasse is a gourmet restaurant of some class and the Jungfrau-Stube is a more informal restaurant. There is also a selection of bars and a nightclub.

****Stella, General Guisanstrasse 10, **t** 033 822 88 71, **f** 033 822 86 71, *www.stella-hotel.ch* (*expensive*). The smallest 4-star hotel in Interlaken, this only has 30 rooms but they, and the public areas, have plenty of style. It also offers the very fine Stellambiente restaurant and an indoor pool.

***Metropole, Höheweg 37, **t** 033 828 66 66, **f** 033 828 66 33, *www.metropole-interlaken. ch* (*expensive*). A large, 95-room, tower-block hotel in the centre of town. The rooms are modern, and some have a south-facing balcony with views of the Jungfrau. Guests enjoy the use of an indoor swimming pool, sauna, solarium, indoor shopping arcade, banking facilities and tourist information office. On the 18th floor is the Top o' Met restaurant with panoramic views.

Post Hardermannli, Hauptstrasse 18, **t** 033 822 89 19, **f** 033 822 00 28, *www.post-harder mannli.ch* (*moderate*). Run by the same family for 30 years, this beautiful, 125-year-old chalet has recently been extensively renovated. The 24 rooms have old-fashioned charm and many have spectacular views of the Alps. Decorated with antiques, farming instruments and prize-winning cow bells.

Backpackers Villa Sonnenhof, Alpenstrasse 16, **t** 033 826 71 71, **f** 033 826 71 72, *www.villa.ch* (*cheap*). This has double, triple and quad rooms, with or without en suite toilets and south-facing balconies, and dormitories.

Eating Out

Bebbis, Bahnhofstrasse 16, **t** 033 821 14 44, **f** 033 821 14 46, *www.bebbis.ch*. A fun restaurant decorated in Swiss chalet style and with a cuisine to match. Live entertainers, too.

dwellers inhabited this area, and you can gain an insight into their lifestyle by visiting this well-presented reconstruction of a prehistoric settlement. What those first settlers called this place no one knows, but the present name was derived more recently – in the 6th century – when, legend has it, an Irish missionary, Beatus, made his home at the entrance to these underground chambers. He reportedly exorcized a dragon from the caves, and preached Christianity to the local heathen population. Visitors venture to a depth of 3,609ft (1,000m) through just a portion of the 5 miles (8.1km) of known paths and trails that wind through numerous caverns and grottos, passing lakes, waterfalls and weirdly wonderful stalactites and stalagmites.

Schynige Platte can be reached on the Schynige Platte Railway SPB trains departing from Wilderswil, one stop from Interlaken Ost on the Berner Oberland Bahnen BOB. This is a curious trip into the high alpine pastures, where you will find such diverse attractions as the **Botanical Alpine Garden** (Alpengarten Schynige Platte; **t** 033 822 28 35, **f** 033 822 28 00, *www.alpengarten.ch; open June–Sept daily 8.30–6; adm*), with over 600 species of alpine flora from above the treeline in their natural habitat; **Teddyland**, where all kinds of teddy bears are displayed in fairytale environments; and the **Lowa Hiking Boot Test Centre** where you can choose from over 200 pairs of boots and test them free of charge for the day.

Jungfraujoch, *see* p.136, and **Grindelwald** or **Wengen**, *see* below and p.135, are reached on Berner Oberland Bahnen BOB trains from Interlaken Ost via either Grindelwald or Lauterbrunnen and Wengen to Kleine Scheidegg.

Schilthorn 007, *see* Mürren, p.139, is reached first by a Berner Oberland Bahnen BOB train from Interlaken Ost to Lauterbrunnen, then take the Post Bus from Lauterbrunnen to Stechelberg and the Schilthornbahn cable car via Mürren.

Brienz and **Thun**, *see* pp.141 and 143, can be reached on a BLS Schifffahrt Thuner– und Brienzersee lake steamer (*t 033 334 52 11, f 033 334 52 12, www.bls.ch*) on the respective lakes.

Grindelwald

The first written mention of Grindelwald is on a document dating from 1146. At that time, King Konrad promised his protection to the Augustine monastery (Augustinerkloster) in Interlaken, which also owned property in Grindelwald. The monks' greed for more and more land occasioned periodic revolts by the citizens of Grindelwald, a conflict that continued until the Reformation in 1528, when the Interlaken monastery was abolished. Thinking that it would augment their independence, the people of Grindelwald allied themselves with the Bernese government – but only on condition that they would not be taxed. The Bernese, however, knew that the monastery was wealthy and didn't want to relinquish this source of revenue. The population of Grindelwald rebelled against this breach of faith, dismissed their Protestant pastor and, in 1528, re-instituted the old faith. Enraged, in their turn, the Bernese dispatched an expedition to Grindelwald that devastated the village.

The late 19th century brought the steam train to Grindelwald, opening the area to convenient travel and bringing in its wake an ever-increasing number of tourists from all over the world.

When you arrive, you will find a beautiful, wide, deep valley squeezed between the north face of the Eiger (and other towering peaks) to the south and lesser peaks to the north, with its only entrances being from Interlaken on the train or from Meiringen on the Grindelwald Bus to the northeast. Needless to say, this area is a winter paradise. There is an impressive choice of ski runs, from beginner to expert levels, covering over 132 miles (213km) and descending from altitudes as high as 9,747ft (2,971m). Grindelwald also has approximately 12.5 miles (20km) of cross-country skiing, and offers a wide variety of other winter sports.

Jungfraujoch, *see* p.136. Grindelwald is a starting point for this famous excursion and Wengernalpbahn (WAB) trains take you to Kleine Scheidegg to begin the trip.

Männlichen, *see* p.138. Grindelwald is one of the two starting points (Wengen is the other); the Gondelbahn Grindelwald-Männlichen gondola cars depart from the Grindelwald Grund station.

Tourist Information

Grindelwald: Grindelwald Tourismus, **t** 033 854 12 12, **f** 033 854 12 10, *www.grindelwald. com* (*open Mon–Fri 8–12 and 2–6*).

Shopping

Grand Bazar, t 033 853 12 88, **f** 033 853 55 88, *www.grandbazar.ch*, in the centre of the village. Has a wide range of top-class souvenirs – including Huggler wood carvings – as well as sports clothes, backpacks, T-shirts and children's clothes.

Bernet Sport, t 033 853 13 09. A member of the INTERSPORT group; has been run by the same family for 100 years; the current owner is a skiing instructor and mountain guide who has climbed every Swiss mountain over 13,000ft (4,000m). The shop offers everything you need, to rent or buy, for skiing, snowboarding, mountaineering and hiking.

Where to Stay and Eat

★★★★Belvedere, t 033 854 54 54, **f** 033 853 53 23, *www.belvedere-grindelwald.ch* (*luxury*). This boasts an enviable location just across the valley from, and almost in the shadow of, the north face of the Eiger. The personality of the Hauser family, owners and operators for over 90 years, is lovingly imprinted on every aspect of this hotel. The 55 rooms are very tastefully appointed and have a modern ambience. The well-equipped spa has both a pool and a jacuzzi with picture windows allowing superb views of the Eiger.

★★★★Kirchbühl & Apartments, t 033 853 35 53, **f** 033 853 35 18, *www.kirchbuehl.ch* (*expensive*). This is a little outside the village, in a more rural environment. It offers 48 very nice rooms, two good restaurants, a sauna, steam bath and whirlpool as well as free entrance to the Grindelwald Sports Centre.

★★★★Spinne, t 033 854 88 88, **f** 033 854 88 89, *www.spinne.ch* (*expensive*). Right in the middle of the village, this has 37 very nice rooms, many with balconies with views over the Eiger. It has four different restaurants featuring Italian/French and Chinese cuisine, two bars, a disco and a wellness centre.

★★★Fiescherblick, t 033 854 53 53, **f** 033 854 53 50, *www.fiescherblick.ch* (*moderate*). This is a charming small hotel that has 25 comfortable, well-equipped rooms, and bed-sitters in the new chalet wing. The Bistro has a special Swiss menu, whilst the gourmet restaurant has 15 Gault Millau points.

Mountain Hostel, t 033 853 39 00, **f** 033 853 47 30 (*cheap*). Located down by the Männlichenbahn gondola station and Grund Station, this is the ideal place for those looking for basic, cheap accommodation. It has 2-, 4- and 6-bed rooms with running water, but the showers and toilets are centrally located. It also has TV, billiards, table tennis, laundry and an Internet corner.

Grindelwald–First

The original Grindelwald-First chair lift, at its inception in 1950, was the longest in Europe. In late 1991 the new system, **Bergbahnen Grindelwald–First** (**t** *033 854 50 50*, **f** *033 854 50 35, www.gofirst.ch*), 3¼ miles (5,226m) in length, was opened. It ascends 3,625ft (1,105m) through three stages: Grindelwald to Bort, Bort to Grindel, and Grindel to First. **First**, at an altitude of 7,113ft (2,168m), sits directly across the valley from four peaks that rise over 13,000ft (4,000m) – the Schreckhorn, Eiger, Mönch and Jungfrau. As a bonus, it is also immediately in front of the famous Grindelwald Glacier. While some may simply want to sit on the terrace of the **Berggasthaus First** (**t** *033 853 12 84,* **f** *033 853 53 12, www.berghausfirst.ch*) to savour the fabulous views, others will want to contemplate a hike. There are some 60 miles (100km) of pathways to choose from, along which over 100 different species of flowers bloom.

The most popular destination, and one that is not too difficult either, is the trek to **Bachalpsee**. Just about an hour away, this mountain lake is particularly popular with photographers as the topography of the land here creates an optical illusion that there is no valley between the lake and the distant mountains. Grindelwald Tourismus even arranges moonlight evening hikes here.

The more adventurous could consider pushing on to **Faulhorn**, another hour or so away and at an altitude of 8,796ft (2,681m). The views range from Grindelwald and its majestic mountains to the lakes of Brienz and Thun and even, in the distance, the Black Forest of Germany. It is possible to stay overnight at the **Berghaus Faulhorn** (*t 033 853 27 13, f 033 853 07 50*), one of the oldest and highest hotels in Switzerland. To return, you have two options. Either return the way you came, or take the path down to Bussalp where there is another mountain restaurant, the **Bergrestaurant Bussalp** (*t 033 853 37 51*), then continue on to Bort – with maybe a stop at the **Berghaus Bort** (*t 033 36 51, f 033 853 35 18, www.berghaus-bort.ch*) for refreshments – from where you can make the final descent back on the Firstbahnen.

At the second, and penultimate, station of **Grindel** you can take a break at the modern **Bergrestaurant Schreckfeld** (*t 033 853 54 30*), before doing a gentle hike to **Grosse Scheidegg**. This is an easy undulating walk of 1½ hours, along which the altitude changes only by 23ft (7m) from 6,414 to 6,437ft (1,955 to 1,962m). When you finally arrive at Grosse Scheidegg don't expect too much of interest; but the **Berghotel Grosse Scheidegg** (*t 033 853 67 16*) makes a welcome resting place until the next Grindelwald Bus (*t 033 854 16 16, www.grindelwaldbus.ch*) arrives to transport you back to Grindelwald. Sit on the left-hand side of the bus if you want to see the Grindelwaldgletscher (glacier) just outside Grindelwald.

Wengen

This dramatically beautiful car-free village at 4,180ft (1,274m), with its stupendous views of the Eiger, Jungfrau and the glorious waterfalls that cascade into the valley below, is reached on a Wengeralpenbahn WAB train from Lauterbrunnen.

In 1834 and 1835 the first licences were issued for the operation of inns over the pass at Kleine Scheidegg to Wengernalp and Kleine Scheidegg respectively. A few years later the first inn was opened in Wengen, and tourism grew. The opening of the railways, Berner Oberland in 1890 and Wengernalp in 1893, brought even more visitors. In 1910 the rail link to Kleine Scheidegg opened up the higher peaks to winter sports.

During the summer time Wengen is surrounded by numerous **hiking** possibilities, and these are detailed in the map *Lauterbrunnental Jungfrau-Region Wanderkarte*, available at the tourist office. The winter season, though, is when Wengen springs to life with a seemingly never-ending selection of **skiing** and **snowboarding** opportunities. Brush up your skills at the **Swiss Ski and Snowboard School** (Schweizer Skschule Snowboardschule; *t/f 033 855 20 22*). Wengen also plays host to the famous **Lauberhorn Downhill Ski Races** – for the 74th time in 2004. Covering 2.65 miles (4,260m), this is the oldest and longest downhill ski race in the World Cup calendar. There are **winter walking trails**, too, and the tourist office has a brochure detailing these.

Tourist Information

Wengen: tourist office, t 033 855 14 14, f 033 855 30 60, www.wengen-muerren.ch (open daily 9–6). Try also www.wengen.com.

Shopping

Photohaus Fritz Lauener, t 033 855 11 54. Carries a full range of Victorinox Swiss Army knives with complimentary engraving, watches, sunglasses and many other souvenirs.
Central-Sport, t 033 855 23 23, **f** 033 855 45 33. A member of the INTERSPORT scheme; offers everything you need, to either rent or buy, for skiing, snowboarding, snowshoes, sledging, mountaineering and hiking.

Where to Stay

****Regina, t** 033 856 58 58, **f** 033 856 58 50, www.wengen.com/hotel/regina (expensive). Dating from 1894, this is a luxurious, traditional mountain hotel and renovated rooms have not sacrificed its character. Relax by the fire, with the family dog, on comfortable furniture in antique-laden, wood-panelled public rooms. There are two fine restaurants, the gourmet Chez Meyer's and Le Grand, plus a beauty centre.
****Silberhorn, t** 033 856 51 31, **f** 033 855 22 44, www.silberhorn.ch (moderate). In a central position, right across from the train station, this has 68 well-furnished rooms and apartments of different sizes, two restaurants with a fine selection of Bordeaux wines, a wellness facility, sun terrace and bars.
***Belvedere, t** 033 856 68 68, **f** 033 856 68 69, www.belvedere-wengen.ch (inexpensive). Built in 1912, this magnificent Art Nouveau hotel has all modern comforts. Most of its 62 rooms have balconies and views.
Residence & Bernerhof, t 033 855 27 21, **f** 033 855 33 58 (inexpensive). Both are located in the centre of the village, with the former offering apartments and studios and the latter tourist accommodation and dormitories. The village restaurant offers typical Swiss mountain specialities.

Eating Out

Sina's, t 033 855 31 72, **f** 033 855 30 72. At the end of the village away from the station; a combination of restaurant, pizzeria and steakhouse, and a lively pub with live music.

Jungfraujoch, see below. Wengen is a starting point for this famous excursion and Wengernalpbahn (WAB) trains originating at Lauterbrunnen take you to Kleine Scheidegg to begin the trip. **Männlichen**, see p.138. Wengen is one of the two starting points – Grindelwald is the other – for this trip that begins on the Luftseilbahn Wengen–Männlichen LWM cable car.

Jungfraujoch

Even today, it would take a knowledgeable eye to see a way, other than climbing, to reach the top of the magnificent Jungfrau at 13,642ft (4,158m). And that is exactly how it seemed back in 1893 when Adolf Guyer-Zeller, a prominent Swiss industrialist captivated by the towering peaks of the Eiger, Mönch and Jungfrau, had the idea of constructing a railway to the top. Work on this project, based on his notes and sketches, began from Kleine Scheidegg in July 1896. It took two full years just to complete the first section of the track, which ran over open ground, to the Eigergletscher station at 7,612ft (2,320m).

From the station onward, the track had to be tunnelled through the mountain. In 1899, a blasting accident claimed six lives. In a subsequent accident, over 29.5 tons

Good Morning Ticket

In order to qualify for a discounted ticket, you must depart from Grindelwald or Wengen at about 7.20am and return from Jungfraujoch before midday; tickets in 2003 cost CHF 113 from Grindelwald and CHF 101 from Wengen.

(30,000 kilos) of dynamite exploded; no lives were lost, but it is said that the blast was heard in Germany. Work continued, and two other intermediate stations, Eigerwand (9,400ft/2,865m) and Eismeer (10,368ft/3,160m), were completed before the final breakthrough out of the rock at Jungfraujoch in February 1912. Europe's highest railway station, at 11,333ft (3,454m), was finally opened on 1 August 1912.

This legendary – and expensive – trip starts at Kleine Scheidegg at 6,762ft (2,061m), where Wengernalpbahn trains arrive from Grindelwald (*see* p.133) or Lauterbrunnen via Wengen (*see* p.135); or on Berner Oberland Bahnen BOB trains from Interlaken (*see* p.130) to Grindelwald or Lauterbrunnen.

Kleine Scheidegg itself, besides being a train junction, is an interesting small complex of hotels, tourist souvenir shops and restaurants. In winter it is perpetually busy with skiers, and rock music blares from bars inside, incongruously, Indian teepees. Between late June and October Switzerland's first – and only – birds of prey show takes place, where you will see raptors soaring gloriously in the mountain skies just a few yards away from the station (*at 11,45, 12.15, and 3, in good weather; CHF 6*).

To continue up to **Jungfraujoch**, change onto a Jungfraubahn JB train (*www.jungfraubahn.ch*). During the first stage of the journey, across open ground to the entrance to the Grosser Tunnel just past the Eigergletscher station, you will be bombarded by a proliferation of alpine vistas so wondrous that you will not know which way to look first. The peaks loom above you, and it will be your first opportunity to see those awesome glaciers close up. There are also tremendous views back across the Lauterbrunnen valley to Mürren and the Schilthorn.

The tunnel, all the way to the top, is 4.4 miles (7,122m) long, but there are two five-minute stops along the way at the intermediate stations of **Eigerwand** and **Eismeer**,

Hiking

Experienced, well-equipped hikers will want to consider taking the new **Eiger Trail** from the Eigergletscher train station. In nearly 3 hours, this will take you up as close as you can get to the Eiger North Face without actually climbing it – although you may see climbers – and winds down to Alpiglen, and on to Grindelwald either by foot or train.

Jungfraubahn JB produce a very comprehensive brochure, the *Wandern*, freely available at most stations, tourist offices, etc., which numbers and details most of the hikes open between May and October throughout the entire Grindelwald, Kleine Scheidegg, Männlichen and Wengen regions.

Eating Out

Top of Europe Glacier Restaurant, Jungfraujoch. An unforgettable experience: the vast expanse of the Aletsch glacier surrounded by numerous snow-capped peaks is a feast for the eyes. The cuisine is fine, too, with a choice of soups, salads, cold plates, meat, fish and vegetarian dishes.
Röstizzeria, Restaurant Bahnhof Kleine Scheidegg, t 033 828 78 28, f 033 828 78 30, *www.roestizza.ch*. Switzerland's own answer to a pizzeria, with variations on one of its famous dishes. This, and such favourites as raclette and *Käseschnitte*, as well as other fast food, can be eaten inside or out. Hot dishes are available from the Grill Station.

each of which offers contrasting panoramas viewed from glassed-in platforms. The first, built into the fearsome north wall of the Eiger, allows you a bird's-eye view of Grindelwald in the valley far below, out over smaller mountains to northern Switzerland and, on occasion, even to the Black Forest in Germany. The second, at Eismeer, is quite different. Looking out eastwards, behind the Eiger and Mönch, the surreal and chilling spectre of eternal ice unfolds before you in the forms of the Grindelwald and Fiescher glaciers. And on closer look, as amazing as it might seem, you may see climbers out there as well. A word of warning here – avoid rushing; this rarefied atmosphere, with 16 per cent less oxygen, affects almost everyone, especially those with respiratory problems. Those suffering from any form of heart trouble should certainly seek their doctor's approval before contemplating this trip.

Once at Jungfraujoch itself the attractions are numerous. In 1996 the **Sphinx observation hall** and terrace were opened, Europe's highest at an altitude of 11,716ft (3,571m); visitors are transported up by way of Switzerland's highest speed lift. From here, you can be entranced by the 360-degree panoramic views. Immediately below you, the vast Aletsch glacier, Europe's largest at 13.7 miles (22km), fills the wide valley between the towering peaks. Inside the glacier is the newly renovated **Ice Palace**, where the ice has been sculpted into beautiful patterns and models. Outdoors, there are hikes in the eternal snow and ice, a summer ski and snowboard park and even opportunities for husky-drawn sled rides.

Or, of course, you could have a meal at the **Top of Europe Glacier Restaurant**. A very new addition is an Indian Buffet, decorated with Bollywood movie posters – certainly incongruous, but with a real rationale. In the past, the increasingly popular Bollywood movies were filmed on location in Kashmir. The political situation between India and Pakistan now makes that impossible, and many are filmed on location in this region. Not missing a beat, the marketing authorities are making a firm bid to attract visitors from the subcontinent to see where their favourite films were made.

Before departing, take the opportunity to send a postcard home, franked by Europe's highest **post office**. Not only does it have a special postmark, it has its own postal code as well – CH-3801.

Männlichen

Männlichen (*www.maennlichen.ch*) is quite remote, and only accessible by transportation from either Grindelwald or Wengen. From Grindelwald (*see* p.133), the Gondelbahn Grindelwald–Männlichen GGM (**t** *033 854 80 80*, **f** *033 854 80 88*) departs from the Grindelwald Grund station. First opened in 1978, it takes 30 minutes to travel 3.4 miles (6.2k) – making it the longest gondola cableway in Europe – lifting you 4,199ft (1,280m) up to Männlichen. The ride is taken in comfortable four-seater cabins.

From Wengen (*see* p.135), the Luftseilbahn Wengen-Männlichen LWM (**t** *033 855 29 33*, **f** *033 855 35 10*) cable car whisks you up 3,051ft (930m) in just five minutes. This was opened in 1954, but was completely renovated in 1992 with a new ropeway and a cabin capacity of 80. A new station has recently been opened just two minutes from the centre of Wengen.

Männlichen, at an altitude of 7,695ft (2,345m), is the mountain that forms a natural barrier between the valleys of the White (*Weisse*) Lütschine river of Lauterbrunnen and the Black (*Schwarze*) Lütschine of Grindelwald. You will note that the valleys form a contrast in themselves. The White Lütschine, the narrower of the two, can boast little of its unprepossessing peaks. The other valley is longer, much broader and is surrounded by a range of highly impressive mountains, including the north face of the Eiger, 13,025ft (3,970m), which forms its south wall. And it is that scene, directly to the south, that holds the greatest fascination. There, alongside the Eiger, tower the summits of the Mönch, 13,448ft (4,099m), and the Jungfrau, 13,642ft (4,158m), with their respective glaciers, the Eigergletscher, Guggigletscher and Giessengletscher.

In the summer you can get up closer to these mountains by taking a fairly easy, relatively flat 1¼-hour hike to Kleine Scheidegg (*see* p.137). In the winter this is the starting point for long, wonderful skiing and snowboarding runs down to either Grindelwald or Wengen.

Mürren

You can reach Mürren either on the Lauterbrunnen–Mürren BLM funicular from Lauterbrunnen to Grütschalp and then on a 3.3ft (1m) narrow gauge non-cog railway covering 2.6 miles (4.25km) to Mürren, or on the Schilthorn cableway from Stechelberg, via Gimmelwald to Mürren.

Traffic-free, like Wengen, but much smaller and more rural, this small village sits on a ledge with simply stunning – and more unfamiliar – views across this steep valley to the Eiger, Mönch and Jungfrau. Mürren is famous for its **winter sports**: the first ski school in Switzerland opened here in 1930, 1937 marked the opening of the first ski lift service in the Bernese Oberland, and today there are around 31 miles (50km) of pistes and more than 16 downhill ski runs. The most famous of these is the 'Inferno Run', first raced in 1928, which covers a distance of 9¾ miles (15.8km) from the summit of Schilthorn and descends 7,054ft (2,150m) down the valley to Lauterbrunnen.

Hot air ballooning is also popular in Mürren. Eduard Spelterini made the first alpine balloon crossing from here on 12 August 1910, eventually landing in Turin, Italy. And one of the most important summer events is the annual International High Alpine Ballooning Competition, which was inaugurated in 1957.

The **Schilthorn 007** cableway (*t 033 823 14 44, f 033 823 24 49, www.schilthorn.ch*) is comprised of four sections: Stechelberg to Gimmelwald, to Mürren, to Birg and finally to the summit of the Schilthorn – a rise from an altitude of 2,844ft (867m) to 9,744ft (2,970m) over 4¼ miles (7km). The longest in the Bernese Oberland, the cableway closes for five days in April and for two to three weeks in November for maintenance.

Tourist Information

Mürren: tourist office, t 033 856 86 86, f 033 856 86 96, www.wengen-muerren.ch (open July–end Sept and mid-Dec–mid-April Mon–Wed and Fri 9–12 to 1–8.30, Thurs 9–12 and 1–8.30, Sat 1–6.30, Sun 1–5.30; mid-Sept–mid-Oct and mid-April–late April Mon–Wed and Fri 9–12 and 2–8.30, Thurs 9–12 and 2–8, Sat 2–6.30; mid-Oct–mid-Dec and late April–early June Mon–Fri 9–12 and 2–5).

Shopping

Abegglen Sport, t 033 855 12 45. Combines as the best souvenir shop in Mürren and the place to rent your winter sports equipment.

Where to Stay

★★★★Eiger, t 033 856 88 00, f 033 856 54 56, www.hoteleiger.com (*expensive*). Established in 1886, and run by the same family ever since, this offers magnificent views of the Eiger, Mönch and Jungfrau from many of the 49 beautifully furnished and well-equipped rooms. The hotel is run with a relaxed personal touch and features an indoor pool, sauna, solarium, a terrace and the Eiger Stübli, an exquisite gourmet restaurant.

★★★Blumental, t 033 855 18 26, f 033 855 36 86, www.muerren.ch/blumental (*inexpensive*). On the main pathway through the village, this has a real mountain hotel ambience. It has 20 rooms, the Grill Room 'Grotte' restaurant, the soundproofed Bliemlichäller bar and disco, and free entrance to the modern village sports centre.

★★★Alpenruh, t 033 856 88 00, f 033 856 88 88, www.muerren.ch/alpenruh (*inexpensive*). Next to the cable car station, this chalet-style hotel has 26 very nice rooms with many having balconies with fine views. It also has a good restaurant and a sun terrace.

Eating Out

Piz Gloria, www.schilthorn.ch (*see below*). Solar driven and revolving once every 55mins, this restaurant at the top of Schilthorn offers diners unparalleled 360° panoramic views. From 8am to 11am you can have the James Bond breakfast for CHF 22.50, including a glass of champagne, and from 11am to 3.30pm there is a variety of soups, cold dishes and hot dishes, including a fine *rösti* and even an Asian dish.

In 1967 the cableway had reached the summit and work had begun on the revolving restaurant, but the company ran out of money. Luckily, the film company planning the next 007 spectacular, *On Her Majesty's Secret Service*, were looking for just such a location. Consequently, the filmmakers finished the building and the revolving restaurant and had use of the cableway for three months before turning everything back over to the Schilthorn Aerial Cableway Company in a deal that suited everyone. In turn, the film brought well-deserved international acclaim to the Schilthorn, making it one of Europe's most popular destinations. This was the first of what are now four mountain-top **revolving restaurants** (this one is called the Piz Gloria), but it is unique in that the isolation of the Schilthorn affords visitors an unobstructed 360° panoramic vista of the surrounding Alps – in excess of 200 peaks, including the Eiger, Mönch and Jungfrau (you can actually see Jungfraujoch just across the valley), plus over 40 glaciers, deep valleys and mountain lakes. Of course, the weather will have a say in what you see but, even on bad days, Schilthorn can be above the clouds and, anyway, swirling winds can change matters very quickly. Other attractions include the James Bond Bar serving an array of lighter snacks, a large octagonal movie theatre showing 10-minute excerpts of the James Bond movie, a multi-vision slide show and a souvenir shop.

The more adventurous can hike all the way back down to Mürren, or start walking at the Birg station. More hiking suggestions, including those from Allmendhubel (reached by funicular from Mürren), are found in the *Mürren Schilthorn Hiking Proposals* brochure readily available in the area. In the winter, those brave enough can actually ski all the way down from Schilthorn.

Trümmelbach (*t 033 855 32 32; open daily April, May, June, Sept, Oct, Nov 9–5, July and Aug 8–6; adm*) is located just 1.3 miles (2km) from Stechelberg, the base station of the Schilthorn cableway, or three stops on the post bus. Trümmelbach, alone, drains the mighty glaciers of the Eiger, Mönch and Jungfrau. Its drainage area of 9.25 sq miles (24 sq km), half of which is covered by glaciers and snow, carries off up to 5,283 gallons (20,000 litres) of water per second that transports as much as 20,200 tons (20,524,148 kilos) of rock and other debris per year through the only glacial waterfalls in Europe that are inside a mountain and still accessible. A lift carries you up inside the mountain, and footpaths, sometimes a little precarious, lead you back past ten different waterfalls, weaving both inside and out of the mountain. The endless current of water can be both visibly and audibly mesmerizing, and the falls' corkscrew paths down the mountain, and the patterns they carve into the rock, are awesome.

This valley is famous for its waterfalls and the **Staubbach**, one the most magnificent just outside the village of Lauterbrunnen, cascades and plunges 945ft (288m) from the rock face above, with much of the water dissipating into fine spray before reaching the valley floor. The water that eventually reaches ground level combines with that of the 70-plus other falls in the valley, and the mountain streams, to feed the eternally fast-flowing White (*Weisse*) Lütschine river.

Brienz

Sitting on the eastern edge of Brienzersee, Brienz would just be a typically pretty Swiss village if it were not for three interesting attractions: one very unusual mountain railway, a long-standing cultural tradition that has made the village famous throughout Switzerland and beyond, and a fascinating open-air museum.

Brienz is 15 minutes or so from Interlaken by train or a 1½-hour sail by BLS steamship from Interlaken Ost. Immediately across from the train station, puffs of steam are the clue that the most well-known attraction of Brienz is just a few footsteps away. These puffs emanate from the small, squat steam engines of the **Brienz Rothorn Bahn** (*t 033 952 22 22, f 033 952 22 10, www.brienz-rothorn-bahn.ch*) at the tiny station tucked in next to the mountain. From the end of May to the end of October

Tourist Information

Brienz: Tourist Information Brienz-Axalp, Hauptstrasse 143, **t** 033 952 80 80, *www.alpenregion.ch* (*open summer Mon–Fri 8–12 and 2–6, Sat 9–12 and 4.30–6, Sun in July and Aug 4.30–6; winter Mon–Fri 8–12 and 2–6, in Feb on Sat 2–5*).

Where to Stay and Eat

Rothorn Kulm, t 033 951 12 21, **f** 033 951 12 51, *www.brienz-rothorn-bahn.ch* (*inexpensive*). Built in 1892 (*see p.142*) entirely of timber; modern amenities in a typical alpine hotel. The restaurant has a range of dishes that nearly equals the views.

Cuckoo About Clocks

Of course, it is impossible to visit Switzerland without noticing cuckoo clocks everywhere, not least in all the souvenir shops. Basically, there are just two types: the mainly brown, relatively undecorated ones that originate in the Black Forest, Germany, and the highly colourful, very decorated Swiss chalet-style ones, often with moving parts and music. Of the latter, the great majority that you will see, ranging in price from a hundred or so to several thousand dollars, are the only genuine Swiss brand ones made by **Lötscher Ltd** (*www.loetscher.ch*) since 1920. All of the moving parts are carved – using three-year-old linden wood to prevent cracking – and painted in Brienz, and then shipped to a factory near Zürich to be assembled. The mechanical movement is chain-driven with a one- or eight-day cycle, and the two typical styles of chalet are based on those from Brienz and Emmenthal. In Brienz, the Kirchofer and Jobin stores sell Lötscher cuckoo clocks.

these little engines pull or push passenger carriages for approximately 1 hour over a distance of 4¾ miles (7.6km) at an average gradient of 22 per cent. Along the way, the train dodges in and out of the forests, passing through six tunnels and allowing tantalizing glimpses of the lake below and the peaks of the Bernese Oberland beyond it. Not least of the attractions is the bewildering array of fauna and rare flora; besides the cows grazing on the rich pastures you may be lucky enough to catch sight of a Golden Eagle or a herd of chamois. Once you disembark at the 7,710ft (2,350m) summit the numerous unhampered views of the surrounding countryside are spectacular. Also at the top you will find the Hotel Rothorn Kulm, where you can indulge in a fondue at the restaurant. Heavy snowfalls can at times prevent the trains from getting father than the midway station at Planalp. If this happens you needn't worry, as there are some delightful hiking paths waiting to be explored.

For most tourists, the least known aspect of Brienz's fame dates back to the early Middle Ages, when a combination of long, dark winter nights and a plentiful supply of suitable linden wood encouraged the citizens to practise the art of woodcarving. It wasn't until the early 19th century, however, that a man called Christian Fischer started selling carved bowls and figures of animals and people to, mainly, British tourists. Fischer started local schools, encouraging young people to take up carving, and by the time of the 1851 and 1859 international fairs in London, Brienzer woodcarvings had become world-famous. Today, the most famous name for woodcarvings, not only in Brienz but throughout Switzerland and even the world, is **Huggler Woodcarvings** (*shop at Fischerbrunnenplatz,* t *033 952 10 00,* f *033 952 10 01, www. huggler-woodcarvings.ch*). The company was started by Johann Huggler (1834–1912), whose surviving carvings of statues and groups are revered to this day. It was his son, Hans Huggler (1877–1947), who introduced in 1915 what is still today one of Huggler's bestsellers: Christmas nativity scenes based on 'real' people of that era. To this day, more than 20 master carvers and their apprentices, who undertake a four-year course, take great pride – not to say infinite care – producing genuinely hand-carved images that are astounding in their detail.

A short bus ride from Brienz station will take you to the **Swiss Open-Air Museum Ballenberg** (Freilichtmuseum Ballenberg; *t 033 952 10 30, f 033 952 10 39, www. ballenberg.ch; open mid-April–Oct daily 10–5; adm exp*), for a look at Swiss rural life as it was experienced through the centuries. In a pleasant natural setting you will find over a hundred restored old buildings, cattle, farming exhibitions and country crafts.

Thun

Thun is situated directly south of Bern, where the River Aare empties into Lake Thun. It has a population of around 40,000 and is, perhaps surprisingly for such a low figure, Switzerland's tenth largest city. With its castle dominating the skyline and the snowcapped Bernese Oberland peaks as a backdrop, it is a quaint medieval town.

Besides the castle and the art museum, there isn't that much to visit. Nevertheless, a trip here is worthwhile just to soak up the atmosphere, and wandering around Thun is a delight. If you want to stay overnight the choice of hotels is limited, and you won't find too many fine restaurants to choose from; however, the nightlife is lively.

As the fastest train trip from Bern takes just 19 minutes, all the sights of Thun can be seen very easily on a day trip from that city.

In the early 12th century the Barons of Thun are first mentioned in historical annals. Very late in the same century Duke Berchtold of Zähringen conquered and expanded the town and also, around 1190, built the castle that still stands today. By 1218 the County of Kyburg, in eastern Switzerland, had succeeded the House of Zähringen, though they ruled less than 50 years. In 1264, Countess Elisabeth of Kyburg granted Thun a City Charter with special privileges, and these documents are now in safe keeping in the Rathaus (town hall). With the 14th century came a barrage of civic problems so severe that Thun became a Bernese country town. Consequently, in 1384 the castle was taken over by the Bernese authorities as the residence for their governors and mayors. Among the highlights of the 15th century was the expansion of the guild that brought with it the construction of the Rathaus and other new Guildhalls. In the 16th century, Thun joined in the Reformation movement. It wasn't until 1835 that the first steamboat came to Thun, with the railway following 24 years later.

Around the Town

The one place of interest in Thun that is not directly in the Old Town is situated just to the south of town on the north side of the Aare basin, the area of water between the river and the lake. The **Museum of Fine Arts** (Kunstmuseum; *Hofstettenstrasse 14, t 033 225 84 20, f 033 225 89 06, www.kunstmuseumthun.ch; open Tues–Sun 10–5, until 9pm on Wed; adm*) is housed in an impressive building, built in 1875. The focus here is on Swiss and international art, with regular exhibitions presented on art history themes or focused on the museum's collections of contemporary 20th-century works.

For all the other sights, start at Freienhofgasse, the main street on the island between the two branches of the Aare; an anti-clockwise route will take you up to the castle and church on the hill, and then back via the Rathausplatz.

Getting Around

The train station is south of the Old Town, a 5min walk from the first branch of the Aare.

Car Hire
Avis, Bernstrasse 40, t 033 437 24 84.
Europcar, Gwattstrasse 9, t 033 334 00 00.

Tourist Information

Thun: Thun Tourismus-Organisation, Bahnhof, t 033 222 23 40, f 033 222 83 23, www.thun-tourismus.ch, in the railway station (open Sept–June Mon–Fri 9–12 and 1–6, Sat 9–12; July and Aug Mon–Fri 9–7, Sat 9–12 and 1–4).

Guided Trips and Tours
BLS Thuner- und Brienzersee, t 033 841 16 43, f 033 841 10 64, www.bls.ch, offer numerous lake steamer services on both lakes Thun and Brienz, which are divided by the town of Interlaken. In fact, most of the places of interest are nearer Interlaken or on Lake Brienz, but you can still take special trips, like fondue cruises, on the lake from Thun.

Market Days
Fair: every second Wed of the month on Bälliz.
Flower and general: Wed and Sat on Bälliz.
Fresh products: Sat mornings at Rathausplatz.
Handicrafts: every fourth Sat (except July) at Mühleplatz.
Flea market: every first Sat (except Jan and Aug) at Mühleplatz.
Geranium: a Tues in May at Waisenhausplatz.
Christmas: mid–24 Dec at Rathausplatz.
Christmas trees: mid–24 Dec on Bälliz.

Where to Stay

★★★Krone, Rathausplatz 2, t 033 227 88 88, f 033 227 88 90, www.krone-thun.ch (moderate). Located in the Rathaus square, this has a delightful medieval exterior. Inside, the 27 spacious rooms are contemporary. It has a sun terrace overlooking the Aare, and French and Chinese restaurants.

★★★★Freienhof, Freienhofgasse 3, t 033 227 50 50, f 033 227 50 55, www.freienhof.ch (moderate). This has a marvellous façade, a long history and a privileged position on the peninsula in the Aare river, in a central location in the old part of town. Its 63 modern rooms have up-to-date facilities.

Emmental, Bernstrasse 2, t 033 222 01 20, f 033 222 01 30, www.essenundtrinken.ch (inexpensive). Classified as a Unique hotel, this has a very pretty chalet-style exterior and has

To the north of Freienhofgasse is a two-storey building with three arches at ground-floor level, one of which is differently shaped from the other two. The **Three Confederates** (Drei Eidgenossen) was the former residence of the lords of Amsoldingen. It was rebuilt in 1409 and became an inn from 1798 to 1920, before being renovated in 1989. There is another arched building next to it; however, it is the odd six-sided tower abutting one corner, and its second-floor balcony, that catches the eye. This is the **Rose Garden** (Rosengarten), a late Gothic burgher's mansion that was built around 1480 for Bartholomäus May. It was subsequently renovated in the 16th and 17th centuries, and again in 1991.

On the south corner, where the street meets the Aare, stands the Freienhof hotel. This started life in 1308 as a municipal shelter for travellers, but was rebuilt in 1783 and again in 1957. On the northeast side of the bridge there is a square, neat house, **Oberherren**, which has a metal terrace overlooking the river. This was once the Overlords' Guildhall, but was rebuilt on its foundations in 1749.

Further north, on Obere Hauptgasse, **Schmieden** was first mentioned in 1437 and was the Smiths' Guildhall; the façade, though, dates from 1779. Much more unusual, however, are the **Church Steps** (Kirchtreppe) that were at one time just a steep path.

been serving travellers since 1898. There are only 11 rooms, comfortable and modern.

Eating Out

Pizzeria al Ponte, Freienhofgasse 16 (*moderate*). As the name implies, this is situated next to the bridge on the island between the two branches of the Aare. Pizza is the order of day, and the menu also includes *antipasti*, soup, pasta, salads, risotto, meat and fish. There is a little terrace next to the river in summer.

Siegfried, Hauptgasse 72, **t** 033 222 15 27 (*inexpensive*). This place is easy to miss as the entrance is down a corridor off the street. Even when you find it, it seems out-of-place – a throwback to the way small Swiss country restaurants used to be. Breadsticks and hard-boiled eggs are on each table, and the menu is pure Swiss.

Kaffeebar Mühleplatz, Mühleplatz 1 (*inexpensive*). This is located right next to the Mühlebrücke and has a rather limited menu of snacks and salads. However, it has a much more impressive list of cocktails and other drinks, and it is a great place to soak up the atmosphere. *Open until 1.30am Fri and Sat.*

Entertainment and Nightlife

Casino Thun, Hofstettenstrasse 35, **t** 033 222 02 90, *www.swisscasinos.ch*, offers punters a choice of 199 slot machines and other games. The Champion's Bar has original exhibits belonging to Swiss sporting stars. *Open 12pm–after 12am.*

Cabaret Borsalino, Obere Hauptgasse 29, **t** 033 223 47 33, **f** 033 223 24 86, *www.nightclub-borsalino.ch*, has a non-stop show from 5pm to 3am, daily.

Musik Park, Scheibenstrasse 49-51, *www.musikpark.ch*, with a tropical design, has it all – international DJs, rock music, a game zone, billiards, a swimming pool and chill-out garden. *Open until 3.30am weekends, and an hour earlier weekdays.*

Nachtwerk, *www.nachtwerk.ch*, opens until 3.30am on Fri and Sat and plays trance, house, hip hop, the greatest hits 1970-90, mainsteam and hardcore music.

Kraftstoff, Scheibenstrasse 21, *www.kraftstoff.ch*, is another dance club that stays open very late.

Indoor Karting, Scheibenstrasse 37, **t** 033 222 83 44, *www.indoor-karting.ch*, has a 360yd (330m) indoor go-karting track, as well as a bar and billiards. *Open until 1am on Fri, Sat.*

These wooden steps, built with a very low rise and covered with a wooden roof, were originally built by master carpenter Johann Boxdörfer, himself from Thun, in 1818.

Once at the top, the dominant building, boasting an impressive clock tower, is the **Town Church** (Stadtkirche) that dates from around 1330 and has frescoes from a century later. In 1738 the master builder Paulus Nader rebuilt it for use as a Protestant church. Three nearby buildings are worth a look, too. The nearest is the **Sexton's House** (Sigristenhaus), a chapel until the Reformation in 1528, rebuilt as a private house in 1537 and then as the Sexton's house in 1822. The **Castle Gate** (Burgtor) is the only city gate to have survived from the 13th century, although the roof was added in 1786. The **Curate's House** (Helferei) is rather imposing, and its medieval core might well once have formed part of the nearby castle. What you see dates from the 16th century and the early 19th century, and it was the official residence of the curate intern between 1725 and 1896.

Higher northwest is **Schloss Thun** (Thun Castle), whose history is documented on p.143. The main attraction here, besides the building itself, is the multi-faceted **Castle Museum** (Schlossmuseum; **t** 033 223 20 01; *open daily April, May and Oct 10–5; June–Sept 9–6; rest of the year 1–4*), which is housed in the formidable tower.

Displayed on several floors, the exhibits are impressively varied and, in addition to giving an insight into the region's cultural development, offer some enlightenment as to how the castle itself evolved throughout the history of Thun. From the tower there are views of the Bernese Oberland in the distance beyond Lake Thun.

Follow the steps down and around to the west of the castle, passing an attractive chalet along the way. Pause here for a moment to admire the views, not only of the Alps, but also of a delightfully haphazard collection of red-tiled roofs below. You will soon come across another of those covered wooden staircases but, as you will note on the descent, this is in less than pristine shape and is covered with graffiti. These steps deposit you back into the Old Town and out onto the pretty **Rathausplatz**. The most important building here is the **Rathaus** (town hall) on the west side that dates from around 1500, with the Archive Tower added in 1585. The present façade dates from a century later, although it was refurbished both in 1762 and 1964. Going around the square clockwise, you will find the **Velschen House** (Velschenhaus), with a white façade and an overhanging wooden roof. This was first mentioned as early as 1406 as home to a man of the same name; later that century the Thorberg Carthusians moved in from 1464 to 1528. Latterly, it has been used as a restaurant. Across the street is a square-looking building, arcaded at ground level and with pretty window boxes hanging from all of the windows. In 1775 Johannes Deci built the **Burghers' House** (Burgerhaus) as a combination of house and business premises. From 1918 it became the headquarters of the Burghers. Across Untere Hauptgasse the building with a terrace outside, **Metzgern**, was mentioned as early as 1361 and was the original Butchers' Guildhall. Much work was done in the late 16th century, and its present look came about in 1770. Directly across from the Rathaus the long façade belongs to the **School on the Square** (Platzchulhaus) that was built in 1793–7 as a hospital, but was used as a school from 1806 to 1909. The last building, with another of those six-sided towers that was rebuilt in 1972, was the former Bakers' Guildhall. Since 1822 it has been the Krone (Crown) hotel.

Between the Rathaus and the Krone a path leads to the inner Aare, and that leads on to the **Mühlebrücke**, a small plaza. Enjoy the tranquillity of the surroundings, then cross the water via the old wooden-covered sluice bridge immediately to the east.

Central Switzerland

Pilatus

This trip from Luzern, the **Golden Round Trip** (Goldene Rundfahrt), encompasses a famous mythical mountain and an impressive array of transportation. You should plan to dedicate a full day to it in order to enjoy it to the full; all information from **Pilatus-Bahnen**, Schlossweg 1 (*t 041 329 11 11, f 041 329 11 12, www.pilatus.com*) or from the Luzern tourist office. As it is a round trip it can be taken in either direction, but only if you visit between May and mid-December, as during the winter months the cogwheel railway is closed.

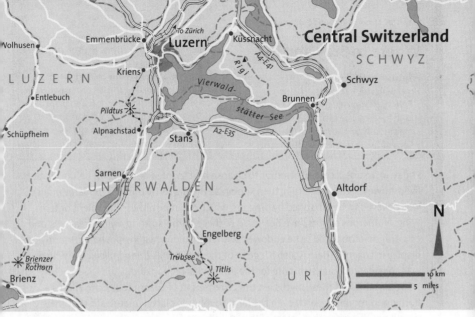

Depart from Luzern on the no.1 bus for the 15-minute, 2-mile (3.1km) trip to Kriens. Follow the signposts to the gondola station, from where a gondola cabin will silently whisk you from Kriens, 1,692ft (516m), through the middle station of Krienseregg at 3,366ft (1,026m) and on to the upper station of Fräkmüntegg, at an altitude of 4,642ft (1,415m). Fräkmüntegg is itself the starting point for numerous hikes, as well as for the longest **toboggan run** in Switzerland (*open April–Oct/Nov; tickets from the gondola car ticket office*). The ultimate stage of the ascent is made by cable car, rising up to the Pilatus Kulm station at an altitude of 6,791ft (2,070m).

Mount Pilatus, the dominant natural landmark of Luzern, stands isolated from the main ranges of the Alps. It is not the prettiest of peaks – in fact it is rather forbidding, both physically and mythically. Legend has it that in the lake on this 'mountain of dragons' are interred the remains of the Roman Governor Pontius Pilate – hence its name. The legend goes on to tell that his anguished spirit surfaced annually, on Good

Tell-Pass Regional Pass for Central Switzerland

Available between 1 April and 31 October from any tourist office or train or boat station, this pass is a necessity for those planning to spend more than two days travelling away from Luzern to attractions in central Switzerland such as the Pilatus, Titlis Rotair and Rigi, for example (*t 041 367 6767, f 041 367 6868, www.tell-pass.ch*).

It gives you two options: either 2 days' unlimited travel on days of your choice within a 7-day time period or 5 days within a 15-day time period. In either case, you receive a 50% discount for travel on the remaining days.

The cost for the 2-day pass is either CHF 135 or CHF 152 for 1st class, or if you have a Swiss Pass or Swiss Card it becomes either CHF 108 or CHF 132 respectively. The cost for the 5-day pass is either CHF 184 or CHF 213 for 1st class, or if you have a Swiss Pass or Swiss Card it becomes either CHF 147 or CHF 170 respectively.

Where to Stay and Eat

Pilatus

Hotel Bellevue, t 41 329 1212, **f** 41 329 1213, *hotels@pilatus.ch* (*inexpensive–cheap*). Built in the shape of a circle and sits perched precariously on the ridge of the mountain. Each of the 27 comfortably furnished double rooms has private bath or shower, toilet and TV.

Hotel Pilatus Kulm (same contact details as above) (*cheap*). The smaller of the two, with a less dramatic location. It is also more basic; the 22 double rooms have hot and cold running water, but showers and toilets are located within separate rooms on each floor.

Friday, in an unsuccessful attempt to cleanse his bloodied hands. Long before Pilate lived, however, this mountain, then known as the Broken Mountain (*fraactus mons*), was believed to be inhabited by dragons, which could be either benevolent or terrifying. Numerous stories have been told of these flame-spitting, flying creatures, and of a dragon-stone, said to be endowed with miraculous healing powers (currently on display in Luzern). There is also a legend of the Moon Milk (*mondmilchloch*), which was considered a universal cure for the infirmities of mankind.

The sum total of these myths led the government of Luzern to declare Pilatus a 'forbidden' mountain, with even the local shepherds placed under oath that they would not approach the waters of the lake. In 1585, however, a determined parish priest from Luzern and some brave citizens ascended Pilatus. Their goal was the exorcism of the spirits there. In continuation of the purgation begun by their mission, the lake was completely drained in 1594. It remained a dry bed for 400 years, until it was dammed again in 1980.

Pilatus, today, is the starting point for numerous hikes, and what you will find are magnificent views: a horizon of glorious mountain peaks and glaciers, Lake Luzern (known locally as Vierwaldstättersee) and its tributary rivers glistening below. On the terrace at the Hotel Pilatus Kulm (*see* above), you will no doubt be enchanted by the black birds with bright yellow beaks and red feet which can be so tame that they will take food directly from your hand. The *Täche* (mountain crows) are found all over Switzerland and tend to live at high altitudes. When they go down to the lower villages it is a warning that snow is on the way.

The journey back to Luzern is attractive, too. As long ago as 1889, a remarkable **cogwheel railway**, which operates on a rack and pinion system, opened between Pilatus Kulm at 6,791ft (2,070m) and Alpnachstad at 1,430ft (436m) on the shores of Lake Luzern. This dramatic trip along the mountainside, which takes 30 minutes when ascending and 40 minutes when descending, still retains the distinction of being the steepest rack railway in the world – with an average gradient of 42 per cent and a maximum of 48 per cent. Down at Alpnachstad you can choose between a quick 20-minute return to Luzern on the Brünig railway or a 70-minute cruise across the lake.

Engelberg

The Engelberg valley was civilized in 1120 when Baron Konrad von Sellenbüren of Zürich founded a Benedictine monastery that was soon renowned for its scientific and artistic activity. The history of the valley and the monastery remained inexorably entwined, with Engelberg retaining its status as a 'state in miniature', under spiritual auspices, up to the time of the French Revolution. Suitably, two brothers from the monastery were the first to climb Mount Titlis in 1744.

However, it wasn't until the middle of the 19th century that Engelberg was commercially developed as a summer tourist resort, with winter sports facilities added at the beginning of the 20th century. Initially, in 1913, a funicular was opened between Engelberg and Gerschnialp, and fourteen years later the first aerial cable car in Switzerland, connecting Gerschnialp and Trübsee, began operation. In the mid-1960s this was extended from Trübsee to the top of Titlis itself. Engelberg's main claim to international fame, though, originates from 1992, when the Rotair, the world's first revolving cable car, was installed between Stand and Titlis.

Engelberg's **Titlis Rotair** (*t 041 639 50 50, f 041 639 50 60, www.titlis.ch; cable cars and restaurants open 8.30–5, last departure up at 3.30 and down at 4.50, everything closed for 2 weeks in Nov for servicing*) not only provides the highest viewpoint in central Switzerland but also, much more innovatively, is the first revolving cable car in the world. Beginning on the valley floor at an altitude of 3,280ft (1,000m), a gondola car glides across the lower pastures and rises up to the first stage, Gerschnialp, at 4,265ft (1,300m), and then continues up to Trübsee at 5,905ft (1,800m). Here you must make a change onto a cable car that whisks you up to Stand – 8,038ft (2,450m) – in just five minutes, and then there's the final leg from Stand to Titlis, at 9,908ft (3,020m).

Tourist Information

Engelberg: Engelberg-Titlis Tourismus, t 041 639 77 77, f 041 639 77 66, welcome@ engelberg.ch, www.engleberg.ch, is located at the Tourist-Centre Engelberg, Klosterstrasse 3 (open in the summer and winter seasons Mon–Sat 8–6.30, Sun 8–6; at other times of the year, between mid-June to mid-Oct, it is the same hours Mon–Sat and Sun 2–6).

Shopping

R. Blatter, t 041 639 50 39, f 041 639 50 30. A delightful souvenir shop that has been run by the same family for nearly 100 years. The son is an expert wood carver and his father a wood-turner, and their handiwork is on sale.
Cristallina Sport, Titlis-Zentrum, t 041 637 11 78, f 041 637 11 80, and Dorfstrasse 39, t 041 637 01 41, f 041 637 47 60, www.cristallina-sport.ch. Has all the equipment you need to rent for either skiing or snowboarding, a snowboard test-centre as well as a wide range of clothes and hiking boots.

Bike'n Roll, Dorfstrasse 31, t 041 638 02 25, f 041 637 11 80, www.bikenroll.ch. Offers crossroad, hardrail, full suspension and freeride bikes, as well as children's bikes, for rent by the hour or day, and also organizes bike tours.

Where to Stay

★★★★**Ramada-Treff Hotel Regina Titlis**, Dorfstrasse 33, t 041 639 58 58, f 041 639 58 59, www.ramada-treff.ch (moderate). A modern hotel with 128 rooms, located right in the centre of the village; has a Swiss/Italian restaurant and the lively Regina Bar.
★★★**Edelweiss**, Terracestrasse 10, t 041 637 07 37, f 041 637 39 00, www.edelweissengelberg.ch (moderate). A few mins from the centre, this charming family-run hotel offers 46 well-equipped rooms and spacious public areas.

Eating Out

No visit to Engelberg is complete without lunch at the top of Titlis, either in the à la carte **Titlis Stübli** or the **Mamma Mia** pizzeria.

Deciding that a spectacular ride over glacier falls and ice crevices among craggy mountain peaks was not sufficiently exciting, the authorities decided to add another thrilling aspect to the last five minutes of the trip. In 1993 the installation of two revolving Rotair cable cars was completed, and these were – and still are – a worldwide innovation. The mechanism used is similar to that of revolving restaurants: shortly after the trip begins the cabin floor begins to revolve, leaving only a central podium and the walls fixed. Thus, the spectacular alpine scenery all around you may be viewed from an unparalleled variety of angles.

At the summit there is a wealth of things to do. In addition to the ever-captivating views that reach out over the Alps and, on a clear day, to the Black Forest in Germany, there are numerous restaurants plus the Ofenbar, considered the highest in Europe. Relax on the sun terrace of the wind-protected Toporama, or take a walk into the **Glacier Grotto** that traverses into the highest point of the Titlis Glacier. You will find that the temperature inside the grotto varies only between –1 and –1.5°C (30.2 and 29.3°F), regardless of the outside conditions. The more adventurous may opt for a walk out onto the glacier, or even take the Ice-Flyer chairlift down to the unique **Glacier Ice Park** and slide down the slopes on snow tubes or other unusual sledges. You can even enjoy an ice-cold drink there at the Sunflower Bar.

On the descent to the valley some may be tempted to stop at **Trübsee**, where, in the summer months and weather permitting, there are enchanting horse-drawn carriage rides around idyllic Lake Trübsee. Most visitors will finish their trip to Titlis the easy way by taking the gentle gondola ride back down to Engelberg. But a more unusual way to descend is to rent a Trotti bike, actually more like an old-fashioned scooter, which can be used on the descent from Gerschnialp to Engelberg. But remember, cows have the right of way!

There is a way, but this is really for those with both a strong stomach and a head for heights, of getting down quickly and then going straight back up: each weekend between May and October **bungy jumping** is available from the cable car that operates between Trübsee and Stand.

Apart from the exciting trip to Titlis, Engelberg – the largest summer and winter resort in central Switzerland – has much more to offer in either season, including other cable and gondola cars. In summer, you can explore over 224 miles (360km) of marked **walking and hiking paths**, many more miles of mountain bike trails and a wide variety of outdoor activities. In winter, downhill and cross-country **skiers** have the run of over 28 miles (45km) of marked ski pistes and 25 miles (40km) of cross-country tracks. Other facilities include a sledge and toboggan run, and indoor pool.

In either season learn more about the history and life of the high alpine valleys at the **Engelberg Museum** (Tal Museum Engelberg; *t 041 637 04 14; open Wed–Sun 2–6; adm*). Arrange, by appointment, a guided tour in English of the **Benedictine monastery**, and its famed library *(Thurs and Sat at 10am; adm)*. Or visit Switzerland's only demonstration dairy operated in a monastery, **Schaukäserei Kloster Engelberg** (*t 041 638 08 88, www.schaukaeserei-engelberg.ch; open daily 9–6.30, Sun and hols until 5pm*).

Eastern Switzerland and Liechtenstein

Rapperswil

Rapperswil is a charming small town with just 7,400 inhabitants, situated some 30 miles (50km) east of Zürich at the other end of Lake Zürich. What little there is to see is mostly found on the hill up by the castle, although the lower town is particularly well preserved. It will not take very long to look around – the attractions have quite odd opening hours – and it's best to visit between April and September. If coming from Zürich, make an early start and then take a leisurely lunch on a lake steamer back to the city.

Start your visit at the tourist office, before strolling north through the lower town to the elaborate steps that lead up to the castle. First, take a look at the **Circus Museum**, in the same building as the tourist office (**t** *055 220 57 57; open April–Oct 10–5 and Nov–Mar 1–5*). Rapperswil has a close connection with the famous Swiss

Tourist Information

Rapperswil: Rapperswil Zürichsee Tourismus, Fischmarktplatz 1, t 055 220 578 57, f 055 220 57 50, *www.rapperswil.ch* (open daily April–Oct 10–5 and Nov–Mar daily 1–5).

Market Days

Rapperswiler market (fresh goods, flowers, spices and pastries): Fri morning Mar–Dec.

Exhibitions and Festivals

Shrove Tues: Eis-Zwei-Geissebei
Late June: blues'n'jazz Rapperswil festival.
4th Sun of Advent: the **Sternsingers**, along with animals from the Knie Zoo, parade through the town for the traditional Christmas play in the town square.

Where to Stay

****Schwanen, Seequai 1, t 055 220 85 00, f 055 210 77 77, *www.schwanen.ch* (*moderate*). This has the best location in Rapperswil on the lakeshore promenade. Some of its 25 modern rooms have balconies overlooking the lake. Also a fine restaurant, brasserie and live music at the bar.

***Hirschen, Fischmarktplatz 7, t 055 220 61 80, f 055 220 61 81, *www.hirschen-rapperswil. ch* (*moderate*). In a traditional building on the main square, this small hotel has much charm. Only 14 rooms, but they all differ in decor and some have four-poster beds.

**Jakob, Hauptplatz 11, t 055 220 00 50, f 055 220 00 55, *www.jakob-hotel.ch* (*inexpensive*). Originally founded in 1830 and located in a car-free area, this was re-opened in 1999 as a charming modern hotel. It has just 20 rooms, all stylishly decorated.

Eating Out

San Marco, Seequai, t 055 211 22 24 (*moderate*). A restaurant and pizzeria, offering 23 different pizzas and an equally wide range of *antipasti* and pasta dishes.

Café Rosenstädter, Fischmarktplatz (*moderate*). You can sit outside on this fine square; besides an interesting menu the speciality here is a large range of Appenzeller beers.

circus, Knie, who have made the town their winter headquarters since 1919. In here you will find memorabilia, models, etc.

Just north of the Fischmarktplatz is the Rathaus (town hall) that was first mentioned in 1429, and past that is the sloping **Hauptplatz**. The street pattern in this area was, in large part, laid out in the 13th century. The original houses were constructed of wood, but, age having taken its toll, these were replaced by stone homes over the course of the 16th and 17th centuries. The architectural harmony you see today is certainly not an accident as construction, renovation and maintenance of all buildings are subject to strict local regulations. This part of town, the social centre of Rapperswil, is also the access point to the Schloss, by way of an impressive double stairway, easily recognizable by the elegant water fountain set between the flights at its base.

Believed to date from the early 13th century, this formidable **Schloss** (castle) sits at the highest point of a narrow promontory, the **Lindenhof**. Just outside the castle entrance is the Liberty of Poland column, topped by an eagle, with the words MAGNA RES LIBERTAS (Freedom Above All) inscribed on it, erected in 1868. Inside, the **Polish Museum** (Polenmuseum; *open April–Oct daily 1–5 and Nov, Dec and Mar on Sat and Sun 1–5, closed Jan and Feb*), founded by Polish exiles and their Swiss friends, presents a wide-ranging array of exhibits. Don't leave the castle before climbing the **Gügeler tower**, which offers magnificent views of the lake and the mountains to the east.

Immediately to the east of the castle is another domineering structure, the Catholic **church of St Johann** with its Renaissance altars and rich treasures. The first church on this site, built in 1253, succumbed to fire in 1882; this new one was consecrated shortly after, in 1885. Be sure to investigate, also, the **Cemetery Chapel** (Liebfrauen-kapelle) just behind the church. It dates from 1489 and has a beautiful wooden ceiling. The cemetery itself, on a lower level, has rather strange metal headstones on many graves.

Not very far away, again eastwards, is the **Museum of Local History** (Heimat-museum; *open July and Aug Wed 4–8, Sat 2–5, Sun 10–12 and 2–5, closed Nov–Mar*), where there are some interesting exhibits, including a model of the town as it appeared around 1800.

Back to the west, follow the Lindenhof along the promontory. From this vantage point, the views are spectacular: the vast expanses of Lake Zürich unfold on either side and the Alps rise majestically in the distance. It also offers the finest perspective of the new **wooden bridge** built in 2001, the longest in Switzerland at 920 yards (841m), connecting Rapperswil to Hurden on the other side of the lake. On the slopes to the north is a **deer park** that was established in 1871 and is home to between 10 and 15 fallow deer. To the south are the expansive **Rose Gardens** (Rosengärten) where, between June and October, 6,000 rose bushes – of 180 varieties – bathe the horizon in a breathtaking display of kaleidoscopic blooms. This also has a distinctive connection to the town; upon Rapperswil's coat-of-arms you will find two rose blossoms.

The **Capuchin monastery**, built around 1606, and other fortifications occupy the western tip of the promontory, and steep steps that run between the monastery and the Rose Garden descend back to the lakeside.

Schaffhausen and the Rhine Falls

Schaffhausen owes its existence to the Rhine Falls (Rheinfall), the largest in Europe. These rapids, formerly known as the upper and lower Laufen, interrupted the transport of goods by water so that all commodities not sold locally had to be moved by horse-drawn carriages around the falls. Count Eberhard III of Nellenburg, anticipating the importance of this site to river merchants of the Rhine, Danube and Aare, founded a town here. His cousin, Heinrich III, who was the German emperor, granted Eberhard the right to mint coins for the new town, *Scafusun*, in 1045. Four years later, Eberhard founded the All Saints Abbey. And in 1080 Eberhard's son, Burkhart, gifted the town to the abbey. The needs of the abbey soon outgrew its structure, however, and in 1104 the Bishop of Constance inaugurated a much larger replacement, which stands today as a magnificent example of the Romanesque style of architecture.

The early 16th century brought the Reformation. In turn, the religious wars which ensued between 1564 and 1585 brought the need for improved fortifications – hence the construction of the Munot. Schaffhausen enjoyed the fruits of prosperity for two centuries longer, especially during the 18th century when a flurry of construction saw, among other things, approximately 150 beautiful bay windows (oriels) added to its

Tourist Information

Schaffhausen: Schaffhausen Tourismus, Herrenacker 15, **t** 052 625 51 41, **f** 052 625 51 43, *www.schaffhausen-tourismus.ch* (*open June– Sept Mon–Fri 9.30–6, Sat 9.30–4; Oct– May Mon–Fri 9.30–12.30 and 1.30–5, Sat 9.30–1.30*).

Tours

Guided **old town** strolls, organized by Schaffhausen-Tourismus, take place mid-April–early Oct on Tues, Thurs and Sat, starting at 2pm; tickets CHF 12.

Shopping

Grieshaber, Vodergasse 84, **t** 052 624 77 31. Has a deer's head as a symbol, and one is on display in this shop that has a wide range of Victorinox products and other souvenirs.

Where to Stay

★★★★★Rheinhotel Fischerzunft, Rheinquai 8, **t** 052 632 05 05, **f** 052 632 05 13, *www. fischerzunft.ch* (*expensive*). Standing within a few feet of the Rhine, this 19th-century building is home to just 10 comfortable rooms, each appointed to the highest standards and decorated in European style with Asiatic influences. Added to this is the chance to experience chef André Jaeger's astounding culinary creations (*see* below).

★★★Zunfthaus zum Rüden, Oberstadt 20, **t** 052 632 36 36, **f** 052 632 36 37, *www.rueden.ch* (*moderate*). Built in the 14th and 15th centuries, this old Guildhall is located just a couple of minutes from the train station. Its 30 rooms and public areas combine historical ambience with 21st-century convenience.

Eating Out

Schaffhausen

Rheinhotel Fischerzunft, Rheinquai 8, **t** 052 632 05 05, **f** 052 632 05 13, *www.fischerzunft. ch* (*very expensive*). A unique restaurant and dining experience. André Jaeger, the owner/chef and president of Les Grandes Tables de Suisse (*www.grandestables.ch*), has combined the best of oriental and French cuisine to create dishes that are not only delectable to the palate, but beautiful to the eye. The dining room has wooden beams, antiques and even a modern art collection.

The Rhine Falls

Schlössli Wörth, Rhenfallquai, **t** 052 672 24 21, **f** 052 672 24 30, *www.schloessliwoerth.ch*. Located in the old fort, this is a charming restaurant with huge picture windows overlooking the falls themselves. Besides a fine menu, there are also daily specials.

houses. Gradually, though, changes in the customs association, the discovery of new salt deposits in Schweizerhalle and, perhaps more importantly, the coming of the railways, altered the economic balance.

All was not lost, however. In 1866, Heinrich Moser constructed a large dam across the Rhine, and the power generated from its hydroelectric works provided Schaffhausen with the spark it needed to play a prominent role in the Industrial Revolution. Unfortunately this attracted the attention of the Allied Forces during the Second World War and Schaffhausen was bombed by the American air force on 1 April 1944.

Today, this town of just over 34,000 people has the ambience of one that time has passed by. On nearly every street, all of which are dominated by the massive Munot fortress towering above, you will find picture-perfect houses with elaborately decorated, painted and sculptured façades. Squares, large and small, are graced by fountains and guarded by statues of the likes of William Tell. Few will know, also, that this northwestern corner of Switzerland is an important wine-growing region.

Schaffhausen

The **Cathedral of All Saints** (Münster zu Allerheiligen; *open daily 8–6*), originally founded by Eberhard von Nellenburg in 1049 and rebuilt shortly afterwards, is one of the finest examples of pure Romanesque architecture in Switzerland. The tower, constructed around 1200, is considered one of the most beautiful in the country, and Count Eberhard is interred in the crypt. The aura of tranquillity extends into the adjoining cloister and herb garden. The former, part 12th-century Romanesque and part 13th-century Gothic, is the largest in the country. It includes a delightful garden and the Noblemen's Cemetery (Junkernfriedhof), in which civic dignitaries and other important townspeople were laid to rest between 1582 and 1874.

There are two museums of some interest next to the cathedral. The **Museum of All Saints** (Museum zu Allerheiligen; *Baumgartenstrasse 6, t 052 633 07 77, f 052 633 07 88, www.allerheiligen.ch; open Tues, Wed, Fri 12–5, Thurs 12–8, and first Sun of month 11–5; adm*) is in an attractive old building and has a mixed bag of exhibits. The **Halls of Modern Art** (Hallen für neue Kunst; *Baumgartenstrasse 23, t 052 625 25 15, f 052 625 84 74, www.modern-art.ch; open Tues–Sat 3–5, Sun 11–5*) are located in an old worsted yarn factory and host large-scale installations by contemporary artists.

High to the east, the imposing **Munot** (*open May–Sept 8–8; Oct–April 9–5; free*), with vineyards around it, is the symbol of Schaffhausen. This highly unusual battlement was constructed between 1564 and 1585 in a prominent defensive position with views over the town, the Rhein and the surrounding countryside. It has a unique circular keep that is protected by thick walls, and a ceiling supported by round, very thick columns and arches. The watchman still resides in the solitary tower and every evening at 9pm he rings a bell that, in days gone by, was the signal to close the town gates and public houses.

The **Fronwagplatz** is the traditional marketplace, and the home of the Fronwagturm tower, adorned with an astronomical clock that dates from 1564 and shows no less than ten different features. Colourful water fountains adorn the Old Town, and nearby is the **Moor's Fountain** (Mohrenbrunnen) that dates from 1535 and is named after Kaspar, the youngest of the Three Holy Kings. Another fine example of this genre, with an octagonal pool and dating from 1632 (replacing the 1522 original), is the **William Tell Fountain** (Tellenbrunnen) to the east.

Beautiful houses are one of the features of Schaffhausen, and just north of Fronwagplatz, at Vorstadt 17, the **House of the Golden Ox** (Haus zum Goldenen Ochsen), which prior to 1608 was an inn, is one of the grandest. Notable among its features are a late Gothic façade decorated with frescoes showing a golden ox and symbols from Babylonian and ancient Greek history. At Platz 7, just to the east, the house of the **Three Kings** (Zu den Drei Königen) dates from 1746 and, in addition to its roccoco façade, is known for the statues of the Three Kings that sit above the second-floor windows. Just to the south, near the corner of Vordergasse and Münstergasse, the **Knight's House** (Haus zum Ritter) is considered the most beautiful in town. Knight Hans von Waldkirch rebuilt it in 1566, commissioning local artist Tobias Stimmer to decorate the exterior. Stimmer worked his magic here between 1568 and

1570 with such mastery that his fresco, brilliantly restored in 1943 by Carl Roesch, has been acclaimed the most significant north of the Alps.

The Rhine Falls (Rheinfall)

A No.1 bus outside Schaffhausen train station will take you in 15 minutes to Neuhausen, where signs will direct you to the falls. You will hear them before you see them and, most probably, will see an upwards rush of foam and spray before you arrive. Niagara Falls they are not; but this 17,000-year-old natural feature, with a width of 164 yards (150m), a height of 75½ft (23m) and a volume of over 153,978.5 gallons (700,000 litres) of water passing over the falls each second, is impressive enough, and the largest in Europe. Steps lead you down by the side of them, and then around to the Schlössli Wörth complex – which from the 12th to 19th centuries was an important trading post on the old salt road from Lake Constance down the Rhine – where you can take a **Rhyfall Mändli** boat (*t 052 672 48 11, f 052 672 49 48, www.maendli.ch; fare CHF 6.50*) around and up to the falls and climb to the top of the famous Känzeli rock in the middle. Whilst on the Känzeli rock it is fascinating to watch the Arlette fish vainly trying, again and again, to jump over the falls on their way upriver. Also from here, **Schiff** boats (*t 052 659 69 00, f 052 659 69 02, www.schiffmaendli.ch*) embark on longer cruises down the Rhine. On 1 August, Swiss National Day, a glorious fireworks display explosively adds a rainbow of illumination to this already magnificent sight.

Stein am Rhein

Stein am Rhein is located at a strategic spot where the Rhine leaves the Untersee – one of the three sections of Lake Constance (Bodensee). Its name means 'Stone on the Rhein'. The Romans built the first bridge over the river here, and a Benedictine monastery has been at Stein since the 14th and 15th centuries. Its medieval connections, however, are its claim to fame, with a fantastic array of wooden-beamed houses that are beautifully and extensively decorated with intricate frescoes and extended bay windows (oriels). It is regarded as Switzerland's best-preserved small medieval town, which means that its small population of 3,000 can be overwhelmed with tourists in the summer season.

Rathausplatz is both the social centre and the main attraction of the town. The Rathaus (town hall) was built between 1539 and 1542, although it has been renovated twice since. The houses around the square, and elsewhere, have the most ornate decorations you are ever likely to see. Originally, the wealthy residents decided that, as testimony to their affluence, they would decorate the exteriors of their mansions with the most detailed frescoes. Many of these were painted between 1520 and 1525 by the German Thomas Schmede. The town is now reputed to have the world's largest concentration of frescoes, and modern-day owners are legally obliged to maintain them in good condition. The small bay windows (oriels) had their practical use, as residents could see what was happening below without being noticed themselves. Worth seeking out are the **White Eagle** (Weisser Adler), the **Fore Crown** (Vordere Krone) and the **Red Ox** (Roter Ochsen) houses.

Tourist Information

Stein am Rhein: Tourist-Service Verkehrsbüro, Oberstadt 9, **t** 052 742 20 90, **f** 052 742 20 91, *www.steinamrhein.ch (open Mon–Fri 9.30–12 and 1.30–5, and in July and Aug on Sat 9.30–12 and 1.30–4).*

Where to Stay

★★★Adler, Rathausplatz 2, **t** 052 742 61 61, **f** 052 741 44 40, *www.adlersteinamrhein.ch (inexpensive)*. In the town hall square and with a beautiful Carigiet façade; two singles, 12 doubles on offer, and also an apartment with two bedrooms. Nice public areas, and a restaurant serving local and French cuisine.

Eating Out

Restaurant Sonne, Rathausplatz 13, **t** 052 741 21 28, **f** 052 741 50 86, *www.sonne.grandstables.ch (expensive)*. Located in a delightful old house that dates from 1463, with a frescoed façade and imposing oriel. Philippe Combe, the chef/proprietor, specializes in poultry, lake or river fish and terrines, with dishes that more than match the splendour of the building. A member of Les Grandes Tables de Suisse.

Don't miss the 1,000-year-old **St George Cloister** (Klostermuseum St Georgen; *t 052 741 21 42; open April–Oct 10–5; adm*) standing next to the river. The frescoes and paintings include one of St George slaying the dragon, and there are wonderfully intricate wooden-beamed ceilings. In the outbuildings is a huge wooden wine press.

The **Museum Lindwurm** (*Understadt 18, t 052 741 25 12, f 052 741 45 82; open Mar–Oct Mon and Wed–Sun 10–5; adm*) is housed in the most delightful blue- and white-painted mansion with, uniquely in Stein, an Empire façade dating from 1819. Actually, the oldest part of the museum dates back to 1279 and the building carried this name as early as 1495, although it was considerably expanded in the 16th century. The urban way of life and agriculture have always been closely intertwined here, and inside you will see how affluent citizens of the middle 1800s lived.

Hohenklingen Castle (Schloss Hohenklingen; *Hansjörg Zaugg, t 052 741 21 37, www.burghohenklingen.ch*) dates from the 13th century and overlooks Stein from a height of 630ft (192m). There is a restaurant there and it can be visited daily with no admission fee.

St Gallen

St Gallen, the seventh largest city in Switzerland, is a thoroughly charming town whose medieval centre co-exists in easy harmony with 21st-century demands.

According to legend, the town was founded in 612 by a roving Irish monk by the name of Gallo. He built a hermitage here that became the foundation for an abbey, the first stone buildings of which were erected in 719. Within this complex, art and culture thrived, and during the 9th and 10th centuries it was one of the foremost centres of learning in the Western world. The growing numbers of visitors attracted tradesmen, and in the mid-14th century a guild constitution gave power over the city to the six trade guilds and the association of powerful businessmen (Zum Notenstein). The manufacture of textiles has played an important role in the history

Tourist Information

St Gallen: St Gallen-Bodensee Tourismus, Bahnhofplatz 1a, **t** 071 227 37 37, **f** 071 227 37 67, *ww.st.gallen-bodensee.ch* (*open Mon–Fri 9–6, Sat 9–12*).

Where to Stay

★★★★Einstein, Berneggstrasse 2, **t** 071 227 55 55, **f** 071 227 55 77, *www.einstein.ch* (*expensive*). Close to the abbey, this classy hotel is also known as the 'Little Grand Hotel'. All its 62 rooms and three suites are quiet, modern and very comfortable. It also has a restaurant with panoramic views over the abbey district and a bar that offers light meals.

★★★Gallo Garni, St Jakobstrasse 62, **t** 071 242 71 71, **f** 071 242 71 61, *www.hotel-gallo.ch* (*moderate*). Easily recognizable by its 2nd-floor oriel, this is a refined and stylish hotel situated close to the exhibition grounds, theatre and concert hall and near the city centre. Affiliated with it is an Italian restaurant named, appropriately enough, Galletto.

★★★Boutique Hotel Jägerhof, Brühlbeichestrasse 11, **t** 071 245 50 22, **f** 071 245 26 12, *www.jaegerhof.ch* (*moderate*). Located in a gracious corner house, this has 41 interesting rooms, along with the first fully organic restaurant in Switzerland, and the biggest wine list in the region.

Eating Out

One of the pleasures of St Gallen is a visit to one of the '1. Stock-biezlie'. These quaint 1st-storey taverns serve tasty local specialities such as St Gallen sausage – made using a singular recipe that dates from 1438 – and *Biber*, a spicy honey cake filled with marzipan. The perfect accompaniment is a glass or two of Rheintaler wine. Typical examples of 1.Stock-biezlie are: **Anker**, Schmiedgasse 20, **t** 071 222 06 96, and **Gastube zum Schlössli**, Zeughausgasse 7, **t** 071 222 12 56.

of St Gallen since the Middle Ages, with linen production superseded by cotton and embroidery in the 18th century.

The main attraction here is undoubtedly the world-famous **Abbey Library of St Gallen** (Stiftsbibliothek St Gallen; **t** *071 227 34 16; open Dec–Mar Mon–Sat 10–5, Sun 10–12 and 1.30–4; April–Nov Mon–Sat 10–5, Sun 10–4; adm; overslippers provided*). This is one of the oldest libraries in the world, and houses a collection of over 100,000 books and manuscripts, some dating back to the 5th century. There are magnificent examples of handwritten books and a collection of 1,650 incunabula (books printed before 1500). The building was constructed in 1758, with a highly elaborate interior completed nearly a decade later in 1767, and it has a glorious elegance. Two tiers of incredible glassed-in bookcases stand beneath intricate ceiling frescoes depicting the first four Œcumenical Councils (Nicaea in 325, Constantinople in 381, Ephesus in 431 and Chalcedon in 451), between side lunettes portraying the Fathers of the Church; below is a lovely inlaid parquet floor. The abbey complex was added to the UNESCO world cultural treasures list in 1983, largely thanks to this extraordinary room.

Adjacent, the **cathedral** (**t** *071 227 33 81; open Mon–Sat 9–6, and after services on Sun*) is dominated by two immense spires. It was constructed by Peter Thumb between 1755 and 1767 as a replacement for the previous medieval structures. The interior design was a collaborative effort by Josef Wannemacher, artist; the Gigel Brothers, stuccowork; and J. A. Feuchtmayer, wood-carving. An extensive restoration undertaken between 1961 and 1967 returning the building to its original condition, most notably uncovering the ceiling frescoes of the chancel and restoring that entire room to its original colours. By the cathedral west entrance is the **Lapidarium** (*open April–Nov daily 2–4, Dec–Mar Sat and Sun 2–4*), where there is a collection of valuable building stones from the 8th to 17th centuries.

Just north is the **St Laurence Church** (*t 071 222 67 92; open Mon–Fri 9.30–11.30 and 2–4*). The first building on this site was a tiny cemetery chapel erected around AD 850, replaced by a larger one dedicated to St Laurence in the 11th century. It is widely held that it was associated in some way with the monastery. In the 13th century it became the parish church, giving the people who worshipped there some degree of autonomy from the monastery. The fire of 1314 destroyed the church and it was a full century later, in 1413, that work commenced on a new Gothic-style building. During the Reformation, in 1527, Holy Communion was celebrated in St Laurence's according to Protestant rites, and it emerged as the town's Protestant church.

The narrow streets and alleys of the **Old Town** to the north, east and west of here remain essentially the same today as when the street plan was laid out following the Great Fire of 1418. Besides being a shopping area these days, the Old Town is famous for beautiful old houses, particularly their extended upper level windows called **oriels**, of which over 100 have been preserved. They were once considered an indication of the wealth of the owner; the affluent cloth merchants would compete among themselves to design the most ornamental and intricate *beau idéal*. Two of the more notable examples along Multergasse are found on the Gothic edifice of Zum Schiff (the Ship), on which the oriel dates from around 1600, and upon Zum Rebstock (the Vine), a structure first mentioned in 1422, renovated in 1793 and embellished with a wooden oriel from 1783. Gallusstrasse and Gallusplatz, west of the cathedral, also have fine examples.

Around the periphery of the Old Town are some other interesting places. Starting clockwise to the north, the former **Convent of St Catherine** (St Katharinen) in Katherinegasse was founded in 1228, but closed three centuries later; it is now used as a lending library for toys. Pride of place here belongs to the calm Gothic cloister. South of that, the **Waaghus am Bohl** or **Kaufhaus**, adorned by an intricate clock, is where merchants took their goods to be weighed from the Middle Ages to the 19th century. Further around, close to the cathedral, the **Karl's Gate** (Karlstor) originates from 1570 and is the only fully preserved gate of the former city walls; it was named in honour of the first person to pass through it, Cardinal Karl Borromäus of Milan.

To the west towards the train station is **Broderbrunnen**, an intricately embellished water fountain at the junction of St Leonhard-strasse and Oberergraben. Further down Leonhard-strasse is a striking Art Nouveau building that now houses the Austrian consulate. Surprisingly, this eccentric building is not alone in St Gallen: these early 20th-century structures are attributable to the wealth generated by the lucrative textile industry. Appropriately, the **Textile Museum** (Textilmuseum; *Vadian-strasse 2, t 071 222 17 44, f 071 223 42 39, www.textilmuseum.ch; open Mon–Sat 10–12 and 2–5, Sun 10–5; adm*) is just around the corner, and displays historical embroidery from the 14th to 20th centuries and European lace from the 16th to 20th centuries.

To the west of the Old Town, and suitably on Museumstrasse, are a group of other museums including Kirchhofer House with Palaeolithic discoveries and the silver collection of Dr Giovanni Züst. On this street, too, is the **Museum of Fine Arts** (Kunst-museum; *Museumstrasse 32; open Tues–Fri 10–12 and 2–5, Sat and Sun 10–5; adm*), one of the finest examples of 19th-century classical architecture in Switzerland. Pride of place belongs to works by Anton Graff, Carl Spitweg and Ferdinand Georg Waldmüller, along with fine examples of Bücklin, Feuerbach and Marées and their German Idealism work; modern art features, too, with some Klee's and Picasso's amongst others, and even work by Jean Tinguely. The **Tonhalle** concert hall and puppet theatre are along here, too.

Vaduz (Liechtenstein)

The city of Vaduz, with a population of around 5,000, is the capital of Liechtenstein, a tiny landlocked country in the centre of Europe between Austria and Switzerland. It is the fourth smallest country in Europe with a land area of just 61¾ sq miles (16,006 hectares) and a population of a mere 33,000.

Historically Liechtenstein was divided into two parts: the Lordship of Schellenberg and the County of Vaduz, each owned over the years by various dynasties of counts. Prince Johann Adam Andreas of Liechtenstein's purchase of first Schellenberg in 1699 and subsequently Vaduz in 1712 earned him a seat in the Diet of the Princes, which was under the dominion of the German Empire. In 1719 Kaiser Karl VI decreed that Schellenburg and Vaduz be elevated to the status of the Imperial Principality of Liechtenstein. It has the distinction of being the only country in the world to still carry the name of its original dynasty.

First a part of Napoleon's Rhine Confederacy and then of the German confederation, Liechtenstein has been a fully sovereign, neutral country since 1866 when the later was dissolved. Since 1924 it has maintained a customs treaty with Switzerland that, effectively, has formed a common economic region between the two small countries in which Swiss customs officers patrol the border with Austria and the Swiss franc (CHF) is the legal currency.

Liechtenstein is a 'constitutional hereditary monarchy upon a democratic and parliamentary basis'. The Prince, as head of state, represents Liechtenstein in its relationships with other countries, whilst the rights and interests of the citizens are protected by a parliament – the Landtag. The first prince to make his permanent residence in Liechtenstein, rather than Vienna, was Franz-Josef II, who reigned from 1938 until his death in 1989. He was succeeded by his oldest son, Prince Hans-Adam II, the reigning monarch.

High German is taught in the schools and used as the official language, but the majority of the natives speak a dialect similar to Swiss German – a derivative that is difficult even for other German-speaking peoples to understand.

Around the Town

Physically, Vaduz is dominated by the very grand castle that is home to the Prince (not open to the public). Best guess is that the original, which was destroyed by

Tourist Information

Liechtenstein: Liechtenstein Tourism, Vaduz, Städtle 37, **t** 02 232 14 43, *wwwtourismus. li (open Mon–Fri 8–12 and 1.30–5.30, Sat April–Oct 10–12 and 1.30–4, Sun May–Sept 10–12 and 1.30–5).*

If you wish to have your **passport stamped** as a memento of your visit, the tourist office staff will oblige, for only CHF 2, with the official Fürstentum Liechtenstein stamp (FL are the initials you see everywhere, which stand for Principality of Liechtenstein).

Guided Tours

One way to learn about Vaduz is to take a **city tour**, organized by the tourist office, which from mid-June to end Sept departs Mon–Fri at 2pm from the Welcome Desk at the bus terminal; tickets CHF 10.

Shopping

Thönys Schuhgeschäft, Städtle 17, **t** 02 232 23 18, **f** 02 233 26 18. The best place to buy Swiss Army knives, or any other souvenir.

Where to Stay and Eat

Half-board recommended.

★★★★Park-Hotel Sonnenhof, Mareestrasse 29, **t** 02 239 02 02, **f** 02 239 02 23, *www.sonnenhof.li (moderate)*. A very comfortable hotel just a short distance from Vaduz. Set in a park, it offers a traditional style, modern facilities, pool and health club, and views of the Rhine and Alps.

★★★Le Real, Städtle 21, **t** 02 232 22 22, **f** 02 232 08 91, *www.hotel-real.li (moderate)*. A small hotel, extremely comfortable and centrally located on Vaduz's one really main street.

troops of the Swiss Confederacy during the Swabian War of 1499, was constructed in the Middle Ages. The present structure dates from the 16th and 17th centuries.

The newest and most important attraction in Vaduz is the **National Art Museum** (Kunstmuseum Liechtenstein; *Städtle 32, t 02 235 03 00, f 02 235 03 29, www.kunstmuseum.li; open Tues–Sun 10–5, Thurs until 8pm; adm*). The building itself, inaugurated in 2000, is an eye-catching cube of anthracite-coloured basalt rock which is stunning enough, but it is actually overshadowed by the exhibits based on the world-famous collections of the Prince of Liechtenstein. Rembrandt's *Amor* and Rubens' *Venus* are the highlights of the Old Masters, and they sit next to important works from modern and contemporary art.

Philately has always been important here, and the **Postage Stamp Museum** (Briefmarkmuseum; *Städtle 37 (in the same building as the tourist office), t 02 236 61 05, f 02 236 61 09, www.pwz.li; open daily 10–12 and 1.30–5; free*) is very popular. Established in 1930, it houses a large collection of stamps issued by Liechtenstein from 1912 onwards, and of swapped stamps from other countries in the International Philatelic Society which date from 1921 onwards. There are numerous other exhibits of items relevant to the design and printing of stamps and the Liechtenstein postal service.

Another local tradition is detailed at the **Ski Museum** (*Fabrikstrasse 5, t 02 232 15 02, f 02 263 23 45, www.skimuseum.li; open Mon–Fri 2–6; adm*). Founded by former ski racer and expert Noldi Beck, its exhibits trace the evolution of skiing from its inception as a necessity for farmers and hunters to what is today almost exclusively a leisure pursuit.

The Prince's presence here shows itself in some unexpected ways, and a visit to the **Prince of Liechtenstein's Court Winery** (Hofkellerie des Fürsten von Liechtenstein; *Fürstliche Domäne, Feldstrasse 4, t 02 232 10 18, f 02 233 11 45, www.hofkellerei.li; open Mon–Fri 8–12 and 1.30–6.30, Sat 9–1*), just a short distance from the centre of Vaduz, is a must. Although covering less than 10 acres (4 hectares), Liechtenstein's wine-making tradition has a long and distinguished history supported by naturally conducive conditions – ideal southwest-orientated hillsides, calcareous soil and a climate that gives out about 1,500 hours of annual sunshine. The most famous of the wines are the dry reds of Süssdruck and Beerli, which can be tasted and bought here.

Graubünden

Scuol

The Lower Engadine valley is in the far eastern part of Switzerland that adjuts into, and is surrounded by, Austria and Italy. It is a by-product of the frequently torrential Inn river; the valley is flanked to the north by the Silvretta range and to the south by the Lischana mountains. Geographical peculiarities have made it remote from other parts of Switzerland, and the historical combination of Rhaetian and Roman influences have bequeathed to the area its distinctive culture and language, Romansch – the fourth official language of Switzerland and still much in evidence here today.

The charm of this valley is its unspoiled villages that have not succumbed to the demands of mass tourism. You will see many houses decorated with *sgraffito* – the elaborate artwork found on the exterior of houses throughout the Engadine.

Scuol, a town of under 2,000 inhabitants at the end of the St Moritz train line, has exploited the local phenomenon of healing waters and revolutionized the traditional concept of the spa.

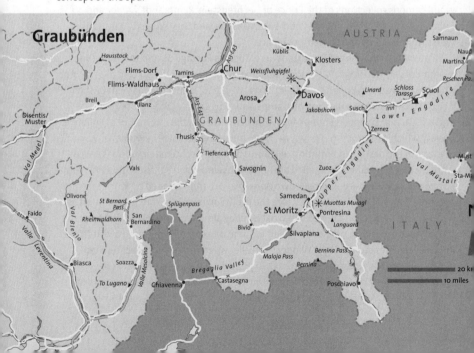

Tourist Information

Scuol: Scuol Information, **t** 081 861 22 22, **f** 081 861 22 23, *www.scuol.ch*, next to the bus station (*open Mon–Fri 8–7, Sat 10–12, Sun 2–4*).

Where to Stay

Scuol

★★★★Belvédere, **t** 081 861 06 06, **f** 081 861 06 00, *www.belvedere-scuol.ch* (*expensive*). Right in the village centre, this gracious hotel has an attractive façade and pleasant gardens with a nice outside pool. Each of the 64 modern and spacious rooms are individually designed, and some have alpine views. There's also a superb restaurant, cosy piano bar and a new wellness centre.

★★★Engiadina, Rablüzza 152, **t** 081 864 14 21, **f** 081 864 12 45, *www.engiadina-scuol.ch* (*moderate*). Near the village centre – 3mins from the spa – in a traditional house that

has been cleverly converted, with many of its 12 rooms furnished in Swiss pine.

Gasthaus Mayor, Postfach 87, **t** 081 864 14 12, **f** 081 864 99 83 (*inexpensive*). A modern comfortable guesthouse with more than adequate facilities, named after the owners.

Tarasp

★★★★Schlosshotel Chastè, Sparsels, **t** 081 861 30 60, **f** 081 861 30 61, *www.relaischateaux. ch/chaste* (*expensive*). A 19-room hotel situated in the shadow of the imposing castle. Pine panelling and a warm, comfortable ambiance. Also a wonderful restaurant and a well-equipped on-site health club.

Eating Out

Schü-San, **t** 081 864 81 43. Incongruously, this pleasant Chinese restaurant and bar overlooks the main pool of the spa. It has a wide-ranging menu including vegetarian dishes, lots of curry and house specialities.

The Spa and Castle

The **Engadin Bad Scuol** (*t* 081 861 20 00, *f* 081 861 20 01, *www.scuol.ch*) is unique in Switzerland, and offers a complete body and mind experience. It comprises different parts: the **bath and sauna landscapes** (*open daily 8am–10pm; adm CHF 25 valid for 2½hrs*); the **Roman-Irish bath** (*open 9.45am–10pm; adm CHF 71 including unlimited admission to the bath and sauna landscape; reservations must be made 24hrs in advance*); and the **therapy centre** (*t* 081 861 20 04), where waters from the Luzius, Sfondraz, Bonifazius and Lishana springs are used to treat any number of ailments.

The **bath and sauna landscapes** make up the majority of the spa. The centrepiece of the **bath landscape** complex is a large, round, indoor pool, equipped with several water fountains, where the water is maintained at a relaxing 93.2°F (34°C). Arranged around this are several smaller pools, including the popular jacuzzi. Next, you will find a brine pool, at 95°F (35°C), whose waters contain 2 per cent natural salt from the springs of the United Swiss Rhine Salt-Works. However, as brine has the capacity for damaging several minerals and stays on the skin, it is advisable to remove spectacles and/or jewellery, and to shower immediately afterwards. The cold-water pool is a chilly 64°F (18°C), but the most unusual pool is outside, reached via an interior channel where you pass through weather-protecting strips. Circular like the large pool, it is sub-divided into three concentric rings. The outer ring is a 'Lazy River' with concrete jacuzzi beds built into the walls, and the two inner rings have jacuzzi jets; the water is a warm 93.2°F (34°C). It is an amazing experience to lay there luxuriating in the water while the snow gently falls around you blanketing the nearby mountains. If all of this gets too much, there is is a solarium inside with wonderfully comfortable lounge chairs: the perfect place for a little snooze.

The **sauna landscape** is just off the bath landscape. This is a mixed sex area and you must dispense with your swimming costume. The only thing that accompanies you further is a towel, although this generally is carried over the arm – not wrapped around you. People of other cultures, particularly North Americans, might tend to believe that this can give rise to pruriency. To the Swiss, however, it is as natural as going to a normal swimming pool, and there is absolutely no embarrassment. An outside sauna gives out 203°F (95°C) of heat; if that leaves you in need of a cooling-off, you can follow up with a dive into the open-air cold pool with a coldwater cascade. At just 64°F (18°C), it is an exhilarating and chilling experience. Along the side of that pool, but back inside, is a glass-encased solarium with comfortable lounge chairs offering complimentary refreshment from a refrigerator filled with bottles of the spa's own natural water.

The **Roman–Irish bath** is a wonderfully sensual experience. At the reception area you will be given a toga to replace your bathing costume and a pair of rubber slip-ons to prevent you slipping on the wet tiled floors. The baths take 2½ hours to pass through, and it is also a mixed sex area. Having changed, you start with two increas-ingly hot dry saunas at 129.2°F (54°C) and 158°F (70°C), which are followed by a shower and an invigorating soap and brush massage – usually performed by a masseuse on the men and by a masseur on the women – that stimulates circulation and peels the skin. Your massage done, have a quick shower and head for the Vapour Baths with the first at 107.6°F (42°C) and the second at 118.4°F (48°C). Shower again and it is time for complete relaxation in two quite large baths, 96.8°F (36°C) and 93.2°F (34°C) respectively. The latter is rather like a small swimming pool, entered via the steps that encircle it, and capped by an intriguing domed roof decorated with rather exotic paintings of mermaids. The penultimate stop – and you will not want to linger long – is the 64.4°F (18°C) Cold Water Pool. After you shower yet again an assis-tant will escort you to the Resting Place. There you will lie for half an hour or so, wrapped in warm towels on contoured air-beds, listening to the soft sounds of nature emanating from the ceiling.

Another sight of national significance within the valley, and one whose command-ing site makes it difficult to ignore, is the **Schloss Tarasp** (Tarasp Castle; *t 081 864 93 68, f 081 864 93 73, www.schloss-tarasp.ch; guided tours in June and early July at 2.30, until late Aug at 11, 2.30, 3.30 and 4.30, until mid-Oct at 2.30 and 3.30, and at other times of the year on Tues and Thurs at 4.30; adm*). In years past, many castles were scattered throughout the Inn valley, although most are now just ruins. But not Tarasp Castle, constructed atop a hill directly in front of the village around the middle of the 11th century by the Tarasp family. In 1900 Dr K. A. Linger, owner of a Dresden cosmetic and pharmaceutical company, purchased it for CHF 20,000. While this was a huge sum at that time, it only represented the beginning of the expense necessary to renovate, restore and furnish the castle. Sadly Dr Linger died, in 1916, shortly before the castle was ready for him to move into. And that presented another problem. Although Dr Linger had bequeathed the castle and its contents to August III, King of Saxony, he declined to take possession in light of the financial burden associated with its upkeep. Resolution was reached when the castle was offered to, and accepted by, an old friend of Dr Linger's, the Grand Duke Ernst Ludwig of Hesse and the Rhine, who had at his disposal the necessary financial means to fund what would be costly ongoing expenses. A grandson of Queen Victoria and brother of the last Empress of Russia, the Grand Duke spent as much time as he could manage during the remainder of his life at Tarasp. At present, the castle is owned by one of his descendants, Princess Margareta von Hessen.

Nauders (Austria)

The village of Nauders in Austria is just a short bus trip or drive from Scuol and is an interesting place to visit in summer. In the Austrian Tyrol, under the shadow of surrounding snow-capped mountains, two lovely valleys stretch towards the horizon and, at the point of their divergence, a quaint village clings to the lower slopes that rise between them. Nauders, on the Reschen Pass at 4,528ft (1,380m), is a fascinating contrast to its Swiss cousins.

Still an active farming community, many of the barns prominently display medallions proudly announcing awards received for prized cattle. Quite incongruously, there is a predominance of hotels, and rather nice ones at that. On closer inspection these have many of the amenities – such as pools, saunas, health clubs and fine restaurants – that you would expect to find in far larger resorts. The reality is that Nauders is in fact a resort village – but with a difference: it successfully combines a working-farm village lifestyle with the infrastructure necessary to attract an international clientele.

Not only is Austria a little more laid back than Switzerland, but prices in general are also quite a bit lower.

Around the Village and into the South Tyrol

Besides exploring the village, which is an absolute delight, the **Museum Schloss Naudersberg** (*www.schloss-nauders.com; guided tours in German May–Oct and Dec–Easter Sun 11, Tues 4.30, Wed 5, Fri 4.30*) is worth a visit. First documented in 1239 as the seat of the Masters of Nauders, it was the seat of a county court from 1300 to 1919. Subsequently abandoned and on the verge of ruin, it was purchased in 1980 by the Köllemann family, who have been restoring it ever since.

Tourist Information

Nauders: Tourismusverband Nauders, Dr.-Tschoggfey-Str. 66, **t** (011 43) 05473 87220, **f** (011 43) 05473 87627, *www. nauders.info* (*open summer Mon–Fri 9–12 and 2–6, Sat 9–6, Sun 9–12; at other times Mon–Fri 9–12 and 2–5*).

Where to Stay and Eat

★★★★**Mein Almhof, t** (011 43) 05473 87313, **f** (011 43) 05473 87644, *www.meinalmhof.at* (*moderate*). With well-equipped rooms, a fine restaurant, an indoor pool and a health club. The delightful owner Hans Kröll takes great care to ensure that all of your needs are met. Members of the family include pet marmots. Full board recommended.

The main summer tourist activity in Nauders is **hiking**, and the tourist office offers the map *Bike- und Wanderkarte Nauders* and a brochure detailing information about walks and hikes (and bike rides) around Nauders. The brochure will tell you that there are no less than 38 marked (strangely 1 to 36 and 40 and 47) hiking trails around the village – and very well marked they are, too. The trails are classified as either blue (very easy, suitable for children and older people), red (moderate) or black (quite difficult). Beware, though, that the classifications have been made by mountain folk with sturdy constitutions and legs like mountain goats! For example, Route 6 (blue) going up to the Grosser Mutzkopf via the Grüner See (suitable, but cold, for bathing) could not be classified as a leisurely stroll. To be fair, though, apart from a few steep stretches the trek goes mostly through pastureland and could not either be classified as mountaineering. And the views – across a panorama that takes in three countries – are stupendous. You will see, immediately to the south, the Reschenpass, beyond which lies the Reschensee reservoir and the Italian South Tyrol. Further around and towards the west, there's a marvellous view back down the Lower Engadine valley towards Scuol in Switzerland.

On your wanderings you may notice huge piles of **firewood** stacked at random intervals. Following Nauders tradition, 132 local families have the rights to the wood, but not to the land, on the slopes around the village. What's more, these rights are tied to a particular property and the fireplaces – up to two – located within that property. Each designated fireplace owns an entitlement to 283 cubic feet (8 cubic metres) of wood. Woodsmen are responsible for cutting the wood, piling it and replenishing the forest; the recipients of the wood must transport it to their homes.

A short excursion into Italy should definitely be on everyone's itinerary. You may be surprised to find that this part of Italy, the **South Tyrol**, is very Austrian in character. That is because it used to be part of Austria, but was handed over to Italy at the end of the First World War. The main attraction in South Tyrol is rather unusual. In the course of the development of an area reservoir, a small village was evacuated. Yet, rising forlornly from the calm waters that have claimed the town, is the top portion of the village church spire, a single reminder of the inhabitants and faith of that community. This eerie scene is one that is often photographed – especially on a clear day with snow-capped peaks in the background. Eerier still, if you are visiting in winter you may be able to cross over on foot across the ice.

Lake Geneva

Lausanne

Lausanne, with a population of 125,00 or 250,00 in the metropolitan area, is the provincial capital of the canton of Vaud in the French-speaking part of Switzerland. It has a dramatic location, being built on three hills – the **Cité**, **Bourg** and **Saint Laurent** – overlooking Lac Léman (Lake Geneva's official name) and the French Alps beyond it.

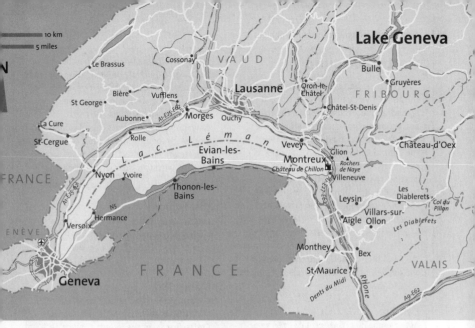

Literary personalities such as Victor Hugo, Jean-Jacques Rousseau and Lord Byron all lived for many years here, as did the musicians Igor Stravinsky, Ernest Ansermet and Clara Haskill. Consequently, Lausanne has deep cultural traditions, and is home to over 20 museums, its own opera company and chamber orchestra, and the Béjart ballet company founded by choreographer Maurice Béjart. There are numerous theatres, too, led by the Vidy-Lausanne Theatre.

Sports-wise, too, it is internationally famous, mainly as the world headquarters of the Olympic Games organization, and many international events are held annually in Lausanne.

Service organizations of banking, insurance and tourism and other multinational companies, such as Alcoa and Reynolds, have made Lausanne their headquarters. The Beaulieu exhibition complex plays host each September to the Swiss National Fair.

As a consequence of all of this, Lausanne is not short on hotels – some of which are pretty luxurious – and there are many top-class restaurants, both in the town and the smaller communities either side of it along the lake.

Lausanne also has the reputation of being Switzerland's youngest city, mainly due to the fact that there are so many schools here, including the university, Federal Institute of Technology and many other professional and private institutions. Such youth has brought with it a lively vitality, and there are numerous clubs and discos, many of which are in the old warehouses of the Le Flon area south of the station.

History

The area in and around Lausanne has an ancient history. A necropolis dating from between 6,500 and 4,500 BC has been discovered beneath the Roman ruins of *Lousonna* at Vidy, and there is evidence that lake dwellers, *lacustrians*, lived in villages built on piles along the lakeshore for nearly 3,000 years.

Getting Around

Lausanne is set upon three levels: **Ouchy** is the area down by the lakeside; the **Old Town**, **cathedral**, many **museums** and the **town hall** and **shopping** area centered around the place de la Palud are found on the upper level; and the **Central Railway Station** (Gare CFF) is nestled between the two. Of course, it is possible to walk or take the bus from one level to another, although the roads are steep and the routes meandering. The fastest and most direct mode of transport is the **Métro** – actually a rather steep funicular that runs from the lake level station of Ouchy to the train station stop and then on and up to the Flon stop by the rue de Grand-Chêne, the closest stop to the Old Town.

Car Hire

Avis, avenue de la Gare 50, **t** 021 340 72 00.
Europcar, avenue Ruchonnet 2, **t** 021 319 90 40.
Hertz, place du Tunnel, **t** 021 323 41 92.

Tourist Information

Lausanne: Lausanne Tourisme, avenue de Rhodanie 2, **t** 021 613 73 73, **f** 021 616 86 47, *www.lausanne-tourisme.ch* (*open Mon–Fri 8–12 and 1–5*). Lausanne Tourisme also has two information desks at the main hall of the train station (Gare CFF), place de la Gare 9 (*open daily 9–7*), and the Metro station Ouchy, place de la Navigation 4 (*open April–Sept daily 9–8 and Oct–Mar daily 9–6*).

The **Lausanne Card**, available from the offices of Lausanne Tourisme, for CHF 15, offers two free days of transport in and around the city, a 20–30% reduction on many museums, a 10% discount on summer excursion tickets and various other discounts at shops and restaurants, etc.

Guided Trips and Tours

A walking tour of the **Old Town** (Vieille Ville), **t** 021 321 77 66, is conducted May–Sept daily at 10 and 3. It departs from the place de la Palud and costs CHF 10. A free, guided tour of the **cathedral** takes place daily July–mid-Sept at 10.30, 11.15, 3 and 3.45.

Trips on **lake steamers** are operated by the **Compagnie Générale de Navigation sur le Lac Léman**, avenue de Rhodaine, **t** 021 614 62 00, **f** 021 614 62 02, *www.cgn.ch*. The most popular will be to Evian-les-Bains, the pretty French town immediately across the lake famous worldwide for its mineral water (*see* p.175). The lake steamers, in effect, act as buses around the lake, west towards Geneva or east to Montreux.

Lost Property

Lost Property Office (Bureau des Objets Trouvés), place Chauderon 7, **t** 021 315 33 85 (*open Mon–Fri 8–12 and 1.45–6, Sat 8–11.30am*).

Market Days

Christmas market: the 10 days before Christmas at the place de la Riponne.
Crafts: first Fri of the month at place de la Palud.
Flea market: Thurs 6am–7pm at the place Chauderon.
Fruit and vegetables: Wed and Sat mornings at the place de la Palud.
St Louis market for flowers and honey: for two days at the end of Aug between 6am to 7pm at Derrière-Bourg.

Exhibitions and Festivals

Late Jan to early Feb: the **Prix de Lausanne**, an international young dancers competition.
Late Mar: **Lausanne Antiques Fair**.
Late Mar: **International Fair of Minerals, Fossils and Gems**.
Late April: the **20km of Lausanne**, a popular running race.
Late April: the **Carnival of Lausanne**.
Late May to early June: the **European Beer Festival** at Ouchy.
Late June: **Fête de la Musique**, free concerts.
Late June: **Fête à Lausanne**, a popular event in the city centre.
June–Aug: **Entrée Libre pour un Eté**, an annual festival of free shows and concerts.
Early to mid-June: **Festival de la Cité**, 250 free outdoor events in the Old City.
Early July: **Athletissima**, an international athletics meeting at the Olympic Stadium.

Late Oct to early Nov: Jazz Festival Lausanne Onze Plus.
Early Nov: Gastronomia, international fair of food, etc.
Mid to late Nov: Antique Dealers show.

Shopping

The principal shopping areas in Lausanne are centered between the place de la Palud and the place St-François. Here you can find everything from large department stores to fashionable boutiques, and much more.

Coutelleries du Petit-Chêne, Petit-Chêne 22, **t** 021 312 01 86, **f** 021 312 22 45, *www.swiss-knife.com*. Has the most extensive collection of Swiss Army knives, as well as numerous pen knives, scissors, kitchen knives, sewing sets with thimbles, corkscrews and an array of collectors' swords.

Heidi's Shop, Petit-Chêne 22, **t** 021 311 16 89, *www.heidi-shop.ch*. Provides quite a contrast, and here there is an excellent array of Lötscher cuckoo clocks, backpacks, mugs, soft toys, dolls, sweatshirts and much else.

Where to Stay

★★★★★Lausanne Palace and Spa, Grand-Chêne 7–9, **t** 021 331 31 31, **f** 021 323 25 71, *www.lausanne-palace.com* (*luxury*). This is a palace by name and by nature. Opened in 1915, it is in the heart of the business and shopping district and yet offers fantastic views over Lake Léman and the Alps. On the exterior is a beautiful, classical façade; the interior features 150 large and spacious rooms and suites, each distinctively decorated with fine fabrics in a traditional style. There are even two toilets in each room, and heated mirrors in the bathrooms that won't steam up! It has the largest wellness centre in the Lake Geneva region, with an indoor pool and specialized beauty treatments.

★★★★Royal-Savoy, avenue d'Ouchy 40, **t** 021 614 88 88, **f** 021 614 88 78, *www.royal-savoy.ch* (*expensive*). This stylish building is set in its own grounds close to the lakeside.

An established hotel with a fine reputation, all of its spacious 99 rooms and 9 suites have been recently renovated, adding modern facilities to the antique decor. Many also have balconies with lake views.

★★★Hôtel du Port, place du Port 5, **t** 021 612 04 44, **f** 021 612 04 45, *www.hotel-du-port.ch* (*moderate*). This hotel, close to the Ouchy Métro stop, has a colourful and irregularly shaped façade. Run by the same family for over 40 years, it has 22 modern rooms and junior suites, some with disabled access and non-smoking.

★★★City, rue Caroline 5, **t** 021 320 21 41, **f** 021 320 21 49, *www.fhotels.ch* (*moderate*). This is in the heart of the Old Town area between the Cathedral and the rue de Bourg. They advertise, and justifiably so, that they offer 4-star service at 3-star prices. The Art Deco lobby sets the style for the rest of the hotel. Fifty guest rooms, some with kitchenettes; each has a bath/shower, a TV with free video, fax and computer connections and a mini-bar.

Jeunotel, chemin du Bois-de-Vaux 36, **t** 021 626 02 22, **f** 021 626 02 26, *www.jeunotel.ch* (*inexpensive*). Situated to the south of the city, by way of a no.2 bus from Ouchy to the Bois-de-Vaux stop. It has a total of 110 rooms offering modern combinations of accommodation, with or without en suite facilities.

Lausanne Guesthouse and Backpacker, chemin des Epinettes 4, **t** 021 601 80 00, **f** 021 601 80 01, *www.lausanne-backpacker.ch* (*inexpensive*). Just a few minutes' walk south of the train station, this is in a gracious old house. It has a range of room combinations, all clean and comfortable: quadruples (with or without sheets), doubles (with or without sheets and with a private or semi-private bathroom) and singles (with a private or semi-private bathroom).

Eating Out

La Grappe d'Or, cheneau-de-Bourg 3, **t** 021 323 07 60, **f** 021 323 22 30 (*very expensive*). This fine restaurant has one Michelin star. In a traditional dining room with a large fireplace, Peter Baermann prepares and presents creative dishes, inspired by the Orient and the Mediterranean, of lake fish and seafood, meats and other seasonal produce. The wine list has fine French and Italian vintages.

La Table du Palace, Grand-Chêne 7–9, t 021 331 31 31, f 021 323 25 71 (*very expensive*). As expected of a restaurant affiliated with the Lausanne Palace and Spa hotel, this one-star Michelin restaurant is one of the finest places to dine in the city. It has a contemporary classical decor, with expansive vistas over the lake and Alps, especially from the terrace on warmer nights. The chef, Eric Redolat, is an advocate of light cuisine that is reminiscent of the region, and presents a tantalizing array of imaginative, exotically flavoured and beautifully presented dishes.

Brasserie Bavaria, rue du Petit-Chêne 10, t 021 323 39 13 (*expensive*). This is a typical German-style drinking house, with painted murals and dark wooden ceilings. Look for a wide selection of foreign beers, sandwiches and breadsticks on the bars, and regional specialties such as *choucroute* and *rösti*.

Le Lacustre, port d'Ouchy-Débarcadère, quai Dapples 1, t 021 617 42 00, f 021 617 42 90 (*moderate*). This French restaurant and brasserie has a terrific location right next to the lake, with stunning views of the French Alps – especially from the large terrace. It has an interesting menu, too, that includes a selection of fish from the lake itself, and a special 4-course *Potence* menu for a minimum of two people at CHF 60pp.

Pinte Besson Chodorge, rue de l'Ale 4, t 021 312 72 27 (*moderate*). In an arched bricked-ceiling cavern dating from 1780, this serves fondues, French and Vaudoise cuisine with ingredients fresh from the market, along with a fine selection of Swiss wines.

Monte-Cristo, avenue du Tribunal-Féderale 2, t 021 311 97 87 (*moderate*). This is a bright, new and lively restaurant whose speciality is tapas. Order these as side dishes, or try the *menu dégustation* with 14 types of tapas, sangria and special house coffee for CHF 60. Latino house music from the DJ on Fri and Sat. *Closed Sun*.

Boccalino, avenue d'Ouchy 76, t 021 616 35 39 (*moderate*). A bright, light, trendy restaurant that has a menu featuring over 120 different types of pizza and 50 types of pasta, with both usually between CHF 17 and 20.

El Chiringuito Café-Restaurant, Saint Laurent 38, t 021 312 73 47 (*moderate*). A Spanish snack bar in the middle of a pedestrian shopping area not far from the Old Town.

Entertainment

The **Casino de Montbenon**, allée Ernest-Ansermet 3, t 021 323 82 51, f 021 315 20 13, just 5mins' walk from the city centre, was built in 1908 and renovated in 1981.

Opera, Music and Dance

Opéra de Lausanne, avenue du Théâtre 12, t 021 310 16 00, www.opera-lausanne.ch.

Orchestre de Chambre de Lausanne, rue St-Laurent 19, t 021 345 00 20, f 021 345 00 21. Led by Christian Zacharias.

Lausanne Sinfonietta, avenue du Grammont 11 bis, t 021 616 71 35.

Association des Concerts de Montbenon, Casino de Montbenon, t 021 318 71 71.

Béjart Ballet Lausanne, chemin du Presbytère, t 021 641 64 80, www.bejart.ch. World-famous ballet.

Nightlife

For **cabaret** shows try:

La Belle Epoque, rue de Bourg 17, t 021 312 11 49. Live shows and music and two spectacular scenes (*open daily from 6pm to 5am*).

Le Tiffany, rue del'Ale 15, t 021 312 52 01 (*open daily from 6pm to 5am*).

Blummell Club of Clubs, Grand-Chêne 7, t 021 312 09 20, with its Midnight Show (*open daily from 6pm to 5am*).

On the **club and bar** scene there is:

Chorus Jazz, avenue Mon-Repos 3, t 021 323 22 33, www.chorus.ch.

The **Cult Club**, place Chaudron 18, t 021 311 95 30, www.cultclub.ch.

Atelier Volant, côtes de Montbenon 12, Le Flon, t 021 624 84 28, www.ateliervolant.ch.

Le Ripp's, place de la Riponne 10, t 021 320 70 51, www.leripps.ch.

L'Akt Music Café, terrasse de la Madeleine 18, t 021 312 00 50, www.l-akt.ch.

Around AD 600, Lausanne was designated a Cathedral City – thus beginning what would become a nearly 1,000-year line of bishops which would end with the Burgundy Wars of the 16th century.

The 12th and 13th centuries brought good times and expansion, and a religious revival occasioned the consecration of the cathedral in 1275. The next centuries were not so kind to Lausanne. With the 14th century came a decline in the city's fortunes and the ravages of the plague. Devastation rained early in the 15th century in the form of the Burgundy Wars that culminated in 1536 with invasion and conquest by the Bernese forces, who ruled for the next two and a half centuries.

The 17th century brought further plagues, which devastated the city four times. Towards the end of the century, the repeal of the Treaty of Nantes gave rise to an exodus of over 1,000 French refugees into Lausanne. In the latter half of the 18th century Lausanne became fashionable, primarily because of Rousseau, and celebrities and European nobility descended in droves. A young Mozart even honoured the city with concerts on two occasions in 1766.

The French Revolution of 1789 brought this peaceful era to an abrupt end. Celebrations by the populace caused consternation in Bern, who sent troops to occupy the town in 1791. One thing led to another and, finally, representations were made to the Directoire in Paris to intervene. After being placed under French protection on 18 December 1797, representatives from the communities in Vaud convened in Lausanne on 24 January 1798, proclaiming a Declaration of Independence. Several days later French troops entered Lausanne to a liberators' welcome. In 1803 the canton of Vaud joined the Swiss Confederation.

The Old Town (Vieille Ville)
The **cathedral** (*open Mon–Fri 7–5.30, Sat 8–5.30, Sun afternoon from the conclusion of the religious service until 5.30*), with its irregular and architecturally diverse façade, dominates the Vieille Ville. Constructed during the 12th and 13th centuries, it has the distinction of being the largest Gothic building in Switzerland; an interesting note is that just four of the five towers included in the original plans were ultimately erected. Present at its consecration in October 1275 were Pope Gregory X and Rudolf of Hapsburg, upon whom, having sworn an oath of allegiance to the Church, was bestowed the title of Emperor. The interior is impressive; note the beautifully sculptured portals, the 16th-century carved choir stalls, numerous sepulchres and 105 stained-glass panes, most of which are set in an glorious circular window.

Outside the cathedral is a terrace, with a welcome water fountain, that offers yet more imposing views of the surrounding countryside. You will also find a rather aristocratic structure, the former **Episcopal Palace** (Ancien-Evêche), adorned by a 13th-century fortified tower, which was home to the bishops of Lausanne until the early 15th century. Today it houses the **Lausanne Historical Museum** (Musée Historique de Lausanne; *place de la Cathédrale 4, t 021 331 03 53, f 021 312 42 68; open July and Aug daily 11–6, all other months closed Mon; adm*). One of the main exhibits is a 28.7 square yard (24 square m) scale model, complete with sound and lighting effects, of the Old Town as it looked in the 17th century. It also features regular temporary exhibitions that can be as diverse as headdresses and bonnets from the late 18th to early 20th centuries to the art of erotic bookplates. There is a very different kind of museum very nearby, the **Mu.dac/Museum for Design and the Applied Arts** (Musée de Design et d'Arts Appliqués Contemporains/mu-dac; *place de la Cathédrale 6, t 021 315 25 30, f 021 315 25 39, www.lausanne/ch/mudac; open July and Aug Mon and Wed–Sun 11–6 and Tues 11–9, all other months closed Mon; adm*). Here, besides applied art, there are contemporary glass sculptures and Egyptian and Chinese pieces, as well as temporary exhibitions.

The other end of the Old Town is dominated by the 15th-century Saint-Maire castle, now the seat of the government of the canton of Vaud. In between, there are any number of quiet cobbled streets full of attractive medieval buildings that have been converted into tempting boutiques, galleries, restaurants and bars. And if you happen to be around here between 10pm and 2am you can hear, from the bell tower, Europe's last nightwatchman shouting out his traditional 'All's Well' cry.

Place de la Riponne and Place de la Palud

Just outside the main doors of the cathedral, the 160 steps of the **Escaliers du Marché** – a wooden roofed stairway similar to two seen in Thun – take you down to another open set of steps that lead into the **place de la Riponne**. This large plaza, adorned by a marvellous fountain from which spout dozens upon dozens of jets of water, is totally dominated by the huge classical façade of the **Rumine Palace** (Palais de Rumine; *place de la Riponne 6*). Named after its donor, this Florentine Renaissance-style structure was built in 1906 as the principal building of Lausanne University. Presently, however, besides being a market place it is also a centre of culture, as it is home to the following museums. The **Cantonal Fine Arts Museum** (Musée Cantonal des Beaux-Arts; *t 021 316 34 45, f 021 316 34 46; open Tues and Wed 11–6, Thurs 11–8, Fri, Sat and Sun 11–5; adm, but free on 1st Sun of month*) displays works by French-Swiss artists like Ducros, Bocion, Gleyre, Vallotton and Soutter from the 18th, 19th and 20th centuries. The **Coin Room** (Cabinet des Médailles du Canton de Vaud; *t 021 316 39 90, f 021 316 39 99; open Tues–Thurs 11–6, Fri–Sun 11–5; adm, but free on 1st Sun of month*) has over 60,000 items from the cantonal collection from antiquity to the modern day. Other exhibits relate to the history of European, Swiss and regional monetary history. The **Cantonal Museum of Archaeology and History** (Musée Cantonal d'Archéologie et d'Histoire; *t 021 316 34 30, f 021 316 34 31, www.lausanne.ch/archeo; open Tues–Thurs 11–6, Fri–Sun 11–5; adm, but free on 1st Sun of month*) has local exhibits from the end of the last Ice Age, through the Bronze Age and the Celts to more modern times, and has an interesting mix of traditional objects, models and thematic explanations in either slide or video shows. The **Cantonal Geological Museum** (Musée Cantonal de Géologie; *t 021 692 44 70, f 021 692 44 75; open Tues–Thurs 11–6, Fri–Sun 11–5; adm, but free on 1st Sun of month*) traces the geological evolution of this region. It features a virtual trip through the Alps, fossils and exhibitions on minerals and crystals. Finally, there is the **Cantonal Zoology Museum** (Musée Cantonal de Zoologie; *t 021 316 34 60, f 021 316 34 79; open Tues–Thurs 11–6, Fri–Sun 11–5; adm, but free on 1st Sun of month*). Also found in *the square is the Espace Arlaud (t 021 316 38 50; open Wed–Fri 12–6, Sat and Sun 11–5),* and this holds temporary exhibitions from the cantonal museums.

Place de la Palud, one of the town's traditional meeting places, is due south of the place de la Riponne, following rue Madeleine out of the plaza and down, past some shops. This really is quite an interesting square. Upon the 17th-century Hôtel de Ville (town hall), the pre-eminent structure, is an ornamental clock which has become a Lausanne landmark. It strikes on the hour between 9am and 7pm with a parade of mechanical figures depicting the region's history. This overlooks the elegant and colourful Fountain of Justice, that dates from 1726. Try to time your visit to coincide with one of two lively market days (*see* p.168). This is also the centre of the modern shopping district, which crosses the busy rue Centrale and extends up to the **place St-François**, dominated by the 13th-century church, with a 15th-century bell tower, of the same name. This once served as the sanctuary of a monastery, but has been Protestant since the Reformation. Place St-François is encircled by pavement cafés, restaurants, shops and the unmistakable central post office.

Ouchy

Just outside the Ouchy Métro, the imposing neo-Gothic castle-like structure to the left, a former defensive building dating from 1893, today houses the 3-Star Château d'Ouchy hotel, surrounded by gardens running down to the lake. Immediately behind, and south, of the hotel are more gardens that lead to the embarkation point for the lake steamers, **Débarcadère d'Ouchy**.

To the west is the **place de la Navigation**, and the **Espace Pierre-de-Coubertin** with a combination of shallow water ponds and fountains abutting the small inner harbour. There is also a children's adventure tower, public chess games and a giant, C-shaped weather vane. It is a also a popular meeting place and, if you are lucky, you may find that you have chanced upon the European Beer Festival.

The main attractions of Ouchy, however, are to the east of the Métro station. Lausanne does not come by one of its nicknames, the Garden City, without reason. And nowhere is this more apparent than along the lakeside promenade of Quai d'Ouchy where, in 1901, nearly 1,100 yards (more than 1km) of trees and flowerbeds were planted. In fact, Lausanne has a total of 790 acres (319.7 hectares) of public gardens, of which 250 acres (101.2 hectares) are at the lakeside. There are over 5 miles (8km) of promenades, and strolling along the Quai d'Ouchy you will see far more than just plants and trees. Interspersed between these are a host of fountains and statues of every kind, including one of General Henri Guisan, leader of the Swiss defensive army in the Second World War. To the north, away from the lake, is an eclectic array of expansive buildings some of which, like the Beau-Rivage Palace and the Royal-Savoy, now serve as luxury hotels. To the south, the Alps glisten in the distance.

As the headquarters of the International Olympic Committee, Lausanne's **Olympic Museum** (Musée Olympique; *quai d'Ouchy 1, t 021 621 65 11, f 021 621 65 12, www. olympic.org; open daily 9–6, but till 8pm on Thurs and closed on Mon Oct–April; adm; audio guides available*), opened in 1993, is the world's greatest centre of information on the Olympic movement. You can reach the museum by taking a pathway that winds its way past an ever-increasing number of Olympian sculptures. Alternatively, if you need a rest, take the escalators up and wander down once you have explored the museum. The architectural futurism of this ultra-modern structure, faced with Thassos marble, is complemented by its use of technology: admission and exit, both to the museum and to the individual exhibitions within, is by a computer-coded key. Permanent exhibitions spotlight a multitude of familiar athletes, their respective events, and, in some cases, the equipment that played a role in their victories. These, as well as whatever temporary exhibits are on offer, are enhanced by a variety of innovative audio-visual effects. This impressive museum is guaranteed to be a winner for children of all ages. In addition to the Olympic Archives, the Olympic Documentation Centre has 150,000 books, 250,000 photos, and film and video totalling 7,000 hours of viewing. There is also a museum souvenir shop, but beware, the prices can hit Olympian heights.

Just north of the Olympic Museum is Switzerland's main photography museum, the **Elysée Museum** (Musée de l'Elysée; *avenue de l'Elysée 18*, *t 021 316 99 11*, *f 021 316 99 12*, *www.elysee.ch; open daily 11–6; adm, but free on the 1st Sat of the month*), located in a picture-perfect 17th-century mansion set in gardens adjacent to the Olympic Museum.

Other Museums and Attractions

Of the other museums in and around Lausanne, the following will be of the most interest; they are listed in a clockwise order starting directly north of the Old Town.

The **Hermitage Foundation** (*route du Signal 2*, *t 021 320 50 01*, *f 021 320 50 71*, *www.fondation-hermitage.ch; open Tues–Sun 10–6 and Thurs until 9pm, and 10–6 on Mon in June; adm exp; No.16 bus to Hermitage*) is housed in a lovely mansion in a landscaped park, built by banker Charles-Juste Bugnion in 1842–50. Donated by his descendants to the city in 1976, it has now been restored and the Bugnion family donated the core of its collection. Look for the Impressionist and post-Impressionist works of the likes of Sisley, Guillaumin, Morren and Puigaudeau as well as works of 20th-century Vaudois artists including Gleyre, Chavannes, Vallotton, Bosshard and Domenjoz. The Vergottis Collection of Chinese porcelain from the 12th to 19th centuries is also on display.

The **Claude Verdan Foundation** (*rue du Bugnon 21*, *t 021 314 49 55*, *f 021 314 49 63*, *www.verdan.ch; open Tues–Fri 1–6, Sat and Sun 11–5; adm; No.5 and 6 bus to the Montagibert stop*) is rather different – it is dedicated to the world of perfume.

The attraction of the **Roman Villa of Pully** (Musées de Pully; *ave S.-Reymondin 2*, *t 021 729 55 81*, *f 021 729 58 94; open April–Oct Tues–Sun 2–5, Nov–Mar 2–5, adm; No.4 bus to the Pully-Gare stop*) is a semi-circular painted mural dating from the 1st century AD.

The **Cantonal Botanic Gardens and Museum** (Musée et Jardins Botaniques Cantonaux; *place de Milan*, *t 021 316 99 88*, *f 021 616 46 65*, *www.botanique.vd.ch; gardens open Mar–Oct daily 10–5.30, closing time one hour later May–Sept; museum open July and Aug daily 11-7, May, June and Sept Wed–Mon 11–6, Oct Wed–Mon 1–5; both free; bus No.1 to the Les Cèdres stop*) are located in the large open area of the place de Milan, directly underneath the strange circular Montriond Mountain. This is a pleasant oasis in the middle of the city.

The **Roman Museum Vidy** (Musée Romain de Vidy; *chemin du Bois-de- Vaux 24,* **t** *021 625 10 84,* **f** *021 625 11 35, www.lausanne.ch/mrv; open Tues–Sun 11–6 and until 8pm on Thurs; adm; buses Nos.1 and 4 to the Bois-de-Vaux stop*) has a permanent exhibition detailing the diversity of everyday life in the Roman city of *Lousonna,* reconstituted on the ruins of a rich house.

The **Crude Art Collection** (Collection de l'Art Brut; *avenue des Bergières 11,* **t** *021 315 25 70,* **f** *021 315 27 71, www.artbrut.ch; open daily June, July and Aug Tues–Sun 11–6, closed Mon the rest of the year; adm; No.2 bus to the Jomini stop*) is an alternative art museum, with exhibits created from all kinds of materials.

Evian-les-Bains (France)

Lake steamers operated by the **Compagnie Générale de Navigation sur le Lac Léman** (*avenue de Rhodaine,* **t** *021 614 62 00,* **f** *021 614 62 02, www.cgn.ch*) set sail from the port d'Ouchy-Débarcadère. The sailing across the lake takes around 40 minutes and is a delight in itself as the French Alps draw ever closer.

Evian is one of those curious places that is world-famous even though most people haven't been there and indeed would be hard-pressed to say where it actually is. The claim to fame, of course, is derived from its most important export, mineral water. It was not until the latter 18th century that the news of Evian's refreshing natural spring water began to circulate throughout Europe. For over a century, the wealthy and the aristocratic flocked to this peaceful mountain town to take the waters by day and indulge themselves in what became a glittering and elegant social whirl by night.

The first Mineral Water development company and the first Spa Water Establishment were both opened in 1826. In 1869, the Public Limited Company of Les Eaux Minérales d'Evian-les-Bains was founded. That same year, Cachat water was approved by the Academy of Medicine and won honours at the Universal Exhibition.

Evian has made an ongoing effort to build upon its natural attributes – the beautiful mountains and lovely lake, refreshing water, pure alpine air, a moderate mountain climate and low atmospheric pressure – by constructing extensive spa and sports facilities. Visitors will also enjoy wonderful restaurants, an array of interesting shops and a variety of cultural activities – not to mention Evian's delightful ambience.

Wander around this very pretty flower-filled town at your leisure, strolling along the lake front promenade and admiring the beautiful houses. Many of the shops may be closed for lunch, but you could enjoy a long, leisurely French meal instead, as many Swiss do. The cuisine in Evian is very much lake-influenced, with char, perch fillets, trout and fera making tasty dishes. And the surrounding high country of the Savoie means that fondue and raclette also feature on menus. The cheeses of Reblochon, Abondance, Vacherin and Tomme are particularly popular, as are the white wines of Marin, Marignan Crepy and Ripaille. The local cherry orchards produce an excellent variety of kirsch, and Muratore liqueur, made from alpine plants, is a local speciality. **Le Franco-Suisse**, place Jean Bernex, is a pleasant restaurant right in the middle of the main pedestrian-only street, specializing in the traditional cuisine of the Savoie.

Montreux and Vevey

While nowadays Montreux is the better known of the two towns, it is Vevey that has the older history. The Romans established a trading post called *Vibiscum* at the junction of the road which led from their Helvetian capital of *Aventicum* (today, Avenches) and the road that connected Lausanne to Martigny, on the way to Italy.

The area that encompasses Montreux and Vevey was, from early on, primarily under the control of the Counts of Savoy, whose presence was symbolized by the nearby Château de Chillon. The year 1536, however, brought dramatic change. On 29 January over 6,000 Bernese troops blitzed the château, subsequently taking control of the whole of the Vaud and bringing with them the Protestant religion. This had far-reaching consequences – in 1685 the French revoked freedom of religion, and many thousands of French Protestants, known as Huguenots, fled to Switzerland, many of them settling in Vevey. In 1798, after more than 250 years of domination by the Bernese, the Vaudois Revolution – which came in the wake of the French Revolution – restored the region's freedom.

In the early decades of the 19th century, artists, writers, musicians and others of like mind began to discover the unique natural charms of this far eastern section of Lac Léman. Beautifully situated, with the peaceful lake and the soaring peaks of the Haute Savoie as a background, it also enjoys a mild climate. The Rochers de Naye at 6,700ft (2,042m) immediately behind (reached by train and famous for their Alpine Garden and Marmot Park) protect the slopes and lake shore from the northerly winds, giving rise to a microclimate which ranks as one of the sunniest in Switzerland. Visitors will be amazed at the numerous vineyards and the abundance of palm trees and tropical flowers that grow along the 9¼ miles (15km) distance from Villeneuve to Vevey – truly meriting its name, the 'Flowered Path'. The springtime is especially delightful when the fields blossom with thousands of fragrant narcissi. Is it any wonder, then, that the likes of Byron, Jean-Jacques Rousseau, Stravinsky and Charlie Chaplin fell in love with this place?

Over the years, Montreux and Vevey have established for themselves a worldwide reputation as a centre for arts and culture. Today, a variety of events and festivals (*see* box opposite) follow one after the other throughout the year.

Around Montreux and Vevey: the Château de Chillon

t 021 966 89 10, www.chillon.ch; open April–Sept daily 9–6; Mar and Oct daily 9.30–5; Jan, Feb, Nov and Dec daily 10–4; adm.

The majority of visitors to Montreux and Vevey will want to see the **Château de Chillon**. Situated on a little island jutting into the lake, this château is a signature landmark, not only for this portion of the Vaud, but for Switzerland as well. You can get there by various means: lake steamer is best, but a no.1 bus is a good alternative from Montreux. The site has long been considered of strategic importance by virtue of its position guarding the narrow stretch of land between the lake and the mountains, along which ran the road that traversed the Great St Bernard Pass and

Tourist Information

Montreux: Montreux-Vevey Tourisme, Pavilion d'information, place du Débarcadère, **t** 0848 86 84 84, **f** 021 962 84 94 (*open Jan–mid-May and mid-Sept–Dec Mon–Fri 9–12 and 1–5.30, Sat and Sun 10–2; mid-May–mid-Sept Mon–Fri 9–6, Sat and Sun 10–5*).

Vevey: Montreux-Vevey Tourisme, place du Marché, La Grenette, **t** 0848 86 84 84, **f** 021 962 84 78 (*open Jan– mid-May and mid-Sept–Dec Mon–Fri 8.30–12 and 1–5.30, Sat and Sun 9–12; mid-May–mid-Sept Mon–Fri 9–6, Sat 8.30–3, Sun 10–2*).

Both share the same website, *www. montreux-vevey.com*, and email, *info@mvtourism.ch*.

Tours

Walking tours of Montreux (April–Sept on Wed, Thurs, Fri and Sat) and Vevey (May–Sept on Wed, Thurs and Fri) take place at 10am, cost CHF 10 and are organized by Montreux-Vevey Tourisme.

Exhibitions and Festivals

Mar: Montreux, **Art Forum**.
April: Montreux, **Montreux Choral Festival**.
May: Montreux, **Golden Rose TV Festival**.
July: Montreux, **Montreux Jazz Festival**.
Aug: Montreux, **Comedy Festival**.
Aug: Vevey, **Festival of Street Artists**.
Nov: Vevey, **St Martin's Fair** – dating from the 1500s and one of Switzerland's oldest.
Nov: Montreux, **Brass Band Competition**.
Dec: Montreux, **Christmas Market** – over 100 chalet-style stalls set up along the quayside.

Shopping

Bazar Suisse, Grand-Rue 24, **t** 021 963 32 74, **f** 021 963 72 87. The best place to buy Swiss Army knives; also on sale are music boxes, toys and cuckoo clocks with lovely carvings.

Where to Stay and Eat

Montreux

★★★★**Eden au Lac**, rue du Théâtre 1, **t** 021 966 08 00, **f** 021 966 09 00, *www.edenmontreux. ch* (*expensive*). This has a wonderful location on Lake Léman, conveniently close to the centre of Montreux. Behind a delightful Victorian façade, the interior has been completely renovated in a Louis XVI decor while preserving the original style. A fine restaurant, too, plus a large garden and pool.

★★★★**Victoria Glion**, Glion/Montreux, **t** 021 962 82 82, **f** 021 962 82 92 (*moderate*). This hotel, on the heights behind Montreux and easily reached by public transport, is a delightful Belle Epoque-style hotel dating from 1869 set in large grounds. Many of the 50 light, airy rooms have lake views and all have modern amenities.

★★★**Splendid**, Grand-Rue 52, **t** 021 966 79 79, **f** 021 966 79 77, *www.hotel-splendid.ch* (*moderate*). This is a charming Victorian hotel in a privileged position across from the lake. The 24 rooms, many with private balcony or loggia, have an old-fashioned ambience. The restaurant offers fine cuisine.

Le Palais Oriental, quai E.-Ansermet 6, **t** 021 963 12 71, *www.palaisoriental.ch*. An unusual oriental restaurant whose specialities include Moroccan, Libyan and Iranian dishes with couscous and curry. Or try the imported Iranian caviar from the Caspian Sea.

Vevey

★★★★★**Hôtel des Trois Couronnes**, rue d'Italie 49, **t** 021 923 32 00, **f** 021 923 33 39, *www. hoteldestroiscouronnes.com* (*luxury*). With a 150-year tradition, this is a charming hotel by the shores of the lake, close to the centre. Its 55 rooms, suites and junior suites are spacious, with traditional decor and balconies overlooking the lake; the public areas are stately and marble-colonnaded. In the summer months, dine on culinary French masterpieces in the terrace restaurant. Also a Puressens spa and health centre with underwater music in the pool.

★★**Hostellerie de Genève**, place du Marché 11, **t** 021 921 45 77, **f** 021 921 30 15, *www.hotel-geneve.ch* (*inexpensive*). A charming small hotel in the centre, just a moment's walk from the lake. It offers 10 pleasant rooms, a shady terrace and a restaurant which specializes in Italian and classic cuisine.

continued on to Italy. It is generally believed that the Romans established an outpost here, although the first documentation of a castle here dates much more recently, from 1150.

First owned by the bishops of Sion, the castle was built as a base from which to collect taxes on the goods that passed along the road. It was enlarged in the 13th century when it came under the control of the Counts of Savoy. It was Peter II of Savoy, the master of Chillon from 1255 to 1268, who was responsible for the size and appearance of the structure as it is seen today.

In 1536, it was captured by the Bernese who used it, amongst other things, as a depot, armoury and residence for their bailiffs. During this period it suffered damage from a violent earthquake that occurred in 1584. The castle remained under Bernese control until the Vaudois Revolution of 1798, following which it became the property of the canton of Vaud.

A century later, in 1897, the renowned restorer and archaeologist, Albert Naef, was appointed as the architect in charge of renovating the château. Seeking to carry out his task as authentically as possible, he consulted numerous archive documents that described much of the work that had been done since the end of the 12th century. What has evolved today is an irregularly shaped oval fortress, guarded by numerous towers and graced by three inner courtyards that are surrounded by a variety of grand rooms that overlook the lake and defensive positions.

The château has inspired countless writers to put pen to paper – Jean-Jacques Rousseau, Shelley, Victor Hugo and Alexandre Dumas, to name a few. The most famous words written about it were composed by Lord Byron in *The Prisoner of Chillon*, his poetic recounting of the imprisonment of Bonivard during the 16th century. This Prior of St Victor's in Geneva was chained for five years to the fifth pillar from the entrance because of his outspokenness in favour of the independence of Geneva. Byron's name is still visible where he inscribed it, upon the third pillar.

Montreux

Montreux is more commercialized and developed than Vevey, with grand hotels lining the lake front interspersed with numerous upmarket boutiques and shops. It is sandwiched between the mountains and the lake, with the railway line separating the **Old Town** (Les Planches) from the new. The former is contained within quite a small area and is worth exploring. The **Historical Museum of the Swiss Riviera** (Musée du Vieux Montreux; *rue de la Gare 40*, **t** *021 963 13 53, www.museemontreux.ch; open daily April–early Nov 10–12 and 2–5; adm*) is located within a collection of 17th-century houses. Its exhibits chronicle the development of the region from the Palaeolithic period to the modern days of tourism.

Of the many celebrities who have settled in Montreux, the rock star Freddie Mercury, of the rock group Queen, is perhaps the most unlikely. Nevertheless, the group recorded their last albums here before Freddie died of AIDS in November 1991, and a bronze statue on the quayside was erected as a permanent memorial to him. If you want to know more, then check out *www.montreux.ch*, and click on the Freddie Mercury tab to find out about Freddie Mercury tours.

Vevey

Vevey has an entirely different character, and the town is somewhat older. The lake front is less commercialized and there are a number of museums that may be of interest, notably the dual **Museum of Old Vevey** (Musée Historique du Vieux Vevey; *t 021 921 07 22, www.vevey.ch/museehistorique*) and the **Museum of the Brotherhood of Wine Growers** (Musée de la Confrérie des Vignerons; *t 021 923 87 05, www.fetedes vignerons.ch*); both are at rue du Château 2 by the lake front (*both open Tues–Sun 10.30–12 and 2–5.30, but closed in the morning Nov–Feb; adm*). The château dates from 1599 and served as a home for bailiffs during the period of Bernese rule. Exhibits, dating from Celtic times, are varied and include memorabilia from the various Vevey Wine festivals, famous local celebrations that were instituted in the 17th century and continue today.

Also worth a visit is the **Jenisch Museum** (Musée Jenisc; *avenue de la Gare 2, t 021 921 29 50; open Tues–Sun 11–5.30; adm*), housed in a neoclassical-inspired building. It has art by Swiss and foreign painters, including 700 works by the Expressionist master Oskar Kokoschka, and the cantonal print room with master prints from many periods.

Les Diablerets

Although the Auberge de la Poste became a modest guest house in 1789 (and is still run by the same family to this day), it wasn't until 1856 that the first hotel saw the beginning of real tourism. Over a century later, in 1964, the first cable car was constructed. Cleverly, Les Diablerets has managed the growth of tourism very well indeed, building upon its original infrastructure, adding new ones and developing a whole array of outdoor activities for every season – all without impinging upon the ambience of this charming country village.

Whatever the season, the highlight of a visit to here is the **Glacier 3000** (*t 024 492 33 77, f 024 492 28 27, www.glacier3000.ch; fare CHF 87*), which has replaced the 1964 cable car. The trip begins outside the village at Col du Pillon, 5,072ft (1,546m), where the first of two cable cars will be waiting to whisk you up to the summit. This, one of the highest vantage points in Switzerland – nearly 10,000ft (3,000m) – offers a vast panorama of mountain peaks, including the Matterhorn at 14,692ft (4,478m) and Mont Blanc at 15,771ft (4,807m). It is also a winter and summer skiing area with a network of chair lifts, ski lifts and cross-country trails.

From June to October, on Saturday, Sunday, Tuesday and Thursday, it is possible to take a short (CHF 10) or long (to the famous Quille du Diable column, CHF 40) husky ride. It is also possible for experienced hikers with the correct equipment to cross the glacier itself. Both start by taking the chair lift down to the ice from Glacier 3000. Most, though, will be content to enjoy a snack or drink while enjoying the views.

In the summer there are over 124 miles (200km) of **hiking paths**. A favourite excursion is to take the cable car up to Isenau, from where a gentle walk of around a half-hour or so will bring you down to Lac Retaud. Really, it is not much of a lake, but the restaurant of the same name not only has some delicious dishes (it specializes in

Tourist Information

Les Diablerets: Diablerets Tourisme, Maison du Tourisme, rue de la Gare, t 024 492 33 58, f 024 492 23 48, *www.diablerets.ch* (*open high season daily 8.30–6.30, other times Mon–Sat 8.30–12.30 and 2.30–6, Sun, hols 9.30–1*).

Exhibitions and Festivals

26 July: Devil's Night – a traditional village festival.
July/Aug: Rösti Festival at Isenau.
Late Sept: International Alpine Film Festival (35th in 2004).
Mid-Oct: Folk Music Festival (20th in 2004).

Shopping

Holiday Sport, t 024 492 37 17. Almost directly across from the tourist office; has a full range of skis, snowboards, snowshoes and sledges available for hire, as well as mountain bikes, hiking boots, etc.

Where to Stay

★★★★**Eurotel Victoria**, t 024 492 37 21, f 024 492 23 71, *www.eurotel-victoria.ch* (*moderate*). A large modern hotel, just outside the village centre. Its 101 rooms are contemporary in style and have all the facilities expected in a 4-star hotel. Pleasant public rooms and fine restaurants, plus an indoor pool and sauna.
★★★**Les Sources**, t 024 492 01 00, f 024 492 01 69, *www.hotel-les-sources.ch* (*moderate*). Just outside the centre of the village within spacious private grounds, this offers 48 double rooms equipped with shower, toilet, telephone, radio and TV. Other amenities are the La Marmotte restaurant, an on-site bar, a lounge and a leisure room with TV/games.
Auberge de la Poste, rue de la Gare, t 024 492 31 24, f 024 492 12 68, *www.aubergedela poste.ch* (*inexpensive*). A typical flower-bedecked Swiss chalet in the heart of the village, which has been run by the same family since 1789. Doubling as a small restaurant (whose speciality is raclette and cheese fondue), it has just 10 rooms – for either one, two, three, four or five people. There is a lavatory in each room, with shower and bath available on the floor.

Eating Out

Fourche, Glacier 3000, t 024 492 33 77, *www. glacier3000.ch*. 'Fourche' means the 'Devil's Fork'. This gastronomic restaurant at just under 10,000ft (3,000m) has fantastic views over the glacier. All the familiar dishes, with fondue, *rösti*, spaghetti and beef prominent.
Les Mazots, Restaurant Fromagerie, Col de la Croix, t 024 492 10 23, f 024 492 10 41, *www.lesmazots.ch*. Located at an altitude of 5,633ft (1,717m), this is a traditional mountain restaurant (*see below*).
Lac Retaud Restaurant, t 024 492 31 29. Overlooking the small lake of the same name, at an altitude of 5,577ft (1,700m) (*see below*). In addition to the usual regional dishes and mushroom specialities, there's strawberries and cream and meringues. Try, also, the home-made *liqueur de maison* and jam. *Closed Nov–early May*.

local mushrooms), but it also serves the home-made fruit-flavoured house liqueur (*liqueur de maison*) that is guaranteed to refresh you – one too many and you might be tempted to take their rowing boat out around the lake. Another easy walk down deposits you on the main road that, if you decide not to wait for the post bus, leads back to the village.

Another interesting possibility is to take the chair lift to Les Mazots, where you will find not only a traditional restaurant, but also the Fromagerie. Here, you can see – and later taste – how the famous mountain cheese L'Etivaz is made.

Those looking for more offbeat ideas might look at the summer and winter adventures offered by the **Centre ParAdventure** (*t 024 492 23 82, www.swissaventure.ch*) and **Mountain Evasion** (*t 024 492 12 32, f 024 492 22 67, www.mountain-evasion.com*).

Winter-sports lovers will have difficulty deciding what to do first in the Les Diablerets area. There are over 75 miles (20km) of ski runs serviced by an array of transportation, including more than 50 ski lifts. And the Swiss Ski and Snowboard School, with offices in the tourist office, is there to help you out. Cross-country skiing, ice-skating, curling, tobogganing and bobsleighing are also available.

Mittelland

Solothurn

The name Solothurn (Soleure in French; *see* regional map, p.207) derives from its Celtic heritage, *Saloduron* – meaning the 'Stronghold of the Salos'. The Romans established a fortress here around AD 370, the remains of which are still visible today. At the northern corner of the Burgundian kingdom, Solothurn flourished in the 10th century. In 1481, it became the 11th canton to join the Swiss Confederation. Consequently, the number eleven has great significance here and, in fact, is referred to as the 'Holy Solothurn number eleven'. Many things here are found in multiples of eleven.

The town's greatest days were between 1530 and 1792. Affluent merchants brought fame and prosperity and, in turn, ambassadors were sent by the French kings – hence the sobriquet 'Ambassadorial Town'. These entrepreneurs built luxurious mansions, many of which can be seen today, harmoniously combining French charm, Italian splendour and German Swiss stability. Quite rightly, Solothurn has acquired the reputation of being Switzerland's best-preserved Baroque town.

Once a year, at carnival time, the town goes wild as citizens, disguised by weird and wonderful masks (*Guggenmusik*), parade through the streets to celebrate *Chesslete*. During this period, when life is turned upside down, the town is re-christened Honolulu. And as incongruous as this may appear, it has its logic. Honolulu is directly opposite Solothurn – on the other side of the world.

Around the Town

The most dominant structure in Solothurn, approached up a stone stairway of eleven steps, is the **Cathedral of St Ursen** (*open 6–12 and 2–7*), which towers above every other building. The inside, somewhat austere, as is the norm for Swiss cathedrals, has eleven bells and eleven altars. Made from greyish/white Solothurn stone, its tower is 216½ft (66m) tall.

Just outside, to the east, stands the **Basel Gate**. From the outside it is impressive and has a central tower, with a portcullis, which is dominated by the figure of a knight.

To the north of the cathedral lie two interesting museums, a collection of churches and the impressive, round Riedholz Tower – one of eleven in Solothurn – that reinforces one of the corner fortifications of the old walls. First, check out the old **Arsenal**'s massive façade that is dominated by a steeply sloping roof, which tapers the levels above the third floor. Two great wooden doors guard the ground floor level.

Tourist Information

Solothurn: Region Solothurn Tourismus, Hauptgasse 69, **t** 032 626 46 46, **f** 032 626 4647, *www.solothurn-city.ch* (*open Mon–Fri 8.30–12, Sat 9–12*).

Where to Stay

****Krone, Hauptgasse 64, **t** 032 626 44 44, **f** 032 626 44 45, *www.hotelkrone-solothurn. ch* (*moderate*). This is a delightful, traditional hotel in the centre of the Old Town directly opposite the cathedral, which offers comfortable, well-equipped rooms, charming public areas and a fine restaurant.

Zunfthaus zu Wirthen, Hauptgasse 41, **t 032 626 28 48, **f** 032 626 28 58, *www.wirthen.ch* (*moderate*). Across from the magnificent clock tower, by Marktplatz, this has a traditional Solothurn façade. Its 14 rooms are bright, open and nicely furnished.

Eating Out

Zunfthaus zu Wirthen, Hauptgasse 41, **t** 032 626 28 48. A wonderful wood-lined dining room, also an outdoor terrace sheltered by an arcade of the traditional façade. Besides daily specials, the menu features many local Solothurn dishes such as perch, fera and trout, and many variations of veal.

Formidable it looks, and formidable it was meant to be. In the old days of the Swiss Confederation, power in a city-state was symbolized by two buildings: the Arsenal, of which this is a perfect example, and the Rathaus (town hall) – just around the corner – that here has an elaborate and ornate façade and was constructed between 1476 and 1711. Although an earlier armoury was located on this site in the mid-15th century, this one, unlike others of its genre, was built solely for military purposes. It is now designated an ancient monument of Switzerland and, appropriately, houses the **Old Arsenal Museum** (Altes Zeughaus; *Zeughausplatz 1*, **t** *032 623 35 28; open May–Oct Tues–Sun 10–12 and 2–5; Nov–April Tues–Fri 2–5, Sat and Sun 10–12 and 2–5*), one of the more fascinating museums in Switzerland. In addition to a vast collection of weapons (one of Europe's largest), the six floors contain an array of intriguing military exhibits, including, but not limited to, uniforms, drums, swords, huge muskets, cannons and even an armoured personnel carrier. The Armour Room, where over 400 suits of armour are lined up in battle order beneath a beautiful wooden-beamed ceiling, is most impressive.

Further north, just outside the old walls, is the traditional façade of the **Fine Arts Museum** (Kunstmuseum; *Werkhofstrasse 30*, **t** *032 622 23 07*, **f** *032 622 50 01*, *www.kunstmuseum.ch; open Tues–Fri 10–12 and 2–5, Sat and Sun 10–5; free*). Several statues of nude women adorn the park in front of it; once inside, look for a fine collection of post-1850 Swiss art represented by the likes of Hodler, Giacometti, Berger and Gubler as well as some Solothurn-born artists. A small collection of Old Masters includes the Solothurn *Madonna*, painted in 1522 by Hans Holbein the Younger.

Another museum, the **Natural History Museum** (Naturmuseum; *Klosterplatz 2*, **t** *032 622 78 21*, *www.naturmuseum.ch; open Tues–Sat 2–5, Sun 10–5; free*), is just south of the cathedral. This, one of the most modern of its kind in Switzerland, operates under the theory that visitors should not just see, but touch also.

To the west of the cathedral is the hugely ornamental Baroque Jesuit Church, and just past this is **Marktplatz**, the social hub of Solothurn. Standing sentry is a colossal clock tower, inhabited by enchanting animated figures designed to lie dormant until the toll of the hour brings them magically to life. There is also another colourful water fountain topped by a well-armed bearded knight – and yes, you've guessed it, one of eleven in Solothurn. If you are visiting on a Wednesday or a Saturday, you will find the streets around here lined with a colourful display of fresh produce.

Two other museums in town are the **Kosciuszko Museum** (*Gurzelngasse 12, t 032 622 80 53; open Sat 2–4; free*), which honours the Polish freedom fighter and hero Tadeusz Kociuszko; and the **Stone Museum** (Steinmuseum; *Hauptgasse 60, by the Jesuit Church, t 032 622 71 45; open May–Oct Sun 2–5; free*), with a collection of religious stonework.

Two Museums Outside Town

The **Schloss Waldegg** (Waldegg Castle; *t 032 624 13 23, www.schloss-waldegg.ch; open Mar–Oct Tues, Wed, Thurs and Sat 2–5, Sun 10–5; Nov–Dec Sun 10–5; adm*) is a marvellous late 17th-century chateau. Built by Johann Viktor von Besenval (1638–1713), a mayor of Solothurn, it gives you a glimpse of the opulent lifestyle of a man of his standing in that era. The **Blumenstein Museum** (Historisches Museum Blumenstein; *t 032 622 54 70; open Tues–Sat 2–5, Sun 10–5; free*) is housed in the summer residence of another patrician family. The exhibits on the ground floor reflect how such people lived in the 18th century, and the first floor offers insights into the lifestyle of Solothurn citizens between the 17th and 20th centuries. Both museums are reached by the no.4 bus.

Ticino

Ascona

Ascona and Locarno, from their respective locations on either side of the Maggia River, could be described as twin towns; but, in reality, they have little in common. Locarno, by far the larger of the two, has its attractions – particularly in the old town. But Ascona, with a population of just 5,000, is a magically pretty town, and most visitors would surely choose to stay there.

Its narrow streets and lanes, dominated by the church's towering spire, meander down, converging with the long and narrow piazza that separates the lake from the town itself. This piazza, the main meeting place of Ascona, is lined with an eclectic array of hotels, restaurants, bars and shops. Adding to the town's peaceful charm, the authorities have made a determined effort to restrict the use of cars insofar as possible. However, you do have to yield to swans and ducks! It is the perfect place to relax, order a cool drink and admire the tranquil and very appealing panorama: pretty villas; yachts, motor boats and lake steamers sliding gracefully over the water; the unusual Brissago Islands; and, wherever you rest your gaze, tree-lined slopes cascading freely into the lake shore. It is no wonder that Ascona has artistic and cultural traditions dating back to the Middle Ages and Renaissance eras. Notwithstanding that, it was at the end of the 19th and beginning of the 20th century that

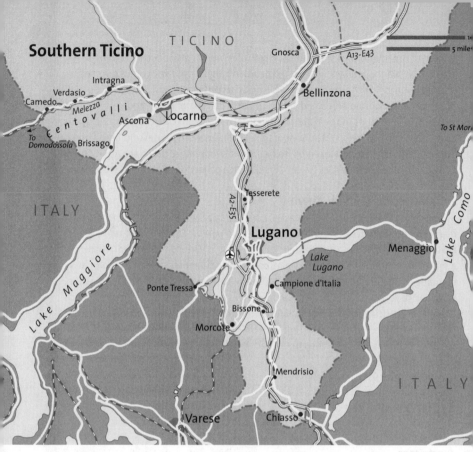

this tiny town, known as *Borgo*, reach its cultural climax. At that time, an influx of philosophers, anarchists and other free-thinkers such as Herman Hesse, James Joyce and Carl Gustav Jung were attracted here. These, and others, have made the hill over-looking Ascona, Monte Verità (the Mountain of Truth), famous in its own right.

Around the Town

The main attraction of Ascona is the pretty town itself, with its delightful pastel-coloured buildings on the famous piazza adjacent to Lake Maggiore and the maze of tiny lanes directly behind it with their boutiques, exclusive shops and galleries.

Notwithstanding that, there are several cultural attractions that are worth exploring. For example, the tourist office itself is housed in the beautifully Baroque **Casa Serodine**. Otherwise known as the Casa Borrani, its stucco decorations by Giovanni Battista Serodine (1587–1626) – brother of the painter Giovanni Serodine (1594–1631) – give it the most elaborate façade of any secular Swiss building.

The majestic bell-tower of the **Sts Peter and Paul Parish Church** (Chiesa parrochiale SS. Pietro e Paolo) dominates not only the adjoining Piazza San Pietro, but also Ascona itself. Look closely at the side facing the lake and you will find the commune's coat-of-arms featuring St Peter's keys and the papal tiara. Although first mentioned in 1264, most of what you see today dates from the 16th century. Inside, there are three magnificent paintings created by Giovanni Serodine between 1600 and 1630, some 15th-century frescoes and a choir enclosed on three sides.

Another church worthy of investigation is located to the northeast, closer to the more modern part of town. The **Church of the Collegio Papio** (Chiesa Mater Misericordiae) dates from the 14th and 15th centuries and is consecrated to Santa Maria della Misericordia. It has an attractive interior, with pride of place belonging to the main altar's polyptych, a unique work dating from 1519 by Giovanni Antonio de Lagaia, a painter from Ascona. The adjacent **Papio College** (Collegio Papio) was bequeathed by Bartolomeo Papio (1526–80) in his will, and Pope Gregory XIII subsequently commissioned the architect Pellegrino Pellegrini to create it. Begun in 1584,

Tourist Information

Ascona: Ente Turistico, Casa Serodine, **t** 091 791 00 90, **f** 091 792 10 08, *www.maggiore.ch* (*open Mar–Oct Mon–Fri 9–6, Sat 10–6, Sun 2.30–5; Nov–Feb Mon–Fri 9.30–12.30 and 2–5.30, Sat 11.30–3.30*).

Guided Trips and Tours

Guided tours of Ascona: April–Oct every Tues at 10am, starting from and organized by the tourist office; CHF 8.

Trenino, t 078 676 16 00: one of those little 'trains' that take you on an interesting tour of Ascona. Climb aboard opposite the Hotel-Restaurant Elvezia on the piazza; CHF 7 fare.

Exhibitions and Festivals

Late June/early July: the **New Orleans Jazz Festival** completely takes over the piazza.
Mid-July: Festival of Ascona – top art events.
Aug: music weeks in Ascona.

Where to Stay

★★★★**Eden Roc, t** 091 785 71 71, **f** 091 785 71 43, *www.edenroc.ch* (*luxury*). Located just to the east of the piazza on the lake, this is undoubtedly the hotel of choice in Ascona. Totally refurbished in 2001, it has the ambience of a beautiful Italian palazzo with its original paintings and works of art co-existing gracefully with unique furnishings. Its 48 deluxe rooms, 33 luxury suites and 3 presidential suites follow this style and you can choose from three restaurants, including the classically French Eden Roc – from whose

terrace you can watch the sun set over the lake – and the new, creative La Brezza. Similarly, there are three pools: indoor, indoor/outdoor and outdoor and, of course, the lake itself, as well as a water-skiing school and boats for hire. Also various health facilities and the Clarins Beauty Farm. The hotel also offers a free shuttle service to and from the train station in Locarno.

★★★**Al Porto**, Piazza G. Motta, **t** 091 785 85 85, **f** 091 785 85 86, *www.hotel-tamaro.ch* (*moderate*). Behind an attractive façade on the piazza; 36 elegantly bright and modern rooms – ask for a lake view. Also a fine restaurant and a pleasant garden.

★★★**Tamaro**, Piazza G. Motta, **t** 091 785 48 48, **f** 091 791 29 28, *www.alperto-hotel.ch* (*moderate*). Right on the famous piazza, this offers charming, stylish accommodation in 51 traditionally decorated rooms, some with a lake view. The restaurant is worth a visit for its gracious architecture, and half-board is available for just CHF 30. *Open Mar–Nov.*

Eating Out

Dining out follows the Italian tradition (*see* p.26).

Grotto Baldoria, Vicolo S. Omobono 9, **t** 091 791 32 98, *s.mauro@bluewin.ch*. Tucked away in one of the side streets off the piazza; the menu is whatever the chef decides he is going to cook that day. The ambience is pleasing and the fare inexpensive.

Elvezia au Lac, Piazza G. Motta 15, **t** 091 791 15 14, **f** 091 791 00 03. A great place for lunch or dinner, with an extensive selection of pizza, *antipasti*, soups, pasta and risotto, as well as meat and fish dishes.

it took four years to complete, and features a magnificent cloister with two sets of arches decorated with numerous heraldic coats-of-arms, most of which belong to cardinal-archbishops from Milan – the jurisdictional power of the era. These days the college is a private school.

Ascona has three entirely different types of museum, in quite different locations. The **Modern Art Museum** (Museo Communale d'Arte Moderna; *Via Borgo 34, t 091 780 51 00, f 091 780 51 02, www.cultura-ascona.ch; open Mar–Dec Tues–Sat 10–12 and 3–6, Sun and hols 4–6; adm*) is arguably the most important and is situated just to the west of the tourist office. Housed in an attractive 16th-century palazzo, it got its start in 1922 when members of a large artists' colony here donated one of their works – 65 in all – to create a future museum. The main collections are those of the Foundations Marianne Werefkin and Richard and Uli Seewald. The Russian Marianne von Werefkin, a joint founder of the Munich expressionist Blaue Reiter movement, has 70 of her works and 160 sketchbooks here. Look, also, for impressive works by Utrillo, Klee and Franc Marc.

On the other side of town, just behind the Hotel Eden Roc, is the small **Epper Museum** (*Via Albarelle 14, t 091 791 19 42; open June/July/Aug Tues–Fri 10–12 and 8pm–10pm, Sat and Sun 8pm–10pm; April/May/Sept/Oct Tues–Fri 10–12 and 3–6, Sat and Sun 3–6; free*). This small museum preserves the artistic heritage of Ignaz Epper (1892–1969) and his wife Mischa Epper-Quarles Van Ufford (1901–78), who settled here in 1932. Ignaz is highly thought of as a major figure of Swiss expressionism, whilst Mischa's sculptures and drawings belong to the more classical French tradition.

Those wishing to learn more about the eccentricities and unusual ideas of those visionaries who flocked to this region beginning in the late 19th century should definitely head for the **Monte Verità Foundation** (Fondazione Monte Verità; *t 091 791 01 81, www.csf-mv.ethz.ch*) and its **Casa Anatta Museum** (*open July and Aug 3–7; April, May, June, Sept and Oct 2.30–6; adm*). This was both the residence and HQ of the 'Co-operative vegetarian colony Monte Verità', and exhibits documents by the utopian visionaries from the north on universal concepts such as truth, anarchy, social utopianism, purification of the body, psychology, dance, music and literature. Take a stroll in the park, also, to the Casa Selma – the 'Russians' House' and the old showers used by the vegetarians – and see the circular painting *The Clear World of the Blessed*, by Elisar von Kupfer, in the recreated wooden house of the Chiaro Mondo dei Beati.

No visitor to Ascona can ignore the presence of Lake Maggiore, and two excursions should definitely be considered. Firstly, take a trip to the **Brissago Islands** (Isole Brissago; *t 091 791 43 61; adm*). They have an ancient history, with Roman remains and the ruins of an early 13th-century church being found there. In 1885 they were purchased by Baroness Antonietta Saint Leger, who built a fine residence and invited her many painter, writer, sculptor and musician friends as guests. More interestingly, for visitors today at least, she turned the larger of the two islands into an exotic garden featuring plant species representative of the Mediterranean, subtropical regions of Asia ranging from China to Korea, southern Africa, North, Central and South America as well as Australia and parts of Oceania. On the small island the spontaneous vegetation is kept in its natural state. Farther afield but not visible is the charming Italian town of Stresa, and its own Borromeo Islands are certainly worth a visit. All of these places can be reached on the lake steamers of the **Navigazione Lago Maggiore**, departing from Ascona.

Centovalli

There may be no towering well-known peaks here, but the Centovalli – valley of a hundred valleys – is still hugely impressive and very beautiful. Starting just west of Locarno/Ascona, with the magnificent village of Intragna as its gateway, this deep, wide valley twists and turns; the Melezza river is joined along its way, from north and south, by waterfalls and tributaries from valleys too numerous to count. Past the border with Italy at Camedo it widens greatly and becomes known as the Valle Vigezzo, before dropping steeply down to the strategically important Italian town of Domodossola.

These valleys have always been remote, and life for the villagers extremely difficult. In fact, a connecting road wasn't built until the late 1800s, and it wasn't until later, in 1923, that the quaint Ferrovie Autolinee Regionali Ticinesi (FART – an unfortunate acronym) train line was opened between Locarno and Domodossola, becoming the international rail connection between the important Gotthard and Simplon railway lines. This is known as the Centovallina in Switzerland and the Vigezzina in Italy.

Historically, families here have been both interconnected and large, with male children named mostly after the saints of the different parishes – and life merely a matter of survival. People's sole recreation was on church feast days when Mass, at which the women sat behind the men, was followed by a processional celebration for the particular saint being honoured. Work, too, was a problem, and these hardy Ticino men had to look to other places to gain financial rewards. Many gained a reputation as highly proficient chimney sweeps (*spazzacamini*), even developing their own language so that they could communicate with each other secretly. Others gathered chestnuts and roasted them in town squares. More went to work in the port of Livorno, Italy, whilst some ventured as far away as California and Australia.

These days, unlike many places in Switzerland, the Centovalli has very little commercialization and this adds to its attraction. **Intragna** is the largest village here and, despite being close to such cosmopolitan towns as Locarno and Ascona, retains an entirely different ambience. The use of local stone in construction makes it look older than it actually is; the village is dominated by the 17th-century 226ft (69m) bell tower of the San Gottardo church – claimed to be the highest in all Ticino. Interestingly, its church records show just how closely knit families were here. They indicate that not once, in the 200 years of recorded marriages until well into the 1800s, did a member of the dominant Selmina/Salmina family marry a person from outside Intragna. In truth, there isn't too much to see, but a walk around the core area outside the San Gottardo church is interesting, not least for the extremely narrow cobble-stoned streets, hardly wide enough for a car to pass along. It is the best place to base yourself for exploring the Centovalli.

Where to Stay

Note: it is a steep walk up from Intragna train station to the centre of the village; free transportation to and from the station is provided by the Hotel Antico.

Antico, t 091 796 11 07, **f 091 796 31 15, *www. hotelantico.ch* (*inexpensive*). A charming hotel in an old property in the heart of Intragna, directly in the shadow of the San Gottardo church's bell tower. The 26 rooms have an old-fashioned feel, which is reflected in the public areas – particularly so in the wooden-beamed dining room. There's also a cosy bar, a private courtyard extension to the restaurant, a refreshing pool and a small children's playground.

Garni Intragna, t 091 796 10 77, **f** 091 796 31 15, *paris@nikko.ch* (*inexpensive*). This is close to the Antico in a similar type of house, and its 12 rooms also have a similar ambience. There is no restaurant, but it shares the Antico's, as it does the pool and children's playground.

Eating Out

Antico, t 091 796 11 07, **f** 091 796 31 15. The best bet for ambience, cuisine and value. For a cost of CHF 30 you get a three-course dinner – maybe even cooked by the owner himself.

The reality is that a car, or even a bus, doesn't give you the best views. This honour undoubtedly goes to the curious **Centovallina trains**, which have large picture windows and a better route, generally with two services an hour. Note, too, the very old and strange carriages – more like tramcars – that sit as museum pieces outside some stations. On its 34-mile (55km) journey between Locarno and Domodossola, it passes 83 bridges and tunnels and negotiates tight curves and steep slopes to the highest station at an altitude of 2,743ft (836m).

Some of the captivating scenery is evident on the short trip from Intragna to Verdasio – just three stops – where a short, sharp walk uphill from the station takes you to the **Monte Camino gondola car station** (*t 091 798 13 93, www.comino.ch*). In six minutes the gondolas take you from 1,804ft (550m) at Verdasio to 3,773ft (1,150m) at Comino, on the north side of the valley. From here there really are wonderful views, both back down to the valley and to distant snow-capped peaks. Just 85ft (26m) higher there is a strange little shrine, dating from the second half of the 15th century, home to the revered Madonna della Segna whose festival day is 6 July.

Although there are signposts to the larger Monte Comino mountain hotel and restaurant, a far more interesting option is to go around and down from the gondola car station to the tiny **Riposo Romantico** (*t 091 798 11 30, f 091 825 33 03*) – actually the highlight of the trip. It is only open from March to October, and the charming couple that run it rely on solar power for lighting and power and wood for heating. They invite you into their home to either eat in their little dining room or out on the south-facing terrace, and the fantastic home-made dishes more than compensate for the limited selection. The speciality, derived from an old family recipe, is the most tasty minestrone – enhanced with *fagioli* (beans) – that is ever likely to pass your lips. The spaghetti is not to be missed, and don't leave without tasting the *Ossi da Mordere*, an almond and honey biscuit – *Ossi* means 'bones' and *Mordere* means 'to bite'. Wash it all down with a glass or two of the local red wine, Nostrano, made from a combination of Bondola and Merlot grapes.

Time, now, to work some of this extravagance off and, suitably, Comino is a fine starting point for a **hike**. The *Locarno-Ascona Dintorni e Valli* hiking map at CHF 15 is useful as all routes are numbered, but it is not absolutely necessary as the paths are clearly signposted. The best idea is to walk back on the generally downhill main path (*sentiero principale*) to Intragna, via Selna, 2,772ft (845m), and Costa, 2,086ft (636m), a walk of about 2½ hours. From Costa either walk on down to Intragna, 1,112ft (339m), or take the easy option on the gondola car. Before setting out, study the colour posters on the walls of the Riposo Romantico, as these explain to you the wide variety of flora and fauna that can – or might – be seen on these slopes.

Of course, the less energetic might decide that a little snooze on the sunny terrace of the Riposo Romantico is in order, before returning to Intragna on the gondola and the Centovallina.

Valais

Crans-Montana

Crans-Montana – actually the two adjoining villages of Crans and Montana – are unique in the fact that, unlike other illustrious villages in the Valais, they are situated on a ledge overlooking the Rhône valley with a Mediterranean microclimate, and not at the end of an adjacent valley. Unique, too, in the fact that they have no discernible

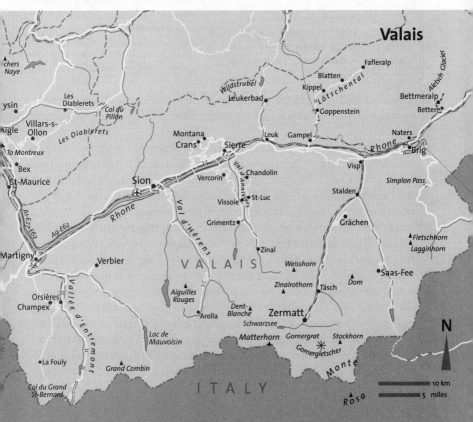

Getting Around

From Sierre: an SMC bus goes to and from the train station to Crans-Montana. The funicular takes just 12 minutes to get from Sierre to Montana.

From Sion: the Postal Bus goes to and from the train station to Crans post office.

Between Crans, Montana and Aminona: a free shuttle bus operates between all the important places in these three villages.

Tourist Information

Crans: t 027 485 08 00, **f** 027 485 08 10 (*open mid-June–early Sept Mon–Sat 8.30–6.30, Sun 10–12 and 4–6, rest of the year Mon–Fri 8.30–12 and 2–4, Sat 8.30–12*).

Montana: t 027 485 04 04, **f** 027 485 04 60 (same opening hours as Crans).

Aminona: t 027 481 01 01, **f** 027 481 01 01 (*open mid-June–early Sept 9.30–11.30 and 3–5*).

For all three : *www.crans-montana.ch*.

Tours

The tourist office offers two interesting tours: on Tues and Thurs between late June and late Sept there is a **mountain walk** for CHF 15, and every Thurs between July and mid-Sept there is a guided **morning on the alpine pasture of Colombire/Merdechon** that departs from the tourist office at 5am and costs CHF 45, including breakfast on the mountain and raclette (and drinks) for lunch.

Shopping

René Rey, t/f 027 481 25 44. In the centre of Crans and part of the INTERSPORT scheme; has everything you might want to rent, including 1,000 skis, snowboards, hiking boots, mountain bikes and golf clubs. What's more, on production of this guide the owner will give you a 25% discount. It also has a fine range of sports clothing.

Where to Stay

★★★★★**Crans Ambassador, t** 027 485 48 48, **f** 027 485 48 49, *www.crans-ambassador.ch* (*luxury*). Directly overlooking the lake in Crans, this has a most unusual and attractive façade. Its 72 beautiful rooms come in different sizes – usually large – and often have big terraces that offer spectacular unobstructed views of the Valaisanne Alps. The restaurants – with a choice of gourmet, regional, diatetic or vegetarian menus – and

history as, until the end of the 19th century, these sun-blessed southern slopes of the Bernese Alps, at an altitude of 4,921ft (1,500m), were nothing but summer pastures for Swiss cows.

This scenario soon changed, though, when two hunting partners from the region, Louis Antille and Michel Zuffrey, realized the area's potential and were behind the opening of the first hotel, the du Parc, in 1893. Within three years the first road suitable for vehicles was opened and, incongruously, within a decade, in 1906, golf was introduced here by the Englishman, Sir Henry Lunn. Two years later Crans-Montana inaugurated the world's highest 18-hole golf course. By 1939 the Plan Bramois golf course, still considered the best in Switzerland, was hosting the first Swiss Open, and has seen such illustrious players as Nicklaus, Ballesteros and Faldo stride its greens. In fact, the specialist magazines *Golf Monthly* and *Golf Magazine* both classified its 7th hole as one of the finest 40 in the world. These days, the sport has progressed to the point that there are three 9-hole courses in the area – one designed by Jack Nicklaus – and a golf simulator, driving swing analyzer and video facilities are also available.

Further progress came quickly. In 1911 the longest funicular in Switzerland, at 2.6 miles (4.2km), was opened to connect to Sierre in the valley in less than an hour. That same year, Lunn's son, Arnold, put Crans-Montana on the world skiing map by swimming pool have terraces with similar views, and there are extensive health and beauty facilities including the Health Centre Mességué-Phytotherm (see p.192; ask about special packages). Relax, too, in the charming Piano Bar.

Hostellerie du Pas de l'Ours, t 027 485 93 33, **f** 027 485 93 34, *www.relaischateaux.com/ pasdelours* (*luxury*). Located in Crans in an attractive building, this has 9 individually furnished suites with jacuzzi and fireplace. The Restaurant de l'Ours, arguably the best in the area and run by the excellent young chef Frank Reynaud, has one Michelin star. The Bistrot des Ours serves great bar food.

★★★Beaureg'Art, t 027 481 21 88, **f** 027 481 21 89 (*inexpensive*). This is the only 'art' hotel in Crans-Montana – it is actually close to the centre of Montana. There are 24 rooms, but 16 of them have been designed by different artists and are, to say the least, quite unusual.

★★Regina, t 027 481 35 22, **f** 027 480 18 68, *www.reginahotel.ch* (*inexpensive*). In the centre of Montana; this is a family-run hotel with 24 pleasant comfortable rooms – ask for one on the southern side with a balcony and great views. The Primavera restaurant offers fine half-board opportunities.

Auberge Crans-Sapins, t 027 483 14 41, **f** 027 483 14 42, *esermet@bluewin.ch* (*inexpensive*).

Near the centre of Crans, this is a small, unpretentious place where all the twin-bedded rooms have private bathroom facilities, whilst the single ones do not. Offers excellent southward views.

Eating Out

Café Restaurant du Centre, t 027 481 36 68. A charming little place full of alpine ambience and serving good value Valaisanne specialities like fondue, raclette and *grillades*. In the high season, there is music nightly.

Le Tirbouchon, t 027 480 26 08. A cosy little wine bar in the middle of Montana where you can find an excellent selection of local vintages – and there are many – with a weekly 'by the glass' list on a board, as well as some interesting choices of *eaux-de-vie*.

Nightlife

The **Casino de Crans-Montana, t** 027 485 90 40, **f** 027 485 90 41. With gaming tables for roulette, black jack, slot machines and restaurants opening for action at 7pm. Minimum age of 18, entrance with photo ID. *Open daily 3pm–3am.*

organizing the Earl Robert of Kandahar Challenge Cup, the first genuine downhill event in the history of skiing. And the skiing scene hasn't looked back; there are now 100 miles (160km) of synchronous pistes, and in 1987 Crans-Montana hosted the World Alpine Ski Championship.

Notwithstanding these outdoor attractions, Crans-Montana has gone one better and established itself as a major shopping venue, with every big designer brand available, as well as all the important Swiss master watch and clock makers. The town also has an impressive Convention Centre, which plays host to the leading lights of the world's political and economic scene.

Not the least of Crans-Montana's attractions are the fantastic views down and across the Rhône valley to a literal wall of snow-capped Valaisanne peaks that stretch as far as the eye can see from east to west. This may be the 'longest' mountain view anywhere in the Alps.

Sightseeing and Outdoor Activities

The **Colombire Alpine Museum** (*Crans* **t** *027 485 08 00, Montana* **t** *027 485 04 04, Aminona* **t** *027 481 01 01; open end June–mid-Sept daily 9.30–5; adm*), reached on the free SMC bus, is well worth visiting in order to explore the secrets of alpine life. Alpine pastures (*alpage*) are stretches of grassy land situated at high altitude and snow-covered in winter. Over 10,000 alpine pastures occupy 20 per cent of Switzerland, and the Valais boasts 700 of them, covering 25 per cent of the canton. In this museum you will learn all about the day-to-day life of both the people and their animals.

Almost everything else to do here, with the exception of shopping, of course, is an outdoor adventure. In the winter **skiers** and **snowboarders** will be in their element. Over 50 slopes – 20 blue, 28 red and 2 black, plus a 2¼-mile (3.5km) floodlit slope from Cry d'Er to Pas-du-Loup – are served by an amazing array of 30 ski lifts, a funitel from Les Vilettes to the Plaine-Morte Glacier, a cable way, 5 cable cars, 14 drag lifts and 6 chair lifts, capable of a capacity of 36,520 people an hour. There is also a 6¼-acre (25,000 sq m) snow park at La Tsa, Aminona, 25 miles (40km) of classic cross-country skiing, 19 miles (30km) of skating area, a 3.7-mile (6km) tobogganing/sledge run, three trails of 6¼ miles (10km) for snow shoe enthusiasts and 37.2 miles (60km) of walking paths. Two Swiss Ski Schools will teach you the necessary skills. Summer skiers, too, can be happy in Crans-Montana, as there are 1¼ miles (2km) of slopes on the glacier of Plaine-Morte, and 3¾ miles (6km) of trails for cross-country skiing in the same area.

In summer **hikers** can choose from 174 miles (280km) of marked paths, including four botanical walks. There are eight marked trails totalling 75 miles (120km) for mountain bikers, as well as a permanent 1½-mile (2.5km) downhill route. Other sports such as archery, beach volley, ten-pin bowling, fishing (seven lakes), horse-riding, water-skiing, paragliding, squash, swimming and tennis are well represented.

Golfers, as has been noted, have a choice of one 18-hole course and three 9-hole courses, and details of green fees etc. can be obtained from the **Golf-Club Crans-sur-Sierre** (*t 027 485 97 97, f 027 485 97 98*) or the tourist office. It might come as a surprise to realize that there are also courses at Leuk, *www.golfleuk.ch*; Sion, *www.golfclubsion. ch*; Verbier, *www.verbiergolf.ch*; Zermatt, *www.golfclubmatterhorn. ch*; Riederalp, *www. golfclub-riederalp.ch*; Saas-Fee; Granges, *www.swissgolfnetwork.ch*, and Obergesteln, *www.golf-source-du-rhone*, in the Valais.

Although it has no natural thermal waters of its own, Crans-Montana can offer the **Health Centre Mességué-Phytotherm** (*t 027 481 48 11, f 027 481 91 55, in the Hotel Crans Ambassador*). Phytotherapy is a plant-based purification and regeneration of the body, and includes medicinal plant-extract baths, individual foot and hand immersions, massages, mudpacks, pressotherapy, liver and kidney poultices, and herbal brews, etc. A team of specialist professional consultants, assisted by masseurs and beauticians, concentrate their dedicated skills on designing treatments, or a course of treatments, customized to your individual needs.

Leukerbad

Leukerbad, at an altitude of 4,629ft (1,411m), has quite a different ambience from its next-door neighbour, the Lötschental (*see* p.195), due to a quirk of nature – thermal hot springs.

Thermal Springs

From an altitude of around 9,842ft (3,000m), rainwater seeps down through the mountains to about 1,640ft (500m) below sea level. After 40 years thermal energy causes the water, by then enriched by calcium and sulphate, to rise up. At a temperature of 123.8°F (51°C) it fills 60 springs at the rate of 857,880 gallons (3.9 million litres) daily.

It wasn't until 1478, when the mineral water springs and baths became the property of the bishop of Sion, Jost von Silenen, that the first inns were opened. In 1850 a road was opened to the village, and that is still the only way to access it as the electric train that started services in 1915 made its last trip in 1967. These days, there are two main ways of enjoying the waters: in the citizen-owned Burgerbad, finally completed in 1989, or at the Alpentherme wellness and medical centre attached to the Lindner Hotel Maison Blanche.

Amongst the many personalities who have visited Leukerbad over the years are Goethe in 1779, Mark Twain in 1878, Pablo Picasso and Paul Valéry in 1933 and James Baldwin, who stayed in the village from 1951 to 1953.

The Baths and Cable Cars

Taking the waters will naturally be high on everyone's agenda. The baths are the largest of their kind in the Alps, and there are two main places to experience them.

The community-owned **Burgerbad** (*t* 027 472 20 20, *f* 027 472 20 21, www.burgerbad. ch; adm CHF 21) is a multi-level, multi-pool, multi-attraction facility that, especially with its new 230ft (70m) water slide, is more along the lines of a water park. There are also sport and wellness facilities, a self-service restaurant and American Bar.

The **Lindner Alpentherme** (*t* 027 472 10 10, *f* 027 472 10 11, www.alpentherme.ch), however, is an altogether more sophisticated place, and offers a wide range of eclectic experiences. Most obvious are the two large pools, both at 96.8°F (36°C), with the open-air one being 360 sq yards (300sq m) and the indoor a third smaller. Both of these have a number of integrated facilities such as neck douches, underwater massage jets, a hot-water pool at 104°F (40°C) and built-in bubble-bath loungers and seats. There is also a competition pool, with four 27-yard (25m) lanes at a slightly lower temperature. Admission to this is complicated: the day is split into four periods and entrance for three hours in each period costs between CHF 13 and CHF 18, with a CHF 3 supplement for each extra half-hour. A half-day ticket, five hours, for the morning costs CHF 19 and afternoon CHF 25, also with a CHF 3 supplement for each extra half-hour. A full-day ticket costs CHF 36.

Undoubtedly, though, the most interesting and sensual experiences are to be had in the **Roman–Irish bath** – one of just two in Switzerland (the other being in Scuol, *see* p.162). Around a separate, elegant Roman-style atrium you will be pampered for over two hours with an array of cold-water, sauna and steam baths ranging from 53.6°F (12°C) to 154.5°F (68°C), a 10-minute massage and finally 30 minutes of rest and relaxation. And all this for just CHF 59.

Tourist Information

Leukerbad: Leukerbad Tourismus, **t** 027 472 71 71, **f** 027 472 71 51, *www.leukerbad. ch* (*open mid-July–Oct Mon–Sat 9–12 and 1.30 –6, Sun 9–11.30; rest of the year closed on Sun*).

Where to Stay and Eat

★★★★Lindner Hôtel Maison Blanche, Dorfplatz, **t** 027 472 10 00, **f** 027 472 10 01, *www.lindner-hotels.ch* (*expensive*). A traditional hotel with a combination of 136 rooms and suites that are well furnished and up-to-date. Also two restaurants, a piano bar, garden terrace, indoor and outdoor thermal pools, grotto bath, sauna, solarium and steam bath, as well as a direct underground connection to, and free use of, the Lindner Alpentherme and the shopping arcade.

★★★Lindner Hôtel de France, Dorfplatz, **t** 027 472 10 00, **f** 027 472 10 01, *www.lindner hotels.ch* (*moderate*). Next to the Maison Blanche and quite different architecturally, this is a medium-sized hotel with 44 comfortable and pleasant rooms. It also has direct access to, and free use of, the Alpentherme facilities.

★★★Hôtel de la Croix-Fédérale, Kirchstrasse 43, **t** 027 472 79 79, **f** 027 472 79 75, *www.croix-federale.ch* (*inexpensive*). Located in a typical chalet in the village centre, this is a small hotel with just 10 traditionally styled rooms.

Château, **t** 027 470 16 27, **f** 027 470 16 42, *www.torrent.ch* (*inexpensive*). Inside a lovely, modern, chalet-style façade, the studios and 2- and 3-room apartments match the ambience: bright, open and with lots of space. The prices are very reasonable, too.

Don't overlook the **Lindner Alpentherme Wellness Centre** either, where you can treat yourself to any number of intriguingly enticing treatments. Some, like massages, etc. are familiar, but others, certainly, are rather unusual. A thalasso treatment of algae and sea salts can be taken in the form of a purifying bath of bubbling seawater, or perhaps as an algae body-pack to enhance the beauty of your skin. Ayurveda – the science of long life – features a range of treatments including synchronized massages, relaxing oil treatments and effective vegetable remedies. These, though, just scratch the surface of the range of treatments available here; others that may entice are hayflower wraps, natural mud packs and aroma baths.

These bathing experiences can be taken individually, or as combination packages with the Lindner Hôtel Maison Blanche, or other hotels.

There are also cable cars in Leukerbad. The **Torrent-Bahnen station** (**t** 027 472 81 10, **f** 027 472 81 16, *www.torrent.ch*) is just outside the village to the east and takes you up to the Restaurant Rinderhütte, at 7,677ft (2,340m). Although with a slightly less dramatic location than the Gemmi, it has spectacular views back across the Valais to the wall of gigantic peaks including the Matterhorn and Monte Rosa. Apart from skiing, its other main attraction is the modern Rinderhütte itself, a great place for lunch. Not only does it have a fine sun terrace, but the menu includes a good selection of local dishes at reasonable prices.

The **Gemmibahn** (**t** 027 470 18 39, **f** 027 470 62 20) takes you up to the ledge that is just north of, and literally overlooking, the village at an altitude of 7,710ft (2,350m). The Berghotel Wildstrubel (**t** 027 470 12 01, **f** 027 470 27 97) offers basic accommodation and a nice terrace restaurant, and there are many good hikes from here – especially around the Daubensee lake.

Incongruously, there is also an 18-hole golf course in Leukerbad, but most visitors will want to try and schedule their time here to coincide with two far more local events. The last Sunday morning in July, at precisely 11am, the annual **Shepherds Festival** enlivens the meadows around the Daubensee. Shepherds arrive with their flocks from both the Valais and Bernese Oberland and, until that hour, the sheep, maybe 1,000 of them, are held back whilst the shepherds spread Gläck – a mixture of bran and salt – around the lakeside. It being a particular favourite of these creatures, they stampede down the mountainside to get to it. Incidentally, they are given this treat just three times during the grazing season – and then only 3.2 ounces (100g) per sheep. Huge wheels of raclette cheese are melted in special raclette ovens and served with boiled potatoes, pickles and onions, all washed down with the local Fendant white wine. Also on show are local bands, yodelling, alpine horn-blowing, flag-throwing and local wrestling competitions.

At the beginning of summer, cows from different regions and farms are led up the mountain to share the same pastures and, as they are not familiar with each other, this leads to territorial conflicts between the animals. Fighting with their horns, a winner finally emerges which then becomes leader of the herd. Very early in August the cows are brought back down to Leukerbad for the annual **Summer Cow Fight**; check with the tourist office for the exact date.

The Lötschental

Surrounded by lofty alpine peaks, this is a beautiful, narrow, attenuated valley (*tal* is the German word for valley), whose people, until the railway reached the head of the valley very early in the 20th century, lived an isolated lifestyle, and still choose to retain a host of centuries-old traditions. Large families equal small fields here: staunchly Catholic families with nine or ten children are not abnormal, and as a consequence, with so many children and such little land to pass down, you will notice that the fields here are particularly small.

The villages of Ferden, Kippel, Wiler and Blatten – each at a slightly higher altitude than its predecessor – have retained their delightful characters. As dramatic as the valley is, however, its apex is even more so. The road comes to a dead end at Fafleralp that, at 5,889ft (1,795m), is literally surrounded by peaks that rise to majestic pinna-cles of between 12,192 and 14,022ft (3,716 to 4,274m) – a sight to be savoured in any season. Switzerland is so small that few places with outstanding natural scenery remain virtually unknown; Lötschental is one of those places.

Outdoor Activities and Festivals

Lötschental is a place most suited to those who enjoy outdoor activities, in summer or winter. During the warmer months the valley offers activities to suit all ages and levels of fitness. Serious hikers will find no end of high mountain trails to explore, either within the valley or venturing as far as Leukerbad and Kandersteg over the mountains. For those intent on exploring in this manner the *Lötschental Touring Map*, available at the tourist office, is a necessity. Visitors seeking easier paths will want to take the cable car to Lauchernalp and walk down from there, with Fafleralp being a

Tourist Information

Lötschental: Lötschental Tourismus, **t** 027 938 88 88, **f** 027 938 88 80, *www. loetschental.ch*, is located next to the cable car station at Wiler, CH-3918 Wiler.

The people of the valley speak a very unusual German dialect, which is difficult for other German-speaking people, let alone foreigners, to understand.

Shopping

Maskenkeller, t 027 939 13 55, **f** 027 939 30 49, *www.maskenkeller.ch*. Located in the heart of Wiler and operated by Agnes and Ernst Rieder-Jerjen, this has the most amazing collection of gruesomely erotic masks – some of which are over 100 years old. The young men of the valley can rent their masks here for the *Tschäggätä* (*see* p.197) – a different one every year to protect their anonymity – and they also have plenty of smaller ones, and models, that make most unusual souvenirs.

Sporthaus Lauchernalp, t 027 939 15 84, *www.sporthaus-lauchern.ch*, in Lauchernalp. Those needing to rent equipment should come here. They also offer instruction in skiing, snowboarding and overland skiing, and provide a variety of ski-adventures, ski-safaris and spectacular heli-skiing.

Where to Stay

Fafleralp, t 027 939 14 51, **f** 027 939 14 53 (*moderate; cash only, no credit cards accepted*). This typical mountain hotel is located in a delightfully isolated position off the road, at the very end of the valley. All of the clean, very comfortable guest rooms, as well as the charming public rooms and dining areas, are lined with wood panelling. Be advised, the road up from Blatten is often closed in winter.

★★★Edelweiss, Blatten, **t** 027 939 13 63, **f** 027 939 10 53, *www.hoteledelweiss.ch* (*moderate*). Located in Blatten, one village back from Fafleralp, this is a fairly large traditional hotel with modern amenities. Its restaurant is famous for its Valais cuisine and fine wines. For those travelling with children, family rooms are available where guests pay extra for children according to their age.

★★★Nest-und Bietschhorn, between Ried and Blatten, **t** 027 939 11 06, **f** 027 939 18 22, *www.nest-bietsch.ch* (*moderate*). One of the largest hotels in the valley. In a traditional house, it offers home-style comforts, a restaurant renowned for its Valais specialities and an in-house sauna. Special excursion packages, including snow safaris, ski-packages and cultural weeks, are also available.

★★★Hotel-Restaurant zur Wildi, Lauchernalp, **t** 027 939 19 89, **f** 027 939 20 19 *www.zur-wildi.ch* (*moderate*). A fairly isolated, small, typical mountain hotel and restaurant reached via the Lauchernalp cablecar. An ideal choice for those interested in summer hikes or winter sports.

Eating Out

Berg-Restaurant Hockenalp, t 027 939 12 45. About 45mins' walk from the Lauchernalp cablecar upper station, this is run by the owner/cook Thomas Murmann. There are no formal opening hours, but he is there most of the time between May and the first snow in the middle of October. His speciality is a delicious cheese bread topped with a fried egg – *Käseschnitte* – washed down with a large glass of white wine, Hocken-Ballon. The brave will finish with Kaffee Perlig – a mind-blowing mix of coffee and a local Schnapps. All the dishes are washed in the outside water fountain.

popular destination. Fafleralp is also the best place for a more gentle hike, particularly up to the small, ice-cold lake of Grundsee and then on to the foot of the large glacier. Similarly, a *Mountainbike-Karte* is available for mountain bikers.

Skiing and/or snowboarding enthusiasts will wish to base themselves close to the **Lauchernalp** cable car (*t 027 938 89 99, www.lauchernalp.ch*), which was opened in 1972. From there a combination of chair lifts and ski lifts rise to Gandegg, at an altitude of 8,858ft (2,700m) – with an upwards extension due for the 2003/04 season. Recent developments have opened up a wide variety of ski runs for beginners through to experts.

With luck your visit will coincide with one of the colourful local traditions. The strangest of these is the *Tschäggätä*. No written records have been found relating to this custom; the tradition has its roots in a story that has been passed down orally through the generations. Legend has it that just across from Wiler, many centuries ago, there was a settlement – *Schurtendiebe aus dem Giätrich* – that was inhabited by very strange people. Under cover of night these people, dressed in often hideously carved wooden facemasks and a fur costume with a large bell tied around the waist, would attack the more prosperous citizens of Wiler. The University of Basel has in fact excavated ruins that confirm that such a settlement did exist. Today, a re-enactment of the tradition continues, but one of the strict rules is that only bachelors can participate. After the 2 February Maria Candlelight Mass the young men prepare themselves, and their expensive costumes, for the festivities, the highlight of which is a carnival parade through Wiler on the Saturday before Ash Wednesday.

Another colourful, but far less grotesque, custom is that of the *Herrgottsgrenadiere* – the 'Red Soldiers'. For many centuries men of the Lötschental worked as mercenaries for foreign armies, and it is recorded that as far back as 1644 six men were killed in the Battle of Lérida, in Catalonia, Spain. They also fought for the Kingdoms of Naples and Versailles, and it is from that era that the red and white uniforms originate. Proud of their service with these armies, the soldiers saved their parade uniforms to wear at church services and parades when they returned to the Lötschental. In further remembrance of those times a white silk banner, bearing a red cross and imprinted with the year 1625, is stored in the archives of the church in Kippel. During the celebrations of Corpus Christi, the descendants of these soldiers don scarlet red frocks with golden buttons, white trousers, a white criss-cross holder for swords and bullets and a peaked cap adorned by a tall feather. After the morning church service, with rifles at their shoulders, they parade through the town accompanied by their famous brass band. The Lötschental women, in their own traditional costumes, join in the festivities, too, and it is a resplendent sight.

If you thought these two customs strange and unusual enough to satiate these people's penchant for the bizarre, you'd be wrong. The New Year brings with it the festival of the Three Kings, *Chinigrosslinu*, during which three young men of military age dress themselves and their steeds in a manner imitating the Three Kings. And not content with 'traditional' tradition, they are chaperoned by two other men dressed in bright and amusing costumes – basically whatever comes to their minds. This colourful entourage is in turn joined by a children's choir, and they go from house to house singing joyous songs until late in the night.

Of course, there has to be a ghost story in the Lötschental. It is the story of Ferden, an old farmer who was killed in mysterious circumstances and whose restless spirit was reputed to return to chase the animals through the mountains and valleys of the Faldum, Resti and Kummen Alps. After days and nights of relentless pursuit the totally exhausted animals gave up red milk. The inhabitants of the village of Ferden, to which these particular Alps belonged, tried in vain to exorcise the farmer's spirit. Finally, the villagers agreed to donate two days' milk production to the poor folk of the valley. This act of generosity must have appeased the spirit of the farmer Ferden, and he bothered them no more. The custom has been celebrated for centuries since in the community house of Ferden, where the women and children receive a gift of cottage cheese and bread, and drink red wine out of wooden cups.

Val d'Anniviers

Situated immediately to the south of Sierre and one of the least known of many such valleys in this area, the Val d'Anniviers is an incredibly beautiful area with numerous attractions.

The road into the valley leads first to Vissoie, a charming little village that is considered the unofficial capital as it controls access to all the other villages. This section concentrates on the villages of St-Luc and Chandolin on the western side of the valley. Other villages, though, have their own attractions: there is Vercorin, Grimentz, with its 15th-century Maison Bourgeoisiale, and Zinal, sitting at the foothills of the imperial crown of five mountains (the Weisshorn, Zinalrothorn, Obergabelhorn, Matterhorn and Dent-Blanche), with its interesting Lée Copper Mine.

The most unusual event in these villages, and others in the valley, takes place on a Saturday in mid to late June and late September. Unfortunately, though, the exact date is variable – you have to check with the tourist office beforehand and be reliant upon favourable weather conditions. June is the time when the cows are taken from the villages up to alpine pastures to feast on the fresh grass, and this ceremony – the *Inalpes* – is quite a celebration. The cows leave the villages at 7am on what can be a rather long procession to pastures (*alpage*) that can be quite remote. Once there, at 10am, the Combats de Reines takes place – the local Valais tradition of cowfighting. These, though, are not the average cows seen grazing all over Switzerland. They are, in fact, the black – often dark brown – Hérens breed that originate in the Valais and the Aosta valley in northern Italy, and have been around for thousands of years. These strong animals have retained their instinct for hierarchy, and all the cows in the herd fight against each other to determine a ranking. The queen, the one that defeats all the others, takes pride of place at the head of processions and retains that position until she, in turn, is defeated. In reality, they don't seriously hurt each other as they stand head-to-head attempting to push the other out of the way. The prizes, suitably enough, are usually cowbells, but the farmer can sell the offspring of a winner for up to ten times the price of an ordinary calf. Winners, too, can go on to competitions, categorized by weight and age, with the winner being called the Queen of the Valais.

In September the reverse process, the ***Desalpes***, takes place when the cows leave the alpine pastures at 9am to return to the village, where more celebrations take place at 11am, as the cows are housed in their indoor barns for the winter.

The Sierre Anniviers tourist office, *www.sierre-anniviers.ch, info@sierre-anniviers.ch*, can arrange accommodation for these events at St-Luc and Chandolin, as well as at Grimentz, Vercorin and Ayer-Zinal. In 2003 this cost, for half board, was CHF 105, CHF 79 and CHF 60 for 3-star, 2-star and 1-star hotels respectively.

St-Luc and Chandolin

In the centre of the village of **St-Luc** there is a very interesting work of art featuring *The Washerwomen (Les Lavandières)*, which reflects an old social custom of this area. In the old days, women were forbidden to enter bars and their only real social meeting place, from which they in turn barred men, was the public washhouse where once or twice a week they could meet and exchange village news and gossip. These washhouses quickly disappeared with the introduction of running water and washing machines, but this dignified sculpture ensures that the custom will forever be remembered.

Also in the village is the station for the **St-Luc to Tignousa Funicular** (St-Luc Chandolin Funiculaire; *t 027 476 15 30, www.funiluc.ch*). Just a short distance above

Tourist Information

St-Luc: Office du Tourisme de St-Luc, **t** 027 475 14 12, **f** 027 475 22 37, *www. saint-luc.ch* (open Mon–Sat 9–12 and 3–6, Sun 9–1.30).
Chandolin: Office du Tourisme de Chandolin, **t** 027 475 18 38, **f** 027 475 46 60, *www.chandolin.ch* (opening hours as above).

Shopping

Chabloz Sports, rue Principale, St-Luc, **t** 027 475 16 18, **f** 027 475 47 18, *www.chabloz-sports.ch*. Has a full range of skis, snowboards, snowshoes and sledges available for hire, as well as mountain bikes. Also good for hiking boots and other sports clothing.

Where to Stay and Eat

St-Luc

★★★Bella-Tola, rue Principale, **t** 027 475 14 44, **f** 027 475 29 98, *www.bellatola.ch* (expensive). This, the luxury hotel of the area, was originally opened in 1859. However, by 1883 demand exceeded supply and this grand building was constructed on the foundations of a Roman villa on the outskirts of St-Luc. These days you can choose from 33 rooms and one suite, each one individually decorated and all the furnishings original and dating from the opening of the hotel. It also has a gourmet French restaurant and the Tzambron, a typical mountain restaurant specializing in regional dishes.
★★Le Beausite, **t** 027 475 15 86, **f** 027 475 50 65 (inexpensive). On the road just before, and under, the village, this is a delightful small hotel and fully lives up to its name. All of its 28 rooms and two studio apartments with kitchenettes are more than comfortable, fully equipped and have balconies with lovely views. The restaurant has a décor of light pine and cuisine that features specialities of the valley.

Sierre

★★★Atlantic, route de Sion 38, **t** 027 455 25 35, **f** 027 456 16 94 (inexpensive). This is a fine place from which to start or finish a trip to the Val d'Anniviers. Besides 37 rooms with modern facilities, it offers a very fine restaurant with a fantastic shrimp dish and a large garden with an oversize swimming pool that is overlooked by vineyards.

the Tignousa station you will find the **François-Xavier Bagnoud Observatory** (*t 027 475 58 08, www.ofxb.ch; open May, June, Sept, Oct 1.15, July and Aug 11.15 and 1.15; adm*). In this, the largest observatory open to the public in Switzerland, you can observe the sun and, on occasion, they have astronomy evenings. From here, the Planet Path (Chemin des Planètes) takes you on a 3.7-mile (6km) walk along a celestial path where you will learn about the planets' dimensions and characteristics, as well as much else. It is a pleasing, gentle walk back from Tignousa to St-Luc.

Back just outside St-Luc the **18th-century Watermills** (Les Moulins du XVIIIᵉ; *t 079 610 92 71; open mid-July to mid-Sept on Wed, Sat and Sun; adm*) are of real interest. Here you will find a corn mill, walnut press, two rye and wheat mills and a cloth-fulling mill. Mills bring to mind bread, and the baking of rye bread in the communal oven is another tradition of St-Luc. Once a year each family prepares, according to recipes passed down through the generations, their own rye bread. You, too, can enjoy this fun, which takes place once a week, by contacting the St-Luc tourist office.

Chandolin, at an altitude of 6,562ft (2,000m), about 1,050ft (320m) higher than St-Luc, has its own attractions, too. The ecosystem is different here to the extent that it has its own micro-climate, and its rich diversity of flora includes several species that are rare even in other parts of the Anniviers, let alone the Valais itself. To explore this subject in detail, it is fun to take one or more of the **Botanical Walks** (Les Promenades Botaniques) between altitudes of 6,561ft (2,000m) and 8,858ft (2,700m). There are 22 information posts positioned along the way that indicate, among other things, that there are no less than 24 species of orchid to be seen, and you may pass the 860-year-old larch tree. Along the way you will find fauna observation posts equipped with binoculars and educational panels. A more detailed guide about the walks can be purchased at the tourist office. In fact, in this area there are over 90 miles (150kms) of hiking paths.

Ella Maillart, 1903–97, was one of the most extraordinary female travellers of the 20th century, having explored, in extremely trying conditions, such places as Asia, China and Tibet. In 1946 she decided that she would spend six months, from the first to last snow, in Chandolin and the ancient chapel has, since 1998, played host to an exhibition that traces the achievements of her life.

Between the end of June and mid-September it is possible to take the Télésiège (chairlift) from Chandolin up to **Tsapé** at an altitude of 8,038ft (2,450m). From here there are some nice walks, particularly up to Lac Noir. The Restaurant Tsapé – at the top station of the chairlift – is a fine place for a breather, particularly during the Fête du Remuage at the end of July.

Saas-Fee

It is strange that two villages, sitting near the ends of adjacent valleys in the far southern Valais, could be so different in character. While its neighbour, Zermatt, is hemmed into a fairly narrow and very steep valley, Saas-Fee sits beautifully in a natural bowl at an altitude of 5,906ft (1,800m). It is surrounded by no less than 13

Tourist Information

Saas-Fee: Saas-Fee Tourism, **t** 027 958 18 58, **f** 027 958 18 60, *www.saas-fee.ch* (*open Mon–Fri 8.30–12 and 2–6.30, Sat 8–7, Sun 9–12 and 3–6, with slight seasonal variations*).

Many all-season packages, put together by the tourist office in brochures and on the website, are available in advance of your visit.

Shopping

Haus der Geschenke, **t** 027 957 25 06, **f** 027 957 18 83, just across from the Ferianart Resort and Spa Hotel. Has by far the widest range of souvenirs and toys in Saas-Fee.

César Sport, **t** 027 957 14 16, *www.cesarsport. ch*, and **Alpin Sport**, **t** 027 957 37 33, *www. alpinsport.ch*. Members of the INTERSPORT scheme; offer everything you need, to either rent or buy, for skiing, snowboarding, mountaineering and summer hiking.

Where to Stay

****Ferienart Resort and Spa, **t** 027 958 19 00, **f** 027 958 19 05, *www.ferienart.ch*

(*expensive*). Behind its chalet-style façade is a warm, stylish and extremely congenial hotel. The rooms and suites are innovatively designed and usually wood panelled, beautifully decorated and extremely well-equipped. Dine in your choice of three restaurants, including the fine Le Gourmet, and afterwards dance to live bands in the bar. There is also an extensive on-site spa and grotto pool.

***Burgener, **t** 027 958 92 80, **f** 027 958 92 81, *www.hotel-burgener.ch* (*moderate*). This is a medium-sized, 30-room hotel in the heart of the village. Cosy and comfortable.

Rendez-Vous, **t 027 957 20 40, **f** 027 957 35 34 (*moderate*). A small hotel that also offers apartments and has modern well-appointed rooms, each with a balcony and bath. Other features are a restaurant, a bar and a sun terrace.

Eating Out

Drehrestaurant Metro-Alpin, **t** 027 957 17 71. At an altitude of 11,483ft (3,500m), this is the world's highest revolving restaurant (*see p.202*).

mountains that rise to over 13,123ft (4,000m), including the Dom which, at 14,911ft (4,545m), is the highest mountain wholly in Switzerland.

This charming glacier village, which has preserved many of its customs and traditions, has a population of just under 1,500. And as recently as 1850 there were just 236 inhabitants, in part because access to the village was difficult. The first road to Saas-Fee was opened in 1951, but then only on the condition that the village itself remained car-free. Of course, Saas-Fee has accumulated its share of shops, but they are manageable in number. It also has a variety of bars and restaurants but, very wisely not wanting to spoil the peaceful and harmonious setting, no noise or music is allowed on the village streets after 10.30pm.

Outdoor Activities

Saas-Fee has a particularly impressive mountain transport system (some of which is closed, though, between seasons). Two large cable cars and three smaller ones, 18 ski lifts, two chair lifts and a 'Metro Alpin' funicular compete for your attention. One particular trip, in winter or summer, is a must: take the cable car from Saas-Fee to Felskinn, at an altitude of 9,843ft (3,000m), then change onto the 'Metro Alpin' – the highest funicular in the world – for the 1,526ft (465m) ascent to **Mittelallin**. On arrival, at an altitude of 11,483ft (3,500m), you will find two 'highest in the world' places. The

Drehrestaurant, which seats 220 people and revolves 360 degrees every hour, is a unique place to enjoy a meal and watch as a panoramic feast of alpine peaks and glaciers slowly reveal themselves to you in all their glory. It is then possible to go down deep into the glacier and visit the world's highest and largest **ice pavilion**. Inside, beneath a ceiling of pure ice that averages a thickness of 33ft (10m), you will learn much about glaciers – and you can touch as well. Regular visitors will notice, too, the effects of almost imperceptible but constant change – the annual movement of both the glacier and ice pavilion is 10.6–11.8 inches (27–30cm).

The overriding appeal of Saas-Fee, regardless of the season, is a magnificent natural setting offering outdoor sports of all kinds. Mountain hikers and mountain bikers will be in their element in the summer. There are over 174 miles (280km) of pathways that vary in difficulty, and the tourist office has brochures, panoramic maps and the *Saastal* hiking map. From Saas-Fee, cable cars ascend to your choice of Plattjen, 8,432ft (2,570m), Längfluh, 9,416ft (2,870m), or Hannig, 7,710ft (2,350m). Each of these has a restaurant/bar where you can indulge in a bit of refreshment before beginning the downhill treks back to the village. Be sure to take along some raw carrots; along the way you are bound to encounter some of Saas-Fee's trademark tame marmots, and these chubby, furry creatures love nothing better than a carrot snack. Alternatively, take the post bus up to Mattmark, where you will see Europe's largest dam, perhaps continuing on to the Monte Moro Pass at 9,409ft (2,868m) before returning to Saas-Fee the same way.

Winter-sports enthusiasts can have the best of both worlds, as the glaciers around Mittelallin allow for summer skiing as well. During winter there are over 62 miles (100km) of ski slopes – 50 per cent red, 25 per cent blue and 25 per cent black runs as well as three off-piste (yellow) runs. There are also 36 miles (60km) of winter hiking paths, and 22 miles (36km) of cross-country ski runs. During summer the runs are reduced to 12.4 miles (20km) of slopes, for average to very good skiers.

Those interested in learning more about the history and culture of Saas-Fee will wish to visit the **Saas Museum** (*open Mon–Fri 2–5; adm*). Housed in an early 18th-century home, the main exhibit is the original study of the German writer Carl Zuckmayer, who adopted Saas-Fee as his second home. Look, also, for traditional costumes, a sacred art collection, folklore articles, a collection of minerals and an exhibition on the history of glaciers.

Zermatt

Life in Zermatt was fairly uneventful until the early part of the 19th century, when the first tourists discovered the Matterhorn in 1820. Eighteen years later a surgeon, Dr Josef Lauber, opened the first inn, the Hotel Cervin, later to be known as the Monte Rosa, which had just three beds. Zermatt, boasting an enviable southern position, yet protected from the wind and with excellent snow conditions, never looked back. These days, the name Zermatt is synonymous with the Matterhorn, and visitors from around the world flock to see the most distinctive, and some say most beautiful, mountain in the Alps. Renowned as both a summer and winter resort, Zermatt is famous, also, for having the longest skiing season in the Alps. The authorities have acted to preserve the character of the village by banning all traffic; motor vehicles must be left at Täsch, 5km down the valley.

As more tourists arrive, so the infrastructure has grown to meet their needs, and this in turn gives rise to other changes. The upmarket shops, hotels, restaurants and discos, originally appendages to scenery and sport, have now become an attraction in their own right. Daylight hours find the few streets crowded with shoppers, and nightfall brings popular bars and discos alive until the early hours of the morning. Zermatt is, therefore, not the quietest of places, but it is somewhere that combines, and uniquely so, dramatically beautiful alpine scenery and unparalleled year-round skiing possibilities with very refined hotels, specialist shops and a lively nightlife.

Mountain Excursions

Without any doubt, the main attraction here is the magical **Matterhorn**. Even in the presence of a host of commanding mountain peaks, thirty-six of which ascend to over 13,000ft (4,000m), it is the magnetism of the Matterhorn, and the Matterhorn alone, which draws huge numbers of visitors from all the corners of the world to Zermatt. At 14,692ft (4,478m), it is not the tallest mountain in the area but, unusually shaped, it stands alone and seems to rise from nowhere.

The easiest way to get unobstructed, and closer, views of the Matterhorn is to start by taking one of the new eight-seat **Matterhorn-Express** gondola cars from Zermatt at 5,315ft (1,620m) up to **Furi** at 6,115ft (1.864m). From there you have two options. Either take the Matterhorn-Express up to **Schwarzee**, 8,471ft (2,582m), where a small lake and a mountain hotel with the same name sit right on the foothills of the Matterhorn. Or, alternatively, take the cable car up to **Trockener Steg** at 9,642ft (2,939m). The sundeck that winds around the restaurant here is not only a great place for refreshments, but also offers glorious 360° views of the surrounding peaks and glaciers. The sheer face of the Matterhorn rises imposingly on one side. To the south stands a veritable wall of mountain peaks, and flowing interminably from them are vast glaciers. Time, now, to take the highest cable car ride in Europe to **Klein Matterhorn** itself, reaching 12,53ft (3,820m). The views from this vantage point are, simply stated, unforgettable, and the panorama that unfolds around you takes in just about everywhere from Mont Blanc to Austria, and everything in between.

This is a great area for summer skiing, and the Theodul Glacier and its surroundings offer a natural amphitheatre of over 8,960 acres (3,626 hectares) of perpetual snow.

A Bird's Eye View of the Matterhorn

The most spectacular views of the Matterhorn are from an **Air-Zermatt helicopter** (**t** *027 966 86 86, www.air-zermatt.ch*). They offer 20-minute trips, for CHF 195 per person, that take you as close as you can get to the summit without actually climbing it. If you are lucky, you might even see climbers. On the same trip, you will also be taken closely over a huge and imposing glacier.

Tourist Information

Zermatt: Zermatt Tourismus, Bahnhofplatz 5, **t** 027 966 81 00, **f** 027 966 81 01, *www. zermatt.ch*, is right outside the railway station (*open mid-June–early Oct Mon–Sat 8.30–6, Sun 9.30–12 and 4–6; the rest of the year Mon–Fri 8.30–12 and 2–6, mid-Dec– mid-June Sat 8.30–12 and 2–6, Oct–mid- Dec and late April–mid-June Sat 9.30–12 and 2–5, mid-Dec–late April Sun 9.30–12 and 4–6*).

Multi-lingual summer and winter information brochures, detailing all manner of activity packages, are available to visitors in advance.

Shopping

WEGA gift shops, Bahnhofplatz and other locations in Zermatt, **t** 027 967 21 66, **f** 027 967 63 94. The best places to buy Swiss Army knives – they will engrave the knives free of charge. Also on sale are clocks, music boxes, watches, cowbells, books, T-shirts, etc.

Bayard, Bahnhofplatz 4 (and at four other locations in Zermatt), **t** 027 966 49 50, **f** 027 966 49 55, *www.bayardzermatt.ch*. Members of the Swiss rent-a-sport rent-and-go scheme; offer everything you need either to rent or buy for skiing, snowboarding, snow-shoeing, sledging, mountaineering, mountain biking and summer hiking.

Where to Stay

★★★★★**Mont Cervin & Residence, t** 027 966 88 88, **f** 027 966 88 99, *www.zermatt.ch/ montcervin* (*luxury*). Opened in 1851, this has been the flagship of the Seiler hotel group since 1855. Located in the centre of the village, it has 132 rooms and suites, and 15 apartments with 1–3 bedrooms, all of which are furnished to the highest standards. Most have balconies and some even have jacuzzis and fireplaces. There is also a Clarins Beauty Salon, indoor pool and health facilities.

★★★★★**Riffelalp Resort, t** 027 966 05 55, **f** 027 966 05 50, *www.zermatt.ch/riffelalp* (*luxury*). At an altitude of 7,290ft (2,222m) and reached via the Gornergrat train with a tram from the station to the resort, this has stunning views of the Matterhorn. Modern in thought but traditional in style, it has 64 rooms and two apartments and such things as its own small cinema, two bowling alleys and a wide – and expanding – range of sports and health facilities. On a plateau with micro-climatic conditions, it even has its own pure spring water.

★★★★**Monte Rosa**, Bahnhofstrasse 80, **t** 027 966 03 33, **f** 027 966 03 30, *www.zermatt.ch/ monterosa* (*luxury*). This, opened in 1839 and taken over by the Seiler family in 1853, is the oldest and most traditional hotel in Zermatt. The traditionally furnished 47 rooms and suites all have modern facilities

There are 15 miles (24.1km) of safe marked runs, including one of 4 miles (6.4km) with a vertical descent of 3,290ft (1,003m).

Another fascinating trip is on a Gornergratbahn (GGB) train – preferably in an open carriage – beginning at the second of Zermatt's train stations located directly across from the main station. From here, the cog-rail trains make a 43-minute ascent to **Gornergrat** at 10,269ft (3,130m), making it Europe's highest totally open-air railway. The initial part of the journey twists and turns through the forested slopes up to the open mountain side, offering ever-changing views of glorious alpine scenery. In the warmer seasons you might see marmots scampering around. Upon reaching Gornergrat, you will marvel at the unparalleled vista of the massive Monte Rosa and her sister peaks, each of which is well over 13,123ft (4,000m). Directly behind you, but in the distance, you will see another range of peaks of equal stature, amongst which is the Dom at 14,911ft (4,545m). Yet even these magnetic mountains will be unable to distract you from the magnificence of the Matterhorn, splendidly isolated in the and lounges, some with balconies with mountain views. Guests also have use of the indoor pool and fitness and health facilities at the nearby sister hotel, the Mont Cervin.

****Alex**, Bodmenstrasse 12, t 027 966 70 70, f 027 966 70 90, www.hotelalexzermatt.ch (*luxury*). This prides itself on being a carefree holiday destination. No pompousness or stuffiness here, but plenty of luxury, with 67 rooms ranging from small singles to de-luxe jacuzzi suites and a cosy atmosphere which is also reflected in the public areas. The romantic grotto indoor pool is next to a health club with pampering treatments, guaranteed to relax body and soul. There's also the very fine Alex Grill restaurant.

***Alpenroyal**, Riedstrasse 96, t 027 966 60 66, f 027 966 60 65, www.alpenroyal.ch (*expensive*). This is a typical mountain-style hotel in an elevated and peaceful location with excellent views of the Matterhorn. A family-run establishment, there are 30 very comfortable rooms, good food and an indoor pool with sauna and whirlpool.

Kulm Hotel Gornergrat, t 027 966 64 00, f 027 966 64 04 (*moderate*). Sitting in splendid alpine isolation at an altitude of 10,286ft (3,100m) and only accessed via the Gornergrat railway, this is the highest hotel in Europe. A typical mountain hotel, the rooms are rather basic, but the views are unparalleled and the restaurant serves wine from the highest vineyard in Switzerland.

Le Mazot, t 027 966 06 06, f 027 966 06 07, www.lemazotzermatt.ch (*inexpensive*). Located by the river, just a couple of minutes from the centre, this has 2 single and 7 double rooms that have excellent facilities. Also a nice restaurant with fondue specialities.

Bahnhof, t 027 967 24 06, f 027 967 72 16 (*cheap*). Right next to the station, this has a mix of rooms ranging from singles to 4 beds – with or without private shower and dormitory accommodation.

Eating Out

Like most mountain resorts in Switzerland, half-board is the better option. This is particularly so if you stay at the Seiler hotels. They have a 'Dine Around' scheme where you can select to eat in any of their hotels with a choice of nine different restaurants that range from the beautiful and traditional Monte Rosa dining room to the outdoor terrace at the Riffelalp, with choices of Swiss, French, Italian, Japanese and American cuisine.

Restaurant Weisshorn, t 027 967 57 72. A nice place right by the bridge next to the church on the main street. A varied menu features such delicacies as home-made soups, cooked in a large pot outside by the tables, as well as *rösti*, fondue and *Käseschnitte*, all at reasonable prices.

distance. Directly in front is the Gornergletscher, and from this vantage point you will be able clearly to define the path along which this massive glacier slowly meanders its way down, as well as its confluences with other, smaller glaciers. Incidentally, the Kulm Hotel Gornergrat here is the highest hotel in the Alps, and its terrace is a great place for a snack.

Another mountain trip starts at the Standseilbahn in Zermatt, just across the river from the Gornergratbahn. The first stage is on the **Métro Sunnegga Express**, a funicular that ascends inside the mountain itself to the plateau of Sunnegga, at 7,546ft (2,300m). From there a gondola cable car travels up to **Blauherd**, 8,619ft (2,627m), and the final stage is by cable car that climbs to **Rothorn** (a common name in Switzerland for a mountain), at 10,180ft (3,103m). Besides being the starting point for numerous walks, it also boasts splendid views in its own right.

Hiking is, of course, a favourite pastime here, and there are numerous routes to choose from; these can last from just an hour or so to a full day. Mountain biking, also, is becoming immensely popular, and there are miles of specially laid-out, well-marked bike trails. Further information regarding both hiking and mountain bike trails is available through the tourist office.

In this wind-protected southern location, Zermatt has three skiing areas that offer excellent snow conditions. There are over 245 miles (394km) of ski slopes, ranging from the simplest to the most complicated runs, that are accessible via an ever-growing myriad of transport alternatives. There are also snow parks, fun parks, sledging runs, snowshoe walking tours and 28 miles (30km) of prepared winter hiking paths.

Western Switzerland

Neuchâtel

Neuchâtel is located on the western side of the lake of the same name, and is in the western, French-speaking part of Switzerland. Close to the French border, it looks to the nearby Jura mountains on one side, and the lake and the peaks of the Bernese Oberland in the distance on the other.

For a fairly small town – it has a population of just under 35,000 – it has a long and interesting history, much of which centres around the **Old Town** (Vieille Ville) and particularly the Collégiale church and the castle. It is low on museums, but the one for art and history is worth a close look. And there are opportunities for boat trips out on the lake, as well as the funicular to Chaumont that offers spectacular views.

Although perhaps not the best place for shopping or nightlife, Neuchâtel does possess some very fine restaurants, and one unique hotel.

History

In the 10th century a fortified township, of which the Prison and Diesse Tower remain as evidence today, were built in Neuchâtel, as was a new castle – from which the name *Neuchâtel* originated. This was constructed on the instigation of Rudolph III of Burgundy and presented in 1011 to his wife, Irmengarde. At the beginning of the 12th century the first Counts of Neuchâtel were titled and, in 1214, granted the city burghers their first charter. It was during this era, also, that the Romanesque wing of the present castle and Romanesque apse and apsidioles of the Collégiale church were constructed. The cenotaph of the Counts of Neuchâtel, dated 1373 and considered a masterpiece of medieval sculpture, can still be admired in the church.

From 1512 to 1529 the territory was occupied, for strategic reasons, by the Swiss cantons, and in 1530 Neuchâtel adopted the Reformation. Henry II of Orléans-Longueville became the first Prince of Neuchâtel at the beginning of the 17th century. In 1707 Mary of Orléans died without leaving an heir, and the citizens chose her successor from among fifteen claimants. It appears they were selective, too, wanting their new leader to be Protestant and strong enough to protect them but

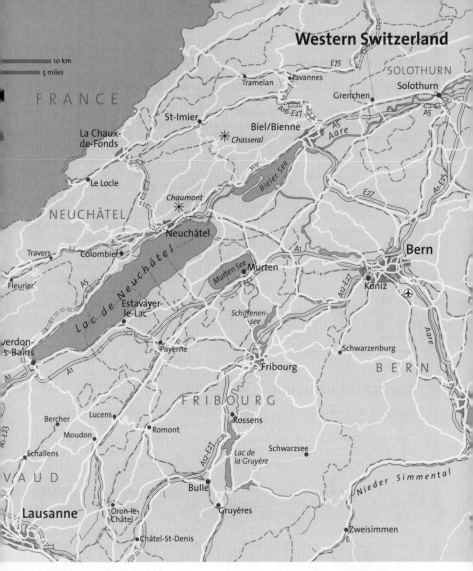

distant enough not to be too meddlesome. Eventually, they settled on Frederick I, King of Prussia, whose entitlement originated through the Houses of Chalon-Orange and Nassau.

The 18th century saw the emergence of industry – especially watchmaking, the manufacture of printed fabrics and lace, commerce, banking and agriculture. The tide of affluence that ensued brought with it many fine houses, most constructed of local yellow stone.

The Napoleonic era brought more changes. The defeated King of Prussia exchanged Neuchâtel for Hanover, and Napoleon elevated his favorite Marshal, Berthier, to the rank of Prince of Neuchâtel – a place he never actually visited. Napoleon's demise allowed the then King of Prussia, Frederick-William III, to retain control of Hanover

Getting Around

The **train station** is situated in the place de la Gare, in an elevated position above the town proper, and although the **Fun'ambule funicular** connects it to the lower part of town it is probably more convenient to take a no.7 or 9 bus to place Pury.

Most **buses** (t 032 720 06 58, *www. tnneuchatel.ch*) start or stop at place Pury. In fact, Neuchâtel is small enough to walk around with ease; however, the No.1 bus is useful as it goes north to the Hôtel Palafitte and south to the Museum of Ethnography. Similarly, the No.7 bus drops you off at the La Coudre stop, north of the city, for the Chaumont funicular. A single fare is CHF 1.60.

Car Hire

Avis, esplanade Léopold-Robert 2, t 032 723 11 67.
Europcar, ch. des Roseaux 5, t 032 724 96 96.
Hertz, rue Pierre-à-Mazel, t 032 725 17 60.

Tourist Information

Neuchâtel: Tourisme Neuchâtelois, Hôtel des Postes, t 032 889 68 90, f 032 889 62 96, *www.ne.ch/tourism* (*open July and Aug Mon–Fri 9–6.30, Sat 9–4, Sun 10–4; rest of the year Mon–Fri 9–12 and 1.30–5.30, Sat 9–12*).

Guided Trips and Tours

Tourist train of Neuchâtel (Train touristique de Neuchâtel) operates daily from May to Oct, with commentaries in French, German and English. It takes you on a 45-minute trip through the Old Town, with a stop at the castle; tickets cost CHF 6.

Market Days

General market: Tues, Thurs and Sat mornings at place des Halles.

Where to Stay

*****Palafitte, rte des Gouttes d'Or 2, t 032 723 02 02, f 032 723 02 03, *www.palafitte.ch* (*luxury*). Behind a bland exterior some distance north of town, you will find an extraordinarily unusual hotel. In the lobby you will be fingerprinted, and your finger then becomes the key to your room. A golf cart parked in the lobby will take you there. All the 40 junior suites are in the form of chalets, and you can select one on stilts directly over the lake itself. Inside, you are met by not just luxury, but a degree of sophistication that almost makes the term high-tech redundant. Expect a plasma TV, home video surround system and an individual 'SIM-pad' remote control for all in-room devices. The screens behind the bed part to reveal a stunning jacuzzi right behind in the bathroom, and on your private deck a ladder leads directly down into the lake – making it your private pool.
*****Beau-Rivage, esplanade du Mont-Blanc 1, t 032 723 15 15, f 032 723 16 16, *www.beau-rivage-hotel.ch* (*luxury*). This has the finest location in Neuchâtel, right by the lakeside and the pretty Mont-Blanc walk, yet just a couple of minutes' walk from the Old Town. The 65 rooms are highly luxurious, and often have views of the Bernese Oberland peaks.
****Beaulac, esplanade Léopold-Robert 2, t 032 723 11 11, f 032 723 60 35, *www.beaulac.ch* (*moderate*). This white rectangular building has a delightful location on the edge of the harbour overlooking the lake.

and reassert his rights to Neuchâtel. Being too distant from his territory, however, he encouraged its incorporation into the Swiss political system. Accordingly, on 12 September 1814 the Principality of Neuchâtel was admitted to the Swiss Confederation as the twenty-first canton. The paradox of a principality within the confederation was short lived, though, as the French Revolution encouraged the citizens of Neuchâtel to follow suit. Fortunately this revolution was bloodless, and Neuchâtel was proclaimed a republic on 1 March 1848.

The 81 rooms and suites – including three disabled ones – are modern and spacious; some have views of the Bernese Oberland.

***La Maison du Prussien**, Gor du Vauseyon, t 032 730 54 54, f 032 730 21 43, *www.hotel-prussien.ch (moderate)*. Situated a little south of town and in its own grounds (take a No.1 bus to the Beauregard stop), this distinguished building used to be an 18th-century brewery. It has just 10 rooms, but they are spacious and quite special, with wooden-beamed ceilings and fireplaces.

**Hôtel des Arts, rue Pourtalès 3, t 032 727 61 61, f 032 727 61 62, *www.hotel-des-arts.ch (moderate)*. This has a good location, just a couple of blocks north of the port and close to the lake. The 40 rooms, four suites and five apartments are all brightly decorated.

Hôtel du Marché, place des Halles 4, t 032 723 23 30, f 032 723 23 33, *www.hoteldumarche.ch (inexpensive)*. Right in the centre of the Old Town, this is a small hotel with just 10 rooms (none ensuite), either single, double or for three, that are clean and simply furnished.

Eating Out

Le Colvert, rte des Gouttes d'Or 2, t 032 723 02 02, f 032 723 02 03, *www.palafitte.ch (very expensive)*. This is the gourmet restaurant of the Hôtel Palafitte, which more than matches the standards of the hotel itself. Directly overlooking the lake, it has a terrace for the warmer months. The *A La Découverte* menu is a 6-course feast for CHF 120, whilst the *Au Plaisir* menu may be better for those with lighter appetites with just 4 courses and costing CHF 80 (CHF 62 without the appetizer). Or choose one of the delicious dishes from the main menu.

Hôtel Dupeyrou, avenue Dupeyrou 1, t 032 725 11 83, f 032 724 06 28, *www.dupeyrou.ch (expensive)*. Located in what is Neuchâtel's most imposing and historic building (*see p.214*), the elegant restaurant here is run by Australian chef Craig Penlington-Montadon and his Neuchâteloise wife, Françoise. The speciality is fish and other seafood, fresh from the market, used to create original and elaborate creations. Eat out on the terrace in good weather.

Beau-Rivage, esplanade du Mont-Blanc 1, t 032 723 15 15, f 032 723 16 16 (*expensive*). The stylish restaurant of the Beau-Rivage hotel has large windows overlooking the lake and the mountains past it. Service here matches the setting, and the dishes featuring the likes of fillet of perch and lobster are beautifully created and presented.

Brasserie du Jura, rue de la Treille 7, t 032 725 14 10 (*moderate*). Just off the place Pury, this has plenty of ambience and is an authentic Neuchâteloise brasserie. One of the specialities here is the local tripe. *Closed Sun.*

Hôtel du Marché, place des Halles 4, t 032 723 23 30, f 032 723 23 33, *www.hoteldumarche.ch (moderate)*. Located in the hotel of the same name, the interior is charming, and there are seats outside for over 150 people in the place des Halles. The cuisine is regional, with such tasty dishes as foie gras of duck with caramelized potatoes. *Closed Sun.*

Café de la Collégiale, t 032 710 02 15 (*inexpensive*). As the name implies, this bright and modern little café is situated right outside the Collégiale church and castle. The menu is small – a selection of croissants, sandwiches and the like – along with an inexpensive daily special. *Open 8.30–5; closed Sun.*

The Old Town (Vieille Ville)

The **tourist office** is just on the edge of the Old Town and is housed in the **Post Office**, at the place du Port, a very impressive building with the names of the countries of the world sculpted around the top.

Just west is the equally impressive **Hôtel de Ville** (town hall; *rue de l'Hôtel de Ville*), that dates from 1784–90; note the two tympanums and the handsome classical columns. On the east side, Minerva and Liberty are depicted either side of a shield decorated with the town's coat-of-arms, and the opposite side has another shield symbolizing Trade and Abundance, protected on either side by two winged and cloud-borne figures. Inside, on the ground floor, there is a model of 18th-century Neuchâtel. Just across the road there is a very large ornamental Louis XVI-style fountain.

The Vieille Ville is to the south, and one of its features are the fountains, similar to those found in Bern and other parts of Switzerland, with their columns topped by brightly coloured statues. The **Justice Fountain** (Fontaine de la Justice) is the closest of them, at the junction of rue de l'Hôpital and Grand'Rue; this was carved by Laurent Perroud in 1545–7 and has recently been restored. It has an octagonal basin and the statue is that of Justice, surrounded by figures representing a pope, a magistrate, an emperor and a sultan that, in earlier eras, represented various forms of government. Just a block or so further south is the **Market Crossing** (Croix du Marché), the most ancient square of the town, where the surrounding 18th-century façades provide a suitable backdrop for the oldest fountain outside the old Neuchâtel town walls. It started life as a watering spot for cattle, but the **Banneret Fountain** (Fontaine du Banneret) was enlarged and in 1581 Laurent Perroud created the figure of the standard bearer that gives it its name. The adjacent Hôtel du Banneret, built in 1609, is considered the finest example of late Renaissance architecture in the region, and has been perfectly conserved. Just to the west, check out the Baroque façade of the Montmollin House at rue des Moulins, and look carefully to the east for the small **passage des Corbets** to spot a very unusual Renaissance spiral staircase.

Neuchâtel's main attractions sit at the top of a steep hill, and a little way up it the **Griffon Fountain** (Fontaine du Griffon), just past the Tour de Diesse, is a suitable place to stop and decide which route to take to them. Actually, until the Reformation in 1530, there used to be a statue of Neuchâtel's patron saint, William, here. The fountain you see today was enlarged in 1664 and on public holidays wine, rather than the usual water, flowed through it. To the south, take note of some fine 18th-century houses in the **rue du Pommier**, which replaced others burnt down in the fire of 1714.

The quick way up to the castle and church is by way of the escaliers du Château, but these are extremely steep and are perhaps better left for the descent. Better, by far, to follow the rue du Château and rue de la Collégiale up to the ramparts and then around to the church itself. Along the way, take time to look at the **Prison Tower** (Tour des Prisons; *open April–Sept 8–6; adm with CHF 1 coin through an automatic turnstile*). This has the distinction of being the most ancient building in Neuchâtel, and it is fascinating to note how easily discernible layers chronicle its constructive history: a white limestone base which dates from Roman times is topped by uncut blocks of granite from around the beginning of the 11th century and finished off by medium-sized white limestone and yellow stone added by 11th- and 12th-century builders. The entire tower was renovated in 1803. There are models of Neuchâtel as it appeared during the 15th and 18th centuries inside, and the top level affords splendid views of the neighbouring district, lake and the peaks of the Bernese Oberland in the distance.

There is little documentation regarding the early history of the **Collégiale church**, but it is known that the building was begun prior to 1185 in the Romanesque style, and was influenced by Basel's cathedral and the Grossmünster in Zürich. A now obliterated inscription on the southern portal identified the founders as Ulrich II of

Neuchâtel and his wife Bertha. It was consecrated on 8 November 1276, a date that probably marks the completion of the western, largely Gothic end. Renovations followed in 1360, 1372 and 1428; in 1530 during the Reformation, Neuchâtel soldiers returning from Geneva stripped the interior of altars and decorative additions. Major alterations were made to the exterior during a general renovation in the mid-19th century, including the destruction of the original church tower in favour of a stone spire. A copy of that tower was grafted onto the northern side of the building, leaving the southern steeple as the only original on the structure.

Inside, stained-glass windows by Clément Heaton were added to the choir in 1905. The wonderful rose window and others on the southern side representing the *Announcement of the Shepherds*, the seal of the Reformer Guillaume Farel and the apostles and their symbols are by Theodor Delachaux, and were installed between 1930 and 1947. The windows on the north and west, of the prophets and Moses and John the Baptist respectively, are creations of Marcel Poncet in 1951. Take a look at the capitals, decorated with Daniel in the lion's den, palmettes, heads of wildcats and even musician eagles and monkeys.

Notwithstanding this, pride of place undoubtedly lies with the gloriously sculpted cenotaph of the Counts of Neuchâtel, considered one of the most remarkable works of art from the Middle Ages and the most important north of the Alps. It was begun on the order of Louis of Neuchâtel in 1372, and consists of no less than 15 carved, painted and almost life-size statues. During the Reformation the Governor prevented its desecration, and between 1678 and 1840 it was actually hidden behind planks before the broken parts were reconstituted and repainted. In fact, what you see today is an amalgamation from different ages: the knights and their ladies at the entrance of the arcades are from the 14th century; the images of Jean and Conrad de Fribourg were created between 1425 and 1458 by Master Matthäus Ensinger; an unpainted Count is thought to be Rodolphe de Hochberg who died in 1487 and the gables topping the cenotaph are clearly from the 15th century.

On the exterior, facing the castle, two smaller apses standing either side of a larger one are Norman. Of the small open **cloister** (*cloître*), only the Romanesque arcades built on to the north wall of the church are original; the rest were renovated in neo-Gothic style in 1875.

Construction of the imposing **château** (*t 032 889 60 11; free guided tours, with commentary in English, French and German, start from the entrance at door No.1, April–Sept Mon–Fri at 10, 11, 12, 2, 3 and 4, Sat at 10, 11, 2, 3 and 4, on Sun and public hols at 2, 3 and 4*) was begun near the end of the 12th century. It was enlarged in several stages over the next three centuries, and renovated extensively following the city-wide fire of 1450. Initially serving as the principal dwelling for the first Lords of Neuchâtel, it became, after 1405, a residence for the governors and a series of councillors. From 1848 to the present it has housed important government offices and it is, in fact, the oldest building in Switzerland that has been in continuous use. In short, in one form or another, the regional authority has made its home in the castle for the past 800 years. The structure is divided into three main sections: the Romanesque tower, the Main Gate and the southern Gallery. The highly ornamental Romanesque section, the oldest part of the château dating back to the 12th century, has an interesting carriage gateway that gave access to the wine cellars – the principal source of income of the counts. The southern Gallery was built in 1488, and has as its main focal point a wall upon which are emblazoned the coats-of-arms of the first thirteen Swiss cantons. Philippe de Hochberg commissioned the construction of the twin-towered Main Gate in 1496–98 as a permanent reminder of his service to the French kings.

Inside there are many notable rooms. The **Antechamber of the Grand Council Hall** has a Robert Flemier painting of *The Blessing of the Plough*. The **Grand Council Hall** itself, built in 1875 over the stables, is where the canton parliament meets. The **Grotto** was originally a stone barrel vault where the Neuchâtel archives were kept, but in 1649 it was ornamented with marble panels painted in grisaille and with the coat-of-arms of Henry II of Orléans-Longueville. The wonderfully wooden-beamed **Knights' Room**, the castle's largest, was once just a cellar before becoming an arsenal; it is now beautifully restored and contains a very large painting by Jules Girardet depicting a battle in front of the Thielle Bridge. The **Department of Agriculture's Vestibule** is noted for its rafters, portraits of magistrates and Marcel Mathy's *Woman with Necklace* sculpture. The parquet-floored – note the tiles evoking the ruling families in the corner – and wooden-beamed **Marie of Savoy Room** is very distinguished, and named after the daughter of the Count of Savoy and niece of King Louis XI of France who married Philippe de Hochberg in 1478. It is dominated by a huge yellow stone fireplace, where painted above it two angels support the Count of Neuchâtel's coat-of-arms. A corridor above the Marie of Savoy room has notable wall drawings featuring coats-of-arms of some 17th-century Neuchâtel governors and the Gallandre family, and a red-chalked image of a mustachioed soldier. Built by, and named after himself, the **Philippe de Hochberg Gallery** dates from 1488; it was enlarged in 1836 and 12 years later when the Republic was founded in 1848 members of the former State Council were imprisoned here. The **State Council Room** on the upper floor of the Romanesque wing was once Count Philippe's bedroom, but since 1848 it is where the five members and the chancellor of the Neuchâtel government convene for deliberations. The wooden ceilings of the **Antechamber of State Council** are particularly decorative and feature the coats-of-arms of Philippe de Hochberg and Marie of Savoy. The **State Room**, seat of the State Court, has a decor that has more or less remained the same since 1691; armorial shields of the rulers and governors of Neuchâtel cover the walls. Look, also, for the handsome Josué Robert clock that dates from 1732. Originally built of wood in the 15th century, the **Castle Chapel** was reconstructed with a stone barrel roof in the 18th century. It is somewhat incongruous that this, with its original Gothic window, is now used as a library.

Before leaving this area, take a walk around the battlements and admire these wonderful buildings from a different perspective.

Three more places are worth seeing back in the lower area of the Old Town. The **rue du Seyon** is an important shopping street, with water channels down one side; in times gone by the Seyon river used to flow through here. At its western end is the **place Pury** where you will find a statue of David de Pury, a major benefactor to the city, responsible for several buildings that are a part of the town's heritage. It is also a major open-air bus terminal. Finally, just south, there is the **place des Halles** surrounded by a wealth of 18th-century buildings. The most notable one is now a restaurant, but it was originally constructed in 1569–75 – with much Renaissance decoration – by Laurent Perroud as a **Covered Market** (Maison des Halles).

Along the Lakeside – South to North

A foot tunnel leads from place Pury to the very pretty **esplanade du Mont-Blanc** and gardens where you will find, just south of the impressive Beau-Rivage hotel, several statues of international artists like Vasarely and Arp.

The **Collège Latin**, a pleasing Empire-style building, is just north on the **quai Ostervald**, and this is now the library where there are important manuscripts of Jean-Jacques Rousseau and other valuable collections. Further along, just before the port, a strange-looking pier juts out into the lake and from here you can undertake an unusual adventure. The **Captive Balloon** (Ballon Captif; *t 032 725 28 00, f 032 725 28 02*) is a tethered hot-air balloon that will take you up to a height of 492ft (150m) from where you can get a 360-degree perspective of the town and its surroundings (*from mid-May to October it flies daily (weather permitting) 9.30am–12am and 12am–2am on Fri and Sat; reserve 48hrs in advance. The flight lasts 15 minutes and costs CHF 30*).

The very picturesque **port** (port de la Ville) is the departure point for cruises on the lake, and also a wonderful place just to pass the time of day. Yachts bob gently at their moorings, and swans and ducks glide effortlessly over the waters or waddle around the promenade begging for lunch.

There are actually three interconnected lakes: the Lac de Neuchâtel, the greatest of them, is in fact also the largest lake located entirely in Switzerland; Lac de Bienne (Bielersee in German) to the north is much smaller; and Lac de Morat (Murtensee in German) to the east is smaller again. Any number of voyages may be made, taking in any combination of the lakes, or just the Lac de Neuchâtel itself. Further information can be obtained from the **Société de Navigation sur les Lacs de Neuchâtel et Morat** (*t 032 729 96 00, f 032 729 96 01, www.navig.ch*).

Immediately north is the home of the **Museum of Art and History** (Musée d'Art et d'Histoire; *esplanade Léopold-Robert 1, t 032 717 79 20, f 032 717 79 29, www.ne.ch/ neuchatel/mahn; open Tues–Sun 10–6; adm, Wed free; every Tues at 12.15pm–1.15pm there are lectures, guided visits and concerts – all in French – for a cost of CHF 4 that includes adm to the museum*). The exhibits here, in 20 permanent and temporary rooms, are both varied and interesting, ranging from paintings – such as the huge one of *Christ Rising to the Heavens* which dominates the lobby – to carriages, household wares and furniture. The main attractions, however, are three 18th-century androids invented by the creative mind of Jaquet-Droz. To see the automatons in action you will either have to time it right (the first Sunday of each month at 2pm, 3pm and 4pm) or, by special and prior arrangement, pay for a private showing.

Take a short stroll down the promenade, quai Léopold-Robert, north from the museum, to admire an array of impressively beautiful houses. These present an unfortunate contrast to the area immediately to the east and fronting the lakeside, which is an eyesore. This was the main site of the 2002 National Exhibition, and as late as the summer of 2003 it was cordoned off and mainly abandoned.

Just North of the Old Town

There are three places worth investigating in this area. The one closest to the Old Town is the **Natural History Museum** (Muséum d'Histoire Naturelle; *rue des Terreaux 14, t 032 717 79 60, f 032 717 79 69, www.museum-neuchatel.ch; open Tues–Sun 10–6; adm, free on Wed*). Modern artwork and sculptures adorn the sandstone façade, and inside you will find a fascinating array of Swiss mammals and birds presented in their natural environment, with a slide show with sound effects for the birds. Look, too, for the giant fossils.

Immediately north, a few blocks away, is the most magnificent, and one of the most historic, mansions in Neuchâtel. Set in French-style formal gardens that slope down westwards towards the lake – which at one time actually reached this far inland – is the grand Louis XVI-style **Hôtel Dupeyrou**. This was built for Pierre-Alexandre Dupeyrou by the Bernese, but Paris-trained, architect Erasmus Ritter in 1765–70. Dupeyrou's close friend was Jean-Jacques Rousseau, and after the latter's death he had the first complete edition of his work published in Geneva in 1788. Two years later, in 1790, he had the second part of those same *Confessions* published in Neuchâtel itself. When Dupeyrou died in 1794 he bequeathed a grand collection of Rousseau's manuscripts to the town library. The 19th century saw the mansion change hands frequently: in 1799 it was sold to Frédéric de Pourtalès, and the state purchased it 14 years later as the home for its new ruler, Marshal Berthier. Three years later it changed hands again and finally, in 1858, the town of Neuchâtel bought it. These days it is leased from the city by an Australian chef and his wife, who run a stylish restaurant on the lower floors under the name Hôtel Dupeyrou (*see* p.209).

There is another very good reason for visiting the Hôtel Dupeyrou, and that is in an inconspicuous part of the courtyard, behind the building. It is quite common for Swiss cities to own their own vineyards, and then lease the rights to produce wines under the city's own name (or even produce their own). So it is here that you will find the **Caves de la Ville de Neuchâtel** (*avenue Dupreyou 5, t 032 717 76 95, f 032 717 70 95, www.cavevillentel.ch*). Its wines have won many prizes and are very good indeed, especially the Pinot Gris and Chardonnay. Taste a few and take a couple of bottles of your favourites home – remember that as about 95 per cent of all wines produced in Switzerland are consumed there, it's not easy or cheap to get any at home. If you are lucky, you may be shown the original cellars of the mansion.

South of the Old Town

The **Museum of Ethnography** (Musée d'Ethnographie; *rue Saint-Nicolas 4, t 032 718 19 60, f 032 718 19 69, www.ne.ch/neuchatel/men; open Tues–Sun 10–6; adm; No.1 bus*) features permanent exhibitions of ancient Egypt and the Himalayas, particularly Bhutan and Tibet; General Charles Daniel de Meuron's 18th-century natural history room; and a 21st-century curiosity room.

Outside Town

Take the No.7 bus from place Pury to the La Coudre stop and then transfer to the **La Coudre/Chaumont Funicular** (*t 032 720 06 00, f 032 724 51 34, www.tnneuchatel.ch; fare CHF 9.20 return*). Opened in 1910, this takes just 13 minutes to transport you from an altitude of 1,696ft (517m) to 3,566ft (1,087m) over a distance of 1.3 miles (2km). This is the only panoramic funicular in the Jura region and from the curious tower at the summit there are unparalleled views over three lakes, the smaller mountains to the west and the peaks of the Bernese Oberland eastwards.

Gruyères

Gruyères is synonymous with Switzerland's world-famous product, cheese. Set on an isolated hill that dramatically controls the broad valley, and with towering mountains looking down upon it, it is a charming, fortified medieval village with an intriguing history and a famous castle.

Nineteen counts of the dynasty of Gruyères resided here beginning in the 11th century and ending when the last, Michael I, left the castle in 1554 and died in exile. The cantons of Fribourg and Bern subsequently divided the county between them, and the castle was used as a residence of the bailiff of Fribourg from that time until 1798. In 1848 it passed into private hands and the families of Bovy and Balland, and the many important artists who also lived there from time to time, left an unusual heritage of their own. Since 1938 the structure has been maintained by the canton of Fribourg.

A walk through this uncluttered pedestrian-only village (population just 1,500) could best be likened to strolling through a living museum. Perched at an altitude of 2,625ft (800m), Gruyères basically consists of just one street with a castle at the end.

Tourist Information

Gruyères: Office du Tourisme, **t** 026 921 10 30, **f** 026 921 38 50, *www.gruyeres.ch* (*open summer daily 9.30–5.30, winter daily 9.30–12.30 and 1.30–4.30*).

Getting Around

Gruyères' train station is not very centrally located and it's either a long uphill walk or a short bus ride up to the village itself.

Where to Stay

***Hostellerie St Georges**, **t** 026 921 83 00, **f** 026 921 83 39, *www.st-georges-gruyeres.ch* (*moderate*). A delightful inn, right in the middle of the village, offering 14 spacious rooms, restaurants, bars and a large covered terrace – all in historic surroundings.
Hôtel de Ville, **t** 026 921 24 24, **f** 026 921 36 28, *www.hoteldeville.ch* (*moderate*). A small but very stylish hotel, also in the centre. Local dishes – *spécialités gruériennes* – are served either in the restaurant or on the terrace.

Eating Out

Le Chalet, **t** 026 921 21 54, **f** 026 921 33 13. A wonderful traditional chalet full of antiques and mementoes where you can sample delightful local dishes, such as fondue 'Château de Gruyères' or raclette with dry meat, all served by girls in authentic Gruyère dress – the *dzaquillon*.

Three gates give access to the village, but most will enter from the north through the Chavonne gate. From this vantage point, where the cobblestone street widens somewhat, the castle, framed by the Dent-de-Broc mountain, dominates the background.

The **Château de Gruyères** (*t 026 921 21 02, www.gruyeres.ch/chateau; open April–Oct daily 9–6, Nov–Mar 10–4.30; adm; request a brochure in English*) is far more than a traditional fortification. Ancient courtyards and rooms mix with an array of traditional art and furniture, including tapestries; don't miss the Medieval Garden.

The other museum of note is the **Museum H. R. Giger** (*Château St Germain, t 026 921 22 00, f 026 921 22 11, www.hrgiger.com; open April–Oct daily 10–6, Nov–Mar Tues–Fri 11–5, Sat and Sun 10–6; adm or combined ticket with upper castle*). Opened in 1998, this houses the largest collection of this artist's work, including his private collection of art on the top floor. Beware, though, some of this is quite erotic and not suitable for young children.

As for the rest of the village, just wander around and discover its charms at your leisure; you could certainly try a cheese fondue or raclette for lunch. You are bound to run across shops trying to sell you some cheese, but you may want to get it directly from the dairy. This is just down the hill from the village, at Pringy-Gruyères, in **La Maison du Gruyère** (*t 026 921 84 00, f 026 921 84 01, www.lamaisondugruyere.ch; open daily 9–7 (6pm Oct–May) and has a visitors' gallery open daily 8–7; adm*). This is a working cheese-dairy where you can see demonstrations of cheese-making three to four times a day between 9am and 3pm. Although it is a commercial dairy, it still adheres to traditions that date back to the 12th century. And, of course, the shop on the premises is only too happy to sell you cheese specialities, and you can eat at the Restaurant de la Fromagerie.

Tours

Touring the Bernese Oberland

This tour can start and finish equally easily in either Bern or Luzern. It takes just a little extra time to start from Zürich and take the train to Luzern, or Basel and start from either Bern or Luzern. From Geneva it is a straightforward train journey to Bern, and from Sion two train changes, at Brig and Spiez, will take you easily to Interlaken. It is not really practical to take this tour from Lugano. *See* map, p.130.

Day 1: Interlaken and Brienz

Morning: From Bern take the train to Interlaken West; from Luzern to Interlaken Ost. If you arrive early, you will have time for a walk around the town before strolling to the Interlaken Ost train station where, on the other side of the underpass, you will find the dock for the BLS Schiffart lake steamers (**t** *033 334 52 11, www.bls.ch*) to Brienz. These operate fairly frequently, more so between late June and early September, and the 1½-hour sailing that crisscrosses **Lake Brienz** (Brienzersee) is a delight. Note the waterfalls at Giessbach, and the elegant Grandhotel Giessbach on the steep hill.

Lunch: On the steamer, *see* below.

Afternoon: On arrival at **Brienz**, the quaint steam engines of the Brienz **Rothorn Bahn** (*see* p.141) are stationed immediately behind the main train station. However, before boarding take a quick walk through this old village, stopping at the Huggler Woodcarvings shop (*see* p.142) to see a real Brienzer tradition. The steep trip on the Rothorn Bahn is rather slow but never boring, as the countryside changes often and there is a wide range of flora and fauna (watch out for the stone eagle). Expansive views extend to the lake in the foreground and the Bernese Oberland peaks behind it. Once at the top, the best bet is to take a seat on the terrace of the Hotel Restaurant Rothorn Kulm that overlooks the lake. Back at Brienz, and if it isn't too late (up to around 6pm until late September), it's possible to return to Interlaken on the lake steamer. Alternatively, a train will take just 20 minutes.

Dinner and Sleeping: In Interlaken, *see* below.

Day 1

Lunch in Interlaken
On the lake steamer (*moderate*) on Lake Brienz; choose a table by the window on the right-hand side of the boat.

Dinner in Interlaken
La Terrasse (*expensive*) – and it does have a terrace – in the Victoria-Jungfrau Grand Hotel is the gourmet restaurant of choice, and has service to match.

The Top O' Met (*expensive–moderate*), on the 18th floor of the Metropole Hotel, has a nice selection of dishes and the town's best views.

Bebbis, Bahnhofstrasse 16, **t** 033 821 14 44, *www.bebbis.ch* (*inexpensive*). A fun restaurant in chalet style with cuisine to match.

Sleeping in Interlaken
Apart from the Victoria-Jungfrau Grand Hotel and Metropole Hotel mentioned above, there are also:

★★★★Stella, General Guisanstrasse 10, **t** 033 822 88 71, **f** 033 822 86 71, *www.stella-hotel.ch* (*expensive*). Only 30 stylish rooms; indoor pool, too.

Backpackers Villa Sonnenhof, Alpenstrasse 16, **t** 033 826 71 71, **f** 033 826 71 72, *www.villa.ch* (*cheap*). Double, triples, quads and dorms.

Day 2: Mürren, Schilthorn 007 and the Trümmelbach Falls

Morning: First take the Berner Oberland Bahnen (BOB) train from Interlaken Ost to Lauterbrunnen (ensure you get in the correct half of the train, otherwise you will end up in Grindelwald). At Lauterbrunnen cross the road to the Lauterbrunnen-Mürren BLM funicular to Grütschalp (be sure to have any heavy luggage loaded separately and it will be transferred on to Mürren, where the hotel staff will pick it up if asked). As this very steep funicular moves off look left, slightly down the valley, to the magnificent Staubbach waterfall that plunges 945ft (288m) down the mountain face. At Grütschalp change to the 3.3ft (1m) narrow-gauge non-cog railway to car-free **Mürren** itself (*see* p.139). Stroll through the village, stopping to admire the views across the valley to the massive Eiger, Mönch and Jungfrau peaks, until you reach the Schilthorn cable car station. From there the cableway rises to its 9,744ft (2,970m) summit, where you will find **Schilthorn 007** (*www.schilthorn.ch*), one of the most important attractions in Switzerland. Its history is fascinating and is related on p.140. From the Piz Gloria restaurant, you can see more than 200 peaks on view, and if you look closely enough you can spot Jungfraujoch across the valley.

Lunch: On Schilthorn, *see* below.

Afternoon: Take the cable car down, this time passing Mürren on the way down to the valley floor at Stechelberg, where a Post Bus takes just three stops to reach the hidden but staggeringly impressive **Trümmelbach Falls** (*see* p.141). The falls drain the glaciers of the Eiger, Mönch and Jungfrau, and are the only glacial waterfalls in Europe that are found inside a mountain and yet are still accessible. A lift takes you most of the way up, and then footpaths take you past endless fast-flowing currents of water whose intrinsic strength and ferocity is awesome. The bus is your best bet back to Stechelberg, and then the cable car will whisk you back to Mürren, via Gimmelwald, for dinner and a night's rest.

Dinner and Sleeping: In Mürren, *see* below.

Day 2

Lunch above Mürren

Piz Gloria, Schilthorn 007 (*moderate*). This offers diners 360° panoramic views. From 8am to 11am have the James Bond breakfast for CHF 22.50, including a glass of champagne, and from 11am to 3.30pm there is a variety of soups, cold dishes and hot dishes.

Dinner and Sleeping in Mürren

****Eiger, t 033 856 88 00, f 033 856 54 56, *www.hoteleiger.com* (*expensive*). Established in 1886, and run by the same family ever since, this offers magnificent views of the Eiger, Mönch and Jungfrau from many of the 49 beautifully furnished and well-equipped rooms. Indoor pool, sauna, solarium, a terrace and the gourmet Eiger Stübli.

***Blumental, t 033 855 18 26, f 033 855 36 86, *www.muerren.ch/blumental* (*inexpensive*). With a real mountain hotel ambience, this has 20 rooms, the Grill Room 'Grotte' restaurant, the Bliemlichäller bar and disco, and free entrance to the village sports centre.

***Alpenruh, t 033 856 88 00, f 033 856 88 88, *www.muerren.ch/alpenruh* (*inexpensive*). Next to the cable car station, this chalet-style hotel has 26 very nice rooms. It also has a good restaurant and a sun terrace.

Day 3: Grindelwald, Männlichen, Kleine Scheidegg, Grindelwald

Morning: From Mürren take the narrow-gauge train to Grütschalp, then the funicular down to Lauterbrunnen and transfer to the train station across the road. From there a BOB train will leave for Interlaken Ost, but be sure to change at Zweilütschinen for the train to **Grindelwald** (*see* p.133). Investigate the main shopping street of the village before walking steeply down through the village to the Gondelbahn Grindelwald–Männlichen GGM. From here gondola cars (often sponsored by Ricola whose colours they are painted in) take 30 minutes to cover 3½ miles (6.2km) up to Männlichen at an altitude of 7,695ft (2,345m) – the longest gondola cableway in Europe. **Männlichen**, *www.maennlichen.ch* (*see* p.138), has a wonderful location on a natural ridge between two valleys, and a wide panorama over the Bernese Oberland. Besides the views, the only thing here is the Berggasthaus Männlichen, and although you wouldn't choose to sleep there it is a delightful place for lunch.

Lunch: At Männlichen, *see* below.

Afternoon: Another form of transport awaits – in the form of the Luftseilbahn Wengen-Männlichen LWM, a cable car that drops steeply down to **Wengen** (*see* p.135). This is a pretty, car-free village with nice views, especially of the waterfalls by Lauterbrunnen. Head directly to the train station, a couple of minutes away, for a train up to Kleine Scheidegg. This journey is very dramatic, with views over the valley and up to Mürren perched on a ridge above the valley, and the train passes close to some awesome glaciers. **Kleine Scheidegg** is a curious collection of train station, hotels, souvenir shops and restaurants as well as the junction for trains to Jungfraujoch. If you are here between late June and late October at either 11.45, 12.15 or 3, just across the tracks you can see, weather permitting, an intriguing falcon show (CHF 6), where these magnificent birds fly freely against a spectacular backdrop of snowcapped peaks. Time now to take the train and descend to Grindelwald.

Dinner and Sleeping: In Grindelwald, *see* below.

Day 3

Lunch at Männlichen
Berggasthaus Männlichen, t 033 853 10 68 (*moderate–inexpensive*). Try specialities like *Käseschnitte*, a fantastic plate of dried meats, or maybe even fondue or raclette.

Dinner and Sleeping in Grindelwald
Grindelwald hotel descriptions are in this box and the box on p.221.
****Belvedere, t 033 854 54 54, **f** 033 853 53 23, *www.belvedere-grindelwald.ch* (*luxury*). This boasts an enviable location just across the valley from, and almost in the shadow of, the north face of the Eiger. The personality of the Hauser family, owners and operators for over 90 years, is lovingly imprinted on every aspect of this hotel. The 55 rooms are very tastefully appointed and have a modern ambience. The well-equipped spa has both a pool and a jacuzzi with picture windows allowing superb views of the Eiger.

****Kirchbühl & Apartments, t 033 853 35 53, **f** 033 853 35 18, *www.kirchbuehl.ch* (*expensive*). This is a little outside the village, in a more rural environment. It offers 48 very nice rooms, two good restaurants, a sauna, steam bath and whirlpool, as well as free entrance to the Grindelwald Sports Centre.

Day 4: Jungfraujoch, Kleine Scheidegg and an Afternoon Hike

Morning: Jungfraujoch is undoubtedly one of Switzerland's premier attractions, but unfortunately this comes at a steep cost (*see* box on p.131 and box on 'Good Morning Ticket' on p.137). Expensive, yes; but an experience that is certainly worth the cost. So, get to Grindelwald station early, and settle down for the trip back up to Kleine Scheidegg where you should change on to a Jungfraubahn JB train (*www.jungfraubahn.ch*) up to Europe's highest railway station at an altitude of 11,333ft (3,160m). The fascinating history of the building of this line and the complex at the top is related on p.136. Once at **Jungfraujoch** – remember to take things slowly because of the thin air – there are a host of interesting things to do including the Ice Palace, hikes in the eternal snow and ice, and even husky-drawn sled rides. Most fascinating, though, are the views directly down and along the Aletsch Glacier that, at 13¾ miles (22km), is Europe's longest. Before leaving, make sure you send your postcards from here, where they will be franked at Europe's highest post office and one that has its own postal code – CH-3801.

Lunch: At Kleine Scheidegg, *see* below.

Afternoon: Head back down to Grindelwald and a little light exercise. To begin this hike, take a Grindelwaldbus to the Berghotel Gross Scheidegg, taking a seat on the right-hand side to admire the Grindelwaldgletscher (glacier). From here an undulating, undemanding footpath that only changes altitude by 23ft (7m) from 6,414 to 6,437ft (1,955 to 1,962m) leads to the penultimate station of the Firstbahnen, Grindel. Another advantage of this hike, besides its easiness, is that it offers a different perspective of the peaks to the south, including the Eiger, Mönch and Jungfrau. Afterwards, you might stop for a drink at the Bergrestaurant Schreckfeld, before returning on the cable car to Grindelwald and some last-minute shopping before dinner. The next day, return to Bern or Luzern by train via Interlaken.

Dinner and Sleeping: In Grindelwald, *see* below.

Day 4

Lunch above Grindelwald

Top of Europe Glacier Restaurant, Jungfraujoch. Offers dishes as fine as its views, and there is even an Indian Buffet if you fancy something more spicy.

Röstizzeria, Restaurant Bahnhof Kleine Scheidegg, **t** 033 828 78 28. Switzerland's own answer to a pizzeria, with different *rösti* dishes. This, and favourites like raclette and *Käseschnitte*, can be eaten inside or out.

Dinner and Sleeping in Grindelwald

Other hotel descriptions in box on p.220.

★★★★Spinne, **t** 033 854 88 88, **f** 033 854 88 89, *www.spinne.ch* (*expensive*). Right in the middle of the village, this has 37 very nice rooms. It has four different restaurants, two bars, a disco and a wellness centre.

★★★Fiescherblick, **t** 033 854 53 53, **f** 033 854 53 50, *www.fiescherblick.ch* (*moderate*). This charming small hotel has 25 comfortable rooms. The Bistro has a Swiss menu; the gourmet restaurant 15 Gault Millau points.

Mountain Hostel, **t** 033 853 39 00, **f** 033 853 47 30 (*cheap*). Located by the Männlichenbahn gondola station and Grund Station, this has 2-, 4- and 6-bed rooms. Also TV, billiards, table tennis, laundry and an Internet corner.

Touring Eastern Graubünden

Graubünden (Grisons in French) is the easternmost canton of Switzerland and, as such, is clearly the most difficult area to reach from the destination cities. Even from Zürich it takes 3½ hours and from Lugano, which is closer, it takes around 4 hours. From Basel, Bern and Luzern the journey time is usually 4½ hours. Geneva and Sion are both the farthest away and present the most difficult trips, with times of over 7 and nearly 8 respectively. *See* map, p.162.

Don't be confused if you start seeing or hearing a rather different language here; Romansch, the fourth – and very much the minority – language of Switzerland, is spoken in the Lower Engadine region, near Scuol.

Day 1: Pontresina

Morning: Unless you are departing from Geneva and Sion, it is quite feasible to get from all the other destinations to **St Moritz** well before midday, and from there it is just a few minutes by train or bus to the nearby town of **Pontresina**. Here, your initial destination is just a couple of train stops away at Punt Muragl Staz, where the Muottas Muragl Bahn (MMB) funicular (*t 081 842 83 08, www.muottasmuragl. ch*) rises to the Berghotel Muottas Muragl, a hotel and restaurant situated at an altitude of 8,058ft (2,456m). Its terrace offers some of the finest views in Switzerland, with the subtly colourful scene of St Moritz and the lakes that meander away from it towards the Maloja Pass directly below you. The snow-white peaks of the higher mountains tower in the distance, casting a long shadow over icy glaciers that lie off the valley leading to the Bernina Pass to the left.

Lunch: At Muottas Muragl (*see* below).

Afternoon: After lunch, it's time for a little exercise. The views continually evolve on an interesting hike around, not up, the mountain to Alp Languard. This takes about 2½ hours and along the way there are enlightening perspectives of the wall of peaks, the loftiest of which is Bernina at 13,284ft (4,049m), across the valley. Among these mountains are massive glaciers with the largest, Vadret da Morteratsch, nearly reaching the valley floor. At Alp Languard there is a restaurant for refreshments, before you make your descent, by chairlift or on foot, to Pontresina and your hotel.

Dinner and Sleeping: In Pontresina, *see* below.

Day 1

Lunch above Pontresina

Berghotel Panorama Restaurant Muottas Muragl, t 081 842 82 32 (*inexpensive*). Accessible only via the Muottas Muragl Bahn; has a traditional mountain ambience and panoramic views.

Dinner and Sleeping in Pontresina

★★★★**Walther, t** 081 839 36 36, **f** 081 839 36 37, *www.hotelwalther.ch* (*luxury*). A magnificent, turreted building, with a Belle Epoque atmosphere.

★★★**Steinbock, t** 081 839 36 26, **f** 081 839 36 27, *www.steinbock-pontresina.ch* (*expensive*). In a 17th-century Engadine house next to the Walther, whose pool guests can use.

Day 2: Pontresina to Scuol

Morning: Set off on an uneventful train trip that starts with a short journey from Pontresina to Samedan, and then continues for nearly 1½ hours through the Upper Engadine to the end of the line at **Scuol** (*see* p.162) in the Lower Engadine. The track follows the Inn river, and the scenery is very pretty indeed, particularly in the latter stages. In this area, unspoiled by mass tourism, you will no doubt notice that the façades of houses are decorated with elaborate art work, known as *sgraffito*. There are just two things to do in Scuol, and as the earliest you can see one is 2.30pm and the other is open until 10pm, there's time to check in to your hotel and have lunch first.

Lunch: In Scuol, at the spa or at one of the hotel restaurants, *see* below.

Afternoon: Now privately owned by Princess Margareta von Hessen, **Schloss Tarasp** (Tarasp Castle; *t 081 864 93 68, f 081 864 93 73, www.schloss-tarasp.ch; guided tours in June and early July at 2.30, until late Aug at 11, 2.30, 3.30 and 4.30, until mid-Oct at 2.30 and 3.30, and at other times of the year on Tues and Thurs at 4.30; adm; easy bus ride from Scuol*) evokes the typical image of a castle and was constructed on top of a hill directly in front of the village around the middle of the 11th century by the Tarasp family. The real highlight of Scuol, though, and unique in all Switzerland, is its spa, the **Engadin Bad Scuol** (*t 081 861 20 00, f 081 861 20 01, www.scuol.ch*), in the centre of town. It offers a 'bath landscape' and a 'sauna landscape' (*open daily 8am–10pm; adm CHF 25 to both, valid for 2½hrs*) and the Roman-Irish Bath (*open 9.45am–10pm; adm CHF 71 including unlimited admission to the bath and sauna landscapes; reserve 24hrs in advance*). A therapy centre also at the spa treats a number of ailments by using the waters from the Luzius, Sfondraz, Bonifazius and Lishana springs. The bath and sauna landscapes make up the majority of the spa; the former consists of a series of indoor pools (including a brine one and a cold-water one), a jacuzzi, outdoor pool and solarium; the latter has an outside sauna and open-air cold pool with a coldwater cascade. The Roman–Irish Bath is an amazing experience, although people should be aware that it includes mixed sex naked areas. It comprises a sauna, a soap and brush massage, and relaxation in large baths; your final stop is a cold-water pool, followed by a period of rest on an air-bed. A detailed description of all the facilities at the spa can be found on pp.163–4.

Dinner and Sleeping: In Scuol or Tarasp, *see* below, and also p.163.

Day 2

Lunch in Scuol

Schü-San, t 081 864 81 43. A Chinese restaurant in the spa; serves curry and house specialities.

Dinner and Sleeping in Scuol/Tarasp

★★★★Belvédère, t 081 861 06 06, f 081 861 06 00, *www.belvedere-scuol.ch* (*expensive*). This central hotel has pleasant gardens with an outside pool. There's also a superb restaurant and a new wellness centre.

★★★★Schlosshotel Chastè, Sparsels, t 081 861 30 60, f 081 861 30 61, *www.relaischateaux. ch/chaste* (*expensive*). A 19-room hotel situated in the shadow of the imposing castle with a warm, comfortable ambience. Also a wonderful restaurant and a health club.

Day 3: Scuol to Nauders (Austria)

Morning: Although the scenery is more or less the same, a day in Austria presents a welcome change of style. First, though, you need to be careful with the bus connections. In 2003 a very early bus, involving two changes, left from the train station at 7.35am and only took 48 minutes, whilst the next bus had just one change but took over 2 hours. It may be best, then, to wait until 10.30am to take the direct bus for a journey time of 51 minutes. In any event, there is no real hurry today. At Martina the bus branches off and passes the rather casual Austrian customs and immigration authorities. **Nauders**, on the Reschen Pass at 4,528ft (1,380m), is a quaint village clinging to the lower slopes in the Austrian Tyrol under the shadow of surrounding snowcapped mountains. It is still an active farming community but, quite incongruously, also a resort village, successfully combining a working farm village lifestyle with the infrastructure necessary to attract an international clientele. In how many other places do you see cows coming and going in the morning and evening past luxurious four-star hotels?

Lunch: In Nauders, *see* below.

Afternoon: The main activity in Nauders during the summer months is **hiking**, and there are no less than 38 well-marked paths around the village. Route 6 (blue) going up to the Grosser Mutzkopf via the Grüner See (suitable, but cold, for bathing) could not be classified as a leisurely stroll. To be fair, though, apart from a few steep stretches, the trek goes mostly through pasturelands and could not, either, be classified as mountaineering. And the views – across a panorama that takes in three countries – are stupendous. You will see, immediately to the south, the Reschen Pass, beyond which lies the Reschensee reservoir and the Italian South Tyrol. Further around, and towards the west, there is a marvellous view back down the Lower Engadine valley towards Scuol. Of curious interest, on the lower slopes and usually near a wide track you will notice huge piles of firewood stacked at random intervals. These have their root in a Nauders tradition, whereby 132 local families have the rights to the wood, but not to the land, on the slopes around Nauders. And, as if that is not complicated enough in itself, those rights are not owned by individuals. Rather, they are tied to a particular property and the fireplaces – up to two – located in that property. Each designated fireplace owns an entitlement to 283 cubic feet (8 cubic metres) of wood.

Dinner and Sleeping: In Nauders, *see* below.

Day 3

Lunch, Dinner and Sleeping in Nauders

★★★★**Mein Almhof, t** (0043) 05473 87313, **f** (0043) 05473 87644, *www.meinalmhof.at* (*moderate*). A charming hotel with much style and ambience, which reflects the fun-loving character of the Kröll family, the owners. Hans Kröll takes great care to attend to your every need. With well-equipped rooms, a fine restaurant, an indoor swimming pool and a health club. Members of the family include pet marmots, who like to be fed carrots from the bar. Full board recommended.

Day 4: Nauders to Samnaun

Morning: This is not a long bus journey in terms of mileage, but the buses only leave every 3 hours and, to make matters more difficult, there is a 2-hour wait at Martina. So to get to Samnaun at a reasonable hour it is necessary to catch an early bus (at 8.43am in 2003). **Samnaun** is one of the most unusual and curious mountain villages in Switzerland. Unusual, in that it is tucked away in the far eastern corner of the country – in a valley with four other villages – and almost surrounded by Austria. In fact, historically it has always been far easier to reach Austria than to get out to the Inn valley and then onto the road to St Moritz and other parts of Switzerland. Even today, the road down to Switzerland – as opposed to going via Austria – is very poor indeed. It is this geographical quirk that, in the late 19th century, led to Samnaun's curiosity value today. At that time, the Swiss government tried to impose taxes on Samnaun's trade with Austria. The citizens of the valley, though, rebelled; and using the argument that as they, effectively, could not trade with the rest of Switzerland, they refused to pay Swiss taxes. The end result is that Samnaun is now a tax-free village. This is its main attraction and the reason why most visitors come here.

Lunch: In Samnaun, *see* below.

Afternoon: Shopping dominates everything in the very narrow, steep valley of Samnaun, and prices are far lower than in the rest of Switzerland; the only real problem is where to look first. In reality, the majority of the over 50 stores are quite small and the range of goods for sale other than alcohol and tobacco is rather limited. The best, and largest, shops are found grouped together near the Hotel Post in the centre of the village, just across from the tourist office. For upscale watches and jewellery go to the Bijouterie; Parfüm-Kosmetik sells duty-free designer perfume and cosmetics; the Duty-Free-Centre offers a wide range of sports watches, cigars, alcohol and spirits and accessories such as Victorinox and camera film etc.; and Sport Mode-Boutique has a large choice of fashionable sportswear featuring every major international designer label, not to mention the biggest selection of skiing and hiking boots, climbing gear and other such outdoor equipment. It takes nearly 3 hours to get to St Moritz by bus, so leave early the next morning. From St Moritz you can make your way back to your destination city.

Dinner and Sleeping: In Samnaun, *see* below.

Day 4

Lunch, Dinner and Sleeping in Samnaun

★★★★**Post, t** 081 861 92 00, **f** 081 861 92 93 (*moderate*). Located right in the centre of the village, this has very spacious and elegantly furnished rooms, a fine health and beauty area and the trendy 'Why Not' nightclub.

★★★**Vital-Hotel Samnaunerhof, t** 081 861 81 81, **f** 081 861 81 82, *www.samnaunerhof.com* (*moderate*). An interestingly designed hotel with 24 rooms, and an extensive health and fitness centre.

★★★**Camona, t** 081 861 82 82, **f** 081 861 82 81 (*inexpensive*). A nice little hotel, with a pizzeria with a pleasant outside terrace.

Touring from Geneva

See maps, pp.167 and 207.

Day 1: Geneva to Montreux

Morning: The day starts with an easy, pretty train trip along Lake Geneva, taking as little as 49 minutes on the fast Italian Cisalpino tilting train or up to an hour and seven minutes on a normal service. As the train station in **Montreux**, see p.178, is a little inconveniently placed, you may need a taxi to your hotel if you have heavy luggage. Next, if you are there between April and October, head back to the station for the short 10-minute train journey to **Aigle**. This is a famous wine town, and vineyards surround you on the short walk up to the fairytale castle. The Château d'Aigle (*t 024 466 21 30, www.chateauaigle.ch; open April, May, June, Sept and Oct Tues–Sun 10–12.30 and 2–6, July and Aug daily 10–6; adm*) dates from the early 13th century. Inside you will find the Vine and Wine Museum (Musée de la Vigne et du Vin) devoted to the history of wine-making. Just across a courtyard dominated by ancient wine presses is a building with an even older heritage. In fact, the Maison de la Dîme was probably constructed at the end of the 12th century. These days it is the setting for both the International Museum of Wine Labels (Musée International de l'Etiquette) with over 800 labels from 52 countries, and La Pinte du Paradis restaurant. Before leaving, taste local wines at a *dégustation* in Cellier Vinicole, just outside the castle.

Lunch: In Aigle, see below.

Afternoon: Back in Montreux, walk along the pretty lakeside promenade lined by pleasant gardens, and look at all the shops across the street. Before heading to the lake steamer dock, near the tourist office, look at the covered market area and the statue of Freddie Mercury (like other artists, the late singer of Queen fame made this area his base). The evocative **Château de Chillon** is just two stops away by lake steamer (see p.176 for opening hours and description).

Dinner and Sleeping: In Montreux and Vevey, see below.

Day 1

Lunch in Aigle

La Pinte du Paradis (*expensive–moderate; closed Mon*). Offers inventive local cuisine.

Café du Château, avenue Cloître 1, t 024 466 24 49 (*inexpensive*). Has a good ambience.

Dinner and Sleeping in Montreux/Vevey

★★★★**Eden au Lac**, rue du Théâtre 1, Montreux, t 021 966 08 00, f 021 966 09 00, *www.eden montreux.ch* (*expensive*). Located on Lake Léman, close to the centre. The interior has been completely renovated in Louis XVI decor. A splendid restaurant, too.

★★★★**Victoria Glion**, Glion/Montreux, t 021 962 82 82, f 021 962 82 92 (*moderate*). This 1869 hotel, on the heights behind Montreux, is decorated in a delightful Belle-Epoque style.

★★★**Splendid**, Grand-Rue 52, Montreux, t 021 966 79 79, f 021 966 79 77, *www.hotel-splendid.ch* (*moderate*). A charming Victorian hotel across from the lake, with an old-fashioned ambience. A fine restaurant, too.

★★★★★**Hôtel des Trois Couronnes**, rue d'Italie 49, Vevey, t 021 923 32 00, f 021 923 33 39, *www. hoteldestroiscouronnes.com* (*luxury*). This 150-year-old hotel has spacious, traditional rooms. In summer, dine on culinary French masterpieces on the terrace.

Day 2: Lausanne and Evian-les-Bains (France)

Morning: It takes less than 30 minutes to get from Montreux to Lausanne. Try and get an early start as this is a busy day. **Lausanne** (*see* p.166) is unusual in that it is situated on three levels that are connected by the Métro – actually a funicular connecting the Old Town at the highest point with the train station at mid-level and Ouchy down by the lake. Your first stop should be the cathedral (*open Mon–Fri 7–5.30, Sat 8–5.30, and Sun afternoon from the conclusion of the religious service until 5.30*), with its irregular, architecturally diverse façade that from this elevated position dominates the area. Constructed during the 12th and 13th centuries, it has the distinction of being the largest Gothic building in Switzerland. Outside the main doors of the cathedral a wooden roofed stairway, the Escaliers du Marché, lead down to the impressive place de la Riponne, a large plaza with a marvellous fountain spurting countless jets of water. A combination of market place and cultural centre, place de la Riponne is dominated by the huge, classical Rumine Palace, home to no less than five museums. Time now to take the Métro down to Ouchy where, at about 12.30pm, a lake steamer will be waiting to carry you across to **Evian-les-Bains** (*see* p.175) in France. The journey takes about 40 minutes. Unlike Switzerland the shops here close for lunch, but Evian is still a very pleasant place to stroll around before eating.

Lunch: In Evian-les-Bains, *see* below.

Afternoon: After lunch, who could resist the opportunity of filling an empty bottle with completely free Evian water flowing out of the mountains? Remember, though, to catch a boat back to Lausanne by around 4pm at the latest in order to have time to visit the **Olympic Museum** (Musée Olympique; *t 021 621 65 11, f 021 621 65 12, www. olympic.org; open daily 9–6, until 8pm on Thurs, and closed on Mon Oct–April; adm exp*), just along the Quai d'Ouchy. This ultra-modern structure, faced with Thassos marble, displays permanent exhibitions spotlighting a multitude of familiar athletes and their respective events.

Dinner and Sleeping: In Lausanne, *see* below.

Day 2

Lunch in Evian-les-Bains
Restaurant Le Franco-Suisse, place Jean Bernex. In the centre of the main pedestrian-only street with a nice terrace; traditional Savoyard cuisine at reasonable prices.

Dinner in Lausanne
See pp.169–70. **Le Table du Palace**, although very expensive, is a wonderful restaurant with expansive views; the **Brasserie Bavaria** has a good ambience and regional specialities; the **Monte-Cristo** has tapas, whilst the **Boccalino** offers 120 different types of pizza.

Sleeping in Lausanne
Select between the hotels on p.169; the hotel of choice is:
*****Lausanne Palace and Spa**, Grand-Chêne 7–9, **t** 021 331 31 31, **f** 021 323 25 71, *www. lausanne-palace.com* (*luxury*). This is a palace by name and by nature. Opened in 1915, it is in the heart of the business and shopping district and yet offers fantastic views over the lake and Alps. Inside are large rooms, each distinctively decorated. There are two toilets in each room, and even heated mirrors in the bathrooms that won't steam up! It has the largest wellness centre in the region.

Day 3: Lausanne to Bern

Morning: Check the schedules for a direct train to **Bern**, Switzerland's capital (*see* p.86), which takes just over an hour. Bern is a city of considerable charm and subtle attractions, with an extensive labyrinth of arcades over 3.7 miles (6km) long, and a colourful array of historic water fountains. Its two symbols are the Clock Tower and bears. A visit to the Clock Tower (Zeitglockentuem) at least five minutes before the hour strikes means you will catch the humorous figure play. The original 12th-century tower, some parts of which still stand, formed the boundary to the first extension of the city. The Astronomical Clock and figure play were not added until 1530. Bern was named after a bear, and these have been formally kept in the city since 1513. The present Bear Pits (Bärengraben; *open summer 8–5.30, winter 9–4*) date from 1857, and are situated in the east of the city, on the other side of the River Aare. Easter is a popular time to visit, when the new cubs make their first public appearances. Next door, the tourist centre operates the innovative Bern-Show with a complex set of movies, slides and inter-active models.

Lunch: In Bern, *see* below.

Afternoon: After lunch, stop at the Münster (cathedral; *t 031 312 04 62; open summer Tues–Sat 10–5, Sun 11.30–5; winter Tues–Fri 10–12 and 2–4, on Sat it closes an hour later and on Sun 11.30–4*), the largest church in Switzerland. This occupies a prime position on a beautiful square near the Aare. Enjoy the views from here, reaching as far as the peaks of the Bernese Oberland in the distance. There are a number of elaborate 16th-century fountains in this area: the Moses Fountain outside the Münster, and, on nearby Kramgasse, the Simson and Zähringer Fountains. Back on the other side of town, the Fine Arts Museum (Kuntsmuseum; *Hodlerstrasse 8–12, t 031 328 09 44, f 031 328 09 55, www.kunstmuseumbern.ch; open Tues 10–9 and Wed–Sun 10–5; adm*) is also worth a visit. The exhibits include some 3,000 paintings and sculptures and nearly 55,000 drawings, including the world's largest collection of works by the Swiss artist Paul Klee (1879–1940).

Dinner and Sleeping: In Bern, *see* below.

Day 3

Lunch in Bern

Altes Tramdepot Brauerei & Restaurant, Gr. Muristalden 6, **t** 031 368 14 15 (*moderate*). A combination of microbrewery and restaurant in a converted tram shed next to the Bear Pits. Meat, vegetarian and wok dishes.

Brasserie Bärengraben, Muristalden 1, **t** 031 331 42 18 (*expensive–moderate*). In one of the 200-year-old customs houses on the Nydeggbrücke. Dine inside, or out on the terrace, on French-orientated dishes.

Dinner in Bern

See pp.91–2. **La Terrasse** is the place to be seen, the **Ringgenberg** has French cuisine, **Le Mazot** is great for Valais specialities, **Bar & Bistro Boomerang's** has Czech and Australian food, and **Brasserie Anker** specializes in *rösti*.

Sleeping In Bern

See pp.89–90. The **Bellevue Palace** is a great luxury hotel, the **Belle Epoque** has a charming ambience, the **Continental Garni** is centrally located, the **City Am Bahnhof** is very good value and the **National Am Hirschengraben** has a charming old-fashioned ambience.

Day 4: Bern to Solothurn

Morning: A direct train to Solothurn takes as little as 37 minutes and there's no need to rush in Solothurn, either. So take a stroll through Bern in the morning, maybe visiting the colourful fruit and vegetable market on Bärenplatz and looking at the nearby Swiss Houses of Parliament. **Solothurn** (*see* p.181) had its greatest days between 1530 and 1792, when French kings sent ambassadors to meet its affluent merchants. Because of this it gained the name 'Ambassadorial Town', and its unique combination of French charm, Italian splendour and German/Swiss stability has left it Switzerland's best-preserved Baroque town. Having been the 11th canton to join the Swiss Confederation, that number has great significance here with many things, curiously, found in multiples of eleven. Once a year, at carnival time, things are turned upside down in this otherwise conservative town, when it re-christens itself Honolulu – as it is exactly on the other side of the world.

Lunch: In Solothurn, *see* below.

Afternoon: Climb the eleven steps to investigate the most dominant structure in Solothurn (its tower is 216.5ft (66m) tall), the Cathedral of St Ursen (*open 6–12 and 2–7*). The interior is austere and that number eleven shows itself in the form of eleven bells and eleven altars. One of the finest attractions in Solothurn is the formidable Old Arsenal Museum (Altes Zeughaus; *Zeughausplatz 1, t 032 623 35 28; open May– Oct Tues–Sun 10–12 and 2–5, Nov–Apr Tues–Fri 2–5, Sat and Sun 10–12 and 2–5*). In addition to a vast collection of weapons – one of Europe's largest – the six floors contain fascinating military exhibits. The Fine Arts Museum (Kuntsmuseum; *Werkhofstrasse 30, t 032 622 23 07, f 032 622 50 01, www.kunstmuseum.ch; open Tues– Fri 10–12 and 2–5, Sat and Sun 10–5; free*) has a fine collection of post-1850 Swiss art and a small collection of Old Masters, including the *Solothurn Madonna* by Hans Holbein the Younger. Marktplatz is the social hub of Solothurn. Standing sentry is a colossal clock tower; when the hour tolls you will see enchanting animated figures come to life. The nearby Jesuit church is adorned with Baroque decorations.

Dinner and Sleeping: In Solothurn, *see* below.

Day 4

Lunch in Solothurn

Zunfthaus zu Wirthen, Hauptgasse 41, t 032 626 28 48. A wood-lined dining room, also an outdoor terrace sheltered by an arcade of the traditional façade. Besides daily specials, the menu features many local dishes such as perch, fera and trout, and variations of veal.

Dinner and Sleeping in Solothurn

★★★★Krone, Hauptgasse 64, t 032 626 44 44, f 032 626 44 45, *www.hotelkrone-solothurn.* ch (*moderate*). This is a delightful traditional hotel in the centre of the Old Town directly opposite the cathedral, which offers comfortable, well-equipped rooms, charming public areas and a fine restaurant.

★★Zunfthaus zu Wirthen, Hauptgasse 41, t 032 626 28 48, f 032 626 28 58, *www.wirthen.ch* (*moderate*). Across from the magnificent clocktower, by Marktplatz, this has a traditional Solothurn façade. Its 14 rooms are bright, open and nicely furnished.

Day 5: Solothurn to Neuchâtel

Morning: This is another short journey, as little as 40 minutes, along the eastern side of the Bielersee and then the larger Lac de Neuchâtel to the historic and pretty town of the same name. In fact, **Neuchâtel** (*see* p.206) wears its proud history unassumingly; but you only have to scratch its surface lightly to unearth some real gems. The best place to start is at the top of the Old Town (Vieille Ville). Here, the construction of the Romanesque Collégiale (Collegiate) church began prior to 1185 at the behest of Ulrich II of Neuchâtel and his wife Bertha. Inside, its stained-glass windows are memorable, but the highlight is the gloriously sculpted cenotaph of the Counts of Neuchâtel, considered one of the most remarkable works of art from the Middle Ages and the most important north of the Alps. Of the small open cloister (*cloître*) only the Romanesque arcades, built on to the north wall of the church, are original. Work began on the imposing Château (*t 032 889 60 11; free guided tours, with commentary in English, French and German, start from the entrance at door No.1, April–Sept on Mon–Fri at 10, 11, 12, 2, 3 and 4, on Sat at 10, 11, 2, 3 and 4, on Sun and public holidays at 2, 3 and 4*) near the end of the 12th century. In constant use for over 800 years, it is the oldest such building in Switzerland. The structure is divided into three main sections: the highly ornamented Romanesque tower, the Main Gate, and the southern Gallery; inside there are many notable and interesting rooms.

Lunch: In Neuchâtel, *see* below.

Afternoon: After lunch, continue exploring more of the Old Town. The **Prison Tower** (Tour des Prisons; *open April–Sept 8–6; adm through an automatic turnstile that will demand a CHF 1 coin*) is the oldest building in Neuchâtel and offers fantastic views. And, as always in Switzerland, the city has its share of colourful water fountains, particularly the Justice, Banneret and Griffon ones. Don't miss the Market Square (place des Halles) in the lower part of the Old Town, surrounded by magnificent 18th-century mansions. The next day, return to Geneva by direct train (1¼hrs).

Dinner and Sleeping: In Neuchâtel, *see* below.

Day 5

Lunch in Neuchâtel

Café de la Collégiale, t 032 710 02 15 (*inexpensive*). As the name implies, this bright and modern little café is situated right outside the Collégiale church and castle. The menu is small – a selection of croissants, sandwiches and the like – along with an inexpensive daily special. *Closed Sun*.

Brasserie du Jura, rue de la Treille 7, t 032 725 14 10 (*moderate*). Just off the place Pury, this is an authentic Neuchâteloise brasserie. One of its specialities is local tripe. *Closed Sun*.

Dinner in Neuchâtel

See p.209. **Le Colvert** in the Hôtel Palafitte and the stylish restaurant of the Hôtel **Beau-Rivage** are excellent choices, as is the **Hôtel Dupeyrou** (actually only a restaurant) in the city's most imposing building.

Sleeping in Neuchâtel

See pp.208–9. The **Palafitte** is, undoubtedly, the most unusual and high-tech hotel in Switzerland and the **Beau-Rivage** has the finest location.

Touring from Lugano

Because of its rather remote geographical location, Lugano is a difficult town to tour from as it means that quite long journeys are required – some of which cross into Italy, sometimes by bus. Another constraint is that some of the trips only operate in the summer months, and that means alternative routes have to be considered for other seasons. These problems aside, this tour includes the most diverse scenery of any and its overnight stops can best be described as eclectic. *See* maps, pp.184 and 162.

Day 1: Lugano to St Moritz

Morning: Between late June and mid-October – and remember that reservations are compulsory and there is a small supplementary charge – take the bus from Lugano train station all the way to St Moritz (in 2003 it departed at 8.40am). Almost immediately, it crosses into Italy, following Lake Lugano before dropping down to the pretty little town of Menaggio on the larger and more beautiful Lake Como. Often, there is a short stop here before the bus continues north, along the west bank of the lake, before a rest stop at the ancient market town of Chiavenna. Ten miles (16km) later the border town of Castasegna is passed, and soon the bus starts climbing up through the dramatic Bregaglia valley, cresting at the Maloja Pass. From there, all the way to St Moritz itself, the road runs to the west of three lakes surrounded by towering peaks – especially to the east. The alternative route is a little more complicated, but not much longer – in time at least. A less than 30-minute train journey to Bellinzona – note the three dramatic castles that will be visited later on the tour – is followed by a 1¾-hour bus trip to Thusis and a further, and very pretty, 1½-hour train ride to St Moritz.

Lunch: In St Moritz, *see* below.

Afternoon: **St Moritz** has a beautiful situation but, in itself, is something of an enigma. In the winter it comes alive, with the many five-star hotels filled by the very rich who come for the excellent winter sports, special events such as horse-racing on the frozen lake, and the casinos. In the summer, St Moritz is much quieter. There are no major places or museums of interest, but the town is worth a visit for an afternoon, if only for its beautiful ambience.

Dinner and Sleeping: In St Moritz, *see* below.

Day 1

Lunch, Dinner and Sleeping in St Moritz

*****Badrutt's Palace**, t 081 837 10 10, *www. badruttspalace.com* (*luxury*). A famous city landmark; home to the glitterati.

*****Suvretta House**, t 081 836 36 36, *www. suvrettahouse.ch* (*luxury*). Mansion-like and set in its own grounds.

****Steffani**, t 081 836 96 96, *www. steffani.ch* (*expensive*). On the central square; comfortable and welcoming.

***Corvatsch**, t 081 837 57 57, *www.hotel-corvatsch.ch* (*moderate*). Family-run hotel with Engadine furnishings. Italian/Swiss restaurant.

***Steinbock**, t 081 833 60 35, *www.steinbock-stmoritz.ch* (*inexpensive*). Central; rustic restaurant serves Italian dishes and grills.

Day 2: St Moritz to Vals

Morning: This trip requires catching a train from St Moritz to Reichenau-Tamins and then another on to Ilanz, from where a bus will take you 12½ miles (20km) along a narrow winding valley to the remote village of **Vals**. This is a curious place with a population of just 1,012, whose Roman Catholic descendants migrated here from the Valais in the 12th century. Vals is most famous for its water, but not just the Valser bottled water sold throughout Switzerland. In fact, it is the spa that brings people here; and their destination is a rather inelegant, un-alpine-looking group of modern tall buildings just past the factory. These were built in the 1960s and collectively form the **Hotel Therme Vals**, which thinks of itself as a one- to five-star hotel. In 1986 the Thermalbad Vals AG company – 100 per cent owned by the community – commissioned Peter Zumthor to construct a new bathing complex, and the results are spectacular. Actually built into the mountainside itself – with alpine flowers sprouting from the meadows on the roof, and hardly identifiable from outside, Zumthor used 60,000 Valser quartzite slabs to produce an interior that is as elegant as it is simple. The ambience here is quiet and peaceful, where people can 'rediscover the primal experience of bathing, cleansing and relaxing in water, the sensation of water on one's skin, at various temperatures and in various settings.' If you want water gadgets, sprays, artificial waves and slides, Vals will be a disappointment.

Lunch: In Vals, *see* below.

Afternoon: It's time to try out the **spa**. It's free for hotel guests, and CHF 28 for others, with no time restrictions. You will find a 42°C Fire Pool; a 14°C cold plunge pool; a flower-scented pool; indoor and outdoor pools at 32°C and 34°C respectively; a rough-hewn spring grotto and steam rock; and a sweat-bath rock, amongst other facilities. Wellness is important here, too, and the area identified by the word *therapie* offers such intriguing treatments as 'natural sea mud pack and aroma cream' and Watsu – a shiatsu massage in body-temperature warm water that lets you float, move and stretch as you experience in-depth relaxation. These, and any number of other enticing treatments, are available on a one-off basis. Take time, too, to walk around the charming village itself, with its old, dark-coloured wooden buildings reminiscent of those found in the Valais.

Dinner and Sleeping: In Vals, *see* below.

Day 2

Lunch in Vals
Take lunch on the terrace built above the spa.

Dinner in Vals
Have dinner at the **Roter Saal** restaurant, or on a half-board basis at the **Chessi**.

Sleeping in Vals
Hotel Therme Vals, t 081 926 80 80, **f** 081 926 80 00, *www.therme-vals.ch* (*moderate–inexpensive*), has a variety of options. In the hotel – there are also small rooms in the Haus Selva – ask for the 19 newly designed rooms going by the name 'Temporaries'.

Day 3: Vals to Münster

There are two ways of getting from Vals to Münster, depending on the time of year and the weather: either part of the way by steam train or all the way by rail.

Morning (option 1): Because of snow conditions, it is not possible to be absolutely certain when the Dampfbahn Furka-Bergstrecke (DFB) steam trains (*t 0848 000 144, f 055 615 30 93, reisedienst@fu-be.ch, www.furka-bergstrecke.ch*) start their service. In 2003, for example, they started on 21 June, with Sat and Sun trips until 13 July and 25 August–5 October, and daily trips 14 July–24 August. Make sure you reserve well ahead. Take the early bus from Vals Therme to Ilanz, then trains from Ilanz to Disentis/Mustér and on to Realp, where you will arrive about 20 minutes before the 11.10 departure. First opened in 1914, this is a fascinating 2-hour trip – but beware that these steam engines do emit smoke and soot. Passing through tunnels, over viaducts and even a folding bridge, the journey is dramatic and the scenery captivating, most especially so when, after the Muttbach-Belvédère station, the huge Rhône Glacier (Glacier du Rhône) dominates northern views. Once at Gletsch, you'll have about three hours to take the bus up to inspect the Rhône Glacier more closely, and a fee of CHF 5 will gain you entry into the Ice Grotto (Eisgrotte) inside the glacier itself. The water melting from the ice here is the beginning of the mighty Rhône river that will eventually find its way down to the Mediterranean.

Lunch (option 1): In Gletsch, *see* below.

Afternoon (option 1): There are plans to re-open the line from Gletsch to Oberwald by 2006; until then take a bus to connect with the 12-minute train trip to Münster.

Morning (option 2): At other times of the year, take the same early bus from Vals to Ilanz, and then trains to Disentis/Mustér, Andermatt and Münster – with trains on the last route tunnelling around the dramatic scenery between Realp and Gletsch. After checking into your hotel, return to the station for the very pretty trip down the valley to Betten, from where you can take the cable car either directly or via Betten (another part of the village, further up the mountain), to the attractive ski village of Bettmeralp. A short walk through the village leads to the cable car up to Bettmerhorn and the strikingly modern Bergrestaurant at 8,694ft (2,650m). After lunch, return to Münster.

Lunch (option 2): At Bettmerhorn, above Bettmeralp, *see* below.

Dinner and Sleeping: In Münster, *see* below.

Day 3

Lunch in Gletsch or Bettmeralp

On the terrace by the Ice Grotto or, more formally, at the nearby **Berghotel Belvédère** (option 1).

At the **Bergrestaurant** on Bettmerhorn, with 360-degree views from its terrace (option 2).

Dinner and Sleeping in Münster

★★★**Hôtel Croix d'Or et Poste**, t 027 974 15 15, f 027 974 15 16, *www.hotel-postmuenster.ch* (*inexpensive*). With a 365-year history, this was once the residence of the Bishop of Sion. It is one of the most beautiful hotels in the valley, and offers traditional cuisine in its charming restaurant.

Day 4: Münster to Stresa (Italy)

Morning: Make an early start, catching a train before 8am to the important junction of Brig. From here, the Italian Cisalpino tilting train takes just under an hour to reach the very pretty Italian resort town of **Stresa**, sitting on the shore of Lake Maggiore under the majestic peak of Mottarone. Take a stroll around; Stresa's ambience is quite different to that found in most Swiss towns. The little triangular Piazza L. Cadorna, shaded by age-old plane trees, is its social hub. Two of Stresa's lakeside villas are open to the public: Villa Pallavicino (1850) and its colourful gardens (*open daily end Feb–early Nov 9–6; adm*), with parrots and a small collection of other animals; and the Villa Ducale (1771), once the property of Catholic philosopher Antonio Rosmini (*d.* 1855); besides the gardens, there's a small museum (*open Tues–Sun 9–12 and 3–6; donation requested*).

Lunch: In Stresa or on the Borromeo Islands, *see* below.

Afternoon: Sitting just out in the lake are three islands, known as the **Borromeo Islands**, of which the two largest are startlingly different from the other. The closest, **Isola Bella**, was until the 1630s nothing but a barren island. Then Count Carlo III Borromeo began developing a Baroque-style palace dedicated to his wife Isabella d'Adda, and work has continued through the centuries. Imposingly intricate, it is furnished with numerous priceless tapestries, furniture and paintings by renowned masters of their respective arts. The grounds are equally intricate, with ten terraces tapered to reflect a cut-off pyramid landscaped with every variety of rare flower, plant and tree imaginable. This marriage of architectural and botanical grandeur is stunning to the eye. In 1501, Count Lancellotto Borromeo obtained **Isola Madre** in perpetual lease. He died, though, in 1513 and it was Renato Borromeo who commissioned the more austere palace here in 1585. The microclimate gives the area a subtropical feel, shown in the rare and exotic plants and flowers, animals and brightly coloured birds – including white peacocks – in the park. The smaller **Fishermen's Island** (Isola Superiore dei Pescatori), situated between the other two, couldn't be more different. It is almost totally covered with old homes on narrow, rambling lanes and occupied by hard-working and frugal inhabitants, many of whom still earn their livelihood from fishing. You can visit the Borromeo Islands (*www.borromeoturismo.it; adm*) easily on a variety of boat services.

Dinner and Sleeping: In Stresa, *see* below.

Day 4

Lunch in Stresa

Try the **Spaghetteria Turistica**, Piazza Cadorna, in the centre of the square, or either of the hotel restaurants on the islands.

Dinner and Sleeping in Stresa

★★★★**La Palma**, Lungolago Umberto I 33, t 0323 32401, f 0323 033930, *www.hlapalma.it*

(*expensive*). A charming hotel in its own grounds on the lake front.

Dinner and Sleeping on the Borromeo Islands

Albergo Ristorante Verbano, Via Ugo Ara 2, Isola Pescatori, t 0323 30408, *www.hotelverbano.it* (*inexpensive*). Has a lot of ambience.

Elvezia, t 0323 30043 (*inexpensive*), on Isola Bella. A nice small hotel.

Day 5: Stresa (Italy) to Intragna

Morning: There are two different methods of getting to **Intragna**. The way of choice is across Lake Maggiore on a Navigazione Lago Maggiore (*www.navigazionelaghi.it*) two-hour sailing to Locarno, from where a FART train takes just a few minutes to arrive at Intragna. Alternatively – and especially if the sailing schedules out of season aren't so convenient – take a train to Domodossola. Next, take a FART train on a truly spectacular trip of less than 1½ hours through the Vigezzo valley in Italy and then the beautiful Centovalli (*see* p.187) to Intragna (*see* p.187). Either way, you should still have time to take a FART train for three stops along the Centovalli to Verdasio, followed by a six-minute gondola car journey (between March and November) up to **Monte di Comino**, where there are two restaurants. The views here are particularly charming.

Lunch: On Monte di Comino, *see* below.

Afternoon: The gondola car stops for lunch, but be sure to catch the first one after, at 2pm, so that you can catch the next FART train from Verdasio to Locarno, and then transfer to a regular train for a 20-minute trip to **Bellinzona**. Bellinzona has an ancient history, with evidence of human presence as far back as the Neolithic period, but it is its strategic location that has always made it important. It is a fact that more alpine passes converge here than anywhere else in the southern Alps – the St Gotthard, St Bernard, Nufenen and Lukmanier, as well as important passes on the east/west axis. The valley is narrow here and, as the gateway to Italy, Bellinzona was an ideal place to fortify before the various routes fanned out again to the south. Although you won't have time to explore them all, there are three castles found on the hillside on the eastern side of the valley that stretches down into the valley itself. The largest and most important of these, the **Castelgrande** (*Monte San Michele*, **t** *091 825 81 45; open daily 10–6; free*) dominates the town and is easily accessible via a small lift (elevator), just a few minutes' walk from the station. With vineyards surrounding it, it is impressively formidable indeed. You can learn more about its history from both a 15-minute film with an English commentary, and by visiting the archaeological/historical museum. The two other castles, those of the di Montebello (with its Civic Museum) and di Sasso Corbaro, are at successively higher elevations to the east.

Dinner and Sleeping: In Intragna, *see* below.

Day 5

Lunch above Verdasio
Riposo Romantico, **t** 091 798 11 30, on Monte di Comino. Home-made food and local red wine (*see* p.188 for full description).

Dinner and Sleeping in Intragna
Antico, **t 091 796 11 07, **f** 091 796 31 15, *www. hotelantico.ch* (*inexpensive*). A charming hotel in an old property in the centre. The 26 rooms have an old-fashioned ambience, and the dining room is wooden-beamed. There's also a cosy bar, a refreshing pool and a small children's playground.

Garni Intragna, **t** 091 796 10 77, **f** 091 796 31 15, *paris@nikko.ch* (*inexpensive*). Close to the Antico in a similar house, with 12 rooms. No restaurant, but it shares the Antico's, as it does the pool and children's playground.

Touring the Valais

The Valais (Wallis in German, Vallese in Italian) in the south of Switzerland is somewhat cut-off from the rest of the country. In fact, it is only accessible from Basel (4–5hrs away), Bern (3hrs), Luzern and Zürich (both 4–5hrs) in the north through a rail tunnel under the Bernese Alps, from Geneva (3hrs) by rail and road connections coming off the eastern end of Lake Geneva, and from Lugano (5¾hrs) by either of two convoluted routes. Sion, though, presents no such problems. *See* map, p.189.

Day 1: Saas-Fee

Morning: The scenery on this trip is full of surprises. From the valley a bus takes you steeply up to the start of the tour at **Saas-Fee** (*see* p.200). The village is car-free, so call ahead to your hotel and they will meet you at the indoor bus station with their little electric bus. Sitting in a natural bowl, Saas-Fee is surrounded by no less than 13 mountains that rise to over 13,123 ft (4,000m). Amble down through the village towards the cable car to Felskinn, at an altitude of 9,843ft (3,000m), then change onto the 'Metro Alpin', the highest funicular in the world, for the ascent to Mittelallin at 11,483ft (3,500m). Here, you will find two 'highest in the world' places. The Drehrestaurant, which seats 220 people and revolves 360 degrees every hour, is a unique place to enjoy lunch and watch as a panoramic feast of alpine peaks and glaciers slowly reveal themselves to you in all their majestic glory.

Lunch: At Mittelallin, *see* below.

Afternoon: After lunch, it is time to delve into the world of permanent ice by going down deep into the glacier to be amazed by the world's highest and largest ice pavilion. Inside, beneath a ceiling of pure ice that averages a thickness of 33ft (10m), you will learn much about glaciers – and you can touch as well. Back in Saas-Fee, you may want to take some time exploring the village's shopping opportunities. If you're staying at the Ferienart Resort and Spa, an hour or two at the spa before dinner is a wonderful way to relax.

Dinner and Sleeping: In Saas-Fee, *see* below.

Day 1

Lunch above Saas-Fee

It has to be the **Drehrestaurant**, t 027 957 17 71, the world's highest revolving restaurant.

Dinner and Sleeping in Saas-Fee

****Ferienart Resort & Spa, t** 027 958 19 00, f 027 958 19 05, *www.ferienart.ch* (*expensive*). Behind its chalet-style façade is a warm, stylish and congenial hotel. The rooms and suites are innovatively designed and usually wood panelled. Dine in your choice of three restaurants, including the fine Le Gourmet, and afterwards dance to live bands in the bar. There is also an extensive on-site spa and grotto pool.

***Burgener, t** 027 958 92 80, f 027 958 92 81, *www.hotel-burgener.ch* (*moderate*). This is a medium-sized, 30-room hotel in the heart of the village. Cosy and comfortable.

Rendez-Vous, t 027 957 20 40, f 027 957 35 34 (*moderate*). A small hotel that also offers apartments and has modern, well-appointed rooms each with a balcony and bath. Other features are a restaurant, a bar and a sun terrace.

Day 2: Zermatt

Morning: As the crow flies, the journey from Saas-Fee to **Zermatt** – at the head of the neighbouring valley to the west – is straightforward. However, by public transport it is more complicated: first a bus (a reservation will save possible disappointment) back down the valley to Stalden, then a train along the slowly rising valley to Zermatt. Note, too, the extra large car park at Täsch on the left; this is a reminder that Zermatt is also a car-free village. Geographically, the village is set in a very narrow valley. It is crowded with all types of hotels and all kinds of shops, many of which advertise international designer names, and this will give you a clue that Zermatt is very much a cosmopolitan village. And, quite the opposite to Saas-Fee, it has a vibrant nightlife. Zermatt's symbol and claim to fame, the magical **Matterhorn** (Cervin in French), slightly crooked-looking, totally dominates the view to the south from the village. On further investigation you'll see that there are more than 36 peaks in this area over 13,000ft (4,000m), but still it is the magnetism of the Matterhorn, standing alone at 14,692ft (4,478m), which continually attracts your attention. There are two places from where you can get closer views but, either way, you have to start by taking one of the new eight-seat Matterhorn-Express gondola cars from Zermatt to Furi at 6,115ft (1.864m). To get to the highest of the two destinations, next take the cable car up to Trockener Steg at 9,642ft (2,939m). There, transfer to the highest cable car ride in Europe to Klein Matterhorn at 12,532ft (3,820m). The views from this vantage point are simply unforgettable, and the panorama that unfolds around you takes in most places from Mont Blanc to Austria. Return by way of Trockener Steg to Furi, and this time change to the Matterhorn Express gondolas up to Schwarzee 8,417ft (2,582m), where a small hotel and restaurant and a little lake sit, literally, on the foothills of the Matterhorn itself.

Lunch: At Trockener Steg or Schwarzsee, *see* below.

Afternoon: Back in Zermatt, few will be able to resist the lure of the shops, if only to window-shop.

Dinner and Sleeping: In Zermatt, *see* below and p.238.

Day 2

Lunch above Zermatt

At the **Restaurant Trockener Steg**, the world's highest pizzeria, or the **Restaurant Hotel Schwarzee**; both have good sun decks.

Dinner and Sleeping in Zermatt

For more hotels in Zermatt, *see* the next page. Fuller descriptions are on pp.204–5.

★★★★★**Mont Cervin & Residence, t** 027 966 88 88, **f** 027 966 88 99, *www.zermatt.ch/montcervin* (*luxury*). Opened in 1851. Central; most rooms have balconies and some jacuzzis and fireplaces. Also a Clarins Beauty Salon, indoor pool and health facilities.

★★★★★**Riffelalp Resort, t** 027 966 05 55, **f** 027 966 05 50, *www.zermatt.ch/riffelalp* (*luxury*). Reached via the Gornergrat train, this has stunning views of the Matterhorn. Modern in thought, traditional in style. Has its own small movie theatre and two bowling alleys.

★★★★**Monte Rosa**, Bahnhofstrasse 80, **t** 027 966 03 33, **f** 027 966 03 30, *www.zermatt.ch/monterosa* (*luxury*). Zermatt's oldest and most traditional hotel. Guests can use the pool and health facilities at the Mont Cervin.

Day 3: Zermatt

Morning: Another fascinating trip is on a **Gornergratbahn** (GGB) train – preferably in an open carriage – beginning at the second of Zermatt's train stations located directly across from the main station. From here, the cog-rail trains undertake a 43-minute ascent to Gornergrat at 10,269ft (3,130m), making it Europe's highest totally open-air railway. The initial part of the journey twists and turns through the forested slopes up to the open mountainside. There, in the warmer seasons, you might see marmots scampering around. At Gornergrat, you can gaze upon the massive Monte Rosa and her sister peaks, each of which is well over 13,123ft (4,000m). Directly behind you, but in the distance, you will see another range of peaks of equal stature; amongst these is the Dom which, at 14,911ft (4,545m), is Switzerland's highest. Yet even these magnetic mountains will be unable to distract from the magnificence of the splendidly isolated Matterhorn. Directly in front is the Gornergletscher, and from this vantage point you can clearly define the path along which this massive glacier slowly meanders its way down. You can go even further and higher, too: on a cable car from Gornergrat to Hohtälligrat and Stockhorn, where the station is at an altitude of 11,178ft (3,407m) and the views are stunning.

Lunch: At Gornergrat, *see* below.

Afternoon: Back in Zermatt, it is time to splash out a little more money than you might initially have intended but, in retrospect, you will be very glad that you did as the trip will remain forever etched in your memory. Air-Zermatt (*t 027 966 86 86, www.air-zermatt.ch*) offer 20-minute **helicopter trips**, for CHF 195 per person, that take you as close as you can get to the summit of the Matterhorn without actually climbing it (but make sure you book in advance). Surprisingly, the helicopter wheels off to the north initially; then, as if magically, you find yourself hovering above a simply massive and majestic glacier whose ice has been weathered into deep canyons that resemble New York skyscrapers. Then the helicopter gains height and heads straight for the Matterhorn itself, gradually circling closer and closer to the summit where, if you are lucky, you might see climbers reaching the summit.

Dinner and Sleeping: In Zermatt, *see* below and p.237.

Day 3

Lunch above Zermatt

Kulm Hotel Gornergrat, **t** 027 966 64 00. With a sun terrace.

Dinner and Sleeping in Zermatt

****Alex, Bodmenstrasse 12, **t** 027 966 70 70, **f** 027 966 70 90, *www.hotelalexzermatt.ch* (*luxury*). Luxurious, with a cosy atmosphere. Indoor pool, health club and the fine Alex Grill.

***Alpenroyal, Riedstrasse 96, **t** 027 966 60 66, **f** 027 966 60 65, *www.alpenroyal.ch*

(*expensive*). A family-run hotel in an elevated peaceful location. Good food, indoor pool.

Kulm Hotel Gornergrat, **t 027 966 64 00, **f** 027 966 64 04 (*moderate*). Accessed via the Gornergrat railway, this is the highest hotel in Europe. Basic rooms, but with unparalleled views; the restaurant serves wine from the highest vineyard in Switzerland.

Le Mazot, **t** 027 966 06 06, **f** 027 966 06 07 (*inexpensive*). By the river. Also a nice restaurant with fondue specialities.

Bahnhof, **t** 027 967 24 06, **f** 027 967 72 16 (*cheap*). Next to the station with a mix of rooms.

Day 4: The Lötschental

Morning: Time, now, for a complete change of ambience, and a short trip back across the Rhône valley onto the southern slopes of the Bernese Alps. The trip takes about three hours, firstly by train to Brig and then on another train that climbs slowly up the north side of the valley, stopping at Goppenstein before disappearing into the tunnel on its way north to the Bernese Oberland. At Goppenstein, a post bus will be waiting to transport you into a mysterious, very beautiful and mostly unknown valley called **Lötschental** (*see* p.195). Your destination is, quite literally, the car park at the end of the road at **Fafleralp**. To save time, call the Hotel Fafleralp – just a few minutes away – ahead of time, or from there, and they will gladly come and pick you and your luggage up. (Remember, in high winter the uphill road between Blatten and Fafleralp is closed.) Head for the next bus back to Wiler, where the Lauchernalp cable car will take you up to **Lauchernalp**. The next destination is entirely unmarked: initially, climb straight up outside the cable car station until you come across the first signposts, then follow the pathway left, westwards, until you reach the first real village where a sign on the wall introduces the Berg-Restaurant Hockenalp.

Lunch: At Lauchernalp, or in your hotel, *see* below.

Afternoon: After lunch, return to Wiler, where you can explore one of the Lötschental's most curious traditions. After the second of February Maria Candlelight Mass it's time for the *Tschäggätä* (*see* p.197); one of the strict rules of this tradition is that only bachelors can participate and they dress in often hideously carved wooden facemasks and a fur costume with a large bell tied around the waist. The masks are usually rented, to protect anonymity, and Maskenkeller (*t 027 939 13 55, f 027 939 30 49, www. maskenkeller.ch*) has the most amazing collection of gruesomely erotic masks – some of which are over 100 years old. They also have plenty of smaller ones, and models, that make unusual souvenirs. Back at Fafleralp there should be time for a gentle, very pretty hike (less than an hour each way) up to the small, ice-cold lake of Grundsee and, on the way back, you might see a couple of the famous black fighting cows – and maybe calves, too – in a field next to the car park.

Dinner and Sleeping: In Fafleralp, Blatten or Lauchernalp, *see* below.

Day 4

Lunch in the Lötschental

The **Berg-Restaurant Hockenalp**, t 027 939 12 45 (*see* p.196), is a real experience (*open May–mid-Oct*); otherwise eat at your hotel.

Dinner and Sleeping in the Lötschental

Take half-board. The **Fafleralp** is the hotel of choice. Full hotel descriptions on p.196.
Fafleralp, t 027 939 14 51, f 027 939 14 53 (*moderate; no credit cards*). A typical mountain hotel, wood-panelled, in a delightfully isolated position at the end of the valley.

★★★Edelweiss, Blatten, t 027 939 13 63, f 027 939 10 53, *www.hoteledelweiss.ch* (*moderate*). A traditional hotel in Blatten. Its restaurant is famous for its Valais cuisine and wines.
★★★Nest-und Bietschhorn, between Ried and Blatten, t 027 939 11 06, f 027 939 18 22, *www.nest-bietsch.ch* (*moderate*). In a traditional house; offers home-style comforts and a restaurant with Valais specialities.
★★★Hotel-Restaurant zur Wildi, Lauchernalp, t 027 939 19 89, f 027 939 20 19 *www.zur-wildi.ch* (*moderate*). A fairly isolated, small, typical mountain hotel and restaurant reached via the Lauchernalp cable car.

Day 5: Leukerbad

Morning: **Leukerbad** is yet another village that sits at the end of a valley branching off the Rhône valley – this time the next valley to the west of Lötschental. Take a bus back to Goppenstein or Gampel-Steg, then a train to Leuk on the valley floor, followed by a bus that climbs steeply, initially, and then evens out as it heads into the rather wide, open area that is Leukerbad, surrounded by large, but not particularly pretty, mountains. The journey usually takes about 2½ hours. Although the mountains play their part, they are not the main attraction here in Leukerbad; that honour goes to the thermal springs that cause water to rise up at a temperature of 123.8°F (51°C), filling 60 springs at the rate of 857,880 UK gallons (3.9 million litres) daily. Before exploring the wonders of these waters, it's time to enjoy an alpine lunch (see below), whilst faced with a timeless view of the Valaisanne Alps, including the Matterhorn and Monte Rosa: the Torrent-Bahnen station (*t* 027 472 81 10, *f* 027 472 81 16, www.torrent.ch) is just outside the village to the east and takes you up to the Restaurant Rinderhütte at 7,677ft (2,340m). Beware, though, the cable car itself closes for lunch, so try and get there before midday.

Lunch: At the Rinderhütte above Leukerbad, *see* below.

Afternoon: Back in Leukerbad, and as it's the final day of the tour, it's time to relax in luxurious surroundings at the **Lindner Alpentherme** (*t* 027 472 10 10, *f* 027 472 10 11, www.alpentherme.ch; adm is complicated, see p.194). Out of the range of different things on offer, the most obvious are the two large indoor and outdoor pools, both at 96.8°F (36°C), with integrated facilities such as neck douches and underwater massage jets. There is also a competition pool, with four 27-yard (25m) lanes at a slightly lower temperature of 78.8°F (26°C). Discerning visitors, however, will plan their trip to coincide with the days that the Roman-Irish bath – one of just two in Switzerland (the other is in Scuol, *see* p.162) – is open. This is an extremely relaxing, sensual, two-hour naked bathe around an elegant Roman-style atrium. On the morning of day 6 take a bus back to Leuk, where you can board a train back to the city from which you started the tour.

Dinner and Sleeping: In Leukerbad, *see* below.

Day 5

Lunch above Leukerbad

The modern **Restaurant Rinderhütte** offers a combination of excellent food and fine views.

Dinner and Sleeping in Leukerbad

Take half-board. Full descriptions on p.194.
****Lindner Hotel Maison Blanche**, Dorfplatz, t 027 472 10 00, f 027 472 10 01, www.lindner-hotels.ch (expensive). A traditional hotel with two restaurants, a piano bar, garden terrace, pools and sauna, as well as free use of the Lindner Alpentherme.

***Lindner Hotel de France**, Dorfplatz, t 027 472 10 00, f 027 472 10 01, www.lindnerhotels.ch (moderate). Next to the Maison Blanche, this medium-sized hotel also has direct access to, and free use of, the Alpentherme.
***Hôtel de la Croix-Fédérale**, Kirchstrasse 43, t 027 472 79 79, f 027 472 79 75, www.croix-federale.ch (inexpensive). Located in a typical chalet in the village centre, this is a small hotel with just 10 traditionally styled rooms.
Château, t 027 470 16 27, f 027 470 16 42, www.torrent.ch (inexpensive). Inside a modern, chalet-style façade, the studios and 2- and 3-room apartments are bright and spacious.

Touring from Zürich

This tour starts from Zürich, which is not very far from Basel, Bern or Luzern. It takes about 3 hours to reach Zürich from Geneva and Lugano, and about 30 minutes longer from Sion. *See* map, p.151.

Day 1: Zürich to Schaffhausen and the Rhine Falls

Morning: Make an early start from Zürich, taking the train for the short trip north to **Schaffhausen** (*see* p.155). Schaffhausen is not a large town, and it is easy to see the important sights and enjoy its elegant atmosphere in a morning. Top of the list is the Cathedral of All Saints (Münster zu Allerheiligen; *open daily 8–6; free*). Originally founded in 1049, but rebuilt soon afterwards, this is one of the finest examples of Romanesque architecture in the country. The adjoining cloister and herb garden have the same aura of simplicity and tranquillity. Entirely different in style, and clearly visible due to its dominant position, is the unusual defensive battlement of the imposing Munot (*open May–Sept 8–8, Oct–April 9–5; free*). Constructed between 1564 and 1585, it is the symbol of Schaffhausen. Note, too, the vineyards on the slopes surrounding the Munot; this area of Switzerland is an important, lesser known wine-growing area. It is impossible not to miss the numerous water fountains (*Brunnen*) around the town, often topped by colourful historical figures such as William Tell. Another feature here are the wonderful old mansions from the 16th, 17th and 18th centuries, adorned by frescoes, statues and, quite often, extended bay windows (oriels). By now it should be around midday, and time to head up to the station, from where a No.1 bus takes you, in just 15 minutes, to Neuhausen. Signs will direct you towards the Rhine Falls, the largest waterfalls in Europe (*see* p.156).

Lunch: At the Schlössli Wörth complex, *see* below.

Afternoon: From Schlössli Wörth, you can take one of the Rhyfall Mändli boats around the Falls to the famous Känzeli rock that stands proudly in the middle of them. The boat waits while you climb the steep steps to get the closest possible look at the 153,978.5 gallons that power past every second.

Dinner and Sleeping: In Schaffhausen, *see* below.

Day 1

Lunch at the Rhine Falls

Schlössli Wörth, Rhenfallquai, t 052 672 24 21, (*expensive–moderate*). Located in the old fort, this is a charming restaurant with huge picture windows overlooking the falls themselves. Besides a fine menu, there are also daily specials. A cheaper alternative is its self-service restaurant next door.

Dinner in Schaffhausen

No question, the **Rheinhotel Fischerzunft** (*expensive*), *see* p.154, offers a culinary experience you will savour for a long time.

Sleeping in Schaffhausen

The **Rheinhotel Fischerzunft** is the hotel of choice, but as it only has 10 rooms the **Zunfthaus zum Rüden** is a good alternative (*see* p.154).

Day 2: Schaffhausen to Stein am Rhein

Morning: Between mid-April and early September the most interesting way to travel between Schaffhausen and Stein am Rhein is on one of the Schweizerische Schiffahrtsgesellschaft Untersee und Rhein boats (*t 052 634 08 88, f 052 625 59 93, www.urh.ch*). Conveniently, the docking point on the Rhine is just a few yards away from the Rheinhotel Fischerzunft, and boats usually depart at 9.10am and 11.10am, but check beforehand. At other times of the year, or if you want a little more time in Schaffhausen, the train offers a faster alternative. Settle down and relax as the boat slowly drifts against the current on a pleasant 2-hour sailing. Few stretches of the Rhine, no matter which country it is flowing through, are not industrialized, but this is one of them. Green hills, in places overlaid with woods, slope gently down to river-banks scattered with quaint houses, often with private docks, and dotted with sleepy, picturesque little towns. There are also a few surprises along the way – lovely reminders of the past. At Diessenhoffen, for example, you will float, perhaps trepidatiously, under a covered medieval wooden bridge.

Lunch: At Stein am Rhein, *see* below.

Afternoon: **Stein am Rhein** is considered Switzerland's best-preserved small medieval town, with rows of wonderful wooden-beamed houses decorated with intricate frescoes. Make your way first to the Rathausplatz, both the town's social centre and its main attraction. The Rathaus (town hall) dominates, and the houses around the square have the most ornate decorations you are ever likely to see, depicting a wide variety of scenes that are, in some instances, decidedly risqué. The houses were decorated to demonstrate their owners' affluence, and this concentration of frescoes is reputed to be the world's largest. The small bay windows (oriels) had their practical use, as residents could see what was happening below without themselves being noticed. There are two very different museums worthy of a visit. The 1,000-year-old St George Cloister (Klostermuseum St Georgen; *t 052 741 21 42; open April–Oct 10–5; adm*) stands on the river and is decorated with frescoes and paintings (including one of St George slaying the dragon) and wonderfully intricate wooden-beamed ceilings. The Museum Lindwurm (*Understadt 18, t 052 741 25 12, f 052 741 45 82; open Mar–Oct Mon and Wed–Sun 10–5; adm*) is where you will see how affluent citizens of the mid-19th century lived.

Dinner and Sleeping: In Stein am Rhein, *see* below.

Day 2

Lunch in Stein am Rhein

Hotel Adler restaurant, Rathausplatz 2, **t** 052 742 61 61 (*expensive–moderate*). A good central choice, serving local and French cuisine.

Dinner in Stein am Rhein

The **Restaurant Sonne**, *see* p.157, is the best restaurant in town, but half board at the **Adler** is another good, and cheaper, choice.

Sleeping in Stein am Rhein

★★★Adler, Rathausplatz 2, **t** 052 742 61 61, **f** 052 741 44 40, *www.adlersteinamrhein.ch* (*inexpensive*). In the town hall square and with a beautiful Carigiet façade; two singles, 12 doubles on offer, and also an apartment with two bedrooms. Nice public areas.

The **Rheinfels**, **t** 052 741 21 44, **f** 052 741 25 22 (*inexpensive*). A good alternative.

Day 3: Stein am Rhein to St Gallen

Morning: It doesn't take too long to travel between Stein am Rhein and St Gallen – between 1½ and 1¾ hours – but you have to be careful about which train you catch as some services stop up to three times, and it may be faster to make one change rather than none. Nevertheless, if you leave around 9am you'll be in St Gallen by 10.30am. **St Gallen** (*see* p.157) is one of Switzerland's largest and most historic cities, and has some wonderful attractions as well as a fascinating medieval centre. Take time to stroll around before lunch. Streets like Marktgasse, Multergasse, Gallusstrasse and Gallusplatz are full of lovely old buildings, many with magnificent extended bay windows (oriels), of which there are more than 100 in St Gallen.

Lunch: In St Gallen, *see* below.

Afternoon: After lunch head for the main attraction here, the world-famous **Abbey Library of St Gallen** (Stiftsbibliothek St Gallen; *t 071 227 34 16; open Dec–Mar Mon–Sat 10–5, Sun 10–12 and 1.30–4; April–Nov Mon–Sat 10–5, Sun 10–4; adm*). This is one of the oldest libraries in the world, with a collection of over 100,000 books and manuscripts, some of which date back to the 5th century. There are magnificent examples of handwritten books and a collection of 1,650 incunabula. Completed in 1767, it has a highly elaborate interior and glorious elegance. Two tiers of incredible glassed-in bookcases stand beneath intricate ceiling frescoes depicting the first four Œcumenical Councils (Nicaea in 325, Constantinople in 381, Ephesus in 431 and Chalcedon in 451); on the ground is a lovely inlaid parquet floor (you are supplied with overslippers to protect it). The library complex is now a UNESCO world cultural treasure, largely on the basis of this extraordinary room. Next to the library, the **cathedral** (*t 071 227 33 81; open Mon–Sat 9–6, and after services on Sun*) is dominated by two immense spires. Unlike many churches it is extremely intricately decorated; especially important are the ceiling frescoes that were rediscovered after an extensive restoration between 1961 and 1967. By the cathedral west entrance is the **Lapidarium** (*open April–Nov daily 2–4, Dec–Mar Sat and Sun 2–4; free*), where there is a collection of valuable building stones from the 8th to 17th centuries.

Dinner and Sleeping: In St Gallen, *see* below.

Day 3

Lunch in St Gallen

One of the pleasures of St Gallen is a visit to one of the '*1. Stock-biezlie*'. These quaint 1st-storey taverns serve tasty local specialities such as St Gallen sausage and *Biber*, a spicy honey cake filled with marzipan. The perfect accompaniment is a glass or two of Rheintaler wine. Typical examples of *1.Stock-biezlie* are: **Anker**, Schmiedgasse 20, **t** 071 222 06 96, and

Gastube zum Schlössli, Zeughausgasse 7, **t** 071 222 12 56.

Dinner and Sleeping in St Gallen

Half board at one of the hotels is a good bet. The **Einstein** has a restaurant that overlooks the abbey district; the **Gallo Garni** has the **Galletto**, an Italian restaurant, and the **Jägerhof** boasts the first fully organic restaurant in Switzerland and one of the region's largest wine lists. *See* p.158 for full descriptions.

Day 4: St Gallen to Schwägalp

As buses don't run to and from Schwägalp other than from late May to late October, this day will have to be dropped at other times of the year, and the tour will go straight on to Day 5.

Morning: Take time, in the morning, to visit a couple more places in St Gallen. First on the list is the **St Laurence Church** (*t 071 222 67 92; open Mon–Fri 9.30–11.30 and 2–4*). The first building on this site was a tiny cemetery chapel erected around AD 850, but this Gothic one dates from the early 14th century. During the Reformation, in 1527, Holy Communion was celebrated in St Laurence's according to Protestant rites, and it emerged as the town's Protestant church. Of the many museums in St Gallen, one, the **Textile Museum** (Textilmuseum; *Vadianstrasse 2, t 071 222 17 44, f 071 223 42 39, www.textilmuseum.ch; open Mon–Sat 10–12 and 2–5, Sun 10–5; adm*), is important as much of St Gallen's wealth is attributable to the lucrative textile industry. In fact you may see a few early 20th-century buildings in St Gallen as testament to this (there is a striking Art Nouveau building nearby, in Leonhardstrasse). The museum displays embroidery from the 14th–20th centuries and European lace from the 16th–20th centuries. Around midday it is time to head for another, altogether different destination – **Schwägalp**, in Appenzell (a canton famous for its cheeses, and also for its wide range of beers and fruity liqueurs). For a journey with the most straight-forward connections, take a train to Herisau and then Urnäsch and then a bus for the last 22 minutes or so of what should be a 50-minute journey. This is an isolated, beautiful location with really only one hotel to check into. Head immediately to the Säntisbahn cable car (*www.saentisbahn.ch*), which will carry you up to the 8,209ft (2,502m) summit of the most panoramic mountain in eastern Switzerland. **Säntis** is a weather station, and has been since 1882; it is also a very modern complex and everything here – including the cable car and the hotel – is wheelchair-accessible.

Lunch: At the top of Säntis, *see below.*

Afternoon: There are many mountain pastures around Schwägalp, and every day between May and October more than 50 herdsmen bring fresh alpine milk to the modern Alpine Demonstration Cheese Dairy. Between 9am and 7pm you can watch cheeses being made in the traditional manner in huge copper vats, and then purchase the end products.

Dinner and Sleeping: In Schwägalp, *see below.*

Day 4

Lunch above Schwägalp

The best option is to help yourself to something at the **self-service restaurant** (*inexpensive*) at the top of Säntis, and then eat out on the terrace and enjoy the panoramic views. Alternatively, eat at the hotel in Schwägalp (*see* below).

Dinner and Sleeping in Schwägalp

***Schwägalp, t 071 365 66 00, f 071 365 66 01, www.saentisbahn.ch (*inexpensive*). It may be the only hotel here, but it is a good one. The 30 rooms are spacious and bright, and you will be served real Swiss traditional dishes at the restaurant – which has a 600-seat terrace.

Day 5: Schwägalp to Vaduz (Liechtenstein)

If you have missed Day 4, you can reach Vaduz from St Gallen by first taking a train to Buchs, and then travelling by bus from Buchs to Vaduz.

Morning: This trip consists of three consecutive bus rides that, collectively, take just 1¾ hours. The first one, from Schwägalp to Nesslau-Neu St Johann, takes just 21 minutes, and is far and away the most dramatic in terms of scenery. The next, to Buchs, lasts an hour and with the exception of a prominent castle is of little interest. And the last, across the river to **Vaduz**, lasts just 16 minutes. Your first stop in this curious little town (*see* p.160) should be at the tourist office, and don't forget to take your passport. Not only will you get tourist information here but, capitalizing on Liechtenstein's curiosity value, they will also stamp your passport as a souvenir, for a small fee. There are a surprising number of attractions here, and one of them is in the same building as the tourist office. Liechtenstein has always made an issue of postage stamps, and they are a favourite of philatelists worldwide. It is no surprise, therefore, that there should be a Postage Stamp Museum (Briefmarkmuseum; *Städtle 37,* **t** *02 236 61 05,* **f** *02 236 61 09, www.pwz.li; open daily 10–12 and 1.30–5; free*) here in Vaduz. It houses a large collection of stamps issued by Liechtenstein from 1912 onwards.

Lunch: In Vaduz, *see* below.

Afternoon: After lunch, head for Vaduz's newest and most important attraction. The National Art Museum (Kunstmuseum Liechtenstein; *Städtle 32,* **t** *02 235 03 00,* **f** *02 235 03 29, www.kunstmuseum.li; open Tues–Sun 10–5, Thurs until 8; adm*) was inaugurated in 2000 and contains the world-famous collections of the Prince of Liechtenstein. On view are Old Masters (the highlights being Rembrandt's *Amor* and Rubens' *Venus*), as well as modern and contemporary works. Also worth a visit is the Prince of Liechtenstein's Court Winery (Hofkellerie des Fürsten von Liechtenstein; *Fürstliche Domäne, Feldstrasse 4,* **t** *02 232 10 18,* **f** *02 233 11 45, www.hofkellerei.li; open Mon–Fri 8–12 and 1.30–6.30, Sat 9–1*). Although covering less than 10 acres (4 hectares), Liechtenstein's wine-making tradition has a long and distinguished history with the dry reds of Süssdruck and Beerli being the most famous. The next day, catch a bus to Sargans or Buchs followed by a train back to Zürich, taking a little over an hour.

Dinner and Sleeping: In Vaduz, *see* below.

Day 5

Lunch, Dinner and Sleeping in Vaduz

Half board recommended at either the **Park-Hotel Sonnenhof** or **Le Real**. As Le Real is in the centre of town, it is a good choice for lunch, too.

★★★★Park-Hotel Sonnenhof, Mareestrasse 29, **t** 02 239 02 02, **f** 02 239 02 23, *www.sonnenhof.li* (*moderate*). A very comfortable hotel just a short distance from, and overlooking, Vaduz. Set in a park, it offers traditional style, modern facilities, pool and health club, and views of the Rhine and Alps.

★★★Le Real, Städtle 21, **t** 02 232 22 22, **f** 02 232 08 91, *www.hotel-real.li* (*moderate*). This small hotel is extremely comfortable and centrally located on Vaduz's one really main street.

Language

The languages used in Switzerland are German (spoken by about 65% of the population); French (about 20%); Italian (about 7%); and Romansch (around 1%, in the canton of Graubünden). German is spoken in a Swiss-German dialect (*Schwyzerdütsch*), in itself very different from other German dialects. High German is the written language.

You will find that most people in Switzerland can speak English, especially people working in the tourist industry and those in large towns and cities.

All words and phrases translated below are in the following order: German, French and Italian.

Pronunciation

German

Vowels

Simple vowels in German are either long or short. They are always long when doubled or followed by *h*, and mostly long when followed by a single consonant. They are, as a rule, short when followed by a group of consonants.

short *i* as *i* in 'it'; **long** *i* as in 'machine'
short *e* as in 'let'; **long** *e* as in 'late'
long *a* as in 'alms'
short *o* as in 'not'; **long** *o* as in 'no'
short *u* as in 'put'; **long** *u* as in 'rude'
short *ä* as in 'fell'; **long** *ä* as in 'mare'
ie as English *ee*
ö as *ur* in 'urn'
ü as German *i* with rounded and protruded lips
e at the end of a word is always pronounced, as an 'er'
äu and *eu* as *oi* in 'boy'
ei and *ai* as *ei* in 'height'
au as *ow* in 'how'

Consonants

Most German consonants are pronounced as in English. Here are some exceptions:
ch as *ch* in 'loch'
j as *y* in 'yes'
s as *z* sound in 'rose'
sp and *st* as *shp* and *sht* when at the beginning of a word
th as English *t*
v as English *f*
w as English *v*
z as English *ts*

French

Vowels

a/à/â between *a* in 'bat' and 'part'
é/er/ez at end of word as *a* in 'plate' but a bit shorter
e/è/ê as *e* in 'bet'
e at end of word not pronounced
e at end of syllable or in one-syllable word pronounced weakly, like *er* in 'mother'
i as *ee* in 'bee'
o as *o* in 'pot'
ô as *o* in 'go'
u/û between *oo* in 'boot' and *ee* in 'bee'

Vowel Combinations

ai as *a* in 'plate'
aî as *e* in 'bet'
ail as *i* in 'kite'
au/eau as *o* in 'go'
ei as *e* in 'bet'
eu/œu as *er* in 'mother'
oi between *wa* in 'swam' and *wu* in 'swum'
oy as 'why'
ui as *wee* in 'twee'

Nasal Vowels

Vowels followed by an *n* or *m* have a nasal sound.
an/en as *o* in 'pot' + nasal sound

ain/ein/in as *a* in 'bat' + nasal sound
on as *aw* in 'paw' + nasal sound
un as *u* in 'nut' + nasal sound

Consonants

Many French consonants are pronounced as in English, but there are some exceptions:
c followed by *e, i* or *y*, and *ç* as *s* in 'sit'
c followed by *a, o, u* as *c* in 'cat'
g followed by *e, i* or *y* as *s* in 'pleasure'
g followed by *a, o, u* as *g* in 'good'
gn as *ni* in 'opinion'
j as *s* in 'pleasure'
ll as *y* in 'yes'
qu as *k* in 'kite'
s between vowels as *z* in 'zebra'
s otherwise as *s* in 'sit'
w except in English words as *v* in 'vest'
x at end of word as *s* in 'sit'
x otherwise as *x* in 'six'

Italian

Italian words are pronounced phonetically. Every vowel and consonant (except *h*) is sounded.

Vowels

a as in English 'father'
e when unstressed is pronounced like *a* in 'fate', when stressed can be the same or like the *e* in 'pet'
i as the *i* in 'machine';
o like *e*, has two sounds, *o* as in 'hope' when unstressed, and usually *o* as in 'rock' when stressed
u as *u* in 'June'

Consonants

Consonants are the same as in English, except:
c when followed by an 'e' or 'i', is pronounced like the English *ch*
g is also soft before 'i' or 'e' as in *gira*
z as English *ts*
sc before the vowels *i* or *e* become like the English *sh*
ch as *k* in Chianti
gn as English *ny*
gli as the middle of the word 'million'

Useful Phrases

hello (informal) *hallo/grütsi salut ciao*
hello (formal) *guten Morgen bonjour buongiorno*
goodbye *auf wiedersehen au revoir arrivederci*
sorry *entschuldigung désolé scusi*
please *bitte s'il vous plaît per favore*
thank you *danke merci grazie*
good *gut bon/bonne buono/a*
how much? *wie viel? combien? quanto?*
yes *ja oui si*
no *nein non no*
WC *toilette toilettes toeletta*
men *Herren hommes signori*
ladies *Damen dames/femmes signore*
help! *Hilfe! au secours! aiuto!*

General

Do you speak English?
Sprechen Sie Englisch?
Parlez-vous anglais?
Parla inglese?

I don't understand
Ich verstehe nicht
Je ne comprends pas
Non capisco

I don't know
Ich weiss nicht
Je ne sais pas
Non lo so

I would like...
Ich möchte...
Je voudrais...
Vorrei...

Speak more slowly
Bitte sprechen Sie langsamer?
Pourriez-vous parler plus lentement?
Parla lentamente

What is your name?
Wie heissen Sie?
Comment vous appelez-vous?
Come si chiama?

My name is...
Mein Name ist...
Je m'appelle...
Mi chiamo...

Transport

I want to go to...
Ich möchte nach... fahren
Je voudrais aller à...
Desidero andare a...

When is the next...?
Wann ist der nächste...?
Quel est le prochain...?
Quando parte il prossimo...?

What time does it leave (arrive)?
Wann fährt er ab (kommt er an)?
A quelle heure part-il (arrive-t-il)?
A che ora parte (arriva)?

From where does the train leave?
Wo fährt der Zug ab?
D'où part le train?
Da dove parte il treno?

How long does the trip take?
Wie lange dauert die Reise?
Combien de temps dure le voyage?
Quanto tempo dura il viaggio?

Single/return ticket
Einfache Fahrkarte/Rückfahrkarte
Un aller simple/aller et retour
Un biglietto semplice/andata e ritorno

Accommodation

a single room
ein Einzelzimmer
une chambre pour une personne
una camera singola

a twin room
ein Zimmer mit zwei Betten
une chambre à deux lits
una camera con due letti

a double room
ein Doppelzimmer
une chambre pour deux personnes
una camera doppia

with shower/bath
mit Dusche/Bad
avec douche/salle de bains
con doccia/bagno

Numbers

one *eins un(e) uno(a)*
two *zwei deux due*
three *drei trois tre*
four *vier quatre quattro*
five *fünf cinq cinque*
six *sechs six sei*
seven *sieben sept sette*
eight *acht huit otto*
nine *neun neuf nove*
ten *zehn dix dieci*
twenty *zwanzig vingt venti*
thirty *dreissig trente trenta*
forty *vierzig quarante quaranta*
fifty *fünfzig cinquante cinquanta*
sixty *sechzig soixante sessanta*
seventy *siebzig soixante-dix settanta*
eighty *achtzig quatre-vingts ottanta*
ninety *neunzig quatre-vingt-dix novanta*
hundred *hundert cent cento*

Days

Monday *Montag lundi lunedì*
Tuesday *Dienstag mardi martedì*
Wednesday *Mittwoch mercredi mercoledì*
Thursday *Donnerstag jeudi giovedì*
Friday *Frietag vendredi venerdì*
Saturday *Samstag samedi sabato*
Sunday *Sonntag dimanche domenica*

today *heute aujourd'hui oggi*
yesterday *gestern hier ieri*
tomorrow *morgen demain domani*

Months

January *Januar janvier gennaio*
February *Februar février febbraio*
March *März mars marzo*
April *April avril aprile*
May *Mai mai maggio*
June *Juni juin giugno*
July *Juli juillet luglio*
August *August août agosto*
September *September septembre settembre*
October *Oktober octobre ottobre*
November *November novembre novembre*
December *Dezember décembre dicembre*

Index

Main page references are in **bold**. Page references to maps are in *italics*.

Also available from Cadogan Guides in our European series...

France

France
Dordogne & the Lot
Gascony & the Pyrenees
Brittany
Loire
South of France
Provence
Côte d'Azur
Corsica
Short Breaks in Northern France

Italy

Italy
The Bay of Naples and Southern Italy
Lombardy and the Italian Lakes
Tuscany, Umbria and the Marches
Tuscany
Umbria
Northeast Italy
Italian Riviera and Piemonte
Bologna and Emilia Romagna
Central Italy
Sardinia
Sicily
Rome Venice Florence

Spain

Spain
Andalucía
Northern Spain
Bilbao and the Basque Lands
Granada Seville Córdoba

Greece

Greece
Greek Islands
Athens and Southern Greece
Crete

The UK and Ireland

England
London–Paris
London Markets

Scotland
Scotland's Highlands and Islands

Ireland
Ireland: Southwest Ireland

Other Europe

Portugal
Madeira & Porto Santo
Malta, Gozo & Comino

The City Guide Series

Amsterdam
Barcelona
Bruges
Brussels
Edinburgh
Florence
London
Madrid
Milan
Paris
Prague
Rome
Venice

Flying Visits

Flying Visits France
Flying Visits Italy
Flying Visits Spain
Flying Visits Switzerland
Flying Visits Scandinavia
Flying Visits Germany
Flying Visits Ireland

Cadogan Guides are available from good bookshops, or via **Littlehampton Book Services,** Faraday Close, Durrington, Worthing, West Sussex BN13 3RB, **t** (01903) 828800, **f** (01903) 828802; and **The Globe Pequot Press**, 246 Goose Lane, PO Box 480, Guilford, Connecticut 06437–0480, **t** (800) 458 4500/**t** (203) 458 4500, **t** (203) 458 4603.